Sally Thompson is Executive Officer of the London Churches Group.

Women Religious

Women Religious

*The Founding of
English Nunneries after
the Norman Conquest*

SALLY THOMPSON

CLARENDON PRESS · OXFORD
1991

Oxford University Press, Walton Street, Oxford OX2 6DP

Oxford New York Toronto
Delhi Bombay Calcutta Madras Karachi
Petaling Jaya Singapore Hong Kong Tokyo
Nairobi Dar es Salaam Cape Town
Melbourne Auckland
and associated companies in
Berlin Ibadan

Oxford is a trade mark of Oxford University Press

Published in the United States
by Oxford University Press, New York

© Sally Thompson 1991

British Library Cataloguing in Publication Data
Thompson, Sally
Women religious : the founding of English nunneries after
the Norman Conquest.
1. England. Convents, history
I. Title 271.90042
ISBN 0–19–820095–1

Library of Congress Cataloging in Publication Data
Thompson, Sally.
Women religious : the founding of English nunneries after the
Norman Conquest / Sally Thompson.
Includes bibliographical references and index.
1. Monasticism and religious orders for women—England—History—
Middle Ages, 600–1500. 2. Convents and nunneries—England.
3. England—Church history—Medieval period, 1066–1485. I. Title.
BX2592.T56 1990
271'.90042'09021—dc20   90–35837
ISBN 0–19–820095–1

Typeset by Pentacor PLC, High Wycombe, Bucks.

Printed and bound in
Great Britain by Bookcraft Ltd
Midsomer Norton, Bath

Preface

WHEN I first started work on the subject of the foundation of English nunneries after the Norman Conquest, I had no idea how long the project would take. My children, who at first were carted round nunnery sites in push-chairs (usually in the rain), are now grown up. Ben, as a preliminary to a history degree, helped to check the footnotes of the thesis which provided the material for this book. Anna learnt to cook, and produced meals when nunneries, not cooking, were on my agenda. I would like to thank them both. Over the years I have had the benefit of much expert help. My particular thanks are due to Professor Christopher Brooke who first suggested the subject, and then provided endless expertise and encouragement as the research progressed; to Brenda Bolton of Westfield College who worked tirelessly to help with the final stages of the doctoral thesis; to Dr Marjorie Chibnall who was kind enough to read the manuscript of the book and give me the benefit of her knowledge and advice. Many others have also helped me on the way: Dr Diana Greenway and Dr Jane Sayers on numerous small points over tea at the Institute of Historical Research, Professor Christopher Holdsworth who advised on questions relating to the Cistercians, and Dr Brian Golding who gave me the benefit of expert advice on the Gilbertines. I am also very grateful to the Master and Fellows of St John's College, Cambridge, for giving me permission to look at their manuscripts and to the archivist, Mr Malcolm Underwood, who was always ready to help. My thanks are also due to the staff at the Institute of Historical Research, and in the manuscript room at the British Library. The completion of the research for this book was made possible by the grant of a Senior Studentship from the Leverhulme Foundation which enabled me to have a precious year working full-time in libraries. Finally, my special thanks are due to the senior members of my family: to my mother who taught me always to look up what I did not know; to my father who taught me never to give up; and most of all to my husband Jim who first encouraged me to take up historical research, and who—despite everything—has managed to stay supportive.

Contents

English Nunneries founded after the Norman Conquest

Abbreviations

For full bibliography with abbreviated references see p. 259.

AASS = *Acta Sanctorum Bollandiana* (Brussels and elsewhere, 1643–).

BIHR = *Bulletin of the Institute of Historical Research.*

BL = British Library.

DHGE = *Dictionnaire d'histoire et de géographie ecclésiastiques*, ed. A. Baudrillart *et al.* (Paris, 1912–).

EETS = Early English Text Society.

EHR = *English Historical Review.*

EYC = *Early Yorkshire Charters*, 12 vols., i–iii, ed. W. Farrer (Edinburgh, 1914–16); iv–xii, ed. C. T. Clay (Yorks. Archaeol. Soc., Record ser., extra ser. 1–3, 5–10 (1935–65); extra ser. vol. iv is Index to *EYC*, i–iii, ed. C. T. and E. M. Clay (1942).

HRH = *Heads of Religious Houses, England and Wales 940–1216*, ed. D. Knowles, C. N. L. Brooke, and V. London (Cambridge, 1972).

KH = D. Knowles and R. N. Hadcock, *Medieval Religious Houses, England and Wales* (2nd edn., London, 1971).

MA = *Monasticon Anglicanum*, W. Dugdale, revd. edn., J. Caley, H. Ellis, and B. Bandinel, 8 vols. in 6 (London, 1817–30, repr. 1846).

MGH = *Monumenta Germaniae Historica inde ab a. c. 500 usque ad a. 1500*, ed. G. H. Pertz, etc. (Berlin, Hanover, 1826–).

PL = *Patrologiae cursus completus series Latina*, ed. J. Migne, 221 vols. (Paris, 1844–64).

PR = Pipe rolls cited by the regnal year, ed., in Pipe Roll Society (London, 1884–).

PUE = W. Holtzmann (ed.), *Papsturkunden in England*, 3 vols. (Abhandlungen der Gesellschaft der Wissenschaftern zu Göttingen, phil.-hist. Klasse, NF 25 (Berlin, 1930–1); 3. Folge, 14–15 (1935–6); 3. Folge, 33 (1952)).

SJC = St John's College, Cambridge.

TRHS = *Transactions of the Royal Historical Society.*

VCH = Victoria History of the Counties of England.

Introduction

IN 1922 Eileen Power published her major work on medieval English nunneries.[1] This studied the period c.1275–1535 and so omitted the era of monastic foundation in the twelfth and thirteenth centuries. Earlier, Lina Eckenstein had worked on the general theme of women and monasticism in a wider European context, but the short section on English nunneries in the twelfth century referred only to the small number of houses which were old foundations, established before the Norman Conquest.[2] The sizeable number of new foundations for women which came into existence during the two succeeding centuries still lacked their historian. After these two seminal works, English nunneries received scant attention in historical studies. Professor Knowles's great history of monasticism is largely concerned with men, and contains only a brief section on the nunneries for the period 1066–1100.[3] He ascribed his 'neglect' of the women to the limitations of the sources available and the sizeable amount of research needed for a detailed study of nuns' houses.[4] Some individual convents have been studied in depth. Work has been done on Stamford Priory, Northamptonshire, and Barking Abbey in Essex.[5] In the last decade research on the nunneries in Yorkshire during the twelfth and thirteenth centuries has been published in pamphlet form.[6] Particular houses of nuns have received spasmodic attention from local historians,[7] while information from a range of English nunneries has been used in an unpublished study of canon law and the religious life for women in twelfth-century England.[8] In

[1] E. Power, *Medieval English Nunneries c.1275–1535* (Cambridge, 1922).

[2] L. Eckenstein, *Women under Monasticism* (Cambridge, 1896), 201–13.

[3] D. Knowles, *The Monastic Order in England* (Cambridge, 1940; 2nd edn., 1963), 136–9.

[4] D. Knowles, *The Religious Orders in England*, 3 vols. (Cambridge, 1948–59), ii. p. viii.

[5] W. M. Sturman, 'History of the Nunnery of St Mary and St Michael outside Stamford', MA thesis (London, 1946); id., 'Barking Abbey; a Study in its Internal and External Administration from the Conquest to the Dissolution', Ph.D. thesis (London, 1961). Marham abbey in Norfolk has been studied in an American thesis: see J. A. Nichols, 'The History and Cartulary of the Cistercian Nuns of Marham Abbey, 1249–1536', Ph.D. thesis (Ohio, 1974).

[6] J. Burton, *The Yorkshire Nunneries in the Twelfth and Thirteenth Centuries* (Borthwick Papers, no. 56; York, 1979).

[7] Details of the many articles in local publications are given in the bibliography. Articles in the VCH are sometimes inadequate and frequently concentrate on the later history of the nunnery when more evidence is available. For a list of the contributors to the sections on religious houses see KH, 3–4. Recent volumes to appear with helpful articles on nunneries are VCH *Cheshire*, iii (1980), VCH *Salop*, ii (1973), VCH *Staffs.*, iii (1970); VCH *Wilts.*, iii (1956) is also very useful.

[8] Z. M. Procter, 'Religious Life for Women in Twelfth Century Canon Law, with special reference to English Houses', M.Phil. thesis (London, 1967).

recent months an important contribution to this field of study has come from America with the publication of Sharon Elkins's book on holy women of twelfth-century England.[9] But there has been no attempt by an English historian to work from the original documents, synthesize the detailed study of the many nunneries founded in the twelfth and early thirteenth centuries, and to relate this expansion to European developments. This is the aim of this book.

The invaluable lists provided in Knowles and Hadcock's *Medieval Religious Houses* indicate the existence of at least 142 nunneries by the third quarter of the thirteenth century.[10] Only ten of these were clearly pre-Conquest foundations, although it is possible that others were in some sense re-foundations of earlier communities.[11] These earlier foundations in many ways form a distinct group. They were abbeys, not priories, and were generally considerably richer than the post-Conquest foundations. They have been excluded from the scope of this study,[12] with the exception of Amesbury, Minster in Sheppey, and Polesworth, which were all re-founded in the twelfth century. The exact date of the foundation of many of the nunneries cannot be pin-pointed with any degree of precision. A large number of houses have no extant foundation charters and can only be dated by the earliest surviving reference. The main period for the foundation of the post-Conquest nunneries was 1100–1250, with the second half of the twelfth century probably seeing the establishment of the greatest number of new communities.[13]

The obscurity surrounding the origins of many of the nunneries is a striking feature. It may in some cases reflect a slow growth, where the initial focal point was provided by an individual anchoress or by earlier links with another religious institution. A study of these

---

[9] S. Elkins, *Holy Women of Twelfth Century England* (University of North Carolina, 1988).

[10] For the lists see KH, 194, 253–5, 270, 272, 278. See also Appendix A where the nunneries are classified alphabetically because of problems with classification based on order. Bretford and Tunstall were short-lived and did not continue as independent priories in the 13th cent.; nor did Ramstede (Ramscombe) which was apparently closed down by Archbishop Hubert of Canterbury in 1198. Spinney, another community which apparently did not survive, is not included in KH.

[11] For example, Hinchingbrooke seems to have developed from an earlier foundation at Eltisley; see Chap. 9, n. 21.

[12] The pre-Conquest foundations which have been omitted are: Barking (*c.*666), Chatteris (1006–16), Romsey (*c.*907), Shaftesbury (?–860, or *c.*888), Wherwell (*c.*986), Wilton (830), and Winchester (*c.*900). For the dates of these, see KH, 253–5. The Franciscan and Dominican nunneries have also been excluded from this book as they were mainly founded in the late 13th and 14th cents.

[13] For the dates of the foundations see Appendix A. The difficulties of establishing when nunneries were founded causes problems for any chronological analysis such as that used in Elkins, *Holy Women.*

origins forms the first part of this book. The second section deals
with the impact of the new orders of the twelfth century, and their
links with English nunneries. The question of the order of many
women's convents poses several problems. While it is a reasonable
assumption that all pre-Conquest nunneries observed some form of
the Benedictine rule, it is made clear by no less an authority than
Abbess Héloïse that this did not easily adapt to the needs of women.
In asking Abelard to write a rule for her community, she pointed out
that the dictates of St Benedict were often not appropriate to her
sex.[14] During the twelfth and thirteenth centuries it seems that a
sizeable number of women's houses varied their allegiance between
the Benedictine and the Augustinian rule.[15] Nor were the nunneries
clearly integrated into the new orders such as that of Cîteaux, Cluny,
or the reformed canons of Prémontré and Arrouaise.

One basic reason for this instability in relation to their order lay in
the difficulties inherent in the women's links with the male religious
for whom the orders were originally founded. Some dependence on
masculine support was an inevitable consequence of the lay status
and inferior position of the female sex. Men were needed to provide
priestly as well as administrative assistance. To meet this need many
of the earlier, pre-Conquest nunneries had been double foundations,
with men and women following the religious life in association. It is
generally thought that such double houses were not a feature of the
twelfth and thirteenth centuries. The double orders of Fontevrault
and the Gilbertines—the English order established by St Gilbert of
Sempringham—are regarded as notable exceptions. But a closer
study of many of the nunneries founded after the Norman Conquest
suggests that their history and development were often linked with
the vagaries of the nuns' dependence on men. Some communities of
women were apparently formed as they were distanced from
monasteries which had earlier provided support. At a number of
other convents it is clear that brothers formed part of the community.
The problems of an individual nun's dependence on male support is
illustrated in the *Life of Christina of Markyate*,[16] a twelfth-century
source which helps to throw some light on the general obscurity
surrounding the early history of religious communities of women.
Christina was a young girl who had to struggle to follow her

[14] *The Letters of Abelard and Heloise*, trans. B. Radice (Harmondsworth, 1974), 159–79,
no. 5.
[15] Uncertainty regarding the order of some nunneries at their foundation is noted in KH,
251. For lists of houses which indicate when other orders were recorded, see ibid. 253–5, 272,
278.
[16] *The Life of Christina of Markyate, a Twelfth-Century Recluse*, ed. and trans. C. H.
Talbot (Oxford, 1959; corr. repr. 1987).

vocation. She was forced to seek help from hermits, bishops, and archbishops. In eventually founding a priory at Markyate in Hertfordshire, she was given vital support by the powerful abbot, Geoffrey of St Albans. Without his help, and the donations of land granted by patrons and benefactors, the small group which formed round Christina might never have stabilized into a permanent community. The third section of the book studies the role of such founders and patrons in the establishment of the nunneries.

This book, therefore, embarks on the study of 139 nunneries founded mainly during the twelfth and the first half of the thirteenth centuries. It analyses their origins, the relationship of the English nunneries to the new European orders of the twelfth century, and the role of founders and patrons both lay and ecclesiastical. Christina of Markyate's friendship with Abbot Geoffrey was not without its critics and clearly gave rise to scandal. The story of Christina is unique, but a study of the nunneries suggests that many communities of women experienced similar difficulties and uncertainties in their attempts to obtain the necessary masculine support. While seeking to remedy previous neglect by concentrating on the history of women religious, the effects of their dependence on men has emerged as a major theme of this book.[17]

[17] In her study Professor Elkins also notes the importance of links with men's houses and of co-operation between the sexes, with men and women leading the religious life in association; see Elkins, *Holy Women, passim*, esp. pp. xvii–xviii.

I

The Genesis of Community

I   Scarcity of Sources

THE shortage of evidence for a study of English nunneries founded after the Conquest has puzzled many historians.[1] Writers struggling to compile articles on particular houses have lamented the lack of sources available. 'Of the early foundation of the priory of Benedictine nuns at Bromhall within the limits of Windsor Forest, nothing is known', wrote Cox in the Victoria County History for Berkshire.[2] Another historian of the nuns, trying to collect evidence for the foundation of a Buckinghamshire priory, could only resolve his problem by stating that: 'The nunnery of Little or Minchin Marlow, *prioratus de Fontibus de Merlawe,* may be said to have no history.'[3] Such a claim is questionable, but an examination of the English nunneries founded in the twelfth and early thirteenth centuries reveals a remarkable scarcity of documentary evidence.

As far as primary sources are concerned, the majority of the nunneries have extant only a minute number of original charters dating from this period. For many houses not a single original charter appears to have survived. Series of charters numbering fifty or more exist for only a handful of nunneries, for example for Nuneaton in Warwickshire, and St Radegund, a Cambridgeshire house; for Lacock in Wiltshire, and the Gilbertine houses of Bullington and Sempringham.[4] Monastic houses often recorded their title deeds by transcribing charters into cartularies or registers. Yet there are

[1] Some of the ideas and information in this chapter were first published in the Cistercian Studies Series, see S. P. Thompson, 'Why English Nunneries had no History. A Study of the Problems of the English Nunneries founded after the Conquest', in J. A. Nichols and L. T. Shank (eds.), *Distant Echoes. Medieval Religious Women,* i (Cistercian Publications, Kalamazoo, 1984), 131–49.

[2] J. Cox, 'The Priory of Bromhall', VCH *Berks.,* ii, 80 (usual spelling Broomhall). Similar remarks about the lack of information were made by VCH authors for Carrow (VCH *Norfolk,* ii, 352); Greenfield and Orford (VCH *Lincs.,* ii, 155 and 209); Keldholme (VCH *Yorks.,* iii, 167); and Lyminster (VCH *Sussex,* ii, 121).

[3] C. R. Peers, 'The Benedictine Nunnery of Little Marlow', *Archaeol. Journal* 59 (1902), 307.

[4] The Nuneaton charters are found among BL Addit. charts. 47,393–53,112. The St Radegund charters are preserved at Jesus College, Cambridge; they are calendared in A. Gray, *The Priory of St Radegund Cambridge* (Cambridge Antiq. Soc., octavo ser. 31; Cambridge, 1898). For a calendar of the Lacock charters see *Lacock Abbey Charters,* ed. K. H. Rogers (Wilts. Rec. Soc. 34; Devizes, 1979). For the Bullington charters see *Documents Illustrative of the Social and Economic History of the Danelaw from Various Collections,* ed. F. M. Stenton (British Academy; London, 1920), 1–74; see also B. Golding, 'The Gilbertine Priories of Alvingham and Bullington; their Endowments and Benefactors', Ph.D. thesis (Oxford, 1979), esp. pp. i, vii; see also ibid., p. i for information about the Sempringham charters, and the smaller numbers surviving for other Gilbertine priories.

surprisingly few such collections belonging to women's convents. Only nineteen are extant, of which two are mere fragments and one is badly burnt.[5] There is evidence of the previous existence of fourteen other cartularies, and short extracts from nine of these have been copied by antiquaries and so survive.[6] But for the vast majority of nunneries a starting-point for the study of their history must be those charters and references transcribed in the *Monasticon Anglicanum*. The revised edition, drawing as it does on the labours of Dodsworth, Dugdale, Tanner, and Oliver, forms a worthy basis for modern study, but is by no means always accurate.[7] Nor is the list of houses complete. One Yorkshire nunnery was so obscure as to miss the attention of both Dodsworth and Dugdale and was first spotlighted in an article written in 1886.[8]

Many of the documents in the *Monasticon* are taken from a version of the charter enrolled in the charter or patent rolls. Such royal records are an important source of information for the nunneries. In some cases, as at Wintney in Hampshire, they provide the main bulk of our evidence for the house.[9] Royal charters of confirmation were obtained by a number of nunneries and can provide valuable information for the date of a foundation as well as for its benefactors and endowment. Information can also be gleaned from other royal records. The pipe rolls are a useful source, and in recording payments to communities of nuns they sometimes provide the earliest evidence of a nunnery's existence.[10] Legal records can also reveal fragments of information, with feet of fines and curia regis rolls giving the names of prioresses and occasionally of chaplains, as well as causes of dispute.

Ecclesiastical records also provide information about the nunneries. Bishops' registers came to be particularly informative, and Eileen Power made great use of them as a source for the history of the nuns

---

[5] These damaged cartularies are those for the nunneries of St Sepulchre Canterbury, and Westwood. That for Nunkeeling (BL Cotton MS Otto C. viii), is described in the Cotton catalogue as 'a burnt lump of little use'. For a list of the surviving cartularies and registers see G. R. C. Davis, *Medieval Cartularies of Great Britain. A Short Catalogue* (London, 1958).

[6] Extracts are extant for Bullington, Castle Hedingham, Haverholme, Legbourne, London Haliwell, North Ormsby, Norwich (Carrow), Stamford, and Studley, see Davis, *Med. Cartls.*

[7] For a brief survey of the monastic sources and the achievement of the *Monasticon*, see KH, 1–3.

[8] W. Brown, 'The Nunnery of St Stephen's of Thimbleby', *Yorks. Archaeol. Journal*, 9 (London and Leeds, 1886), 334–7.

[9] PRO, C53/124, membr. 31, calendared in *Cal. Chart. Rolls, 1327–41*, 391–7.

[10] This is the case at Broomhall in Berks., where a reference in the roll of 1157 × 1158 indicates that the priory was in existence some 45 years earlier than the date generally given. See *The Great Rolls of the Pipe for the 2nd, 3rd and 4th Years of the Reign of King Henry II, 1155, 1156, 1157, 1158*, ed. J. Hunter (London, 1844), 151; cf. KH, 256. For a discussion of pipe roll evidence and the problems of dating see *HRH*, 11–12.

in the later Middle Ages. However, the earliest extant are those for Lincoln and York, no other diocese having a register pre-dating 1250.[11] Evidence for the period before the bulk of registers was compiled has to be gleaned from scattered episcopal *acta*.[12]

It has been pointed out that the study of ecclesiastical organization in the twelfth century involves collecting widely dispersed fragments of evidence and asking questions which they were not designed to answer.[13] This is certainly true of the nunneries. The basic source material for the convents founded after the Conquest is provided by charters. The main purpose of the bulk of these charters was to record a grant of land or rent. If the document survives only as a cartulary copy, or in the form of an *inspeximus* in the royal records, or as a transcript made by an antiquary, witness lists are frequently omitted, making them virtually impossible to date.[14] In some cases, as for example at Clementhorpe in Yorkshire, what appear to be foundation charters have survived in the form of documents drawn up at the initiation of a convent to record its endowment and to name its principal benefactors.[15] It has been convincingly pointed out, however, that carefully constructed foundation charters can be misleading, involving an artificial telescoping of events as a simplified record for posterity.[16] The set phraseology of many of the charters, developed from an earlier period when there was more reliance on living memory, can also cause particular problems.[17] Even the earliest charters of a particular house usually refer to the community as already in existence. The historian must decide whether this was just a conventional form of wording or whether it reflected a real beginning.

[11] For a list and description of extant episcopal registers see D. Smith, *Guide to the Bishops' Registers of England and Wales. A Survey from the Middle Ages to the Abolition of Episcopacy in 1646* (Royal Hist. Soc.; London, 1981). The Lincoln register for Bishop Hugh of Wells is largely composed of institutions, ordinations of vicarages, etc., and has no information about general business or visitations; see *Rotuli Hugonis de Welles episopi Lincolniensis* AD *MCCXXIX–MCCXXXV*, ed. W. P. W. Phillimore and F. N. Davis, 3 vols. (Cant. and York Soc.; London, 1907 [1905]–1909).

[12] For a note on the current research into episcopal *acta*, with bibliography, see *English Episcopal Acta I. Lincoln 1067–1185*, ed. D. Smith (London, 1980), pp. vii–ix and xxix–xxx.

[13] M. Brett, *The English Church under Henry I* (Oxford, 1975), 3. It has also been pointed out that sources for the history of women frequently present particular problems; see J. Verdon, 'Les Sources de l'histoire de la femme en Occident aux xe–xiiie siècles', *Cahiers de civilisation médiévale* 20 (1977), 219–51.

[14] For a general discussion about the untrustworthy nature of many 12th cent. documents see M. Clanchy, *From Memory to Written Record. England 1066–1307* (London, 1979), chap. IX and esp. 257.

[15] *EYC*, i, 278, no. 357.

[16] V. H. Galbraith, 'Monastic Foundation Charters of the Eleventh and Twelfth Centuries', *Cambridge Hist. Journal* 4 (1934), 205–22.

[17] Clanchy, *Written Record*, 257; see also *passim* for the slow change of emphasis from oral to written.

Such intrinsic weaknesses in the source evidence (from the point of view of a present-day student) is further compounded by the problem of forgery.[18] A sizeable number of the remarkably large series of charters for Wix Priory in Essex were forged,[19] and it would be rash to suppose that this house was unique. Other nunneries have charters issued under suspicious circumstances or displaying suspicious characteristics. At Armathwaite, an entry on the patent rolls states that charters of the nunnery had been destroyed, yet a mere seven years later the king is obligingly confirming a very long charter full of privileges which claimed that the house was founded by William II.[20] Similarly, at Minster in Sheppey, one charter described on the rolls as lost is then recalled in remarkable detail.[21]

Apart from the shortage of charter evidence and the difficulties of interpretation, the lack of sources is compounded by the fact that nunneries generally attracted little attention from monastic chroniclers. Henry II's refoundation of Amesbury as a priory of the order of Fontevrault was reported by several chroniclers, presumably because of the royal involvement.[22] Other houses receive brief notices because of proximity or the incidental involvement of the monastery compiling the record. The small priory of Bungay in Suffolk is mentioned in the *Chronicle of John de Oxenedes*, and the *Chronicle of Meaux* goes into some detail about a dispute with the nuns of Swine, also in Yorkshire.[23] But in general nunneries singled out for particular attention by monastic chroniclers are those which were in some way linked with the community of monks. Thus the St Albans' historians record the foundation of Sopwell and St Mary de Pré, two

[18] For a discussion of the question of forgery, with bibliography, see A. Morey and C. N. L. Brooke, *Gilbert Foliot and his Letters* (Cambridge Studies in Medieval Life and Thought, N.S. 11; Cambridge, 1965), chap. VIII. See also C. N. L. Brooke, 'Approaches to Medieval Forgery', *Journal of the Society of Archivists* 3 (1965–9), 377–86, and Clanchy, *Written Record*, 248–57. Also *Fälschungen im Mittelalter*, Schriften der Monumenta Germaniae Historica, Band 33, 6 vols. (Hanover, 1988 [5 vols. so far, 6 = Index, to come])

[19] C. N. L. Brooke, 'Episcopal Charters for Wix Priory', in *A Medieval Miscellany for D. M. Stenton*, ed. P. Barnes and C. Slade (Pipe Roll Soc.; London, 1962), 45–63. The Wix charters are the subject of current research.

[20] *Cal. Pat. Rolls, 1467–77*, 392 (1473); printed *MA*, iii, 271–2, no. 3; and ibid. *1476–85*, 208 (1480), printed *MA*, iii, 271, no. 1.

[21] *Cal. Chart. Rolls, 1327–41*, 112–16 (1329). This confirmation has the appearance of being an amalgamation of several charters.

[22] See *Gesta Regis Henrici Secundi Benedicti Abbatis. The Chronicle of the Reigns of Henry II and Richard I (AD 1169–1192) known commonly under the name of Benedict of Peterborough*, ed. W. Stubbs, 2 vols. (Rolls ser. 49; 1867), i, 165. See also 'The Chronicle of John Brompton', in R. Twysden, *Historiae Anglicanae Scriptores X . . .* (London, 1652), 1119; and *Giraldi Cambrensis Opera*, ed. J. S. Brewer, J. F. Dimock and G. F. Warner, 8 vols. (Rolls ser. 21; 1861–91), viii, 170.

[23] *Chronica Johannis de Oxenedes*, ed. H. Ellis (Rolls ser. 13; London, 1859, repr. 1969), 69; *Chronica Monasterii de Melsa a fundatione usque ad annum 1396*, ed. E. A. Bond, 3 vols. (Rolls ser. 43; 1866–8), ii, 12–22.

communities founded by the abbey, as well as recounting the virtues
of the recluse Christina of Markyate and the help given to her by
their abbot.[24]

As well as the shortage of evidence for the communities of women,
there is also a remarkable lack of information about individual nuns.
Two prioresses, Lucy and Amphelisa, had their deaths recorded in
the mortuary rolls of their respective houses, Castle Hedingham and
Lillechurch (Higham).[25] Both these rolls date from the first decades
of the thirteenth century,[26] and the ladies must presumably have
been of some importance. But a striking feature of English nunneries
founded after the Conquest is the lack of evidence about their
inhabitants. There seem to have been few women of spiritual vision
or stature following a religious vocation in the twelfth and thirteenth
centuries, or if there were, they have left no trace on the records.[27]
The account of the life and religious virtues of Christina of Markyate
is unique.

There may also have been particular practical reasons why the
number of documents which have survived for the nunneries is so
small. Fire seems to have been a major hazard. References to fires
occur at a sizeable number of houses and sometimes it is explicitly
stated that documents were burned.[28] Floods could also constitute a

[24] See the account in *Gesta Abbatum Monasterii Sancti Albani*, ed. T. H. Riley, 3 vols.
(Rolls ser. 28; 1867–9), i, 80–2 (Sopwell), 201–5 (St Mary de Pré), and 98–105 (Christina and
Markyate Priory).

[25] BL Egerton MS 2849 (Castle Hedingham roll). In this magnificently illuminated roll, 122
entries commemorate the death of Lucy who is described as prioress and foundress. For a
consideration of her possible identity see pp. 180–1. The Lillechurch (Higham) roll is preserved
in the library of St John's College, Cambridge, SJC MS 271. In this the death of the prioress
Amphelisa is mourned by some 378 other religious communities. For a recent study of
fragments of two mortuary rolls see C. R. Cheney, 'Two Mortuary Rolls from Canterbury:
Devotional links of Canterbury with Normandy and the Welsh March', in D. Greenway, C.
Holdsworth and J. Sayers (eds.), *Tradition and Change. Essays in Honour of Marjorie Chibnall
presented by her Friends on the Occasion of her 70th Birthday* (Cambridge, 1985), 103–14.

[26] For the probable dating of the Castle Hedingham manuscript, *c.*1230, see *New
Palaeographical Society. Facsimiles of Ancient Manuscripts etc.*, ed. E. Thompson, G. Warner,
F. Kenyon, and J. Gilson, 1st ser. 2 (London, 1903–12), 126. The date generally given for the
Lillechurch roll is *c.*1265 × 1298, see M. R. James, *A Descriptive Catalogue of the
Manuscripts in the Library of St John's College, Cambridge* (Cambridge, 1913), 317–18,
no. 271. But there was an earlier prioress Amphelisa dating from the time of Bishop Gilbert de
Glanville (1185–1214), see SJC archives D 46.41; also *Registrum Hamonis Hethe, Diocesis
Roffensis*, AD 1319–52, ed. C. Johnson, 2 vols. (Cant. and York Soc., 48–9; Oxford, 1948), i,
27. An early 13th-cent. date is confirmed by internal references in the roll to Henry, prior of
Colchester and Godfrey, prior of Launceston, who both lived in the first decade of the 13th
cent., see *HRH*, 160, 169.

[27] This is noted by Eileen Power who wrote: 'For some reason which it is impossible to
explain, monasticism did not provide in England during the later Middle Ages any women
of sanctity or genius who can compare with the great Anglo-Saxon abbesses' (Power, 502).
A similar point is made in Knowles, *Monastic Order*, 136.

[28] See Power, 171–2. In addition to the cases she cites, fires appear to have occurred at

problem. The nuns of Stratford, Middlesex, had their lands flooded on many occasions and the women at Crabhouse in Norfolk seem to have abandoned their original site because of similar hazards.[29] There is evidence of serious floods at several other nunneries.[30] Political troubles might also lead to the destruction of documents. At Ickleton the records of the prioress were said to have been destroyed in the rebellion of 1381,[31] and the nunneries situated on the northern border clearly suffered from Scottish raids.[32] It would not be difficult to identify similar accidents and natural hazards for monasteries of monks and canons, but it is possible that the nuns were particularly vulnerable, with unsuitable sites and less robust buildings.

Poverty could be an underlying cause of susceptibility to accident and the scarcity of surviving documents, for lack of adequate resources seems to have been a major problem for the nuns. Claims of financial difficulty, particularly when made in the context of taxation, have to be treated with caution. Marham Abbey in Norfolk, founded in 1249, did not qualify for the Norwich taxation of 1254; probably because of this it was also omitted from the taxation of 1291, although by that date the nunnery had acquired considerably more endowments.[33] Its poverty may well have been more apparent than real. The majority of nunneries founded after the Conquest, however, do seem to have been poor.[34] Direct evidence of their financial state in the twelfth and thirteenth centuries is not easy to find. Many, like Marham, are not mentioned in the returns for the taxation of Pope Nicholas IV.[35] The figures that are given, incomplete as they are, vary from a temporal income of ten shillings a year for St Margaret's Ivinghoe in Hertfordshire, to nearly £200

Broomhall (KH, 256), Buckland (*Cal. Close. Rolls, 1231–34*, 402), Castle Hedingham (*PR 3 Richard I*, 32), Catesby (*Cal. Lib. Rolls, 1245–51*, 345) and Malling (*The Historical Works of Gervase of Canterbury*, ed. W. Stubbs, 2 vols. [Rolls ser. 73; 1879–80], i, 485).

[29] *Cal. Pat. Rolls, 1358–61*, 175; M. Bateson, 'The Register of Crabhouse Nunnery', *Norfolk Archaeology* 11 (1892), 4.

[30] For evidence of other floods see Power, 176–7. It has been suggested that proximity to the sea was a reason for the dereliction of the nunnery of Swine: see G. Duckett, 'Charters of the Priory of Swine in Holderness (among the Rawlinson MSS in the Bodleian Library)', *Yorks. Archaeol. Journal* 6 (1879–80), 114. It is also probable that Godstow Nunnery was badly flooded: see D. Ganz, 'The Buildings of Godstow Nunnery', *Oxoniensia* 37 (1972), 151.

[31] VCH *Cambs.*, vi, 232.

[32] The nuns of Holystone and Lambley appear to have been driven out by the Scots in the 14th cent. (KH, 281).

[33] Nichols, 'Marham Abbey', 32–7.

[34] For a discussion of the poverty of the Yorkshire convents in this period see Burton, *Yorks. Nunneries*, 24–6. For the financial difficulties of the women in the later Middle Ages see Power, 161–236; see also ibid. 96–130 for an account of the property and income of the nunneries.

[35] For an assessment of the taxation see R. Graham, 'The Taxation of Pope Nicholas IV', *EHR* 23 (1908), 434–54.

annual revenue for Godstow Abbey in Oxfordshire.[36] Godstow, however, founded by a noble lady and favoured by Henry II, was exceptional. As well as adding to the vulnerability of site and buildings and the likelihood of hazards such as fire and flood, poverty would jeopardize both the collection and the survival of documents. The payment of scribes as well as the provision of wax and ink was expensive, more so possibly than the parchment unless this was of very fine quality.[37] Enrolment on the royal records would also have involved payment. Financial difficulties may have prevented the nuns from obtaining charters in the first place, and subsequently lessened the likelihood that documents they did possess were safeguarded by being recorded on the charter or patent rolls. An analysis of existing sources suggests some correlation between the wealth of a house and the number of documents which have survived. With the exception of Hinchingbrooke, none of the apparently poorest houses have a series of charters or a cartulary surviving.[38]

There may also have been other problems peculiar to the nuns which help to explain the shortage of documents and the relative obscurity of the women's convents. Knowledge and understanding of Latin seems to have presented considerable difficulties. It has been pointed out that in the thirteenth century there are some references to ignorance of Latin, while in the fourteenth century nearly all episcopal injunctions to nunneries are in French. By the fifteenth century the Alnwick visitation records provide evidence of the complete incomprehension of Latin in some houses, with even the prioress not able to understand episcopal mandates. There is no comparable evidence for such ignorance in the men's houses visited by the bishop.[39] Such lack of learning might well have an effect on the keeping and survival of records. In 1440, the prioress of Langley in Leicestershire informed the visiting prelate that she had in her possession the foundation charter for her house, but that she was unable to understand it.[40] A similar difficulty in understanding

---

[36] KH, 264 (Ivinghoe); 259 (Godstow).

[37] Clanchy, *Written Record*, 93–4.

[38] For Hinchingbrooke there was a register which was destroyed by fire in 1830 (Davis, *Med. Cartls.* 55, no. 490). A number of charters are also extant: see *Index to the Charters and Rolls in the Department of Manuscripts, British Museum*, ed. H. J. Ellis, ii, *Religious Houses and Other Corporations and Index Locorum for Acquisitions from 1882–1900* (London, 1912), 387–90.

[39] Power, 246–51.

[40] *Visitations of Religious Houses in the Diocese of Lincoln. Records of Visitations held by William Alnwick, Bishop of Lincoln AD MCCCCXXXVI–MCCCCXLIX*, ed. A. H. Thompson, 2 vols. (Cant. and York Soc. 24; London, 1919), ii, pt. 1, 174.

muniments is given by the author of the English version of the cartulary of Godstow as the reason for his labours:

And, for as muche as women of relygyone, in redynge bokys of latyn, byn excusyd of grete undurstondyng, where it is not her modyr tonge: Therfore, how be hyt that they wolde rede her bokys of remembraunce and of her munymentys wryte in latyn, for defaute of undurstondyng they toke ofte tymes grete hurt and hyndraunce.[41]

If charters and muniments written in Latin were unintelligible, this would have militated against their transcription into cartularies and registers, and so lessened the likelihood of the documents' preservation.

The lack of surviving sources for the early history of nunneries may also be explained by their dependence on chaplains. By the very nature of their religious calling a community of women depended on the services of priests to celebrate Mass and for other devotional needs. Men were clearly required to help in other ways, managing the nunneries' estates, working as labourers, acting for the women in law suits, and writing their charters. There is little direct evidence as to who wrote these. An occasional witness list is terminated by a name, always masculine, coupled with the statement that he was the scribe.[42] In the medieval period the art of writing was thought of as a laborious task similar to that of manual labour.[43] It always remained distinct from other aspects of literacy,[44] and it may well have been considered unsuitable for women.[45] It would seem that the nuns did not always find it easy to obtain the services of chaplains who could remedy such deficiencies. When the prioress of Langley returned the original mandate to Bishop Alnwick instead of the certificate he requested, she made it clear that her chaplain was equally unable to

[41] *The English Register of Godstow Nunnery*, ed. A. Clark, 2 vols. (EETS; London, 1911), i, 25. A similar attempt to make a cartulary intelligible is found at Canonsleigh in Devon, where there are detailed summaries in French in the manuscript: see *Cartulary of Canonsleigh Abbey (Harleian MS3660). A Calendar*, ed. V. London (Devon and Cornwall Rec. Soc., N.S. 8; 1965 for 1962), p. xxxi.

[42] e.g. BL Addit. chart. 48,093 (Nuneaton chart. dating from *c.*1240 × *c.*1250). For a discussion of the question as to whether the clerical last witness of a charter was frequently the scribe, see J. H. Hodson, 'Medieval Charters. The Last Witness', *Journal of the Society of Archivists* 5 (1974–5), 71–89.

[43] See examples cited in P. Schmitz, *Histoire de l'Ordre de Saint Benoît*, 7 vols. (Gembloux, 1942–6; 2nd edn., i–ii, Maredsous, 1948–56), ii, 64–5.

[44] Clanchy, *Written Record*, 88.

[45] In the Bodleian Library a MS from the nunnery of Winchester contains a reference to a *scriptrix*, and was apparently written by a nun (Oxford, Bodleian MS Bodl. 451 fo. 119ᵛ). This dates from *c.*1100. It may reflect the higher degree of literary activity in those nunneries founded before the Conquest. In the 15th cent. the editor of the *Paston Letters* has shown that only one of this group of literate ladies was able to write, and her skill was limited: see *Paston Letters and Papers of the Fifteenth Century*, ed. N. Davis, 2 vols. (Oxford, 1971), i, pp. xxxvii–xxxviii.

understand it.[46] Similarly the translator of the Godstow register, labouring to rewrite Latin in a language intelligible to the nuns, referred to the difficulties the women had in finding learned and trustworthy men to advise them.[47] Problems in obtaining literate chaplains at any point in the nunneries' history must have had damaging repercussions on the production and preservation of documents. One earlier hint of such difficulties is found in the Lillechurch mortuary roll recording the death of the prioress of Lillechurch (later Higham) priory. This magnificent document contains entries from some 378 religious houses mourning her death, and those for several houses of nuns are written in an unformed and sprawling hand suggestive of a beginner in the art of writing.[48]

The scarcity of sources is a fundamental aspect of a study of women's convents founded in the twelfth and first half of the thirteenth centuries. As well as reflecting particular problems facing the nuns— their general poverty, their lack of skill in Latin, the language of documentation, and some difficulties in obtaining literate chaplains— the dearth of evidence may also reflect the diverse origins of many of the houses of women which came into being in the twelfth and thirteenth centuries. The question of when a monastery was founded may be less significant than asking how it was founded.[49] This is true of many nunneries which appear to have developed slowly, and whose diverse origins are unlikely to be encapsulated in a foundation charter. The suggestion that some nunneries had shadowy beginnings is not novel. Writing in 1870, one historian of the priory of Little Marlow in Buckinghamshire pondered its early history. He wrote:

Whether it owed its being to the labour and devoted self-sacrifice of a recluse, or sprang at once into comparative affluence by the generosity of a rich and noble patron, or was a branch of some larger nunnery, are points that cannot be solved with the scanty records that we as yet possess regarding this religious house.[50]

Lack of sources frequently precludes firm answers about individual houses, yet cumulative evidence can provide some insights into the genesis and foundation of nunneries which 'had no history'.

[46] *Lincoln Visitations*, ii, pt. i, 174.

[47] *Cartl. Godstow*, i, 25.

[48] Lillechurch mortuary roll, SJC MS 271. The hand for the Wroxall entry is particularly unformed.

[49] This point was made in relation to a priory of Augustinian canons: see J. C. Dickinson, 'The Origins of St Augustine's Bristol', in, *Essays in Bristol and Gloucestershire History*, ed. P. McGrath and J. Cannon (Bristol and Glos. Archæol. Soc.; 1976), 112–13.

[50] W. Birch, 'Account of the Nunnery of Little Marlow', *Records of Buckinghamshire* 4 (Aylesbury, 1870), 65.

2 Hermits and Anchoresses

It is clear that several nunneries developed round a hermit or an anchoress. The process by which a recluse attracted followers who then required a greater degree of organization, and their subsequent formalization into a religious community, has been described as the slide to cenobitism.[1] Such a development was not uncommon in men's communities, and several Augustinian and Cistercian houses grew up round hermitages.[2] Evidence suggests that in the twelfth and thirteenth centuries a sizeable number of women led the life of an anchoress.[3] The *De Institutis Inclusarum* of Ailred of Rievaulx, a treatise written in response to requests from his sister who was leading the life of a recluse, appears to have fulfilled a real need in providing guidance for such anchoresses.[4] It is not possible to estimate how many recluses subsequently came to follow a more cenobitic form of religious life, but the starting point for a study of such an evolution must be the *Life of Christina of Markyate*.

The story of Christina falls into three parts: her private vow of dedication to God as a young girl and the subsequent conflict with her parents, her time as a dependant of other recluses, and her own life as the head of a group which later developed into a priory of nuns. It provides a portrait of an individual, not simply a type of feminine holiness.[5] The text of the *Life* survives in a fourteenth-century manuscript, damaged by the fire in the Cotton Library in the

[1] L. Genicot, 'L'Erémitisme du xie siècle dans son contexte économique et social', in *L'Eremitismo in Occidente nei secoli xi e xii* (Miscellanea del Centro di Studi Medievali, 3rd ser., 4; Milan, 1965), 66–9. For a summary of his argument, see C. J. Holdsworth, 'Christina of Markyate', in D. Baker (ed.), *Medieval Women, Studies in Church History*, Subsidia 1 (Oxford, 1978), 188.
[2] For examples see H. Dauphin, 'L'Érémitisme en Angleterre aux xie et xiie siècles', *Eremitismo in Occidente*, 279–83. See also J. Herbert, 'The Transformation of Hermitages into Augustinian Priories in Twelfth-century England', in W. J. Shiels (ed.), *Monks, Hermits and the Ascetic Tradition, Studies in Church History* 22 (1985), 131–45.
[3] A. K. Warren, *Anchorites and their Patrons in Medieval England* (Univ. of California Press, 1985), 18–21.
[4] For the text of this, with an introduction to its content and compilation, see C. H. Talbot, 'The *De Institutis Inclusarum* of Ailred of Rievaulx', *Analecta Sacri Ordinis Cisterciensis* 7 (Rome, 1951), 167–217. For evidence of its popularity and a list of the extant MSS, see ibid. 169–70 and 175–6. For a note on English anchorite rules see Warren, *Anchorites and Patrons*, 294–8.
[5] It has been suggested that the *Life* deserves recognition as 'perhaps the twelfth century's most effective and revealing personal history of a woman': see R. W. Hanning, *The Individual in Twelfth Century Romance* (New Haven and London, 1977), 50.

eighteenth century. The text is incomplete, breaking off in mid-sentence.[6] One of the puzzling features about its account of Christina's life is the lack of evidence it provides for the nunnery at Markyate which is known to have developed round her. The usual explanation is that the story terminates at an earlier point in the recluse's history before the formation of the priory.[7] Talbot noted that the manuscript consisted of twenty-three leaves, two quires of eight and one of seven, and concluded that probably one leaf and a whole gathering were missing and a sizeable proportion of the text was lost.[8] The account refers to occasions which can be dated *c*.1140, and Markyate was dedicated some five years later.[9] But an alternative interpretation is that the story does cover the formative period of the community, although this is not the author's concern. It is not clear that the account terminates in 1140, and it may well include later events. Perhaps the missing gatherings from the only extant manuscript of the *Life* contained blank pages or another manuscript. It is clear that the *Vita* reveals the existence of a church and a cloister, and in the later part mentions Christina's monastery (*monasterium*).[10] Such wording suggests the priory at Markyate. It is apparent that regular services were being held, shared by the community.

A reinterpretation of other evidence also suggests that the *Vita* may be a more complete account than has hitherto been supposed. It was apparently dedicated to some worthy person whose name is lost.[11] While the incomplete nature of the manuscript precludes any certainty, the most likely person to receive the dedication of the *Life* was Abbot Geoffrey of St Albans. Christina's friendship with the Norman abbot and their mutual dependence is one of the main themes of the account, and at one point the author states that the recluse would not leave her cell and St Albans to go to a more famous establishment because 'she revered you above all others'.[12] This must surely refer to Geoffrey. It suggests that the *Life*, or parts of it, must

[6] For a description of the MS of the *Life* (BL Cotton MS Tiberius E. i (ii), fos. 146–67) see Talbot, *Life of Christina*, 1–4.

[7] The author of the account of Markyate in the VCH knew of the *Life* only through Roscarrock's account of it, and dismissed it as of little interest: see VCH *Beds.*, i, 358, n. 10, and Talbot, *Life of Christina*, 1, n. 2.

[8] Talbot, *Life of Christina*, 4–5.

[9] Ibid. 14–15.

[10] Ibid. 178, 180. The word *monasterium* is in distinct contrast with the earlier use of *heremum*.

[11] Ibid. 5.

[12] 'Tum quia te super omnes sub Christo pastores in terra fortissime diligebat sicut (iugi) experimento probasti' (ibid. 126, BL Cotton MS Tiberius E. i (ii), fo. 158ᵛ).

predate the abbot's death in February 1146, and so could be dedicated to him.[13]

It is probable that much of the account was written while Christina was still alive, making use of her reminiscences. This would seem to be compatible with the freshness of detail and vivid character of the personal anecdotes which are such a feature of the work. It is not clear when Christina died. The history of St Albans, the *Gesta Abbatum*, states that Abbot Robert de Gorron (1151–66) took a mitre and sandals embroidered by the Lady Christina when he visited the pope.[14] But the fact that Christina had made the sandals does not necessarily mean that she was alive; nor can this be inferred from the reference in the pipe roll of 1155 × 1156 which records a payment made to her.[15] It is quite possible that this merely refers to an earlier payment and does not provide firm evidence that she was alive at that date.[16] If the *Vita* was dedicated to Abbot Geoffrey, and the death of the heroine took place before 1156, it is not safe to conclude that the account leaves out some fourteen years of Christina's life and omits the time when the community at Markyate developed into a priory. Bishop Alexander consecrated the church at Markyate in 1145,[17] a mere five to six years after incidents clearly covered by the *Vita*. The appearance of a pilgrim, a Christ-like figure, at the end of the manuscript of the *Life*, suggests the culmination of spirituality appropriate to the final stages of the biography.[18] The *Vita* could be substantially complete, covering most of the life of the recluse and the development of the community at Markyate. Far from being largely irrelevant to the history of Markyate nunnery,[19] the *Life of Christina* may in itself provide a testimony to the vigour of the eremitical community and the minimal and gradual nature of the changes required for it to develop into a priory.

[13] Talbot suggested that the *Life* was written at the instance of Abbot Robert de Gorron (1151–66), (Talbot, *Life of Christina*, 9–10); but the evidence for Christina's links with him is scanty, and Abbot Geoffrey would seem a far more likely candidate.

[14] *Gesta Abbatum*, i, 127. The Latin is *fecerat*.

[15] *PR 2–4 Henry II*, 22. The entry reads 'et in blado quod rex dedit Dominae Christinae de Bosco l s'. This wording would seem to suggest payment to a recluse, suggesting it might date from an earlier period.

[16] For the difficulties of using pipe roll evidence and the possibilities of misleading longevity see *HRH*, 11–12.

[17] *Acta I Lincoln 1067–1185*, 30–1, no. 49. It has been pointed out that the time when a monastic church was dedicated in relation to the foundation of the community could vary considerably, e.g. from 7–17 years: see A. Binns, *Dedications of Monastic Houses in England and Wales 1066–1216* (Studies in the History of Medieval Religion, 2; Woodbridge, 1989), 9–10.

[18] For the importance of this pilgrim, see Holdsworth, 'Christina', 191–2.

[19] Talbot concluded that the *Life* omitted at least fourteen years of Christina's life during which the community at Markyate was placed 'on a canonical footing' and the church was consecrated (Talbot, *Life of Christina*, 4).

It has been argued that the *Life* could not have been dedicated to Abbot Geoffrey of St Albans because it is critical of him.[20] This attitude might be explained by the identity of the author. It is possible that the biography is the product of the eremitical community grouped round the hermit Roger who features in the *Life* as sheltering Christina, and who eventually designated her as his successor. A passage in the account reveals that at least five other hermits lived with Roger.[21] At one point Christina is described as the hermit's 'Sunday daughter', implying that there may have been other female followers.[22] Reading and writing were regarded as a duty for those following the solitary life,[23] and it is quite feasible that one of the hermits could have undertaken such a task. Such authorship would explain the detailed knowledge of Christina and her life-story, a knowledge which included some incidents which could only have been revealed by a close relationship with the lady herself. It could also explain the links with the abbey of St Albans, and at the same time the element of detachment and criticism. One of the hermits in the community may, like Roger, have been a monk at St Albans, thus explaining references in the account to 'our monastery', and yet still have been capable of writing a life of the recluse which contained some criticism of the abbot.[24] The links hermit Roger maintained with the abbey seem to have been somewhat nebulous in his lifetime, even if the abbey claimed him at his death.[25] His hermitage was not on land belonging to St Albans, and there is no suggestion that he made any reference to the abbey when he nominated his successor. Nor does he seem to have looked to St Albans for support for Christina; the account makes it quite clear that initially Abbot Geoffrey had not met the recluse and knew nothing of her.[26]

It is a possible hypothesis that the *St Albans Psalter*, as well as the *Life of Christina of Markyate*, was the product of the hermit community. It, too, is a work which testifies to the links with the abbey, while displaying interesting discrepancies with the practices of the monks. Differences between the calendar in the *Psalter* and those

---

[20] Talbot, *Life of Christina*, 9.

[21] Ibid. 108–9. Their names are not given.

[22] Ibid. 106–7.

[23] R. M. Clay, 'Further Studies on Medieval Recluses', *Journal of the British Archaeol. Assoc.* 16, 3rd ser. (1953), 74.

[24] Compare Talbot's suggestion that the author of the *Vita* may have been attached to Christina's community as a chaplain or confessor (Talbot, *Life of Christina*, 7). Another possibility is that the references to 'our monastery' were added later by the writer of the Tiberius MS, who came from St Albans.

[25] *Gesta Abbatum*, i, 101. For a description of Roger and his virtues, see ibid. 97, where it is claimed that the hermit was under obedience to the abbot.

[26] Talbot, *Life of Christina*, 134–5.

of the abbey were noted by the editors, as was the misspelling of the patron saint's name.[27] It has been shown that the main hand of the *Psalter* is not found in other local books; nor is it particularly of the St Albans type. The set of miniatures, the glory of the manuscript, was the work of the Alexis Master, an independent professional artist who travelled widely between centres.[28] The main evidence for the linking of the *Psalter* with the hermit community rather than the abbey, is the entry for the obit of hermit Roger, which places particular emphasis on his importance. The hand is similar to that in the main text, and the wording certainly suggests a strong bond with him.[29] Similarities between the *Psalter* and the *Life of Christina* are striking. In addition to the common theme of the Alexis story, the illustrations in the *Psalter* of the episode on the road to Emmaeus reflect Christina's encounter with the mysterious pilgrim described in the *Life*.[30] These similarities could merely reflect a common homage to the lady of Markyate and her story, but it is also a possibility that both bear witness to the strength and identity of the community of recluses grouped near the abbey of St Albans.

Whatever the authorship of these monuments of literary and artistic skill, the main emphasis of the *Life of Christina* is to stress the heroine's spiritual qualities; it does not provide direct evidence of the formation of the priory of Markyate. Nevertheless insights may be gleaned from the background even if they are not the author's main concern. Before Roger's death, he made Christina his heir.[31] This designation was regarded with apprehension by the young lady, implying the exercise of some authority over others who had been disciples of the hermit. The *Life* indicates that as her fame grew, the number of Christina's followers increased.[32] No figure is given, but the account of the understandable terror of the women at the apparition of a headless body tells of a flock of maidens trying to

[27] *The St Albans Psalter*, ed. O. Pächt, C. R. Dodwell, and F. Wormald (London, 1960), 23–5. It should be noted, however, that the priory was not a cell of St Albans, and so the calendar used might not conform in every respect to that of the abbey. For the relationship between Markyate Priory and the abbey of St Albans see pp. 57–8.

[28] *Manuscripts from St Albans Abbey 1066–1235*, ed. R. M. Thomson, 2 vols. (Woodbridge, Suffolk, 1982), i, 25–7.

[29] For an analysis of the hands see ibid. 25. The entry reads 'Obitus Rogeri heremite monachi sancti albani; apud quemcunque fuerit hoc psalterium fiat eius memoria maxime hac die' (*St Albans Psalter*, 278 and plate 10). Goldschmidt suggested that the wording of this obit indicates that Roger was the scribe of the MS (ibid. 29–30). Other hermits, Azo and Ailward, are also commemorated in the Psalter (ibid. plates 4 and 9).

[30] Holdsworth, 'Christina', 191–2. For the popularity of the Alexis story see A. Gieysztor, 'La Légende de Saint Alexis en Occident: Un idéal de pauvreté', in *Études sur l'histoire de la pauvreté*, ed. M. Mollat (Publications de la Sorbonne, Série Études, 8, Paris, 1974), 125–39.

[31] Talbot, *Life of Christina*, 108–11.

[32] Ibid. 144–5.

shelter round their leader.[33] The word used for these followers is *puellae* rather than *sanctimoniales*,[34] and Christina herself is referred to as *domina* rather than prioress.[35] She is also given the title of *domina* in the charter of Bishop Alexander marking the consecration of the church, although her followers are described as nuns (*sanctimoniales*).[36] It is probable that the change from a community grouped round a holy recluse who exercised considerable authority, to a nunnery with its more formal organization, was a slow and almost imperceptible process.

While Christina's influence was based on her charisma and the legacy from hermit Roger, her successors would clearly come to need a more formal title and to be elected prioress. Christina's profession probably marked a stage in the progression from recluse to head of a community of nuns, but it is not easy to date this ceremony,[37] nor to determine its significance. The *Vita* refers to it on two occasions and with apparently different emphasis. At one point the suggestion is that the recluse was anxious to make her profession, with the hint that she feared to die while still unprofessed.[38] This time the ceremony seems to have been postponed, and when the *Life* returns to the theme the author implies that the lady was persuaded into the consecration by the pleading of Abbot Geoffrey.[39] The essentials for Christina, in making her profession, seem to have been the vow of virginity, which in view of her temptations apparently caused her much anxiety,[40] and the stress on obedience. Bishop Alexander of Lincoln performed the ceremony and the obedience promised was probably to him rather than to the abbot of St Albans. Christina's biography suggests that before agreeing to this profession, she had been tempted to withdraw to a quieter spot, presumably to follow a

[33] Ibid. 178–9.

[34] In his translation Talbot sometimes used the word 'nun' where 'maiden' might be a more accurate rendering, e.g. Talbot, *Life of Christina*, 140–1. The word *sanctimonialis* is used once to describe the life led by Lettice, a relative of the abbot of St Albans (ibid. 152–3).

[35] She is also described as *domina* in the pipe roll reference to a payment being made to her (*PR 2–4 Henry II*, 22).

[36] *Acta I Lincoln, 1067–1185*, 31, no. 49. In the charter recording agreement with St Paul's about the foundation of Markyate, the word used for the head of the women is *magistra*. See *Early Charters of the Cathedral Church of St Paul, London*, ed. M. Gibbs (Camden 3rd ser. 58; London, 1939), 119–20, no. 154.

[37] Talbot suggested *c.*1131, as this mention of her profession follows the invitation for Christina to go to head the new community at Clementhorpe (founded *c.*1125 × 1133) (Talbot, *Life of Christina*, 15), but the chronology is not clear.

[38] Ibid. 124–5.

[39] Ibid. 144–7.

[40] Ibid. 126–9. For a study of her visions and the temptations, some of them specifically sexual, which she underwent in the course of her vocation, see Holdsworth, 'Christina', 197–202. For a study of the concept of virginity see J. Bugge, *Virginitas. An Essay in the History of a Medieval Ideal* (The Hague, 1975).

more contemplative rather than a cenobitic life.[41] The ceremony may well have marked a further stage in her acceptance of the responsibilities of a growing community. It is doubtful if it constituted a turning point as regards her status.[42] She clearly regarded the private vow of dedication to God which she had taken many years earlier as of great importance. The story of her life is her struggle to keep it. Her profession at St Albans and her consecration may have represented a public acknowledgement of this private dedication rather than a crystallization of any particular form of her way of fulfilling this vow.[43]

Attempts to distinguish between the different forms of religious vocation may, at this date, imply lines of demarcation which did not in fact exist. It is generally held that the main distinction between a hermit and an anchorite is that, while both led a solitary life, the former had freedom of movement and the latter was enclosed within strict geographical limits.[44] It has been argued that such distinctions can have a flavour of artificiality.[45] The *Life of Christina* certainly suggests an easy transition from the life of an anchoress to that of a hermit. During her initial stay in Roger's cell, it is clear that the recluse was strictly enclosed as befitted an anchoress.[46] The *Vita* implies, however, that the picture was a changing one. Roger himself was probably not so restricted, and it is possible that as his heir Christina enjoyed more freedom. The account does not indicate rigid enclosure for either Christina or her followers.[47] As the ceremony of

[41] Talbot, *Life of Christina*, 146–7.

[42] Compare the view put forward by Dauphin that it was this ceremony which made her a nun (Dauphin, 'L'Érémitisme en Angleterre', 310). It is interesting that the *Ancrene Wisse* itself refers to a ceremony of 'professiun' and vows taken by an anchoress, see p. 32. A 12th-cent. *ordo* for the consecration of a virgin (the word 'nun' is not used) is printed in *The Pontifical of Magdalen College, with Appendix of Extracts from other English MSS of the Twelfth Century*, ed. H. A. Wilson (Henry Bradshaw Soc. 39; London, 1910), 84–6. The importance of the tradition of a consecrated virgin has been stressed by Noreen Hunt. She pointed out that a virgin as such was regarded as being in a state of innocence, and monastic profession was almost a subsidiary element: see N. Hunt, 'Notes on the History of Benedictine and Cistercian Nuns in Britain', *Cistercian Studies* 8 (1973), 157–77, esp. 159.

[43] For the general significance of the 'contract of dedication to God' and the similarities between the private and solemn vow, see Procter, 'Religious Life for Women', 25–34.

[44] For studies on English hermits and recluses see F. Darwin, *The English Mediaeval Recluse* (London, 1944), where the author gives credit to Gerald of Wales for spotting the essential difference—'heremitae solivagi aut anachoritae conclusi' (ibid. 4, n. 3). See also the basic work of R. M. Clay, *The Hermits and Anchorites of England* (London, 1914). For more recent studies see H. Mayr-Harting, 'Functions of a Twelfth-Century Recluse', *History* 60 (1975), 337–52; and Warren, *Anchorites and Patrons*.

[45] J. Leclercq, '*Eremus* et *eremita* pour l'histoire du vocabulaire de la vie solitaire', *Collectanea Ordinis Cisterciensium Reformatorum*, 25 (Rome and Westmalle, 1963), 24–5. The terminology is also discussed in A. K. Warren, 'The Nun as Anchoress: England 1100–1500', in *Distant Echoes*, 198–9.

[46] Talbot, *Life of Christina*, 102–5.

[47] Ibid. 140–1.

enclosure for an anchoress came increasingly under episcopal control[48] boundaries may have become more rigid, but at this date the lack of a clear-cut distinction between a hermit and an anchorite is further illustrated by the fact that Roger himself was described as both.[49]

The whole development of the community at Markyate, which took several years, is only revealed by the survival of the *Life of Christina* and its echoes in the *Gesta Abbatum*. The surviving charter evidence, the consecration charter of Bishop Alexander of Lincoln and the confirmation charter of the dean and chapter of St Paul's,[50] provides no clue of the anchoretic origin of the nunnery except for the implicit witness to the importance of the Lady Christina and the absence of the title of prioress. For other nunneries evidence of similar origins has to be sought out, and is often merely hinted at. In the case of the nearby convent of Sopwell, the account of the house's foundation in the *Gesta Abbatum*, which stresses the role of the abbot of St Albans, states that he was first attracted by the sanctity of two ladies following a religious life at Eywood, housed only in rough shelters. Abbot Geoffrey granted endowments, provided buildings, and founded a community of nuns strictly under the control of the abbey and situated near its gates.[51] An examination of charter evidence for the priory provides some corroboration for the *Gesta's* suggestion of an eremitical origin. A register of St Albans, compiled in the fourteenth and fifteenth centuries, contains early charters relating to the nunnery of Sopwell. One of these records the donation of a certain Henry d'Aubigny to 'the cell near St Albans first founded by hermit Roger'.[52] The confirmation charter of Henry's son makes it clear that the place referred to is Sopwell.[53] The mention of hermit Roger is intriguing. If he is the same man as the protector of Christina, as seems probable, it raises the possibility of Sopwell having an origin linked to that of Markyate.[54] Perhaps Roger started his life as a hermit near the abbey where he had been a monk, only to move subsequently. Perhaps the ladies at Sopwell formed part of his community.

[48] For the enclosure of anchoresses see Warren, *Anchorites and Patrons*, partic. 92–124. For the role of the bishops see ibid. 53–91.

[49] He is called a hermit in *Gesta Abbatum*, i, 97, and an anchorite by William of Malmesbury: see *Willelmi Malmesbiriensis monachi. De Gestis Pontificum Anglorum*, ed. N. E. S. A. Hamilton (Rolls ser. 52; 1870), 314, n. 1.

[50] *Acta I Lincoln 1067–1185*, 31, no. 49 and *Early Charts. of St Paul's*, 119–20, no. 154.

[51] *Gesta Abbatum*, i, 80–2. It has been suggested that the two recluses can be identified with names given in the *St Albans Psalter* of Avicia, prioress of Sopwell, and a nun Adelisia (Clay, 'Recluses', 74), but it is not clear that this identification is valid.

[52] BL Cotton MS Tib. E. vi (ii), fo. 204. This grant is printed in *MA*, iii, 365, no. 2.

[53] Ibid.; *MA*, iii, 365, no. 4.

[54] It is suggested in *VCH Herts.*, iv, 422, n. 2 that the *Gesta* may have confused the origins of Markyate and Sopwell. But the *Life of Christina* confirms the link between Roger and Markyate.

The picture given in the *Life of Christina* of men and women grouped round hermit Roger, has an interesting echo in the wording of Henry d'Aubigny's charter. He makes his grant to the hand-maidens and slaves of God, the men and the women serving God at the cell near the abbey.[55] Confirmations of Henry's charter reveal that his daughter was a member of this group.[56] It is unfortunate that it is not possible to date these charters with any precision. Henry was alive in c.1107–32, and was probably dead before 1146 as the confirmation charter of his son is witnessed by Abbot Geoffrey.[57] He may have been a nephew of Abbot Richard, Geoffrey's predeces-sor.[58] This, combined with the reference to hermit Roger, certainly suggests an earlier date for the existence of a community at Sopwell than that of c.1140 given in the *Gesta* for the foundation of the priory.[59] A group linked with a hermit had apparently formed before the abbot took action to establish the nunnery.

Crabhouse in Norfolk is another convent where there is evidence that the community originally developed round a recluse. An account of the origins of the nunnery, probably spiced with legend, is contained in the register.[60] It is written in French and suggests that two anchoresses played their part in the development of the priory. A maiden was inspired to live a solitary life. Others gathered round her, but eventually difficulties, culminating in a great flood, forced them to abandon the site. What happened then is not clear, but it seems as if one member remained and lived the life of an anchoress or hermit at nearby Wiggenhall. It was only after this that the community subsequently developed with the help of a lay patron and a house of canons.[61] It is impossible to verify the details of an account such as this. The hand appears to date from the thirteenth and fourteenth centuries, and if, as has been suggested, the purpose of the account was to instruct ladies of the convent,[62] it may embody valid tradition. The similarity with the *Life of Christina* and the gradual development of Markyate Priory indicate an inherent probability.

---

[55] BL Cotton MS Tib. E. vi (ii), fo. 204; printed in *MA*, iii, 365, no. 2. The Latin reads 'ancillis Dei et servis Dei'.

[56] Ibid.; *MA*, iii, 365, nos. 3 and 4.

[57] Henry is mentioned in two charters of Henry I: see *Regesta Regum Anglo-Norman-norum, 1066–1154*, 3 vols., ii *Regesta Henrici Primi 1100–1135*, ed. C. Johnson and H. A. Cronne (Oxford, 1956), 65, no. 812, note, and 257–8, no. 1738. For his son's confirmation charter see BL Cotton MS Tib. E. vi (ii), fo. 204; printed *MA*, iii, 365, nos. 3 and 4.

[58] For the probable pedigree of the family see L. C. Loyd, 'The Origin of the Family of Aubigny of Cainhoe', *Beds. Hist. Rec. Soc.* 19 (1937), 110.

[59] *Gesta Abbatum*, i, 80.

[60] BL Addit. MS 4733, fos. 1–54. See also Bateson, 'Reg. Crabhouse', 1–63.

[61] Bateson, 'Reg. Crabhouse', 2–5 and 12–14.

[62] Davis, *Med. Cartls.*, 33, no. 284.

Other evidence provides a measure of corroboration. The legend mentions Alan fitz Richard as one patron of the community, and the pipe rolls confirm the existence of such a man who was apparently alive in 1179–81.[63] Some early charters of Crabhouse also provide hints of an anchoretic origin. They refer to a *domina* Leva, who, like Christina, is not given the title of prioress although she is described as a nun.[64] She was the daughter of Godric of Lynn and the hermitage of Wiggenhall was granted to her. It has sometimes been assumed that this Leva was the first anchoress in the legend, but this is questionable.[65] The grant to her was made at the end of the twelfth century, and the wording suggests that she was probably associated with the later growth of a community of nuns round the hermitage of Wiggenhall.[66] The development of an independent nunnery at Crabhouse was apparently linked with the transfer of the cell of canons at Norman's Burrow to the priory of Castle Acre towards the end of the twelfth century. The significance of such links with communities of men is studied in a later chapter. While it is not possible to establish a definite chronology for the early history of the community,[67] it would seem clear that the origins of the nunnery of Crabhouse were linked with the vocation of recluses and the hermitage of Wiggenhall.

A small group also formed the nucleus of the community of Kilburn in Middlesex, where a hermit called Godwyn had built a hermitage. This was under the care of the abbey of Westminster and was granted by Abbot Herbert (1121–*c*.1136), at Godwyn's request, to three maidens—Emma, Gunilda, and Christina.[68] According to the short account in the history of the abbey written by John Flete in

---

[63] Bateson, 'Reg. Crabhouse', 13; *PR 26 Henry II*, 23 (1179 × 1180) and *PR 27 Henry II*, 87 (1180 × 1181).

[64] These charters are preserved in the Castle Acre register, BL Harl. MS 2110, fo. 82ᵛ; printed *MA*, v, 69, no. 4 and 70, no. 5, where the name is incorrectly given as Lena. In the charter recording the subsequent grant of Norman's Burrow to Castle Acre it is stated that the hermitage at Wiggenhall had been held by the 'hermit Joñ' (Ibid., fo. 60ᵛ, printed *MA*, v, 69, no. 1). It is not clear whether this name should be expanded in the masculine or feminine form. The probability is that it refers to a male hermit, John.

[65] Bateson, 'Reg. Crabhouse', 2–3.

[66] One charter recording a grant of land to the nuns refers to 'monialibus Deo servientibus et servituris in heremo iuxta Wigehale' (BL Harl. MS 2110, fo. 82ᵛ, printed *MA*, v, 70, no. 6). These charters probably date from the last decades of the 12th cent.

[67] It is suggested in KH, 279 that the flood mentioned in the register may have taken place *c*.1200. But the sequence of events in the account suggests it was earlier. A very different chronology is assumed by one historian of the nunnery who places the origins of the community before the Conquest with the women then being disrupted by the Domesday Inquest. He omits to cite any evidence. See A. Jessopp, 'Ups and Downs of an old Nunnery', *Frivola* (London, 1896), partic. 33 and 36–7.

[68] Abbot Herbert's settlement is recorded in a cartulary of Westminster dating from the reign of Edward I (BL Cotton MS Faust. A. iii, fos. 325ᵛ–326ᵛ, printed in *MA*, iii, 426, no. 1).

the fifteenth century, the ladies were the handmaidens (*camerae*) of Queen Matilda.[69] The queen was noted for her piety, and her servants may well have been inspired by her example.[70] A possibility is that they retired to a life of seclusion after Matilda's death in May 1118.[71] The record of the abbot of Westminster's grant indicates that the hermit Godwyn played an important role. The women were clearly under his tutelage and were to remain so. It is stated, however, that after the hermit's death, the women should, with the assent of the abbot, choose a suitable elderly man to be their mentor.[72] As with Christina of Markyate, the death of the recluse who had originally provided the focus of the group would have necessitated a greater degree of organization and the formalization of authority, and must have marked an important stage in the development of the priory. The abbot's charter itself already implies some degree of organization. Endowments were transferred to the women and the Bishop of London's blessing was obtained. A document setting out the rights of Westminster Abbey over the cell, in which the bishop agreed to its exemption from episcopal jurisdiction, also probably dates from this period as part of the establishment of the convent at Kilburn.[73] As at Markyate it is difficult to categorize the nature of the community. The women are referred to in Herbert's charter as *ancillae Dei* or *puellae*. They are not described as nuns (*moniales*), and they were led by a hermit. Yet the charter clearly envisages a continuing and growing community.

There are other convents of women where, as at Kilburn, the focal point seems initially to have been provided by male hermits. At Blithbury in Staffordshire, early charters record grants being made to two monks, Guthemunde and Saxe, who were probably hermits.[74] The group at Blithbury apparently came to include women, and a

---

[69] *The History of Westminster Abbey by John Flete*, ed. J. A. Robinson (Cambridge, 1909), 87–8. For Flete and his history see B. Harvey, *Westminster Abbey and its Estates in the Middle Ages* (Oxford, 1977), 12–18.

[70] She had been brought up at Wilton nunnery. An account of her unhappy childhood is given in D. Baker, ' "A Nursery of Saints": St Margaret of Scotland reconsidered', *Medieval Women*, 123–4.

[71] The possibility that the origins of the community go back as early as this is also indicated by the obligation on the part of the nuns to pray for the soul of Abbot Gilbert (? 1085–1117 × 1118) 'Liber Niger Quaternus', Westminster Abbey Muniments Book 1, fo. 125. Abbot Herbert's grant dates from 1128 × 1134.

[72] BL Cotton MS Faust. A. iii, fos. 325ᵛ–326ᵛ; printed in *MA*, iii, 426, no. 1.

[73] *The Letters and Charters of Gilbert Foliot*, ed. A. Morey and C. N. L. Brooke (Cambridge, 1967), 491, no. 463. Professor Brooke noted the possibility that it is a charter of Bishop Gilbert the Universal (1128–34).

[74] These charters have been preserved in the transcriptions of Randulph Holme (BL Harl. MS 2044, fo. 123; printed in *MA*, iv, 160, nos. 2 and 1). The dedication of the community to St Giles could be an indication that they were hermits, as St Giles, a French saint, was himself a hermit; see *The Oxford Dictionary of Saints*, ed. D. H. Farmer (Oxford, 1978), 173–4.

confirmation of a grant to the two men refers to nuns and to those of both sexes who might be received in the future.[75] In the same county, the origin of the nunnery of Farewell appears to have been similar. At the petition of Roger, Geoffrey, and Robert, three hermits, and the brothers of Farewell, the church and endowments were granted to a community of nuns there.[76] A charter of the bishop, presumably of an earlier date, had confirmed the church of Farewell to the 'men serving God in that place', and makes no mention of any women.[77] It is possible that the nuns merely replaced a masculine hermit community rather than sharing a common origin, but it would seem likely that at Farewell too, the development of a community of women was initiated by a small group of hermits.

The obscurity of the early history of several other nunneries may both conceal an eremitical origin and in part be explained by it. At Cheshunt in Hertfordshire no evidence survives for the foundation of the house. However, an isolated charter records a grant by Conan, Earl of Richmond, of a hermitage at Cheshunt to the church of John the Baptist and three brothers serving God there.[78] There is nothing specific, apart from its location, to associate the hermitage with the development of the community of women, yet it raises the possibility of a link. The nunnery of Cheshunt was in existence by 1183, when Pope Lucius III took it under papal protection.[79] An entry on the pipe roll of 1165 × 1166, which appears to refer to it, suggests that the community was in existence much earlier, at a date closer to the earl's grant.[80] The origins of the priory of Rowney, also in Hertfordshire, are veiled in similar obscurity. This house was said by a later source to have been founded by the earl.[81] Its dedication to

---

[75] BL Harl. MS 2044, fo. 123; printed in *MA*, iv, 160, no. 1. The Latin reads: 'Guthmundo et Saxi monachis et monialibus ibi manentibus locum de Blytheburgh, cum terra, et cum suis pertinentiis, et omnibus illis qui, vel quae ibidem accipientur ad serviendum Deo, et sancto Egidio . . . ' The charter is witnessed by Bishop Roger de Clinton and can be dated 1129 × 1147.

[76] *MA*, iv, 111, no. 1.

[77] Ibid., iv, 111, no. 2. It is interesting that this grant refers to the men as 'canonicis fratribus conversis ibidem Domino servientibus' and makes no specific reference to hermits.

[78] *EYC*, iv, 40–1, no. 35 (with facsimile). It is dated by the editor, who notes that the community has not been identified, as Oct. 1156 × Apr. 1158.

[79] The bull, dated 18 Dec. 1183, is copied in the register of Bishop Fitz James (1506–22); see London Guildhall MS 9531/9, fos. 37ᵛ–38.

[80] *PR 12 Henry II*, 77. See also *PR 13 Henry II*, 141, where the entry is underlined for deletion. The name *Cestrehunt* appears to refer to this nunnery, although the entries are under Glos., rather than Herts. (Later in his reign Henry granted alms to the nuns of Cheshunt from Winchester (*PR 32 Henry II* [1185 × 1186], 177). The suggestion of an earlier date for the nunnery is endorsed by a letter of Alexander III to Gilbert Foliot which can be dated 1163 × 1181 and refers to a young lady entering the convent when pregnant (*Foliot Letters and Charters*, 527, no. 25).

[81] See a confirmation charter of Henry VI (*Cal. Pat. Rolls, 1452–61*, 503–4 [1459]).

John the Baptist could suggest an eremitical genesis, and is the same dedication as that of the church in Conan's charter.[82] Whether Rowney was originally linked with the Cheshunt hermitage must, in the absence of clear evidence, remain a matter for conjecture.

At Flamstead, in the same county, the date of the nunnery's foundation is uncertain. The priory was certainly in existence in 1163 when it obtained a papal bull.[83] The traditional date given for the foundation is *c.*1150, but there is no precise evidence for this. To add to the possibilities of confusion Roger IV de Tosny who died in 1209 is described in one charter as the 'patron and founder' of the house.[84] But he was a minor at the death of his father in 1162, and another charter implies the foundation was earlier by referring to a grant made to the priory by his grandfather, Roger III, who died *c.*1157 × 62.[85] The dedication of the nunnery of Flamstead to St Giles in the Wood may indicate an eremitical origin,[86] and the *Life of Christina of Markyate* provides clear evidence of the existence of a recluse at Flamstead in the early part of the twelfth century. Alfwen, the anchoress there, sheltered Christina in her escape from the importunities of a would-be husband and the trials of the world.[87] There is no direct evidence to link the priory of nuns at Flamstead with an earlier anchoretic community, but such a link is a possibility.[88]

In addition to these Hertfordshire convents, there are other houses where the presence nearby of hermitages or anchorages may be significant. A grant of 1227 to Holm Cultram reveals that a

[82] *EYC*, iv, 40–1, no. 35. John was regarded as the archetypal hermit; see Binns, *Dedications*, 32.

[83] *PUE*, iii, 586, no. 494 (Herts. County Record Office, 19684). See also 587, no. 496 (1166 × 1179). On questions relating to Flamstead I am grateful for the help of Chris Butterill who is working on the cartulary.

[84] *The Beauchamp Cartulary Charters, 1100–1268*, ed. E. Mason (Pipe Roll Soc.; London, 1980), 210, no. 370 (1162 × 1209). Although the second Roger to hold the manor of Flamstead, he is Roger IV de Tosny: see *The Complete Peerage*, by G. E. C.; revised edn. V. Gibbs, H. A. Doubleday, Lord Howard de Walden, G. H. White, and R. S. Lea (London, 1910–59), xii (i), 765–9. For a family tree of the Tosny family of Flamstead see *Cartl. Beauchamp*, p. lx.

[85] Flamstead Cartulary, Herts. Record Office, MS 17,465, fo. 3. There is also a reference to his ancestors in a grant printed in *MA*, iv, 300, no. 1.

[86] See n. 74. He may have been a saint to whom women felt particular devotion: see Binns, *Dedications*, 30.

[87] Talbot, *Life of Christina*, 92–3. Alfwen's reported use of the plural when she denied Christina's presence at Flamstead to those searching for her, stating that she was 'not here with us', could indicate the presence of a small community (ibid. 94–5).

[88] Talbot argued that the priory of nuns could not be linked with the hermitage (Talbot, *Life of Christina*, 92, n. 1). Sharon Elkins suggests that the site at Flamstead was not the same as that of Alfwen's cell, but there seems no evidence to indicate this (Elkins, *Holy Women*, 190, n. 39). It is not possible to determine whether an entry on the pipe roll of 1155 × 1156 (*PR 2–4 Henry II*, 21) refers to a recluse at Flamstead or at some other place in the county.

hermitage in the forest of Inglewood was probably in existence as early as the reign of John, if not before.[89] The origins of Armathwaite Priory in Inglewood are unknown, and the obscurity is made greater by the patently forged charter which claimed that the founder of the house was William II.[90] Apart from this doubtful evidence of antiquity, the earliest mention of the nunnery occurs in the *Mappa Mundi* of Gervase of Canterbury, which dates from *c.*1201.[91] No evidence survives to link the hermitage with the nunnery, but the possibility of a connection must remain. It is interesting that a thirteenth-century manuscript of Ailred's *De Institutis Inclusarum* belonged to Holm Cultram.[92] At Northampton, Leland records a tradition that the community had moved from Fotheringay to the abbey of Delapré.[93] It is clear that the church of Fotheringay belonged to the abbey, confirming the suggestion of a link between the places.[94] There was a hermitage at Fotheringay in the last quarter of the twelfth century,[95] which may have been of earlier date, and again it is a possibility that this was linked with the early history of the nuns.

At other nunneries later evidence indicates that there were anchoresses linked with the community. Such an association is not hard to explain. The inevitable dependence of the anchoress on others for material and spiritual support, and the common aims of those following the solitary and the cenobitic life, would encourage the forging of such links. Some nuns became anchoresses as a progression to a more advanced form of the religious life.[96] It is also a possibility that religious houses deliberately forged links with hermitages, and that the episcopal hierarchy encouraged such integration into a more traditional structure.[97] Near Davington nunnery in Kent, there is fifteenth-century evidence of an anchoress

---

[89] *The Register and Records of Holm Cultram*, ed. F. Grainger and W. G. Collingwood, (Cumberland and Westmorland Antiq. and Archaeol. Soc., Rec. ser. 7; 1929), 76, no. 217 (1215).

[90] *Cal. Pat. Rolls, 1476–85*, 208; printed in *MA*, iii, 271, no. 1. See also p. 164.

[91] For the value of the *Mappa Mundi* as a source see D. Knowles, 'Gervase of Canterbury and the *Mappa Mundi*', *Downside Review* 48 (Exeter, 1930), 237–47. In its earliest form the *Mappa* probably dates from *c.*1201. For the reference to Inglewood see *Gervase of Canterbury*, ii, 441. Another early reference to the house is contained in a charter dating from *c.*1200 × *c.*1229: see *The Register of the Priory of St Bees*, ed. J. Wilson (Surtees Soc. 126; 1915), 86.

[92] Oxford Bodleian MS Hatton 101 (SC 4048). For a list of the surviving MSS see '*De Institutis Inclusarum*', 175–6.

[93] *The Itinerary of John Leland*, ed. L. T. Smith, 5 vols. (London, 1907–10), i, 4.

[94] *Regesta Regum Scottorum*, ed. G. W. S. Barrow, 2 vols. (Edinburgh, 1960), i, *The Acts of Malcolm IV, King of Scots 1153–65*, 279, no. 274.

[95] Clay, *Hermits and Anchorites*, 236–7.

[96] For comments on this type of anchoress see Warren, 'The Nun as Anchoress', 197–8.

[97] This point is made by Professor Holdsworth; see Holdsworth, 'Christina', 189 and n. 18.

whose cell was attached to the north side of Faversham church, a mere half-mile away from the nunnery.[98] Sometimes such cells were handed on to a successor, so this could imply the earlier existence of an anchorage. It is possible this was linked with Davington. A surviving obituary calendar of the nunnery records the deaths of anchoresses as well as nuns.[99] The date of these obits is not given, but some of the names in the calendar refer to thirteenth-century prioresses, and this could indicate the existence of a cell linked with the nunnery before the fifteenth century. How early such a link was made, and whether it was in any way associated with the origins of the priory, it is not possible to determine.

No attempt can be made to ascertain the number of nunneries which evolved from a community of recluses. Sometimes an apparent link with a hermitage could reflect a common origin; in other cases it might merely illustrate the sizeable number of cells for men and women wishing to follow a solitary vocation.[100] At Fosse in Lincolnshire, a fragment of evidence reveals the ambiguity. A chirograph in the Kirkstead cartulary, dated 1184, refers to the recluse (*inclusa*) and the nuns of St Peter quitclaiming ten shillings to the nuns of Fosse.[101] St Peter's Church was situated at the north end of Torksey near the house of Augustinian canons.[102] This charter provides the earliest reference to the nuns of Fosse, as well as evidence for the existence of nuns and a recluse at St Peter's. A charter of Bishop Hugh of Avalon, dating from *c.*1187 × 1198, confirmed to the anchoress of St Peter's and her companions (*ancillis*) the place where they lived in the north of the churchyard.[103] The

---

[98] 'Anchorites in Faversham Churchyard', *Archaeologia Cantiana* 11 (1877), 24–6 (no author given).

[99] This list is bound in BL Cotton MS Faust. B. vi(i), fos. 102–107ᵛ. The references to anchoresses are on fos. 102ᵛ and 107ᵛ. The list includes prioresses of other Kent nunneries, but whereas for other houses it is stated to which nunnery the prioress belonged, for Davington Priory itself merely the lady's name is given. Further evidence that the list derives from Davington is given by the references to Robert de Campania, grandson of the founder (ibid., fos. 103 and 105).

[100] At Polesworth in Warwickshire, architectural evidence suggests that an anchorage may have been attached to the church in the 13th cent. and still have been used in the 15th cent. (Clay, 'Recluses', 79). For a discussion of the possible association of the nunnery of Tarrant with anchoresses, and the question of whether such a link dated back to the foundation of the convent, see p. 33. Other nunneries which appear after their foundation to have anchorages attached or nearby are: Bristol, Carrow, Hampole, Nun Appleton, and Clementhorpe (York); see the lists in Clay, *Hermits and Anchorites*, 216–17, 234–5, 256–7, 258–9, 260–1.

[101] Kirkstead cartulary, BL Cotton MS Vesp. E. xviii, fo. 214ᵛ.

[102] A papal bull of 1186, confirming grants to Torksey Priory of canons, included the church of St Peter as part of its endowment. For this bull, which provides evidence about the early history of the priory of canons, see B. Dodwell, 'A Papal Bull for Torksey Priory', *BIHR* 52 (1979), 87–90.

[103] *English Episcopal Acta IV, Lincoln, 1186–1206*, ed. D. M. Smith (London, 1986), 132–3, no. 201.

probability is that the anchoretic community at St Peter's merged into the nunnery of Fosse: how far it was fundamental to the development of the priory of women is not clear.

The *Life of Christina of Markyate*, the Crabhouse register, and fragmentary charter evidence, indicate that in several cases recluses provided the focal point for the subsequent formation of a priory of nuns, and that the link between Christina and the convent of Markyate was by no means unique. A major testimony to the importance of anchoresses and the development of communities round them is provided by the *Ancrene Wisse* (the 'Anchoresses' Guide' or 'Rule').[104] This treatise, compiled initially for three women living the life of anchoresses, is a lengthy exhortation to a life of prayer and privation. It is written in English, in a West Midland dialect, and probably dates from early in the thirteenth century.[105] The existence of thirteen manuscript copies of the Rule is a clear indication of its popularity.[106] The evidence of the *Ancrene Wisse* also suggests that the transition from a group of anchoresses to a community of nuns was an easy process, with no rigid lines of demarcation dividing the different forms of vocation. While the original Rule was written for three sisters, another version probably drafted only a few years later, and possibly by the same author, envisages a larger community numbering at least twenty.[107] It is not clear how far the three sisters had initially lived a communal life. Reference is made in the Rule to their mutual support and encouragement, and it would appear that the decision to leave the world and to follow this form of religious life had been a joint one.[108] Nor is it clear that all elements of community life were removed, and it is possible that the sisters shared one household.[109] Even if they were separate, the anchoresses clearly had contact with

[104] For the basic text of the Rule I have used the Moreton edition, which provides both the middle English and a translation: see *The Ancren Riwle: a Treatise on the Rules and Duties of Monastic Life*, ed. T. Moreton (Camden Soc.; London, 1853). For recent research and comments on the Rule see *The English Text of the Ancrene Riwle edited from BM MS Cotton Cleopatra C. vi*, ed. E. J. Dobson (EETS 267; Oxford, 1972); and E. J. Dobson, *The Origins of Ancrene Wisse* (Oxford, 1976).

[105] E. J. Dobson, 'The Date and Composition of *Ancrene Wisse*', *Proceedings of the British Academy* 52 (1966), 181–208.

[106] For the different texts of the *Ancrene Wisse* and their affiliations, see E. J. Dobson, 'The Affiliations of the Manuscripts of *Ancrene Wisse*', in N. Davis and C. L. Wrenn (eds.), *English and Medieval Studies presented to J. R. R. Tolkien* (London, 1962), 128–63.

[107] For a discussion of these changes, their significance, and the argument that the corrector and revisor of the Cleopatra and Nero MSS was the same man, and in fact the author, see Dobson, 'Date of *AW*', *passim*, and particularly 201–3.

[108] *Ancren Riwle*, ed. Moreton, 226–9, 192–3.

[109] Dobson, *Origins of AW*, 169. He argues that the early multiplication of the MSS is more likely to indicate the existence of several groups rather than that the three sisters were

their maidservants and exercised authority over them.[110] The terminology used in the Rule suggests no sharp contrast between anchoress and nuns—the anchoresses were to take vows of obedience, chastity, and stability, the word 'professiun' being used.[111]

It has been pointed out that many of the provisions of the *Ancrene Wisse* bear a close resemblance to Augustinian constitutions drawn up at a similar date for the Dominican convent of St Sixtus in Rome.[112] Yet it is also true that such resemblance to another rule should not obscure what have been described as the 'anchoretic springs of the treatise'. Its author drew on many strands of influence in writing his guidance for the women, and to delineate the *Ancrene Wisse* in terms of an existing rule is too restrictive.[113] The aim of a recluse did not, of course, present any intrinsic challenge to the monastic ideal. Both represented, in general terms, a renunciation of the world to enable a closer union with God.[114] The rule of silence within the monastic order was both a witness and a safeguard of the vital element of solitude within the communal life. Strict enclosure came to be a feature of the worthy nun as well as of the anchoress.[115] Sometimes it may reflect an anchoretic origin. At both Kilburn and Sopwell the sources make clear that the members of the community, gathering as they had round anchoresses, were strictly enclosed.[116] It is not surprising that there was transition between the different forms of vocation. It is clear that the *Ancrene Wisse* was soon adapted for a much larger group apparently organized on a more communal basis. The use of the word 'cuuent' and the mention of unity and community of life in a passage inserted in the Corpus manuscript shows that the initial emphasis on a solitary life had undergone some

sufficiently separate to need individual copies of the Rule. In a 9th-cent. rule it was stated that there should never be less than two or three recluses grouped together (Clay, *Hermits and Anchorites*, 128–33).

[110] *Ancren Riwle*, ed. Moreton, 424–9.

[111] Ibid. 6.

[112] Dobson, *Origins of AW*, 94–103.

[113] A. Barratt, 'Anchoritic Aspects of *Ancrene Wisse*', *Medium Aevum* 49 (1980), 32, 44–6. He suggests that the Carthusian influence should not be underestimated, and that the author of the Rule was a person of eclectic taste.

[114] For the similarity of the two ideals, and the distinctions of status, see *Dictionnaire de droit canonique*, ed. R. Naz (Paris, 1935–), v, s.v. *Ermites*, partic. 415–16.

[115] For a study of the effects of enclosure on women religious see J. T. Schulenburg, 'Strict Active Enclosure and its Effects on the Female Monastic Experience (ca 500–1100)', in *Distant Echoes*, 51–86. See also R. Grazeau, 'La Clôture des moniales au xiie siècle en France', *Revue Mabillon*, 58 (1974), 289–308.

[116] At Sopwell the nuns were enclosed 'sub clave et sera ac sigillo Abbatis' (*Gesta Abbatum*, i, 81). At Kilburn an entry in the curia regis rolls implied the inability of the prioress to attend court as 'inclusa est' (*Curia Regis Rolls*, PRO texts and calendars (London, 1922–79), v, 22 [1207]).

modification.[117] As well as in itself illustrating the ease of transition from anchorage to priory, the *Ancrene Wisse* was probably used by communities of nuns as well as by groups of anchoresses.

The question as to which group of women inspired the *Ancrene Wisse* has not been easy to answer.[118] Arguments have been put forward for the ladies of Kilburn, Middlesex, and for those at Tarrant in Dorset. The main evidence for Kilburn is the known existence there of three anchoresses. In view of the probable ubiquity of such groups, however, this carries little conviction, and the dating of the original version of the Rule as probably between 1215 and 1222 eliminates the possibility.[119] The argument for Tarrant is based on the statement in a Latin manuscript of the Rule, dating from the fourteenth or beginning of the fifteenth century, that it was written by Simon of Ghent, Bishop of Salisbury (1295–1315) for his sisters, the anchoresses of Tarrant.[120] Such authorship must refer to the Latin version of the Rule. There is no clear evidence for the existence of anchoresses at Tarrant as distinct from the community of nuns there. The only hint of a link with recluses is the grant in the thirteenth century to the house of Tarrant of a hermitage nearby at Mannington,[121] but there is no mention of anchoresses. In view of the fragmentary nature of the sources, this does not rule out the possibility that anchoresses were associated with the nunnery in the early thirteenth century, but it may be that this later version of the Rule was simply for the edification of the nuns or for their chaplains.[122]

More convincing is the suggestion that the convent of Limebrook in Herefordshire provides the background for the *Ancrene Wisse*. The case for the identification of the treatise with this area rests

[117] The text of this passage is printed in *The English Text of the Ancrene Riwle. Ancrene Wisse, edited from MS Corpus Christi College Cambridge 402*, ed. J. R. R. Tolkien (EETS 249; 1962), 130. For a translation of the passage with comment on its significance see Dobson, *Origins of AW*, 267–71.

[118] For a summary of the various hypotheses up to the work of Professor Dobson see '*De Institutis Inclusarum*', 169, n. 7.

[119] For the dating of the Rule see Dobson, 'Date of AW', partic. 206. For a summary of the suggested dates for the early MSS of the Rule see Dobson, *Origins of AW*, 121–2, n. 2. The question of a link with Kilburn is discussed in R. W. Chambers, 'Recent Research upon the *Ancren Riwle*', *The Review of English Studies* 1 (1925), 15–22.

[120] Magdalen College Oxford Latin MS 67 (MA). See *The Latin Text of the Ancrene Riwle edited from Merton College MS 44 and BM MS Cotton Vitellius E. vii*, ed. C. D'Evelyn (EETS 216; 1944), pp. xi–xiv.

[121] *Cal. Chart. Rolls, 1226–57*, 232 (1237) and 272–3 (1242).

[122] In using the words 'sororibus suis anachoritis', the bishop may simply have been reflecting the terminology of the Rule itself, and referring to the nuns at Tarrant in a spiritual rather than a literal sense. This is suggested in Dobson, *Ancrene Riwle*, p. clxxi, n. 3. Tarrant was not the only nunnery to possess a version of the Rule, for Canonsleigh was given a copy by their foundress, Matilda de Clare (ibid., pp. xxv–xxvi).

largely on linguistic grounds, which indicate that the main group of manuscripts were produced in north Herefordshire or south Shropshire. The internal evidence of the Rule suggests that the author was a member of an Augustinian community, and it is argued that Wigmore Abbey fits both the geographical location and this Augustinian emphasis.[123] Limebrook Priory is situated about four miles from the abbey.[124] Little is known of its origins. In the fourteenth-century cartulary of the Mortimer family, a charter of Roger de Mortimer, which can probably be dated *c.*1252 × 1256, confirms land to the nuns of Limebrook.[125] It is incomplete, as the folios which would have contained the opening sentences are lost. But in the charter is a reference to an earlier grant made by Roger's grandfather to the church of St Leonard Sutelsford, or La Derefaud, and those living there. This charter has been cited as revealing the existence of an earlier community of women at La Derefaud, but this appears to be an error, as the passage refers only to brothers.[126] The dedication of the church there to St Leonard, a hermit, might imply an eremitical emphasis,[127] and it is possible that the group of brothers were hermits, but the charter does not in fact provide evidence of anchoresses at La Derefaud or Limebrook.

The dating of the early history of the priory of nuns is, however, compatible with the date of the *Ancrene Wisse*. The earliest reference to the nuns of Limebrook occurs in an eyre roll of 1221.[128] This description of the women as nuns does not necessarily mean that by that date they were a fully organized priory. The group there could be the sizeable community implied in the Corpus revision of the *Ancrene Wisse*. There is a hint in the sources that some form of religious settlement for women had existed at Limebrook some decades earlier at the end of the twelfth century. In a sixteenth-century genealogy of the Lingen family, lords of the area, it is stated that Ralph de Lingen was the 'first founder' of the priory of

---

[123] Dobson, *Origins of AW, passim* and particularly chaps. III and V.

[124] For a map of the area see ibid. 176.

[125] BL Harl. MS 1240, *Liber Niger de Wigmore*, fo. 40. For a description of this secular cartulary see Davis, *Med. Cartls.*, 150, no. 1292. For the dating of the charter see Dobson, *Origins of AW*, 214–17.

[126] Professor Dobson transcribes the Latin as 'sororibus quondam existentibus apud La Derefaud' (Dobson, *Origins of AW*, 218). But an examination of the text shows that the word is 'fratribus' and that throughout the charter the reference is to brothers not sisters forming the community at La Derefaud (BL Harl. MS 1240, fo. 40).

[127] For St Leonard see *Dict. of Saints*, 244–5. He was a saint whose popularity increased in the first half of the 12th cent. and his patronage was frequently invoked for hospitals; see Binns, *Dedications*, 29–30.

[128] *Rolls of the Justices in Eyre for Lincolnshire 1218–1219 and Worcestershire 1221*, ed. D. M. Stenton (Selden Soc. 53; 1934), 647, no. 1524.

Limebrook.[129] He is known to have died in 1190.[130] Professor Dobson has suggested that the author of the *Ancrene Wisse* was Ralph's son Brian, who is described in the same genealogy as a secular canon of the abbey of Wigmore. If the authorship of Brian de Lingen could be proved beyond doubt, the link between Limebrook and the *Ancrene Wisse* would be established.[131] The absence of such proof does not rule out the possibility that the nunnery developed from anchoretic origins. The wording of the Rule and the early multiplication of manuscripts suggests the existence of several small groups of recluses linked with each other.[132] The pipe rolls record the existence in the early thirteenth century of a recluse, Margaret, who lived within the jurisdiction of the Sheriff of Herefordshire and the March of Wales, possibly under the patronage of Roger de Montgomery.[133] The pressures on fragmented groups or individuals to unite and merge for a more communal form of vocation must have been considerable. In the twelfth century these were convincingly set out by the Abbot of Barnoldswick when he persuaded some recluses at Kirkstall to join his community and provide the new site for his abbey. He argued that, as laymen without a leader, the change to monasticism would improve the quality of their vocation.[134] Such instability may have been a particular feature of groups of women recluses. It is interesting that there is little evidence for the existence of female hermits. For women the enclosed life of an anchoress provided more security and protection, but even then the evidence of the *Ancrene Wisse* suggests the possibilities of a rapid transition to a more cenobitic life.

Cumulative evidence indicates, therefore, that the call to a solitary life provided the initial impulse for many cells which subsequently developed into nunneries. For some a mere fragment of information

---

[129] BL Harl. MS 1087, fo. 66, printed in *MA*, iv, 182. For a discussion of this genealogy see Dobson, *Origins of AW*, 195–209.

[130] *PR 2 Richard I* (1190 × 1191), 46. For references to Ralph on the pipe rolls see Dobson, *Origins of AW*, 205–9.

[131] For the detailed arguments justifying the claim of Brian de Lingen see Dobson, *Origins of AW*, chap. VI, partic. 343–68. The suggestion that he included his own name as a hidden signature in the text of the Rule is intriguing, but as Professor Dobson himself admits, not fully proven.

[132] It has already been noted that in Hertfordshire it would seem that hermit communities which eventually developed into Markyate and Sopwell were linked (see p. 23), and that there were also anchoresses at Flamstead. Evidence for other networks of hermit communities is given in Mayr-Harting, '12th Century Recluse', 337.

[133] *PR 5 John*, 55 (1202 × 1203); *PR 14 John*, 158 (1211 × 1212). For the suggestion that the recluse, Margaret, may have been linked with Roger de Montgomery see Dobson, *Origins of AW*, 235–6.

[134] See E. K. Clark, 'The Foundation of Kirkstall Abbey', *The Publications of the Thoresby Soc.* 4, *Miscellanea* (Leeds, 1895), 177–8.

hints at such an origin, and the scarcity of evidence precludes any proof. At Ankerwyke in Buckinghamshire only the name survives to suggest that the priory was originally linked with an anchorage. At Gokewell in Lincolnshire, an early charter refers to the 'nuns of Eskdale'.[135] A famous hermitage was sited as Eskdale, near the abbey of Whitby,[136] and it is a possibility that the women who came to form the community at Gokewell originally had links with this.

For many convents, the evidence is complex and inconclusive. At St Sepulchre in Canterbury, the community appears originally to have been linked with a parish church. According to a later source, the priory was founded by Archbishop Anselm in the church of St Sepulchre.[137] It seems that this church was parochial as well as conventual,[138] and this could hint at an anchoretic origin, with a group of recluses attached to a parish church. Such links may have been quite common. At Sempringham the young ladies under the care of St Gilbert were housed next to the church, and the *Ancrene Wisse* refers to anchoresses sheltering under the eaves of the church.[139] The archbishop wrote letters to a group of six women apparently living the life of anchoresses under the care of a certain brother Robert.[140] There is nothing specific to link this cell with Canterbury other than the interest and concern of the archbishop, but such a link is a possibility. St Sepulchre may have developed round anchoresses. But another fragment of evidence which could relate to the origins of the priory, is the entry in Domesday Book revealing the existence of a group of nuns holding land from the abbey of St Augustine close to Canterbury.[141] As this does not conflict with what is known of the site of the nunnery of St Sepulchre, it may refer to women from this community and suggest the possibility of some association with the abbey. Yet another question

[135] BL Egerton chart. 622, printed in *EYC*, vi, 204, no. 105 (not from the original), and dated by the editor as −1175. He is not able to offer any explanation for the name Eskdale (ibid., p. xiii).

[136] Godric of Finchale had a hermitage there: see *Reginald of Durham. Libellus de Vita et Miraculis S. Godrici Heremitae de Finchale*, ed. J. Stevenson (Surtees Soc. 20; 1847), 58. For references at a later date to an Eskdale hermitage and the mid-12th-cent. legend of the murdered hermit see *EYC*, ii, 355–6.

[137] See the 14th-cent. chronicle of William Thorne, printed in Twysden, *Scriptores*, 1893. For an edition with translation of Thorne's chronicle, see *William Thorne's Chronicle of St Augustine's Abbey, Canterbury*, ed. A. H. Davis (Oxford, 1934).

[138] W. Urry, *Canterbury under the Angevin Kings* (London, 1967), 211.

[139] *The Book of St Gilbert*, ed. R. Foreville and G. Keir (Oxford, 1987), p. xix; *Ancren Riwle*, ed. Moreton, 143.

[140] *PL*, clix (1854), 167–8 and 257–8. These ladies, all with Anglo-Saxon names, are described as *ancillae Dei*. The suggested date of the letters is −1109: see Clay, 'Recluses', 74. It has been pointed out that the known recluses of the 12th cent. were apparently all English or Anglo-Danish: see Mayr-Harting, '12th Century Recluse', 337–8.

[141] Urry, *Canterbury*, 62 and note.

is posed by the dedication of the convent to St Sepulchre. Such a dedication was sometimes used for hospitals, but is unique, in England, for a nunnery.[142] Lanfranc had founded two hospitals at Canterbury,[143] and another possibility is that the priory of St Sepulchre originally had links with a hospital. Such nebulous beginnings would not dispense with the necessity for a patron to stabilize the community with permanent endowments. The *Valor Ecclesiasticus* records that alms were given to the poor by the nuns of St Sepulchre on the anniversary of the death of William Calvel their founder.[144] A William Calvel lived in the early years of the twelfth century, and was known to the archbishop.[145] It is probable that he played an important part in the development of the community, possibly with his role obscured by the prestige of Anselm.[146] Links with hospitals, links with monks and canons, and the role of founders and patrons in the establishment of nunneries, are examined in the following chapters in an attempt to explore further the genesis of religious communities of women founded after the Norman Conquest.

[142] Examples of hospitals with this dedication are Hedon (Newton), and Hereford: see KH, 362, 363. See also Warwick which was of the order of the Holy Sepulchre: KH, 178–9.

[143] Ibid. 349–50.

[144] *Valor Ecclesiasticus temp. Henry VIII auctoritate regia institutus*, 6 vols. in 4 (London, 1810–34), i, 30.

[145] Urry, *Canterbury*, 62.

[146] For examples where the role of prestigious founders is exaggerated because of their social importance, see pp. 163–5.

3   Links with Hospitals

IN the twelfth and thirteenth centuries there were many similarities between hospital and monastery. The fundamental purpose of a medieval hospital was religious in the sense that it was concerned with the care of the soul as much as with the body.[1] Nor was provision of hospitality and alms the prerogative of hospitals alone, for this was also an important function of religious houses.[2] It has been shown in a study of the Augustinian canons that the distinction between hospitals and small priories could be one of degree rather than kind, and it is sometimes not possible to differentiate between them.[3] The original foundation of St Bartholomew in London seems to have included both a hospital and a priory within one inchoate institution. Tensions arose and the hospital gained a greater degree of independence and subsequently developed separately.[4]

Such bipartite development within a community shows that by the late twelfth century a distinction was made by contemporaries between hospital and priory. In view of this possibility of differentiation, the difficulties of demarcation between nunnery and hospital are striking. In the case of women seeking to follow a religious vocation, there was no criterion of priestly status to help distinguish between a hospital inmate, veiled and living under a Rule, and a nun. Nunneries were sometimes under the authority of a master (*magister*)—a title frequently associated with hospitals, while sisters at hospitals were sometimes ruled by a prioress. The possibilities of confusion are tacitly illustrated by Knowles and Hadcock, who classify a number of feminine communities as 'nunneries, or hospitals of sisters'.[5] The question is whether such ambiguity merely reflects a lack of knowledge about a particular establishment, or whether it indicates a genuine blurring of function and organization. The previous chapter has shown that the distinctions between communit-

---

[1] The basic study of English hospitals is R. M. Clay, *The Medieval Hospitals of England* (London, 1909). For the ecclesiastical nature of medieval hospitals see ibid., pp. xvii–xviii.

[2] For example the *Regularis Concordia* drawn up in c.970 laid great stress on the provision of charity: see *Regularis Concordia. The Monastic Agreement*, ed. T. Symons (Nelson Med. Texts, 1953), partic. pp. xxxvii and 61.

[3] J. C. Dickinson, *The Origins of the Austin Canons and their Introduction into England* (London, 1950), 145. He cites as examples Reigate, Peterstone, and Wymondley which are referred to as both hospital and priory.

[4] See N. J. Kerling, 'The Foundation of St Bartholomew's Hospital in West Smithfield, London', *The Guildhall Miscellany* 4 (iii) (1972–3), 137–48.

[5] KH, 288–9.

ies of anchoresses and communities of nuns may sometimes imply lines of demarcation which are too rigid. It seems that this was also true of nunneries and hospitals.

Examples exist of hospitals apparently modifying their original purpose and changing into priories of canons.[6] It appears that some nunneries originated in the same way, and that similarities between hospital and nunnery may sometimes reflect a common origin. A study of a community of women which seems to have modified the emphasis of its original foundation, and developed from a hospital into a priory, illustrates the gradual nature of such a change and the difficulty of delineating it. St Mary de Pré in Hertfordshire was founded at the end of the twelfth century by Abbot Warin of St Albans. The account of its foundation in the *Gesta Abbatum* states that the establishment of a church on this site was the outcome of a vision by a certain layman as to the sanctity of the spot where the bones of St Amphibalus had met with the relics of St Alban.[7] Abbot Warin (1185–95), following the dictates of this spiritual insight, built a church to commemorate the saintly meeting, establishing there a community of leprous women. A close reading of the account indicates that some at least of these women had previously been inmates of the nearby hospital of St Julian.[8] It appears that women were removed from the proximity of the men at St Julian's and enclosed in separate buildings at St Mary de Pré.[9] The abbot's foundation charter has been preserved and sets out the original endowment of the community in considerable detail.[10] Much of the provision was in the form of alms rather than the land or rents necessary to enable an independent existence. Allowances of food and drink were to be received from the abbey, and the women, described as *infirme femine*, were to be given old cloaks and tunics belonging to the monks.[11] Both the endowment and the terminology

---

[6] This appears to have been the case at Newstead-by-Stamford, Elsham, and Creake as well as probably St Gregory's, Canterbury: see Dickinson, *Austin Canons*, 146–8. See also M. Rubin, *Charity and Community in Medieval Cambridge* (Cambridge, 1987), 137–8.

[7] *Gesta Abbatum*, i, 199–201.

[8] This hospital was founded by Abbot Geoffrey (1119–46) for a master and leprous brothers: see KH, 388.

[9] For a discussion of the association of men and women following the religious life, and the general movement towards the separation of the sexes see Chap. 4.

[10] The charter is transcribed in *Gesta Abbatum*, i, 202–4. Mutilated fragments of what appear to be the original are preserved in the Public Record Office: see PRO, E40/11,538 and E40/15,365.

[11] It may be this provision of cast-off tunics, up to the number of thirteen, which led to the statement in KH, 264 that the foundation was to provide for thirteen leprous men as well as women. But the text seems to suggest that the old clothing was to provide for the women: see *Gesta Abbatum*, i, 203.

suggest a hospital rather than a priory, and a fragment of an early charter, dating from the time of Abbot Warin, describes the community of St Mary de Pré as a hospital.[12] The view has been put forward that the establishment changed to a nunnery in the fourteenth century as leprosy died out,[13] but this would seem to be an over-simplification. The change appears to have been more gradual and to have started well before the fourteenth century. A record of King John's reign refers to leprous nuns, and several thirteenth-century charters also mention nuns as part of the community.[14] Papal bulls of 1256 refer to the prioress and convent of leprous women belonging to the Benedictine order.[15] Some thirteenth-century documents refer to the church (*ecclesia*) of St Mary de Pré. The use of this general term adds to the difficulties of any attempt to delineate a change from hospital to nunnery. Other terminology is also often not precise—in 1349 a letter of the prior of Christ Church, Canterbury, stated that the prioress and sisters of the hospital of Thanington were not professed to the religious life.[16] The title of prioress does not seem, therefore, to be reserved for the head of a priory of nuns.[17] Despite such ambiguities, the weight of evidence suggests that St Mary de Pré changed from a community of sick women to a community of religious.

There may have been considerable pressures towards such a change. At the hospital of Thanington, a bull of Alexander III forbade the prior and convent of Christ Church to admit any who were not infected.[18] It would seem that healthy women were asking for admission into the community and consequently papal intervention attempted to prevent any such modification of the hospital's original purpose in caring for the sick. Healthy women may also have

---

[12] PRO E40/11,069.

[13] See W. Page, 'The History of the Monastery of St Mary de Pré' (*St Albans and Herts. Arch. and Archaeol. Soc. Transactions*, 1; N.S. 1895–1902), 12–13. See also KH, 264–5. Compare VCH *Herts.*, iv, 428 which describes the foundation as a nunnery.

[14] *Rotuli Chartarum in turri Londiniensi asservati*, 1 (1199–1216), ed. T. Hardy (Record Commission; London, 1837), 127a. The description 'moniales leprose' is also used in a 13th-cent. charter (BL Addit. chart. 19,279). For another charter which refers to nuns as part of the community see BL Addit. chart. 19,962. This can be dated *c*.1218 × 1245 as William de Husseburn, seneschal of St Albans, was a witness.

[15] The bulls are calendared in *Regesta Pontificum Romanorum inde ab a. post Christum natum 1198 ad a. 1304*, ed. A. Potthast, 2 vols. (1874–5; repr. Graz, 1957), ii, nos. 16,550 and 16,616. They are printed in *MA*, iii, 356, nos. 4 and 5. No. 6 (Potthast, no. 16,630) dated 23 Dec. 1256, makes no reference to leprosy.

[16] *Literae Cantuarienses. The Letter Books of the Monastery of Christ Church Canterbury*, ed. J. Sheppard Brigstocke, 3 vols. (Rolls ser. 85; London, 1887–9), ii, 300, no. 777.

[17] Prioresses are recorded at other hospitals, e.g. at St John Baptist, Reading, and St Bartholomew, Dover: see KH, 386, 356.

[18] *Literae Cant.*, iii, 75–6, no. 971 (1164).

wanted to enter St Mary de Pré. A further possibility is that the natural processes of recovery may have lessened the original emphasis of providing for those who were ill. If some of the inhabitants of the Hertfordshire community merely suffered from minor skin complaints, and, having recovered, wanted to remain, they would have been difficult to distinguish from nuns. Yet another possible reason for such a change is suggested by the development at the house of Gilbertine canons at Clattercote, which in the mid-thirteenth century changed from receiving the sick to admitting the healthy because their maintenance was less expensive.[19]

The account of the foundation shows that the women at St Mary de Pré were, from the outset, veiled and enclosed.[20] For those who had leprosy the transition to a religious life, and the change from 'mulieres leprose' to 'moniales leprose' would in many ways have been a natural process. Lepers were marked by their disfiguring disease, a malady coloured with Biblical associations, and set apart for a life withdrawn from the world. The permanence of their affliction had important implications for the organization of hospitals.[21] Hospital inmates who were lepers and thus unable to leave the institution may well have identified increasingly with the religious life. The change to a priory might in some ways have been a spontaneous development with action being needed, as in the intervention of the pope at Thanington, for the institution to maintain its original purpose and care for the sick. As leprosy died out in the fourteenth century,[22] so Thanington itself seems to have become an institution resembling a priory rather than a hospital.[23] It would seem that in the late thirteenth and fourteenth centuries similar modifications of purpose took place at other establishments originally founded as hospitals.[24] It may well be that some ambiguity of status remained at St Mary de Pré. Fourteenth-century regulations issued by the abbots of St Albans suggest that in their view further organization was required to regularize the life of the community. Abbot Thomas de la Mare (1349–96) decreed that no more sisters were to be received, and that

[19] VCH *Oxon.*, ii, 105.

[20] *Gesta Abbatum*, i, 202.

[21] L. F. Le Grand, 'Statuts d'hôtels-dieu et de léproseries. Recueil de textes du xiie au xive siècle', *Collections de textes pour servir à l'étude et à l'enseignement de l'histoire* (Paris, 1901), pp. xxv–xxvi.

[22] For the general chronology of leprosy in England see Clay, *Hospitals*, 36; see also ibid. 43–7 for the question of the decline of the disease in the 14th cent. and later.

[23] KH, 397.

[24] e.g. at Ilchester in Somerset, originally founded 1217 × 1220 as a hospital for poor travellers and pilgrims. In 1281 it is described as a priory and in the 14th cent. there are references to nuns as well as sisters; see KH, 366 and 288, and VCH *Somerset*, ii, 156–8.

those who were there could become nuns if they so wished.[25] The impression given by his edicts is that the community consisted of women who were largely illiterate, with rivalry between nuns and sisters, but not much distinction of education or role. If such regulations mark the final organization of St Mary de Pré into a nunnery, it is clear that the development had started much earlier. Apart from the evidence of terminology, the papal bulls of 1256 indicate that rebuilding was taking place[26] and this may mark a stage in the evolution of the house into a priory of nuns.[27]

Evidence from St Mary de Pré suggests that a community founded for sick women could develop within a short period of time into an institution resembling a priory, and that the distinction between hospital and nunnery was by no means always clear. Apart from the question of illness, the general obligation of the religious to dispense charity—an obligation stressed in the Benedictine rule—could further blur any demarcation between hospital and a community of nuns. There is evidence to suggest that some nunneries placed considerable emphasis on almsgiving and hospitality. At Nuneaton in Warwickshire, the reason given for the grant of a church in 1255 was to facilitate this house's work of hospitality and service to the poor.[28] It is possible that this was a mere formula justifying the gift, but claims about the provision of hospitality were not always used at this date to justify such grants, and so it should not be dismissed as a meaningless stereotype.[29] Other evidence confirms that Nuneaton was concerned with charity. In 1292 a charter of the Bishop of Winchester referred to the nuns' support of a hospice for the poor and infirm, and the evidence of the *Valor Ecclesiasticus* indicates that alms were given within the monastery as well as at the gate.[30] Evidence of concern with charity is also available for the Yorkshire priory of Marrick. A series of charters, though not in their original form, survive for this house, and a number of them provide specifically for help for the infirm and weak.[31] Evidence from the

[25] *Gesta Abbatum*, ii, 401–2. Abbot Thomas's sister became a nun at St Mary de Pré (ibid. 373). Regulations for the house were also issued by Abbot Richard (1326–35): see ibid. 213–14. The *Gesta* states that before this no certain rule had been professed.

[26] Potthast, ii, nos. 16,550, 16,616, and 16,630: printed in *MA*, iii, 356–7, nos. 4, 5, and 6.

[27] This is suggested in A. E. Levett, 'The Accounts of St Mary des Prés (Pray)', in *Studies in Manorial History by Ada Elizabeth Levett*, ed. H. M. Cam, M. Coate, and L. Sutherland (Oxford, 1938), 287.

[28] *Calendar of Entries in the Papal Registers relating to Great Britain and Ireland*, i, *Papal Letters 1198–1304* ed. W. H. Bliss, (London, 1893), 315.

[29] See the petition for the granting of a church to the poverty-stricken London convent of Haliwell printed in *Foliot Letters and Charters*, 245, no. 172.

[30] BL Addit. chart. 47,398 (17); *Valor Eccl.*, iii, 77.

[31] The charters are printed in 'Charters of Marrick Priory', ed. T.S. (?Thomas Stapleton), *Collectanea Topographica et Genealogica*, 8 vols. (London, 1834–43), v, 100–24 and 221–59. Examples of those providing for charity are 122, no. 8 and 113, no. 4 (early 13th cent.).

Valor Ecclesiasticus supports the suggestion that almsgiving was important for the community at Marrick. A total of £9. 4s. 7d. seems to have been devoted to this purpose—a sizeable proportion of the nunnery's income.[32]

Such concern for almsgiving and charity provided a logical framework for links between hospitals and priories. Some nunneries clearly had dependent hospitals associated with them. At Castle Hedingham in Essex, the nearby hospital seems to have become linked with the nunnery.[33] The hospice of Rerecross on Stainmore was given in c.1171 to the nuns of Marrick.[34] Other nunneries had hospitals appropriated to them at a later date in the fourteenth and fifteenth centuries, presumably as a source of finance, or for administrative convenience.[35] Examples exist, however, of an apparent association of nunneries and hospitals in which it is not so clear that they were originally independent establishments subsequently linked together. There is a distinct possibility that the foundation of the nunnery of St Bartholomew in Newcastle was in some way associated with the foundation of a hospital. Early evidence for this nunnery is preserved in the *Liber Cartarum* of the corporation of Newcastle upon Tyne. A charter records the confirmation given by Earl Henry, son of King David of Scotland, of a grant to the nunnery. The grant apparently consisted of all the holdings and buildings of a certain burgess, named Aslach.[36] He appears to have been a man of some means and it is probable that he was the founder of the hospital of St Mary, Westgate. The surviving fragment of the cartulary of this hospital is also preserved in the *Liber Cartarum*, and one charter states that Aslach founded the hospital as a secular and subsequently entered the religious life.[37] Yet the confirmation of Henry of Scotland uses terminology which suggests Aslach entered St Bartholomew's.[38]

The origins of both nunnery and hospital are obscure, nor is it

---

[32] *Valor Eccl.*, v, 237.

[33] VCH *Essex*, ii, 184.

[34] KH, 387. Some of the nunneries founded before 1066 had links with hospitals. These may sometimes have given an institutional form to the nuns' provision of charity, e.g. at Barking Abbey where the abbess founded the hospital of Ilford in c.1140 (ibid. 366). For examples of hospitals which developed as 'monastic by-products' of priories of canons, see Dickinson, *Austin Canons*, 146.

[35] e.g. St Bartholomew, Newcastle (Gateshead hospital), and Seton (the hospital of St Leonard, Lancaster): see KH, 360, 368.

[36] For the *Liber Cartarum* see *Early Deeds Relating to Newcastle upon Tyne*, ed. A. M. Oliver (Surtees Soc. 137; 1924), pp. ix–xi. Earl Henry's charter (ibid. 49, no. 68) is also printed in *Reg. Regum Scot.*, i, 152–3, no. 32.

[37] *Newcastle Deeds*, 9–10, no. 1.

[38] 'Sciatis me dedisse et concessisse Deo et Sancte Marie et Sanctimonialibus de Novo Castello pro salute anime mee et antecessorum meorum Aslach burgensem meum de Novo Castello Scilicet se et omnes res suas tam in terris quam in pecuniis . . .' *Reg. Regum Scot.*, i, 152, no. 32.

clear whether the foundation of the hospital preceded that of the priory, and what, if any, was the connection between them. A tradition, recorded in Fordun's *Scotichronicon*, suggests that a nunnery was in existence in Newcastle at the end of the eleventh century, and that Agatha, mother of Queen Margaret of Scotland, took the veil there.[39] There appears to be no evidence to verify this, or to equate such an establishment with the nunnery of St Bartholomew. This convent was certainly in existence by 1143 × 1149 when Bishop William of Ste Barbe confirmed land to the nuns there.[40] Earl Henry's confirmation of Aslach and his possessions can be dated 1141 × 1151.[41] It is not clear whether the hospital was founded by this date. Reference in the earl's charter to the grant made to the nuns of Aslach's buildings could refer to the hospital, but it is by no means clear. The hospital of St Mary was certainly founded by c.1153,[42] and may have been in existence earlier, but the probability is that the community of St Bartholomew's was the older foundation. The dedication to this particular saint, a favourite patron of hospitals,[43] may suggest that the house had a particular concern for the provision of alms or for the care of the sick. That Aslach himself wished to enter the community could further support this view. The presence of men together with women was common in hospitals.[44] Another charter referring to a man entering the house to follow the religious life at St Bartholomew's has survived. The wording of this grant also does not suggest a mere death-bed repentance and the entry of a dying man into the community.[45] A possibility is that the group originally embraced both men and women and was concerned with practical charity. A degree of specialization may subsequently have been introduced, with the hospital developing as a more formalized institution under the

[39] KH, 262.

[40] *Durham Episcopal Charters 1071–1152*, ed. H. S. Offler (Surtees Soc. 179; 1968), 131–5, no. 33. The editor favours a date of 1144.

[41] *Reg. Regum Scot.*, i, 152, no. 32.

[42] *Newcastle Deeds*, 9–10, no. 1. This charter can be dated by the witness of archdeacon Rannulf: see John Le Neve, *Fasti Ecclesiae Anglicanae 1066–1300*, rev. edn., 3 vols., ii, *Monastic Cathedrals (Northern and Southern Provinces)*, compiled by D. Greenway (London, 1968–77), 39–40.

[43] Clay, *Hospitals*, 252–3. Eight hospitals were founded under his patronage during the period 1066–1215: see Binns, *Dedications*, 31.

[44] For notes on individual hospitals see KH, 339–410. A sizeable number of these were for men and women ('fratres et sorores').

[45] The grant of Toki son of Toki was confirmed by Bishop Hugh du Puiset. It was made when the donor 'se religioni in Domo illarum coram nobis reddidit', see T. Madox, *Formulare Anglicanum* (London, 1702), 50, no. xcii. The date of this charter is c.1155 × 1174, and the grant of a man with the same name is mentioned in a confirmation charter of Henry II: see *Newcastle Deeds*, 49–50, no. 69. For a bibliography on the question of grants *ad succurrendum* see G. Constable, *Medieval Monasticism. A Select Bibliography* (Toronto, 1976), 125, nos. 776–9.

patronage of Aslach.[46] There may have been some dispute over this development of the hospital. A charter of Henry II, which can be dated before 1165 and possibly as early as 1158, confirmed land and alms to the church of St Mary, Newcastle, and to the hospital and brethren there.[47] No mention is made of the nunnery. But another royal charter dating from 1166 × 1173 confirmed the hospital to the nuns of St Bartholomew and St Mary, suggesting that it formed a part of the nunnery's endowment.[48] This may represent an attempt on the part of the nuns to retain control over the hospital. If so it does not seem to have been successful. In 1183 a bull of Lucius III set out the hospital's possessions at some length and made no reference to the nuns.[49] The probability is that by this date the hospital was established as an independent institution. The community of St Bartholomew, Newcastle, presents interesting similarities with the foundation of St Bartholomew in London. In both cases it remains unclear whether hospital or priory was founded first, and it is probable that initially the two institutions formed part of one establishment. It may well be that both at Newcastle and in London the original foundation should not be categorized as either hospital or priory, but was altogether a more amorphous community subsequently propagating into two independent institutions.[50]

At Bristol, evidence suggests a similar confusion between hospital and nunnery and the possibility of links between them. The *Monasticon* outlines the problem and simultaneously dismisses it with the statement 'of this nunnery, sometimes called a hospital, very little is known'.[51] According to a later tradition, the foundress of the nunnery, dedicated to St Mary Magdalene and situated on St Michael's Hill, was Eva fitz Harding, the widow of Robert fitz Harding.[52] He was a rich citizen who became lord of Berkeley and played an important part in the foundation of St Augustine's abbey,

---

[46] An alternative view, which assumes that the hospital was founded first and then simply appropriated to the nunnery, is set out in W. H. Knowles, 'The Hospital of St Mary the Virgin, Newcastle upon Tyne', *Archaeologia Aeliana* (N.S. 15; 1892), 194–5.

[47] This charter is preserved in an *inspeximus* of Edward III, calendared in *Newcastle Deeds*, 54, no. 72.

[48] Ibid. 49–50, no. 69.

[49] Ibid. 52–4, no. 71.

[50] A similar development with a priory as well as a hospital apparently deriving from an earlier foundation, took place at Canterbury with Archbishop Lanfranc's foundation there of a community dedicated to St Gregory (KH, 349–50 and 152). The foundation charter of St Gregory's, printed in Dickinson, *Austin Canons*, 280–2, refers to the foundation of a church—*ecclesia*—with six priests, who cared for a hospital near the church. A priory and a hospital subsequently developed.

[51] *MA*, iv, 589.

[52] This tradition is recorded in *The Maire of Bristowe is Kalendar by Robert Ricart, Town Clerk of Bristol 18 Edward IV*, ed. L. T. Smith (Camden Soc., N.S. 5; 1872), 22. See also J. Smyth, *Lives of the Berkeleys*, ed. J. Maclean, 3 vols. (Gloucester, 1883), i, 44 and 59.

Bristol.[53] It is also claimed that Eva became the prioress of her nunnery.[54] Charter evidence confirms the existence of a Lady Eva, wife of Robert,[55] and some documents preserved in the cartulary of St Mark's hospital, Bristol, refer to the hospital of St Mary Magdalene.[56] This suggests that Eva fitz Harding's house was, for part of its history at least, a hospital. Further evidence is provided by charters, one which can be dated *c.*1235 × *c.*1248, recording grants made to the house of St Mary Magdalene on the hill of St Michael, and the brothers and sisters serving there.[57] It would appear that Eva fitz Harding's community was concerned with the provision of hospitality or other forms of practical care. The dedication itself suggests this, for Mary Magdalene was a saint frequently invoked as a patron of hospitals.[58] The house seems to have subsequently developed into a priory of nuns, with no particular concern for practical charity. In 1284, a visitation return of Bishop Giffard of Worcester described the inhabitants of the community as nuns, nor is there anything in the brief entry in the register to suggest they cared for the poor or sick.[59]

It is a possibility that the ambiguities and uncertainties surrounding the early history of the community on the hill of St Michael may mask a link with the abbey of St Augustine, and that the two establishments were originally associated. The founders were husband and wife, and Eva was given an important place in the traditions of the abbey. It is said that she was buried in St Augustine's by the side of her husband.[60] She is described as 'foundress' in records of the abbey, and a sizeable almsgiving—to fifty poor men—

---

[53] For an article on the foundation of the abbey, see Dickinson, 'St Augustine's Bristol', 109–26.

[54] *Ricart's Kalendar*, 22.

[55] e.g. she witnesses charters of her husband Robert in the mid-12th cent.: see *Descriptive Catalogue of the Charters and Muniments . . . at Berkeley Castle*, ed. I. H. Jeayes (Bristol, 1892), 8, no. 11 and 15, no. 25.

[56] *Cartulary of St Mark's Hospital Bristol*, ed. C. D. Ross (Bristol Rec. Soc., 21; Bristol, 1959), 205–7, nos. 327–31.

[57] BL Addit. chart. 6518. This can be dated by the witness James la Warre, mayor of Bristol: see *Cartl. St Mark's Hospital*, 282. This description of the house as on the hill of St Michael makes it clear that the charter relates to Eva's foundation. Possibilities of confusion exist as a leper hospital for women, also dedicated to St Mary Magdalene, was apparently founded in the manor of Bedminster, south of the River Avon, before 1219 (KH, 347). Eva's foundation is also described as a hospital, with brothers and sisters, in two charters preserved in the cartulary of St Augustine's abbey (fo. 174). A microfilm of this cartulary is deposited with the Glos. Record Office (MS 1071).

[58] For the association of Mary Magdalene with hospitals and lepers, see Clay, *Hospitals*, 249–52. For the medieval Mary Magdalene as a patron saint see also Binns, *Dedications*, 33–4.

[59] *Episcopal Registers. Diocese of Worcester. Register of Bishop Godfrey Giffard Sept 23rd 1268–August 15th 1301*, ed. J. Willis Bund, 2 vols. (Worcs. Hist. Soc., 1902 [1898–1902]), ii, 234.

[60] *Ricart's Kalendar*, 22. The necrology of the abbey of St Victor, Paris, records the death of

marked the anniversary of her death.[61] Had she been foundress of a separate community it is probable that her burial would have taken place within the confines of her foundation. It may be that women were originally linked with the abbey's provision of alms. St Augustine's seems to have been concerned with such almsgiving on a considerable scale, for the abbot and canons undertook the daily feeding of one hundred poor in the almonry constructed at the beginning of the thirteenth century by Maurice de Gaunt.[62] The hospital of St Mark subsequently developed from these beginnings to provide the dispensation of charity in a separate establishment.[63] The suggestion of a link between women and the charitable activities of a great monastery is strengthened by evidence from other houses. At Bury St Edmunds, an entry in Domesday Book describes nuns there in terms suggesting that they were part of the community of the abbey and were in some way connected with charity.[64] At Evesham, five nuns apparently attached to the abbey in the early twelfth century were probably serving in the almonry,[65] while at St Albans the regulations of Abbot Paul at the end of the eleventh century caused nuns to be housed in the almonry or nearby.[66]

Although there is no firm evidence that the foundation of St Mary Magdalene, Bristol, was originally linked with the provision of alms and associated with the abbey of canons,[67] it is suggestive that the origins of other nunneries indicate similar links. At Derby, the nunnery of Kingsmead, or de Pratis, was situated a mile away from the Augustinian canons of Darley. The canons had previously lived at

Robert and calls him canon of the house as well as its founder: see Dickinson, 'St Augustine's Bristol', 111. It is a possibility that his wife entered the religious life with him. For examples of married partners both entering a religious house see pp. 84–5, 156.

[61] 'Abbot Newland's Roll of the Abbots of St Augustine's Abbey by Bristol', ed. I. H. Jeayes, *Bristol and Glos. Archaeol. Soc. Trans.* 14 (1889–90), 125–6. One hundred poor were fed at the anniversary of Robert fitz Harding.

[62] *Cartl. St Mark's Hospital*, p. xii.

[63] For the development of the hospital as an independent institution see ibid., pp. xii–xv. It is interesting that even at St Mark's modifications later took place which resulted in the religious aspect of the life there being stressed at the expense of the establishment's eleemosynary function.

[64] For a discussion of the curious collection of people mentioned in the Domesday entry, and the suggestion that they may have been dependants of the abbey, see M. D. Lobel, *The Borough of Bury St Edmunds. A Study in the Government and Development of a Monastic Town* (Oxford, 1935), 12–13.

[65] VCH *Worcs.*, ii, 116. The reference to the nuns is in the Evesham cartulary, BL Cotton MS Vesp. B. xxiv, fo. 41ᵛ.

[66] *Gesta Abbatum*, i, 59. For the links between the abbey of St Albans and different communities of nuns see pp. 56–61.

[67] Leland records other confused traditions of hospital and nunnery in Bristol with his reference to 'an hospitall of olde tyme where of late a nunrye was caullyd S. Margarets' (Leland, *Itin*, v, 89).

St Helen's in Derby, moving in *c.*1146 to a new site.[68] They left behind them a small community which came to be described as a hospital. The women of Kingsmead clearly had links with the canons. A charter of Bishop Walter Durdent, dating from *c.*1154 × 1159, conceded the care of the virgins to the abbot. Apparently he had constructed their dwelling and the bishop recognized his right to consecrate the nuns.[69] Links with the abbey are also implicit in the later settlement of Bishop Richard Peche, outlined in an episcopal charter which probably dates from *c.*1180. The bishop confirmed the grants to the nuns and stated that they held endowments in their own right and owed no obedience to the abbey.[70] The wording of the charter suggests that there had been problems over the nuns' dependence on the canons of Darley and that this settlement was to give them a novel autonomy.[71] Perhaps the move of the canons to a new site on the Derwent outside the city represented for them a change to a more contemplative life. It is interesting that Albinus, first Abbot of Darley, is referred to in one charter as *magister canonicorum,* a description possibly reflecting his earlier title and suggestive of a hospital rather than an abbey.[72] There is also a hint that the women may have been involved in some form of practical care. The preamble to Bishop Richard's charter refers to the needs of Martha as well as to the vocation of the more contemplative Mary.[73] A charter dating from the early thirteenth century reveals a link between the nuns of Kingsmead and the hospital of St Helen, as it refers to the prior of St Helen's who is also master of the nuns.[74] Although such an explanation is by no means proven, a distinct possibility is that originally the community at St Helen's had embraced both men and women, perhaps associated together in the provision of hospitality or alms, and subsequently expanded to form three more specialized communities—an abbey of canons at Darley, a community of nuns at Kingsmead, and a hospital at St Helen's.

---

[68] KH, 156. For the early history of the abbey see *The Cartulary of Darley Abbey,* ed. R. Darlington, 2 vols. (Derby Archaeol. Soc.; 1945), i, pp. ii–v.

[69] *Cartl. Darley,* ii, 595–97, no. 02.

[70] Ibid., i, 176–8, no. D15. I have followed the editor in identifying Bishop R. of the charter as Richard Peche (1161–82) rather than Roger of Weseham (1245–56).

[71] For other examples of nunneries apparently obtaining a greater degree of independence towards the end of the 12th cent. see Lillechurch, p. 132, the Premonstratensian nunneries, pp. 140–2, and Harrold, pp. 152–5.

[72] *Cartl. Darley,* i, pp. iv–v.

[73] Ibid., i, 177, no. D15. The Biblical allusion is to Luke 10: 38–42. For a discussion of the roles of Martha and Mary as types of monastic vocation see C. J. Holdsworth, 'The Blessings of Work: the Cistercian View', in D. Baker (ed.), *Sanctity and Secularity. The Church and the World, Studies in Church History* 10 (Oxford, 1973), 64–6.

[74] BL Wolley chart. viii. 51 calendared in *Descriptive Catalogue of Derbyshire Charters in Public and Private Libraries . . .,* ed. I. H. Jeayes (London, 1906), 302, no. 2,383.

Evidence that some nunneries may, at their inception, have been linked with institutions resembling hospitals is more explicit at Carrow in Norwich. One source ascribes the foundation of the priory to two sisters who were members of a hospital in the city. The cartulary for Carrow is no longer extant, but extracts from it have been preserved by Tanner. One entry states that the house was founded in 1146 by Seyna and Lescelina, 'sorores moniales de hospite Sancte Marie et Sancte Johannie in Norwich'.[75] The existence of such an establishment is confirmed by a charter of King Stephen referring to a grant made by him to the church of St Mary and St John and the nuns there. The king gave the nuns twenty-five shillings' worth of land and expressed the wish that they should found their church on this site.[76] His charter was probably drawn up, c.1136 × 1137, some ten years before the date given in the extract for the foundation of Carrow.[77] Such a discrepancy would be explained if the nunnery developed from an earlier institution. Nothing specific in the royal charter suggests that the church of St Mary and St John was a hospital, but the use of the word in the Tanner manuscript, apparently taken from the cartulary, cannot be dismissed lightly. It would seem a possibility that women originally serving in an institution concerned with hospitality, almsgiving, or the care of the sick, should subsequently wish to modify their vocation and form a priory of nuns situated outside the walls of Norwich.

The statement that Carrow nunnery was founded by two sisters, nuns of the hospital of St Mary and St John, implies that nuns served in hospitals. If nuns were sometimes concerned with practical charity and the care of the sick, initially forming part of the community within a hospital, it would provide a further explanation for the apparent confusion between the two types of institution, and for modifications of emphasis within them. It would also explain similarities of terminology, such as the use of the title 'prioress' within some hospitals. Fragments of evidence from the pipe rolls confirm that in the twelfth century nuns played their part in

---

[75] Oxford, Bodleian Tanner MS 342, fo. 149ᵛ, printed in W. Rye, *Carrow Abbey... in the County of Norfolk* (privately printed, Norwich, 1889), app. 1, where it is transcribed as 'sorores moniales de hospitali...'.

[76] This charter is printed in *Reg. Regum*, iii, *Regesta Stephani . . . 1135–1154*, ed. H. A. Cronne and R. H. C. Davis (Oxford, 1968–9), 226–7, no. 615. Some doubts have been expressed as to its authenticity, but it has been suggested that the expanded wording of the text—'et volo quod in ipsa terra fundent ecclesiam suam'—may be the result of a deliberate emphasis on the royal role in the foundation: see E. Hallam-Smith, 'Aspects of the Monastic Patronage of the English and French Royal Houses c.1130–1270', Ph.D. thesis (London, 1976), 73.

[77] For difficulties of detail in relation to the date of 1146 see *HRH*, 216, n. 2.

hospitals. One entry refers to the nuns of the hospital of Barton.[78] It is difficult to identify this institution,[79] but the wording certainly suggests that nuns were serving in a hospital.[80] Other pipe-roll entries record payments to the nuns of Richmond.[81] There appears to be no other evidence of a nunnery of that name, and these could refer to nuns attached to the hospital at Richmond.[82]

The association of a religious vocation with the care of travellers and of the poor and sick, was given a particular form with the establishment of the order of St John of Jerusalem.[83] Women as well as men joined the order, and a hospital dedicated to St Mary Magdalene was founded for women at the headquarters of the order in Jerusalem.[84] The original purpose of the Hospitaller sisters as well as of the brothers was to care for pilgrims and those in need. It has been suggested, however, that by the end of the twelfth century such concern with practical charity had tended to give way to the foundation of more contemplative communities for women.[85] Regulations for the important house of Sigena in Aragon, founded in 1188, give little evidence of concern for the sick, other than those of the community.[86] A study of the house of Aconbury in Herefordshire shows, however, that the care of the sick still seems to have played a part in the vocation of the English sisters of the order in the first part of the thirteenth century. Aconbury was founded by Margaret de Lacy, daughter of William de Braose, on land granted to her by King John shortly before his death.[87] The community was to be of the order of the Hospital of St John. But its foundress was horrified when

---

[78] *PR 2–4 Henry II* (1155 × 1156), 38.

[79] The entry is for the counties of Notts. and Derby, where there is no other evidence of the existence of such a hospital. The name Barton is a common one: see *The Concise Oxford Dictionary of English Place Names*, ed. E. Ekwall (Oxford, 1960), 28–9.

[80] An alternative explanation is that the hospital was for sick nuns, but if so it is probable that they would have been described as *moniales leprose*; cf. the entry referring to the establishment of such a hospital in Lincolnshire (*PR 28 Henry II* [1181 × 1182], 60).

[81] The entries referring to them are in the account rendered by Rannulf de Glanville for the honour of Earl Conan, 1171–82: see *PR 18 Henry II* (1171 × 1172), 5–*PR 29 Henry II* (1182 × 1183), 56.

[82] The hospital of St Nicholas, Richmond, was founded by 1172. Very little is known of its history: see VCH *Yorks.*, iii, 322.

[83] For a general background to the order with bibliography see E. J. King, *The Knights of St John in the British Realm*, revd. and cont. by Sir Harry Luke (London, 1967).

[84] For the influence of the Hospitallers and their use of this dedication see Clay, *Hospitals*, 249–50.

[85] J. Delaville Le Roulx, 'Les Hospitalières de Saint Jean de Jérusalem', *Comptes rendus des séances de l'année 1894* Académie des inscriptions et belles-lettres, (4th ser. 22; Paris, 1894), 138–40.

[86] Ibid.

[87] For an account of the early history of Aconbury see W. Rees, *A History of the Order of St John of Jerusalem in Wales and on the Welsh Border* (Cardiff, 1947), 60–1. King John's grant

she discovered that the sisters of the order were liable for service abroad, for she felt that this would seriously impair the efficacy of her spiritual provision for the souls of her family. She tried to get the order changed to that of the Augustinians. This resulted in a lengthy dispute and a series of papal bulls which reveal that Margaret argued for the change on the grounds that her original endowment to the Hospitallers had been a mistake caused by women's ignorance. She pleaded that as the Augustinian rule was used in the services held by the community, it would be a simple matter to change to that order.[88] Eventually she gained her wish, and Aconbury provides an interesting example of a convent of women changing order on the initiative of the founder.

The change also probably caused a modification of emphasis within the community from hospital to nunnery. The thirteenth-century cartulary for Aconbury, and several original charters which have survived, reveal interesting terminology. Some of these charters, drawn up when the house still belonged to the Hospitallers, record grants made to St John of Aconbury and the sisters serving God there.[89] One refers to the brothers and sisters who form the community,[90] and another grant, enrolled in the cartulary, gives a certain Sister Constancia, apparently the head of the house, the title of *magistra*.[91] Such wording is indicative of a hospital rather than a nunnery, and Aconbury is frequently described as a hospital, particularly in documents dating from the first half of the thirteenth century.[92] It could be argued that this merely reflects the original allegiance of the house to the order of Hospitallers, but a phrase in a papal bull of 1233 suggests that the inhabitants were concerned with the care of the needy. The pope ordered that if the members of the community were to transfer to other houses, some of the older

---

is recorded in *Rotuli Litterarum Patentium in Turri Londinensi asservati 1201–1216*, ed. T. Hardy (Record Commission; London, 1835), 199b. It is possible that it indicates a sign of royal repentance for his treatment of the Braose family.

[88] The papal bull of 8 April 1233, which outlines the situation, is calendared in *Cal. Pap. Lett.*, i, 134, and printed in full in J. Delaville Le Roulx, *Cartulaire général de l'Ordre des Hospitaliers de S. Jean de Jérusalem 1100–1310*, 4 vols. (Paris, 1894–1906), ii, 451–2, no. 2,047. For other bulls relating to the dispute see ibid., nos. 2,059, 2,086, 2,138, 2,140. The bull which finally released the house at Aconbury from obedience to the Hospitallers is dated 16 July 1237 (ibid., no. 2,167). Letters patent of the bishop of Worcester, executing the mandate, are preserved in the Public Record Office (PRO, E326/8712 and E326/8713).

[89] PRO, E315/55, fos. 22 and 28; for a description of this cartulary see Davis, *Med. Cartls.* 3, no. 9. For the charters see PRO, E326/4020, and E326/6158.

[90] PRO, E315/55, fo. 39. This charter is printed in *MA*, vi, (i), 490, no. 7.

[91] PRO, E315/55, fo. 42ᵛ.

[92] e.g. PRO, E326/4020, E326/891, and E326/6158.

women were to remain behind to look after the poor and sick.[93] Charters which apparently date from the second half of the thirteenth century, however, generally refer to the prioress and nuns of Aconbury,[94] and there is nothing to suggest a particular concern with alms or practical care. It would seem probable that the change of order modified the emphasis of the community at Aconbury towards a greater stress on prayer and contemplation.

A study of the primary sources, fragmentary as they are, presents a confusing picture. They suggest that the demarcation between a hospital and a nunnery was by no means always clear. It is generally held that in the late thirteenth and fourteenth centuries some institutions, previously established as hospitals, modified their function and purpose as leprosy died out or the requirements of travellers changed. It would seem that changes had also occurred much earlier. Particularly in the first decades of the twelfth century, nunneries and hospitals may have been less specialized institutions. Nuns may have served in hospitals and some nunneries may have had a particular concern with dispensing charity or looking after the sick. Women linked with communities of men may well have played a special role in such practical care. In some cases the origin and development of a nunnery seem to be linked with that of a hospital, and yet the links are often not clear and are difficult to establish. The nunnery of Baysdale in Yorkshire seems to have grown out of a previous settlement at Hutton where a hospital was in existence in the twelfth century.[95] It is not known whether this was founded before or after the move of the nuns to Nunthorpe and then to Baysdale.[96] It is a possibility, however, that the nuns' change of site was linked with the foundation of a more contemplative community. Such origins are shrouded in obscurity, and any conclusions must be tentative. A move from eleemosynary activities to a more withdrawn religious life would seem to reflect a general trend. A study of the new orders suggests that there was a similar movement for the women following the Premonstratensian and Arrouaisian rules. Caring for

[93] 'Remanentibus ibi vetulis mulieribus ad pauperum Hospitalis et . . . infirmorum obsequium, in aliis monasteriis reliquas collocare procures . . .' (*Cartl. de L'Ordre des Hospitaliers*, ii, 452, no. 2,047).

[94] e.g. PRO, E326/5774 (1263) and E326/8696 (1258). See also some charters of Katherine de Lacy, daughter of the foundress, copied on a roll preserved in the Public Record Office (PRO, Exch. KR [Transcripts of deeds and charters] E132/2/11).

[95] VCH *Yorks.*, iii, 158. For the hospital see ibid. 314. The site of this was at Hutton Lowcross. There is some confusion about the early site of the nunnery which has been identified as Hutton Rudby (*EYC*, ii, 463 and Burton, *Yorks. Nunneries*, 43), as well as Hutton Lowcross (*EYC*, i, 445). As Hutton Lowcross was in the fee of Adam de Brus who granted a licence for the foundation of the nunnery (*MA*, v, 508, no. 1) it would seem the more likely.

[96] The date of the move to Baysdale was probably c.1190 × 1211: see Appendix A.

the poor and sick was probably left to lay sisters serving in hospitals, and in the thirteenth century detailed regulations were laid down for the organization of these establishments.[97] In the preceding century, however, the situation was probably much more fluid, and the distinction between a nunnery and a hospital, as well as that between a nun and a sister, less finely drawn.

[97] Apart from the Hospital of St John of Jerusalem the extant regulations for hospitals date mainly from the 13th cent.: see Le Grand, *Statuts d'hôtels-dieu*, p. xi. It is interesting that the early statutes for a Paris hospital, drawn up *c.*1220, decreed that the sisters were to be tonsured 'ut moniales': see ibid. 44.

4 Links with Monasteries: The Question of Double Houses

A study of the growth of communities round recluses, and of the links between nunneries and hospitals, has indicated the importance of association between men and women religious. A twelfth-century source, the *Book of Different Orders and Callings in the Church*, suggests that such association was widespread.[1] It makes special reference to women who 'sweetly take up Christ's yoke with holy men or under their guidance'. Unfortunately the section dealing with these women was either never written or was subsequently lost. As communities formed, so the lay status of women inevitably resulted in dependence on men to administer the sacraments of mass and confession. Moreover, in a society where women were regarded as inferior and weak,[2] the need for male help would not be confined to priestly ministrations, but was also required in practical spheres such as the acquisition and organization of endowments.

In earlier periods one solution to the problem of intrinsic female dependence had been the foundation of double monasteries for monks and nuns. The institution took many forms and a strict definition is difficult to establish.[3] While the early history of double houses may have been associated especially with Gaul, a flowering of such convents occurred in Anglo-Saxon England in the second half of the seventh century. These English double houses, for example Whitby, Minster in Sheppey, and Wimborne, included both men and women as part of their community under the authority of an abbess, usually a lady of high rank. The degree of association between the

[1] *Libellus de diversis ordinibus et professionibus qui sunt in aecclesia*, ed. G. Constable and B. Smith (Oxford, 1972), 4–5. This was written in the second quarter of the 12th cent., probably in the diocese of Liège. For a note on syneisactism, a particular form of chaste association between the sexes, see G. Constable, 'Aelred of Rievaulx and the Nun of Watton: An Episode in the Early History of the Gilbertine Order', *Medieval Women*, 220, n. 49. For Robert of Arbrissel's apparent use of this penitential practice see pp. 114–15.

[2] In England the status of women seems to have diminished following the Norman Conquest: see D. M. Stenton, *The English Woman in History* (London, 1957), 28–30.

[3] See J. Godfrey, 'The Double Monastery in Early English History', *Ampleforth Journal* 79 (1974), ii, 19–32. He points out that though the double monastery in 7th-cent. Gaul was a clearly established institution, it did not conform to a single pattern, but took on various forms, with sometimes the abbess in overall control and sometimes the abbot. A brief survey of the history of double houses is given in *Dict. de droit canonique*, iii, 972–4, s.v. 'Cohabitation; Les Monastères doubles'. I would agree with Sharon Elkins that the use of the term 'double monasteries' can be misleading (Elkins, *Holy Women*, p. xviii).

sexes may have been slight, yet it is the partnership which is the main characteristic of the institution.[4] Double houses have been defined as consisting of two communities, one of monks and one of nuns, established in the same place but not necessarily within the same boundary, observing the same rule, and together forming a legal entity under one authority.[5] Decrees legislating against men and women leading the religious life in close proximity can be traced back to the early history of monasticism. For example, in 506 the Council of Agde forbade men to place nunneries in the neighbourhood of masculine cloisters for fear of Satan's cunning and people's gossip.[6] Unease was also apparent in the tenth century. Double houses appear to have played no part in the monastic revival of that period, and its leaders were clearly sensitive to the dangers inherent in any partnership between the sexes.[7] Several of the nunneries founded before the Conquest secured priestly support by the provision of chaplains endowed with prebends. The holders of these were probably secular clerks and increasingly came to be nonresident,[8] thus avoiding the dangerous implications of a double house.

It has generally been held that the establishment of double houses was only revived in England with the spread of some of the new orders of the twelfth century.[9] The Gilbertines, unique as an English order, provide the clearest example.[10] But a close study of both Benedictine and Augustinian communities of women suggests the possibility of the earlier existence of forms of double organization, and the association of men and women following the religious life. The evidence is not clear, with sources often merely hinting at the presence of women linked with a monastery, or of monks and canons associated with a community of women. Such vagueness and

---

[4] M. Bateson, 'Origin and Early History of Double Monasteries', *TRHS*, N.S. 13 (1899), 137–98.

[5] Schmitz, *Ordre de St Benoît*, vii, 45–6. See also ibid., i, 298–300.

[6] 'Monasteria puellarum longius a monasteriis monachorum, aut propter insidias diaboli aut propter oblocutiones hominum, collocentur', J. D. Mansi, *Sacrorum conciliorum nova et amplissima collectio*, ed. L. Petit and J. B. Martin, 54 vols. in 59 (Paris, 1901–27, repr. Graz, 1960–1), viii, 329.

[7] The major document of the reform movement, the *Regularis Concordia* drawn up in the 1970s, expresses concern on the part of King Edgar and Archbishop Dunstan lest association between the sexes should involve scandal: see *Reg. Concordia*, 2, and 4–5.

[8] See A. H. Thompson, 'Double Monasteries and the Male Element in Nunneries', in *The Ministry of Women. A Report by a Committee Appointed by his Grace the Lord Archbishop of Canterbury* (London, 1919), app. viii, 149–56. For a note on prebends at nunneries see also Power, 144.

[9] U. Berlière, 'Les Monastères doubles aux 12ᵉ et 13ᵉ siècles', *Mémoires de l'Académie Royale de Belgique*, 2nd ser. 18 (Brussels, 1923), 3–32, esp. 11–12.

[10] For the Gilbertine order see pp. 73–9.

ambivalence is not in itself surprising, and could reflect growing unease about such partnership between the sexes. Such suspicion would obscure the importance of links between men and women and the possibility that some communities of women developed from double monasteries. Great abbeys such as St Albans had groups of women linked with them, apparently following the religious life under their shelter. Some communities of Augustinian nuns seem to have had early links with nearby houses of canons. This could merely be the association of two institutions, but in some cases the establishment of an independent convent of women may have reflected growing concern about the partnership of the sexes resulting in a move towards their separation. Other Benedictine and Augustinian nunneries seem, in the twelfth century, to have had men forming part of their communities. This chapter explores the question of links between houses of men and women religious, and the possibility of the existence of forms of double organization at some Benedictine and Augustinian nunneries. The development of the order of Sempringham, with its establishment of double houses for nuns and canons, is set against this background.

The grouping of women seeking to follow a religious vocation near an established monastery of monks or canons is readily understandable. Close proximity would facilitate spiritual and material guidance as well as practicalities such as the administration of the sacraments. It has been suggested that in Germany and Holland the majority of great Benedictine abbeys had a dependent community of women associated with them.[11] Several of the English Benedictine monasteries had links with groups of nuns. The most notable example is that of St Albans. This abbey was involved with the foundation or development of at least three different communities of women in the course of the twelfth century. Sopwell was the closest to the monastery, situated less than half a mile from the abbey buildings. The account of the foundation of Sopwell by Abbot Geoffrey describes it in terms of the abbot helping recluses.[12] But it is possible that the establishment of the priory there represents a regularization of a community of women formerly associated with the monastery.[13] For from the ninth to the eleventh centuries women

---

[11] Schmitz, *Ordre de St Benoît*, vii, 50. The importance of links with monasteries and the need to be near men who could act as spiritual directors has also been noted in a recent study of French nunneries: see M. Parisse, *Les Nonnes au Moyen Age*, ed. Christine Bonneton (Paris, 1983), partic. 51.

[12] *Gesta Abbatum*, i, 80–2. For the probable anchoretic origins of this community see p. 23.

[13] The suggestion that some of the women may have previously formed part of the monastic community is also made in L. F. Rushbrooke Williams, *History of the Abbey of St Alban* (London, 1917), 59. See also KH, 265.

who led a religious life, or at least claimed to do so, seem to have been linked with the abbey. This is clear from the history of St Albans, the *Gesta Abbatum*. In writing his account, the author was clearly disturbed by the scandalous proximity of women to the church. A certain Abbot Wulnoth and then Abbot Paul (1079–99) were shown by the St Albans historian to have taken steps to bring a greater degree of discipline and propriety into the lives of these nuns (*sanctimoniales semi-saeculares*).[14] Abbot Paul apparently placed them under a rule and compelled them to wear black habits. He gathered them together and housed them in the almonry and places nearby.[15] After outlining these laudable measures the *Gesta* says no more about the subsequent fate of the nuns. There is nothing in this official account of the foundation of Sopwell to suggest that any of the nuns had previously been associated with the abbey. The author merely states that the abbot was impressed with the sanctity of two recluses living in a rough shelter at Eywood, and so he gathered them together with others, provided them with buildings, and ensured that they were strictly enclosed under his authority. By organizing the ladies under a rule at Sopwell, Abbot Geoffrey may have been continuing the efforts of his predecessors such as Abbot Paul. A site in the vicinity of the abbey may have been thought preferable to having women more closely associated with the monks in the almonry.

The *Life of Christina* and the account in the *Gesta Abbatum* both make it quite evident that links between the community of women and the monastery of St Albans played an important part in the development of the priory at Markyate. It was at the abbey that Christina, as a young girl, was first inspired to take the private vow of dedication[16] which was so to upset her parents' plans of a suitable marriage and lead to her struggles to follow her vocation. The friendship between the recluse and Abbot Geoffrey is one of the main themes of the *Vita*, and it is shown to be a relationship of mutual dependence and enrichment.[17] According to the *Gesta*, the abbot, as a result of this friendship, endowed the community at Markyate with buildings, and when fire destroyed this settlement was sufficiently generous to provide a second time.[18] The picture given in the St Albans account is that the abbot was in a material sense the founder of the nunnery of Markyate. It is quite clear, however, from other

[14] *Gesta Abbatum*, i, 11.
[15] Ibid., i, 59.
[16] Talbot, *Life of Christina*, 38–9.
[17] For an article which explores the theme of friendship between Christina and Abbot Geoffrey see C. N. L. Brooke, 'St Albans: The Great Abbey', in R. Runcie (ed.), *Cathedral and City. St Albans Ancient and Modern* (Thetford, 1977), partic. 59–62.
[18] *Gesta Abbatum*, i, 95, 103.

evidence that the priory was not a cell of St Albans. Charters from the archives of St Paul's in London show that the nunnery was situated on land belonging to its canons and that they acted as patrons. Their consent was needed for the election of the prioress.[19] Nor is there evidence that the convent was ever visited by St Albans in the thirteenth century. Moreover, the priory was subject to episcopal jurisdiction, a situation hardly suggestive of institutional links with this great abbey, proud as it was of its exemption.[20] The impression given throughout the *Life of Christina* is of personal friendship between the abbot and the lady recluse rather than of institutional dependence. But an interesting feature of the *Life* is the suggestion of frequent and easy communication between the two communities. Christina's brother, a monk of St Albans, stayed with his sister at Markyate for some time before he died.[21] Christina also had contacts with other members of the abbey. Indeed, it is suggested that she had been the cause of many of them entering religion.[22] Once Christina's friendship with the abbot had blossomed, the *Vita* stresses the mutual dependence and frequent meetings between them. Although it is probable that on most occasions Geoffrey visited her, the account certainly implies that Christina also went to the abbey.[23]

Evidence about the endowment of the priory at Markyate is scanty, but there is little to suggest that the bulk of it had been obtained through the generosity of the abbot of St Albans. The *Gesta*, however, expresses considerable resentment at the expense involved in the support of women by Abbot Geoffrey.[24] Whether this was a real cause of concern to contemporary members of the monastery, or rather reflected later views of St Albans historians is difficult to decide. The reason given for the discontent is financial, but the somewhat coy reference to the strength of friendship between Christina and Geoffrey, combined with the suggestion that it might have caused scandal if their sanctity had been less apparent, suggests that the author had other grounds for unease.[25] The *Vita* also refers to doubts about their relationship, and the very vigour of its attack on scandalmongers implies that such worries may have been widespread.[26]

[19] *Early Charts. of St Paul's,* 119–21, nos. 154–5. It is a popular misconception that Markyate was a cell of St Albans. It is described as daughter house of the abbey by the editors of the Psalter: see *St Albans Psalter,* 24–5.

[20] For the question of the abbey's exemption see J. Sayers, 'Papal Privileges for St Albans Abbey and its Dependencies', in D. A. Bullough and R. L. Storey (eds.), *The Study of Medieval Records. Essays in Honour of Kathleen Major* (Oxford, 1971), 57–84.

[21] Talbot, *Life of Christina,* 158.   [22] Ibid. 126.

[23] Ibid. 140.   [24] *Gesta Abbatum,* i, 103.

[25] Ibid., i, 105.   [26] Talbot, *Life of Christina,* 174–6.

The *Gesta* reveals an even greater degree of resentment when describing the foundation of the community at St Mary de Pré by Abbot Warin of St Albans (1183–91).[27] It states that the church was founded to the detriment of the abbey and that many murmured against it.[28] The particular burden of complaint seems to be that the abbot had diverted revenues from the monastery to endow the community of women.[29] The foundation charter of St Mary de Pré, as preserved in the *Gesta*, shows that although the abbot kept a considerable measure of control, receiving promises of obedience from the inmates, the monastery of St Albans seems to have had little direct concern for the women enclosed there. The *magister* of the house was initially a layman, and the chaplains, although given hospitality at the monks' table, were not full members of the monastery.[30] Nevertheless, there is a hint in the sources that the establishment of this house can also be linked to a desire to separate the sexes. The *Gesta* states that the leprous women were taken from the hospital of St Julian, apparently a hospital for men, and were strictly enclosed in their new buildings.[31] The implicit suggestion is that their former association with the men of the hospital was undesirable.

If the monks of St Albans appear to have had little direct involvement in the care of the women at St Mary de Pré,[32] evidence suggests that the position was different earlier in the twelfth century. At Sopwell, the strictly enclosed nuns were inevitably dependent on masculine support for the management of the priory's estates and rents[33] as well as for priestly services. It was decreed that a mature monk of the abbey was to act at the *magister* of the nuns, exercising authority under the control of the abbot.[34] In 1163 the abbey seems to have tried to extend its jurisdiction over nuns. Abbot Robert de Gorron (1151–66) obtained a bull from Pope Alexander III giving

[27] *Gesta Abbatum*, i, 199–205. For its original foundation as a hospital see pp. 39–40.

[28] 'Sic igitur ecclesiam Sanctae Mariae de Pratis (licet multi contradicerent, quos contrivit) in hujus detrimentum ecclesiae fundavit.' (Ibid., i, 215).

[29] Ibid., i, 205.

[30] Ibid., i, 202–4.

[31] Ibid., i, 202. For an article on the hospital of St Julian see VCH *Herts.*, iv, 464–7. It was founded by Abbot Geoffrey and there seems to be no evidence that the original foundation included women. But as already suggested (see Chap. 3), men and women were often associated together in hospitals.

[32] After giving an account of the 14th-cent. reforms instituted at the house, the *Gesta* declared that until then the inmates had possessed no certain rule (*Gesta Abbatum*, ii, 213–14). This does not suggest vigorous oversight on the part of the monks during the 13th cent.

[33] In the early 13th cent., some charters relating to the nunnery are witnessed by William de Husseburn, seneschal of St Albans, suggesting he may have had some oversight of the nuns' temporal administration, e.g. PRO, Anc. Deed E40/996, and E210/125.

[34] This is set out in the papal bull of 1156: see *PUE*, iii, 244–5, no. 107.

the abbot of St Albans the right to bless nuns—not just those at the cell of Sopwell but other nuns as well.[35] This privilege can be seen as an aspect of the general thrust to increase the power and rights of the abbey,[36] but it also implies that links with the nuns were considered desirable, and that the abbey was wanting to extend such jurisdiction. It is not clear what other nuns are referred to, or whether this right was ever exercised. It is possible that other communities of women were attracted to the abbey for protection and the provision of priestly support. Perhaps St Albans wished to extend its jurisdiction to the community at Markyate. But the sources are silent. Only at Sopwell is there evidence of the abbot exercising the right to receive nuns into the religious life.[37]

This study of the relationship between the great abbey of St Albans and the communities of women situated nearby underlines the importance of individual abbots, particularly Abbot Geoffrey. The *Gesta Abbatum* suggests that the monks were not happy with their abbot's support of feminine vocation. It is only in the case of the foundation at Sopwell that the account makes no reference to opposition or unease on the part of the monastery. If the establishment of the community there involved the removal of the women from a closer liaison with the abbey, such reticence would need no further explanation. It is not possible to determine when association with women came to be resented. The *Life of Christina of Markyate* certainly suggests that in the first half of the twelfth century contact between the abbey and the maidens was frequent and generally welcome. The privilege granting St Albans the right to bless nuns implies that in the middle of the twelfth century such a right was desired. The part played by the abbey of St Albans in establishing communities of women following a religious vocation should not be underestimated. The establishment of a nunnery at Sopwell, virtually in the shadow of the abbey, may reflect the organization of women previously attached to St Albans into a separate and strictly enclosed community. The development of the priory at Markyate was also undoubtedly helped by links with the monastery. Although Christina and her followers were less dependent, it was the support of Abbot Geoffrey which ensured the growth of an anchoretic community into a priory, and the *Life of Christina* provides valuable evidence of the frequency of contact between women and the abbey in the mid-

[35] 'Ut, sicut Deo dicatas virgines intra cellam de Sopwella ad ius tuum pertinentem fultus apostolice sedis presidio benedicitis, sic tam illas quam alias, que tuo subsunt regimini, tam tu quam successores tui benedicendi liberam habeatis facultatem.' (Ibid., iii, 290, no. 148).

[36] For the shower of papal privileges bestowed by Adrian IV on St Albans see Sayers, 'Papal Privileges', 59–62.

[37] *Gesta Abbatum*, i, 232 (1212).

twelfth century.[38] Although not the original intention of the founder, the establishment of the church of St Mary de Pré enabled the development of a third priory of women linked with St Albans. But the comparative lack of involvement of the monks with this community is suggestive. It may in part reflect the more practical orientation of the original foundation. But it probably also indicates that by the end of the twelfth century there was altogether less association between monks and nuns, and that the men were increasingly unwilling to accept the care of such women and the responsibility for them.

St Albans Abbey was not the only Benedictine monastery to play an important part in the foundation of communities of nuns. The abbey of Peterborough was responsible for the establishment of a convent at Stamford.[39] Abbot William of Waterville granted the church of St Michael at Stamford to the nuns and was described as founder of the priory.[40] Fragments of evidence hint at an earlier origin and it is a possibility that, as at St Albans, nuns were following a religious life in association with the monastery before they were established in a separate church.[41] The foundation documents stress the subjection of the community of women to Peterborough, and the extent of control exercised by the abbey is striking.[42] A promise of obedience made by the prioress and convent of Stamford, and preserved in the Peterborough registers, states that the nuns and all their belongings were at the disposal of the abbot and monastery.[43] It is clear that the abbot was to govern the reception of nuns, and the prior of Stamford, who was to oversee the community of women,

[38] This support was important as it is clear that some anchoretic groups did not survive.

[39] For a short history of the priory see VCH *Northants.*, ii, 98–101. For more detailed recent research see Sturman, 'Stamford'.

[40] For an account of the foundation in Hugh Candidus see *The Chronicle of Hugh Candidus, a Monk of Peterborough*, ed. W. T. Mellows (London, 1949), 128. The extract from the chronicle referring to Stamford is printed in *MA*, iv, 260, no. 1.

[41] A reference to King Stephen's grant to the nuns suggests a date before 1154: see *Liber Feodorum. The Book of Fees commonly called Testa de Neville*, PRO Texts and Calendars, 2 vols. in 3 (1920–31), i, 196. Similarly a deed of the time of Abbot Robert (1214–22) refers to a pension dating from William's predecessor Abbot Martin of Bec (1132–55) (Madox, *Form. Ang.*, 371, no. dclxvi). If the foundation did date from Martin's time, he may have been influenced by the practice at Bec where a small group of pious women lived under the protection of the abbey, see A. A. Porée, *Histoire de l'Abbaye du Bec*, 2 vols. (Évreux, 1901), i, 183–4.

[42] A charter of Abbot William referred to the nuns as 'in subjectione nostra et consilio, rebus suis tam interius quam exterius disponendis' (BL Cotton Vesp. E. xxii, fo. 39ᵛ; London Soc. of Antiquaries MS 60, fo. 154. For a description of these registers of Peterborough see J. D. Martin, *The Cartularies and Registers of Peterborough Abbey* (Northants. Rec. Soc.; 1978). The charter is printed, with some inaccuracies, in *MA*, iv, 260, no. 2.

[43] *MA*, iv, 261, no. 6. For a shorter version of a similar promise of obedience see BL Cotton MS Vesp. E. xxii, fo. 39ᵛ.

was to hold office at the will of the abbot and monks.[44] The authority of the prior in relation to the prioress is not clear, but with the prior acting as representative of the abbot his authority probably overshadowed that of the woman. His jurisdiction involved spiritual concerns as well as the administration of estates and other temporal matters.[45] The first known priors were monks of Peterborough, and in 1243 the precentor of the abbey was admitted as *magister* of the nuns. Monks sometimes acted as proctors for the women in law suits.[46] Some charters dating from the first part of the thirteenth century refer to the counsel and consent given by the prior,[47] and in the registers of Hugh of Wells, Bishop of Lincoln, the patronage of churches is described as belonging to the master and convent of St Michael Stamford.[48] It would appear that the dominant role in the community was taken by the prior, or *magister*, himself a monk of the abbey.

There are indications that the nuns attempted to obtain a greater degree of independence from Peterborough. According to a charter preserved in the registers of the abbey, an agent employed by Stamford to obtain a confirmation of privileges from the pope exceeded his instructions. He obtained the insertion of clauses abrogating the abbatial sanction for the election of a prioress, and annulling the payment of certain pensions to the abbey.[49] It is hard to believe that such action was entirely due to an opportunist agent: it seems more likely that he would have acted in the belief that the prioress and convent supported his initiative. Nothing is known of the involvement of the prior in this saga, but it is suggestive that Prior Henry of Fiskerton resigned in 1229, a possible date for the incident.[50] In the event, such presumption brought little reward. The prioress and nuns had to write to ask the help of the Archbishop of Canterbury and his suffragans, requesting their intervention to restore the convent to the friendship of its neighbours, and

[44] BL Cotton MS Vesp. E. xxii, fo. 39ᵛ; *MA*, iv, 260, no. 2.

[45] The position and authority of the prior are discussed in Sturman, 'Stamford', 245–58.

[46] *Rotuli Roberti Grosseteste, episcopi Lincolniensis. AD MCCXXXV–MCCLIII*, ed. F. N. Davis (Cant. and York Soc. 10; 1913), 69. An example of a monk of Peterborough acting as proctor for the nuns is given in PRO Anc. Deed E326/8779.

[47] e.g. PRO Anc. Deed E210/3614; E210/3672.

[48] *Liber antiquus de ordinationibus vicariarum tempore Hugonis Wells, Lincolniensis episcopi 1209–35*, ed. A. Gibbons (Lincoln, 1888), 46.

[49] BL Cotton MS Vesp. E. xxii, fos. 39ᵛ–40. An account of the dispute is given in VCH *Northants.*, ii, 98. The date of it is not certain as Archbishop Richard and Prioress 'A' mentioned in the charter could indicate 1174 × 1181 or 1229 × 1230 (*HRH*, 220). I would disagree with Sharon Elkins that this incident gives no indication that subjection to Peterborough was onerous to the women, although it certainly suggests that they could not exist without the abbey's support (Elkins, *Holy Women*, 52).

[50] *Rot. Wells*, iii, 173.

renouncing all claim to papal privileges thus unworthily obtained.[51] Presumably life without the support of the monks of Peterborough had proved impossible.

In contrast to the degree of control exercised by the abbots of both St Albans and Peterborough over their dependent communities of women, the abbey of Westminster seems to have allowed the community at Kilburn a considerable degree of autonomy. This was probably a reflection of the anchoretic origins of the priory,[52] and suggests again that the women of Sopwell and Stamford may have had previous links of dependence with the nearby monasteries. There is no evidence that the hermit Godwyn, who grouped maidens together under his tutelage at Kilburn, had previous links with Westminster. The organization outlined in the foundation charters of Kilburn is clearly to provide for the women on a permanent basis after the hermit's death. They are then to select a mature man as their mentor. The advice, and presumably the consent, of the Abbot of Westminster was to be obtained, but the monastery's control seems to have been less autocratic than that of St Albans over Sopwell. It is stipulated that the abbot and prior were not to force anyone to enter the community without the women's consent. The chaplain, too, was not to be admitted against their wishes.[53] The Abbot of Westminster clearly played a part in the establishment of a priory of nuns at Kilburn. According to the history of the abbey written by John Flete, Abbot Herbert was the founder of the cell and granted the site of the new community as well as some lands and rents.[54] Later abbots confirmed his grants and continued to supply allowances of food to the women.[55] But the men who succeeded hermit Godwyn as *magister* of the nuns do not seem to have had any particular connections with the abbey. One is described as *Magister* Alexander of St Paul's,[56] and an agreement drawn up between Westminster and the bishop in 1231 explicitly provided for a secular priest to hold the office of *magister* and *custos* of the nuns.[57]

[51] BL Cotton MS Vesp. E. xxii, fos. 39ᵛ–40.

[52] See pp. 25–6.

[53] BL Cotton MS Faust. A. iii, fos. 325ᵛ–326ᵛ; printed *MA*, iii, 426, no. 1.

[54] *Flete*, 87.

[55] Ibid., 94, 97. See also BL Cotton MS Faust. A. iii, fos. 327–329. These charters are printed in *MA*, iii, 426–7, nos. 2, 4, 5, and 6. At the Dissolution the nuns were said to receive a weekly allowance from the abbey of 40 gallons of beer and 18 loaves of bread (*Valor Eccl.*, i, 432).

[56] *Curia Regis Rolls*, v, 22 (1207). It is possible that he can be identified with Alexander of Norfolk, a canon of St Paul's: see Le Neve, *Fasti*, rev. edn., i, *St Paul's London*, 91. It is interesting that Flete describes the women as canonesses (*Flete*, 87). This suggests that they did not follow the same rule as the monks, and could indicate a link with St Paul's.

[57] BL Cotton MS Faust. A. iii, fo. 329, printed in *MA*, iii, 428, no. 9. For a discussion of the role of bishops in relation to nunneries see Chap. 10.

Another community of women which owed its foundation in some measure to an abbey of Benedictine monks was the priory of Thetford in Norfolk. The site had been occupied by a small cell of men dependent on the abbey of Bury St Edmunds.[58] According to the account of its foundation preserved in the registers of Bury, the two surviving inhabitants of the cell wished to withdraw because of the great difficulties they were experiencing, and they suggested that nuns should take their place. Abbot Hugh (1157–80) apparently needed some persuading. The implication is that he was reluctant to undertake responsibility for women. But the advocacy of the Bishop of Norwich, together with the support of the sheriffs of Norfolk and Suffolk, convinced him of the worthiness of the women and the desirability of supporting them.[59] As at St Albans, there are hints that women had previously followed a religious life in the shelter of the abbey. In Domesday Book an entry refers to the presence of nuns apparently connected with Bury.[60] The women who came to Thetford had previously been living at Ling, and there is nothing to link them with the abbey apart from the fact that their chapel appears to have had the same patron saint, St Edmund.[61] This could reflect the popularity of the saint rather than any particular association with the abbey of Bury. Yet it is interesting that, as at St Albans, there are tenuous hints of links between the women and the monastery's infirmary. The prioress of Thetford undertook to pay four shillings per annum to the infirmary of the abbey, and the *custos domus infirmorum* witnessed the charter of Abbot Hugh which set out the endowment to the nuns.[62] In 1176 × 1177, the pipe rolls record a royal payment to the nuns, and the entry immediately follows the record of a payment to the sick of St Edmund.[63] It is by no means clear that there was a continuous tradition of women with a religious vocation associated with the abbey of Bury, possibly in caring for the sick, but it must remain a distinct possibility. Be that as it may, the monks were clearly responsible for providing the initial endowment of the nuns of Thetford, and it appears that they also provided weekly supplies of bread and beer.[64]

---

[58] A short account of the history of the priory is given in VCH *Norfolk*, ii, 354–6.

[59] Abbot Hugh's charter is preserved in the Lakenheath register, BL Harl. MS 743, fos. 271ᵛ–272ᵛ. It is printed in *MA*, iv, 477–8, no. 1, from the version in a 15th-cent. register, Cambridge UL MS Ff. ii 29. For a description of these registers see *The Archives of the Abbey of Bury St Edmunds*, ed. R. M. Thomson (Suffolk Rec. Soc. 21; 1980).

[60] See Chapter 3, n. 64.

[61] VCH *Norfolk*, ii, 355.

[62] BL Harl. MS 743, fos. 271ᵛ–272ᵛ.

[63] *PR 23 Henry II*, 124. The question of general links between nuns and hospitals is studied in Chap. 3 of this book.

[64] BL Harl. MS 3977, fos. 26–26ᵛ. For a revision of these arrangements in 1369 see VCH *Norfolk*, ii, 355.

Several groups of women, therefore, depended in some way on a Benedictine monastery for their foundation as organized convents, and in some cases the nuns may have originally been linked with the men's monastic community. The founding of the cells of Sopwell and Stamford particularly may have reflected a regularization of the life of women associated with the monks, and the desire to remove them further from the parent abbey. Although separate establishments in terms of geographical location and identity, these two communities maintained close links with the monasteries during the twelfth and early thirteenth centuries, and were in some measure dependent on them. The sources, partly perhaps because of unease about the association of the sexes, are by no means clear. It may be that other nunneries were originally linked with communities of monks with virtually no evidence surviving to document such a liaison. At Wothorpe, near Stamford, evidence from the continuator of Pseudo-Ingulf reveals the presence of nuns next to a cell of monks from the abbey of Crowland. Abbot Joffrid is recorded as giving the men power to hear the confessions of the neighbouring nuns.[65] The unreliability of the source is notorious,[66] but the author gives an interesting amount of detail, and it is clear that in 1086 Crowland held land in Wothorpe.[67] The fragment would seem to provide a further illustration of links between nuns and monks, even if it does little to elucidate the nature or extent of the association.[68]

For at least one Augustinian monastery there is clear evidence to show that a priory of women evolved from a double house of both canons and nuns. At Moxby in Yorkshire,[69] the prioress, giving evidence in a plea of *quo warranto* in the reign of Edward I, stated that in the time of Henry II the nuns had been linked with the canons of Marton, but that they then separated, with certain lands being assigned to the women.[70] The date when this happened is not clear. A charter of Henry II in favour of the nuns of Moxby was issued, probably in January 1158.[71] It outlines gifts made to the nuns, and

[65] 'Sanctimonialium sororum suarum juxta commanentium', 'Petri Blesensis continuatio ad Historiam Ingulphi', in *Rerum Anglicarum Scriptorum Veterum*, ed. W. Fulman (Oxford, 1684), i, 115.

[66] For a note on the problems of Crowland's early history see *The Ecclesiastical History of Orderic Vitalis*, ed. M. Chibnall, 6 vols. (Oxford, 1969–80), ii, pp. xxv–xxvi.

[67] VCH *Northants.*, i, 319b.

[68] It is not clear whether there are links between these women and the 12th cent. community of nuns at Wothorpe. For the association of this foundation with the order of Arrouaise see p. 155.

[69] For Moxby see Burton, *Yorks. Nunneries*, 7–8; see also VCH *Yorks.*, iii, 239–40.

[70] *Placita de quo warranto temporibus Edw. I, II, and III in curia receptae scaccarii Westm. asservata*, ed. W. Illingworth (Record Commission; London, 1818), 190.

[71] This is printed in *EYC*, i, 328, no. 419 from an *inspeximus* version on a charter roll of Edward II. The date is confirmed by evidence in the pipe roll of 1157 × 1158 which shows the remittance of the rent to the nuns in accordance with the charter: see *PR 2–4 Henry II*, 146.

may record the first establishment of the women at Moxby. A later grant of the king refers to the canons and nuns of Marton.[72] References such as this, and the proximity of Moxby to Marton, may indicate that even with the establishment of the nuns at Moxby, a complete separation was not intended. The suggestion of a continuing association is also implicit in a grant of Hugh du Puiset which was made jointly to the canons of Marton and the nuns of Moxby.[73] Perhaps the division of the two communities was a gradual process, and separate ownership of endowments was not stabilized until the beginning of the thirteenth century. A royal writ of 1223 ordered the sheriff to permit the prioress and nuns to hold the land of Huby according to the charter of Henry II.[74] If this refers to land previously granted jointly, it could indicate a more complete separation of the nuns from the canons.[75]

One reason behind the move of the nuns to Moxby and their eventual organization as an independent community, was probably unease about forms of double organization. There are hints that such disquiet was a factor in the establishment of other communities of women belonging to the Augustinian order. At Crabhouse in Norfolk, it has already been noted that the community probably originated around an anchoress.[76] It is clear that the women became linked with the Augustinian canons of Norman's Burrow.[77] Roger, prior of the canons, issued a charter granting the hermitage of Wiggenhall to the nuns. The preamble of the charter referred to the evils threatening the church and the need for scandal to be avoided.[78] In about 1181, Godfrey de Liseurs, the son of the founder of the cell, transferred Norman's Burrow to Castle Acre Priory.[79] An agreement between the Cluniac monks there and the canons and the nuns is preserved in the Castle Acre register. This states that the men of Norman's Burrow were to give up their rights in the hermitage to the nuns, and that the ladies should be allowed to celebrate in their own chapel with their own chaplains in return for a payment to the

---

[72] *EYC*, i, 329, no. 420. Farrer dates this charter 1180 × 1181. The possibility of an earlier date is raised by the reference to the grant in Huby in the pipe roll of 1166 × 1167 (*PR 13 Henry II*, 78). This would seem to refer to the land eventually obtained by the nuns.

[73] *PR* (Chancellor's Roll), 8 *Richard I* (1196), 261.

[74] *Rotuli Litterarum Clausarum in Turri Londinensi asservati*, ed. T. Hardy, 2 vols. (Record Commission; London, 1833–4), i, 534b.

[75] Compare the view of Farrer who suggests that this may be the land in Riseborough which was originally granted to the nuns (*EYC*, i, 329).

[76] See pp. 24–5.

[77] For Norman's Burrow see *KH*, 101 and *VCH Norfolk*, ii, 358–9.

[78] BL Harl. MS 2110, fo. 82ᵛ; printed *MA*, v, 70, no. 5.

[79] The charter of Bishop John confirming the transfer of Norman's Burrow to Castle Acre (BL Harl. MS 2110, fo. 125ᵛ, printed *MA*, v, 70, no. 8), probably dates from *c*.1181 as it has similar witnesses to another charter of this date (ibid., fo. 125ᵛ).

Cluniac monastery.[80] Perhaps the separate endowment of the women, and the move of the canons to Castle Acre, was linked with a desire to achieve a separation of the sexes, and thus to lessen the chance of scandal hinted at in Prior Roger's charter.

At Marton, and possibly also at Crabhouse, the origins of the nunnery were closely associated with a community of Augustinian canons. Other foundations may have been similarly linked. At Grimsby in Lincolnshire, a priory of nuns was situated near the house of canons at Wellow. The early history of both communities is obscure. According to tradition both had royal founders, and both were thought to belong to the Augustinian order.[81] There is indeed some evidence of links between the two houses. In the late twelfth and first half of the thirteenth centuries there are examples of the canons acting both as proctor and *magister* for the nuns.[82] There are similar hints of association between other Lincolnshire houses. The nuns of Gokewell were situated near the canons of Thornholme, whose priory was probably founded in the reign of Stephen.[83] In 1163 a bull of Alexander III confirmed Gokewell as one of the possessions of the canons.[84] Brothers and a canon of Thornholme acted as witnesses to a charter recording grants to the nuns.[85] It is also interesting that the hands recording the Thornholme and Gokewell entries commemorating the death of the prioress of Lillechurch in the Higham mortuary roll seem to be identical.[86] It would appear that, on this occasion at least, a member of the priory of men acted as scribe for the nuns.

Interesting links, therefore, exist between some Benedictine and Augustinian monasteries and communities of women following a religious vocation. It is possible that such links merely reflect co-operation between independent foundations and the involvement of canons or monks in the care of nearby nuns.[87] But in the case of

[80] BL Harl. MS 2110, fos. 125ᵛ–126.

[81] KH, 179 and 280.

[82] A bull of Pope Lucius III shows that a certain Brother 'G', a brother of Wellow, acted as proctor for the nuns (*PUE*, iii, 469, no. 367). 'G' had the temerity to sell some of the nuns' property without their permission. In 1232 the *magister* of the nuns was also a member of the Augustinian abbey (see *Rot. Wells*, iii, 202).

[83] KH, 176. For the foundation date of Gokewell see Appendix A.

[84] *PUE*, i, 357, no. 95.

[85] BL Egerton chart. 622. This is printed, not from the original, in *EYC*, vi, 204, no. 105.

[86] SJC MS 271, Lillechurch Mortuary Roll. The entry follows that of Thornholme and was omitted in the table printed in C. E. Sayle, 'The Mortuary Roll of the Abbess of Lillechurch, Kent', *Proceedings of the Cambridge Antiquarian Soc.* 10 (1898–1903), 383–409.

[87] This is the probable explanation of the links between the canons of Kirkham and the nuns of Yedingham, Yorkshire. Prior Andrew of the Augustinian house frequently witnessed charters for the nuns and on one occasion is described as their *magister* (*EYC*, i, 306–7, nos. 390–2). There seems to be no other suggestion that the early history of the houses was

Moxby it is explicitly stated by the prioress that the nuns had originally formed one community with the canons. It has been suggested that the development at Moxby might be explained by the influence of the new orders,[88] several of which are known to have established double houses. The origins and development of these Continental movements are studied in the next chapters. While there is no evidence of a link between Moxby and one of the new orders of canons such as those of Prémontré or Arrouaise, or even of the English order of Sempringham,[89] it is possible that a nunnery which remained independent of any institutional link with a double order might still imitate similar forms of organization. What seems clear is that, far from being unique, Moxby was indicative of a more general trend in the twelfth century from an earlier association of the sexes towards the formation of more separate communities for women. A study of other houses shows that, in the twelfth century, there were several where both men and women formed part of an early community which subsequently developed as a nunnery.

At Blackborough in Norfolk, a Benedictine house, early charters enrolled in the fourteenth-century cartulary[90] suggest that when the community was first founded male members were at least as important as female. The charter of Roger de Scales and Muriel his wife, which probably marks the foundation of Blackborough, refers only to monks, and makes no mention of women.[91] William, one of their sons, entered the community,[92] and it would seem that the original foundation was for men. But the confirmation charters of Robert, another son, indicate changes. One such charter refers to the sisters and brothers who formed the community at Blackborough, while others just mention women.[93] It could be argued that such changes of wording merely suggest that a community of women replaced an earlier one of men,[94] and that an isolated reference to sisters and brothers is insufficient evidence to conclude the existence

linked. But the evidence suggesting a link with male religious at Moxby and possibly Grimsby, and Fosse, as well as Newcastle and Swine, leads me to question Sharon Elkins' assertion that in the North, as distinct from the South, only rarely were religious men the founders of nunneries: see Elkins, *Holy Women*, 91.

[88] Burton, *Yorks. Nunneries*, 7–8.

[89] Dr Burton suggests that Arrouaise was a more likely model than Sempringham (ibid., 48, n. 29).

[90] BL Egerton MS 3137. For a description of the cartulary see Davis, *Med. Cartls.*, 8–9, no. 57. A brief background history is given in VCH *Norfolk*, ii, 350–1.

[91] BL Egerton MS 3137, fo. 30; printed in *MA*, iv, 206, no. 1. Another charter of Roger which just refers to the brothers is also transcribed on this page of the cartulary.

[92] Ibid., fo. 31; printed in *MA*, iv, 207, no. 4.

[93] Ibid., fos. 30v–31; printed in *MA*, iv, 206–7, nos. 3 and 2.

[94] This happened at Canonsleigh in Devon, as well as at Thetford: see pp. 171–2 and p. 64.

of a double community. But other charters, including one of Robert, are directed to a certain Hamo Walter and Matilda his mother together with those who serve God at Blackborough,[95] suggesting that both sexes were important members of the community. Later grants made by Robert's sons refer only to nuns.[96] The chronology of these changes is not clear, but it would seem that the early community for men was founded in *c.*1150 and that women were established at Blackborough by the end of the century.[97]

Swine in Yorkshire is another priory where evidence suggests the existence of some form of double community. It was apparently founded as a Benedictine house by Robert de Verli in the decade *c.*1143 × 1153.[98] A charter recording the grant of the church, transcribed by Dodsworth, refers to him as Brother Robert de Verli.[99] In all probability he can be identified with *magister* Robert of Swine who witnesses several early charters and was clearly in a position of authority in the priory.[100] Apart from the suggestion that the founder was following the religious life, there is evidence of the presence of a sizeable number of other men apparently belonging to the community. A notification of Henry II to Swine referred to the master of the house, canons, brothers, and nuns.[101] The existence of canons at the priory is confirmed by the evidence of witness lists,[102] and also by the record of a dispute between Swine and the abbey of Meaux in the first half of the thirteenth century. This reveals the presence of at least two canons and seven brothers or *conversi*.[103] In 1267 × 1268 the visitation returns of Archbishop Walter Giffard of York show that canons and brothers still formed part of the community at Swine. Reference is made to walls separating the sexes

[95] BL Egerton MS 3137, fos. 30–30^v and 33–33^v.

[96] Ibid., fo. 31^v. Some later charters referring only to women are printed in *MA*, iv, 207, nos. 5 and 6.

[97] KH, 256; see also Appendix A.

[98] For the dating see Appendix A. A background article for the priory is given in VCH *Yorks.*, iii, 178–82. For a note on the question of claims of the priory to be Cistercian see pp. 106 n. 80, 110.

[99] Oxford, Bodleian MS Dodsworth, vii, fo. 259. It is printed in *EYC*, iii, 75–6, no. 1, 360. The editor suggests that Robert was a priest of the church of Swine and perhaps the brother of the 'real founder' of the house who was a member of the Verli family and whose name is unknown.

[100] He acted as witness to some charters of Rievaulx, Bridlington, and Nunkeeling: see *EYC*, ix, 242, no. 160 (1175 × 1176); ibid., iii, 59, no. 1,338 (1157–*c.*1180); see also Oxford, Bodleian MS Dodsworth, vii, fo. 256, printed *EYC*, iii, 55, no. 1,333 but without witnesses.

[101] 'Magistrum ejusdem domus et canonicos et fratres et sanctimoniales ibidem Deo servientes' (*EYC*, iii, 78, no. 1,363 [1181]).

[102] For example a Nun Cotham charter is witnessed by Philip, canon of Swine: see Oxford, Bodleian MS Top Lincs. d 1, fo. 6^v; Magister Robert witnessed a charter together with Alexander his canon: see *Abstracts of the Charters . . . of Bridlington Priory*, ed. W. Lancaster (privately printed, Leeds, 1912), 195.

[103] *Chron. Meaux*, ii, 15–22, partic. 19.

and to windows through which food and drink were passed.[104] There is a distinct possibility that Swine was the mother house of other communities. Evidence from the cartulary of Nun Cotham Priory in Lincolnshire suggests that it was initially a daughter house of the Yorkshire convent. A charter of Alan de Monceaux, the lay founder of Nun Cotham, referred to a grant to the nuns of Swine living at Cotham. Another charter of the convent of Swine recorded their donation of the church of Burgh to the nuns of Cotham, using the metaphor of mother and daughter.[105] Similarly, an isolated charter hints at links between Swine and Catesby in Northamptonshire. It records the prioress and convent of the Yorkshire house quitclaiming any right they might have in the churches of Ashby and Basford to their sisters, the nuns of Catesby, who are described as belonging to their order.[106] There is no evidence to suggest that Swine maintained any links with either of these houses, both of which also appear to have numbered brothers among their community.[107] This probably reflects the general organizational weakness of the nunneries which made it difficult for them to retain control over associated foundations.[108]

Several other convents provide evidence that men formed part of their community in the twelfth century. Moreover, as some of them are entitled canon, they cannot have been lay brothers.[109] At Legbourne in Lincolnshire, there are references to individual canons apparently linked with the priory,[110] although it is not possible to

---

[104] *Register of Walter Giffard, Lord Archbishop of York 1266–79*, ed. W. Brown (Surtees Soc. 109; 1904), 147–8. Windows were used as a guarded means of communication in Gilbertine houses: see R. Graham, *St. Gilbert of Sempringham and the Gilbertines* (London, 1901), 54–7; see also *Book of St Gilbert*, 33.

[105] Oxford Bodleian MS Top Lincs. d 1, fos. 12ᵛ and 13ᵛ.

[106] 'De ordine nostro'—see charter PRO E326/421.

[107] The brothers of Nun Cotham are mentioned in a letter of Alexander III (cf. *PUE*, iii, 31, attrib. to Alexander IV, see p. 104, n. 69); see also Oxford, Bodleian MS Top Lincs. d 1, fos. 1–2, printed in *MA*, v, 676–7, no. 4. The cartulary of the house also contains other references to brothers: see Oxford, Bodleian MS Top Lincs. d 1, fos. 25, 27, 32ᵛ. A letter of Bishop Gravesend referring to the canons and lay brothers of Catesby is enrolled in Sutton's register: see *The Rolls and Register of Bishop Oliver Sutton 1280–99*, ed. R. M. T. Hill, 8 vols. (Linc. Rec. Soc., 1948–86), ii, 5.

[108] The difficulties are well documented in the case of Langley, Leicestershire, founded as a daughter house of Farewell in Staffordshire: see VCH *Leics.*, ii, 3. Problems arose, and eventually papal judges delegate decreed in 1209 that the prioress of Langley should be elected by the prioress of Farewell and the convent of Langley, and that the mother house would renounce all other rights over the Leicestershire community: see J. Sayers, *Papal Judges Delegate in the Province of Canterbury 1198–1254* (Oxford, 1971), 175. The evidence from Swine suggests it is unwise to assume, as Sharon Elkins does, that Farewell was the only nunnery to establish a daughter house (Elkins, *Holy Women*, 53).

[109] For a discussion of the status of brothers in Gilbertine nunneries see p. 74.

[110] e.g. Gerard, canon of Legbourne, witnessed a charter dating from *c.*1160 × 1179 (Oxford, Bodleian MS Linc. chart. 1165); Reginald, a charter of the mid-12th cent.

estimate the number there at any one time. At Stixwould, in the same county, evidence from the cartulary and some original charters[111] demonstrate the presence of canons and of other men who are described as brothers (*fratres*) of the house. A charter of 1172 is witnessed by Thomas, who is given the title of canon, and four other brothers of Stixwould.[112] Their status is not clear, but the fact that the whole convent of brothers and nuns at Stixwould acted as witnesses to a charter suggests that men were important members of the community as well as women.[113] Men apparently entered the convent of Stixwould to follow the religious life and presumably to become full members of the priory.[114] Other houses also appear to have men joining them. At Wykeham in Yorkshire, William de Octon gave half a carucate of land to the nuns when his nephews were received into the house.[115] The size of the grant suggests that they were not unimportant additions to the community. At Greenfield in Lincolnshire there is also evidence of the presence of men as well as nuns. A grant of a certain Anfrid de Haugh, dating from early in the reign of Henry II, refers to the nuns of Greenfield and their brothers,[116] and a later confirmation charter reveals that Anfrid himself was entering the house to serve God both in life and in death.[117] His daughter was already a member of the priory[118] and the wording of his charter does not suggest that this was a grant *ad succurrendum*, but that he was joining the community during his lifetime.

It appears, therefore, that in several priories of nuns men formed part of the community to a degree hitherto unrecognized. This raises the question as to the status of such brothers. Many are simply

(*Transcripts of Charters relating to the Gilbertine Houses of Sixle, Ormsby, Catley, Bullington, and Alvingham*, ed. F. M. Stenton [Linc. Rec. Soc. 18; Horncastle, 1922], 105, no. 5); Roger, canon of Legbourne, witnessed a 12th-cent. charter (BL Addit. chart. 7524).

[111] BL Addit. MS 46,701; for a description see Davis, *Med. Cartls.*, 106, no. 931. Some of the original charters preserved in the BL are printed in *Danelaw Docs.*, 279–89. Other charters for the house are held in the Bodleian Library, Oxford.

[112] *Danelaw Docs.*, 284, no. 380. It is clear that Canon Thori was also a canon of Stixwould: see ibid. 80, no. 122. At least eight brothers are mentioned in the witness lists of Stixwould charters in terms suggesting they belonged to the community, in addition to the two who are given the title of canon: see ibid., 283–4, 288.

[113] Ibid., 282, no. 378 (early Henry II).

[114] Ibid., 283–4, no. 380 (1172).

[115] *EYC*, ii, 373–4, no. 1,065 (1170 × c.1185). For references to a *magister* and canons of Wykeham see ibid., i, 300, no. 383 (1160 × 1176).

[116] *Danelaw Docs.*, 92, no. 140. See also ibid., 95, no. 145, which refers to the convent of nuns and brothers at Greenfield. For a background history of Greenfield see VCH *Lincs.*, ii, 155–6.

[117] *Danelaw Docs.*, 92–3, no. 141.

[118] See a charter transcribed in the Collections of Gervase Holles, BL Lansdowne MS 207 A, fos. 217–217ᵛ.

described as *fratres*—an epithet which provides little indication as to their standing or role. But fragments of evidence suggest that they could be men of means. At St Radegund in Cambridge, one of the brothers of the house, called Sturmi, can probably be identified with the man of the same name who granted the advowson of the church of All Saints to the nuns.[119] In Buckinghamshire, a charter of the priory of Little Marlow, which dates from before the end of the twelfth century, reveals that a certain Michael Parmenter of London, a man of some substance, entered the house. His daughter was already a nun there. Michael then decided that he would rather dedicate himself to the service of the Lord in a masculine community, and the nuns released him from all his obligations to them, except for a rent to be paid to Waltham Abbey.[120] This was the monastery he then entered as a *conversus*.[121] The status of such brothers in communities of women should not be underestimated. In a house of men the lay recruits would be more likely to be relegated to a secondary position by the very presence of the choir monks—a group in clerical orders. Nuns in Anglo-Norman society, being themselves lay and often illiterate, as well as mere women, would be less likely to cause a diminution in prestige or position. In the twelfth century, brothers attached to several Benedictine and Augustinian nunneries may have been fuller members of the community than the description of them as lay brothers might suggest.[122] In the absence of archaeological or other evidence, it is impossible to determine whether the brothers lived within the same boundary as the women, or to ascertain details about the degree of separation between the sexes. It is clear that such communities formed one organizational unit, and even if in separate buildings, must at least have been in close geographical proximity. It would seem that the association of men and women following a religious life was more prevalent than

---

[119] Gray, *St Radegund*, 144, no. 383 and 90, no. 79a. The interpretation suggested in VCH *Cambs.*, ii, 218 is that he was brother of the prioress. For other evidence of brothers at the house see Gray, *St Radegund*, 135, no. 323.

[120] His charters are transcribed in a Waltham cartulary, BL Harl. MS 391, fos. 104–104^v: see *Early Charters of the Augustinian Canons of Waltham Abbey, Essex, 1062–1230*, ed. R. Ransford (Studies in the History of Medieval Religion, 2, Woodbridge, 1989), 390–1, nos. 566–7.

[121] Waltham cartl. BL Cotton MS Tib. C. ix, fo. 229. I am grateful to Dr R. W. Ransford for these Waltham references.

[122] In Benedictine abbeys there appears to have existed a class of fully monastic *conversi*. The term was originally applied to those who entered a monastery in later life: see Knowles, *Monastic Order*, 754–5 and 419–20, and idem, *Relig. Orders*, i, 286. For the argument that the early Cistercian and Carthusian lay brothers were probably full members of the community distinguished by their lay status see J. Dubois, 'L'Institution des convers au xiie siècle, forme de vie monastique propre aux laïcs', in *I Laici nella 'Societas Christiana' dei secoli xi e xii. Miscellanea del Centro di Studi Medievali*, 3rd ser. 5 (Milan, 1965), esp. 260–2.

has hitherto been recognized, particularly in the early part of the twelfth century. The origins of a sizeable number of nunneries were linked with communities of monks and canons, and the shortage of evidence about such links may in itself reflect growing unease about the partnership between the sexes.

This discussion of forms of double organization in England provides a background to the work of St Gilbert of Sempringham, the founder of a double order for nuns and canons.[123] Gilbert, born in Lincolnshire, was a member of the household of Alexander, Bishop of Lincoln, before returning to Sempringham as a parish priest.[124] It is probable that he had no intention of founding a religious order for women. His biographer suggests that he only came to help women who wished to follow a religious vocation when he was unable to find men with sufficient commitment.[125] Be that as it may, he encouraged the vocation of a group of maidens and enclosed them in buildings adjoining his church. Like Christina of Markyate, these women began their religious pilgrimage as anchoresses.[126] In response to the practicalities of the situation Gilbert, acting on the advice of a Cistercian abbot, added lay sisters to his growing community. It was hoped that these would provide the ladies with the necessary servants and at the same time lessen the danger of their being corrupted by the worldliness of secular village girls. For similar practical reasons, lay brothers, modelled on the Cistercians, came to be added to the order to provide the necessary masculine help.[127]

The burden of this growing community became too heavy for Gilbert, and in 1147 he went to Cîteaux to ask the Cistercians to accept responsibility for those under his care.[128] But this was

[123] Until recently the basic study of the order has been Graham, *St. Gilbert*. The *Book of St Gilbert* is a welcome addition to the literature of the order, and Dr Brian Golding is currently working on a book on the Gilbertine houses. For a recent article stressing the developing ideology of the order see S. Elkins, 'The Emergence of a Gilbertine Identity', in *Distant Echoes*, 169–82. See also Elkins, *Holy Women*, 125–44.

[124] The main source for the biography of Gilbert is the *Vita* written by an anonymous canon of the order as part of the campaign for his canonization: see the *Book of St Gilbert*. For details of St Gilbert's life see ibid., pp. xv–xxvi.

[125] Ibid., 30–1. For comments on the suggestion that his concern for women was a practical development see Elkins, 'The Gilbertines', 170.

[126] The *Life* emphasizes that they were enclosed and cut off from the temptations of the world—'Hoc modo constructis rite domibus religioni competentibus et claustro circumquaque clauso, inclusit ancillas Christi solitarie victuras sub pariete ecclesie beati Andree apostoli, in vico de Sempringham . . .' *Book of St Gilbert*, 32.

[127] Ibid., pp. xx and 36–8. For a note on the Cistercian influence on the lay brothers see Elkins, 'The Gilbertines', 181, n. 10, and for a discussion of the general question of the Cistercian influence, ibid., 177–80.

[128] *Book of St Gilbert*, pp. xxi and 40–5.

refused,[129] and so Gilbert obtained support for his task of the *cura monialium*, by adding resident canons to the order. In the words of Gilbert's biographer, these were needed because convents of women had to be ruled by monks or clerics who could not only help with their administration but take concern for their souls.[130] The story of the revolt of the lay brothers at Sempringham suggests that the arrival of these canons modified their position, and reinforces the probability that lay brothers held positions of some importance in a community of women. The leader, Ogger, and his fellows felt that their status was diminished by the introduction of canons to the order.[131] In this they may well have been right.

The majority of houses founded during the main period of Gilbertine expansion in the middle decades of the twelfth century seem to have been double establishments, with canons and lay brothers as well as nuns and lay sisters forming one community.[132] Men and women led the religious life in association within the same organization and charters refer to the nuns and their brothers, clerical and lay, or to the convents as being of both sexes.[133] It is not easy to ascertain the degree of separation and the degree of common living in the early Gilbertine houses. The main sources for the order date from the late twelfth or early thirteenth centuries, and may stress the element of separation as a reflection of the increasing concern at such association between the sexes. The story of the nun

[129] In my view they refused because at that date nuns had not been fully accepted into the order: see p. 94. See also *Book of St Gilbert*, pp. xl–xli. For a different interpretation of the significance of this refusal, see B. Golding, 'St Bernard and St Gilbert', in B. Ward (ed.), *The Influence of St Bernard: Anglican Essays with an Introduction by Jean Leclercq* (Fairacres, Oxford, 1976), 44–6.

[130] 'Hoc autem nutu Dei et consilio fecit virorum sanctorum et sapientum, quoniam, sicuti patrum decreta diffiniunt, necesse est ut monasterio puellarum, presidio et administratione monachorum vel clericorum regantur, eo quod salubre sit Christo dicatis virginibus si patres eis spirituales eligantur, quorum non solum gubernaculis tueri, sed etiam doctrinis possint edificari', *Book of St Gilbert*, 46. Cf. the reason given for the earlier inclusion of lay brothers: 'sane quoniam sine solatio virili parum proficit sollicitudo feminea' (ibid. 36). Sharon Elkins points out the developing element of justification for Gilbert's action in including men in the order: see Elkins, 'The Gilbertines', 173–7.

[131] For the revolt of the lay brothers see *Book of St Gilbert*, pp. xxiv, lv–lxii, 77–85, 135–63. See also D. Knowles, 'The Revolt of the Lay Brothers of Sempringham', *EHR* 50 (1935), 465–87. Professor Knowles's puzzlement at the amount of credence given to the 'handful of illiterate lay brothers' (ibid. 465) would be in part explained if they were respected members of the community.

[132] These double houses were: Alvingham (1148 × 1154), Bullington (1148 × 1154), Catley (1148 × 1154), Chicksands (c.1147 × 1153), Haverholme (1139), North Ormsby (1148 × 1154), Sempringham (St Mary, ? 1139), Sixhills (1148 × 1154), Watton (1151 × 1153).

[133] e.g. *Danelaw Docs.*, 50–1, nos. 77–8; *Gilbertine Charts.*, nos. 8, 26 (Bullington); ibid., nos. 12, 28 (Catley); *MA*, vi, (ii), 949, nos. 2 and 3 (late copies) (Haverholme); 'Charters relating to the Priory of Sempringham', ed. E. M. Poynton, *The Genealogist* (N.S. 15; 1899), 159, no. 2; (N.S. 16; 1900), 225.

of Watton, the scandal of her liaison with a brother of the house and her subsequent pregnancy, is an important early source for Gilbertine history.[134] These events must have taken place in the late 1150s or early in the next decade, and the saga suggests that the separation of the sexes was not as complete as the subsequent regulations implied. It is also clear that there was some contemporary concern about the proximity of male and female Gilbertines. When the lay brothers of Sempringham rose in revolt against Gilbert and appealed to the pope, the possibility of scandal was one of the charges they laid against the founder of their order.[135] The archbishop and several bishops wrote to Alexander III to assure him that the nuns and canons were in fact separated, but at the same time it would seem that stricter measures were taken to ensure that men and women lived apart.[136]

Even this may not have been enough. It is significant that the majority of Gilbertine houses founded towards the end of the twelfth century and later were for canons only.[137] The only double house to be founded after the middle of the twelfth century was Shouldham. This could be regarded as a special case. Its founder was the powerful lord, Geoffrey fitz Peter, and one of the main purposes of the foundation was to provide a suitable memorial to his wife Beatrice de Say who had died in childbirth, and had been first buried in the priory of Chicksands.[138] It is also interesting that even during the lifetime of Gilbert houses were founded for canons only.[139] Malton in Yorkshire, founded in 1150, may in part have been established to provide the canons with a retreat from the cares of looking after women. In a letter to the priory St Gilbert stressed that the purpose of the community was that the order might be 'protected and exalted through the strictness of their religious observance'.[140] But at least part of the work of Malton Priory was the care of the sick and poor.

[134] For an article on this story and its significance as early evidence for the internal arrangements of the houses of the order see Constable, 'Nun of Watton', 205–26. See also *Book of St Gilbert*, pp. liv–lv.

[135] *Book of St Gilbert*, pp. lv–lvii.

[136] The episcopal letters are printed in *Book of St Gilbert*, 135–63. For a table of the letters and notes on them see ibid., pp. lxxxv–xc.

[137] e.g. the houses of: Bridge End (1188 × 1199), Clattercote (changes from hospital to priory 1258 × 1279), Ellerton (−1207), Fordham (−1227), Holland Marsh (c.1180), Marlborough (?−1199 × 1200), Mattersey (c.1185), Newstead by Ancholme (?−1171), Owton (possibly only a grange, 1204), York (c.1200). For these and the other small 13th-cent. foundations for canons see *Book of St Gilbert*, pp. xxxvi–xxxvii.

[138] Shouldham was founded in c.1197 × c.1198. For the circumstances of the foundation see Graham, *St Gilbert*, 40–1; see also *MA*, vi (ii), 974–5. It is sometimes claimed that the 14th century foundation of New Biggin at Hitchin was a double priory (*Book of St Gilbert*, p. xxxvii) but this is not clear.

[139] Gilbert's biographer claimed that by his death nine double houses and four houses of canons had been founded (ibid. 54–5).

[140] Ibid. 164–5. The cartulary of Malton is preserved: see BL Cotton MS Claud. D. xi. The

Three hospitals—those of Malton, Broughton, and Norton, were linked with the priory.[141] The Gilbertine house of St Katherine's, Lincoln, founded by Bishop Robert de Chesney soon after 1148, was also apparently associated with the care of a hospital. Charters dating from the end of the twelfth century refer to grants to the canons and brethren and poor of the hospital. The hospital was an earlier foundation, and the charter evidence, as well as the juxtaposition of priory and hospital, would suggest that the episcopal purpose in establishing this Gilbertine house was to provide for those in need.[142] This eleemosynary function may explain the apparent presence of sisters within the community,[143] even though the priory was not founded for nuns and the charters refer only to men. Clattercote in Oxfordshire is another example of a Gilbertine foundation where the care of the sick—members of the order afflicted with leprosy—was the primary purpose of the community. It seems to have been for men rather than for both sexes, and in the mid-thirteenth century it developed into a priory for canons.[144] The establishment of hospitals was proudly listed by Gilbert's biographer as a major achievement of the saint.[145]

The care of women seeking to lead a religious vocation was the primary purpose of St Gilbert of Sempringham in establishing his communities and developing the structure of his order. This was recognized by contemporaries. William of Newburgh declared that he held the palm among those who were concerned with women.[146]

original grant of the founder Eustace fitz John was made to God and the canons of the order of Sempringham who serve God according to the Augustinian rule: see ibid. fo. 36, printed *MA*, vi (ii), 970, no. 1 (*c*.1150).

[141] The hospital at Malton seems to have been founded at the same time as the priory (KH, 376), Broughton was also founded by Eustace fitz John and linked with the canons, while Norton was probably granted to the priory *c*.1189 to enable the priory to provide food for the poor (ibid. 348, 381).

[142] *Cal. Chart. Rolls 1327–41*, 52; for date see *Acta I Lincoln 1067–1185*, 97, no. 163, and *Book of St Gilbert*, p. xxxi, n. 1. For an article on the priory see R. E. Cole, 'The Priory of St Katherine without Lincoln, of the Order of St Gilbert of Sempringham', *Associated Archaeol. Soc. Reports and Papers* 27 (2) (1904), 264–336, and for the foundation of the hospital of St Sepulchre see KH, 371.

[143] Women seem to have formed part of the community: see *MA*, vi, (ii), p. xcvii, cap. 6, where it is stated that the community numbered twenty sisters and sixteen brothers; the charters, however, only refer to canons and brothers so the women may have had lesser status; see also Cole, 'Priory of St Katherine', 267 and 323–7.

[144] The hospital at Clattercote was founded in the middle of the 12th cent. and a bull of Innocent III refers to it as 'conventui domus leprosorum sancti Leonardi de Clatercota ordinis de Sempyngham': *The Letters of Pope Innocent III (1198–1216) concerning England and Wales. A Calendar with an Appendix of Texts*, ed. C. R. and M. G. Cheney (Oxford, 1967), no. 1,057. For the priory see also VCH *Oxon.*, ii, 105.

[145] *Book of St Gilbert*, 54–5.

[146] *Chronicles of the Reigns of Stephen, Henry II and Richard I*, i, *Historia Rerum Anglicarum of William of Newburgh*, ed. R. Howlett (Rolls ser. 82; London, 1884, repr. 1964), 55.

It is also reflected in the *formulae* of the charters. Many which record early grants made to the Gilbertine houses refer to nuns serving God as the beneficiaries of the donation and make no explicit mention of the brothers.[147] Later charters however generally record that grants were made to the 'monialibus et fratribus clericis et laicis'. Others refer to the prior and convent, or state that the grant was made to the canons of the house.[148] These changes in terminology could reflect a modification in the status of the women. Masculine members of the community increased in importance, and as the concept of double houses became less acceptable, the later foundations of the order were for men only. It is possible that one of the houses established at the end of the twelfth century did in some way adhere to the original purpose of the order and provide for the care of nuns. The proximity of the priory of Gilbertine canons established at York next to the existing community of nuns at Clementhorpe is suggestive. The Gilbertine house was founded in c.1200 through the grants of Hugh Murdac, archdeacon of Cleveland.[149] It was clearly a quite separate community from that of the nuns and there is no specific evidence of any links between them. But its situation, adjoining the nunnery buildings, may be significant. If it was, and the canons did help with the *cura monialium*, the silence of the sources about any such care for women illustrates in itself the modification of Gilbert's original ideal.

The Gilbertine double houses were concentrated in Lincolnshire and Yorkshire, with one of their priories being situated in Norfolk.[150] This is similar to the geographical distribution of the other communities, not belonging to the order, where the presence of canons has been noted. The majority of these, though by no means all, were situated in Lincolnshire. A contemporary source suggests

---

[147] e.g. at Alvingham (*Acta I Lincoln 1067–1185*, 43–4, no. 67); Bullington (*Danelaw Docs.*, 3, no. 2; 14, no. 19; 22, no. 32; 38–9, nos. 57–8; 62–3, nos. 95–6); Chicksands (BL Harl. chart. 45 I 7); Haverholme (*Acta I Lincoln 1067–1185*, 24–5, no. 37); North Ormsby (*MA*, vi [ii], 963, nos. 2–3; *Gilbertine Charts.*, 41–2, nos. 5–6); Sempringham (Poynton, 'Sempringham Charts.', xvi, 153, no. 52; *MA* vi [ii], 947, no. 2); Watton (*MA* vi [ii], 954, nos. 2, 3, 4, and 6; *EYC*, ii, 406, no. 1,109). See also *Book of St Gilbert*, p. li.

[148] e.g. Bullington (BL Harl. chart. 52 H. 28); Catley (*Gilbertine Charts.*, 84–5, no. 18; 89, no. 28); North Ormsby (ibid. 48–9, no. 20; 54, no. 32, and to the convent 45–7, nos. 15, 16, 17); Sempringham (Poynton, 'Sempringham Charts.', xv, 159, no. 2; xvi, 156, no. 59; xv, 223, no. 12 [convent of both sexes]; Sixhills (*Gilbertine Charts.*, 6–7, nos. 14–15; 22, no. 39; 33, no. 60); Watton (*EYC*, i, 40, no. 33; 55, no. 49; ii, 37, no. 681; 254, no. 917; 408–9, no. 1,112). The growing importance of men within the order is also pointed out in *Book of St Gilbert*, pp. lii–liv. Some grants are to brothers alone, i.e. *Danelaw Docs.*, 60, no. 92. Cf. the statement made in 1407 that the brothers had never formed a *conventus*, that they had always been removable at the will of the Master of Sempringham, and, apart from personal requirements, held none of the property except for the use and profit of the nuns (*Gilbertine Charts.*, p. ix).

[149] *MA*, vi [ii], 962, no. 1.

[150] For the primarily local development of the Gilbertine order see *Book of St Gilbert*, pp. xxvi–xxx.

some confusion as to which priories were Gilbertine. The *Mappa Mundi* described thirteen houses as having white canons and nuns ('canonici albi et moniales').[151] Nine of these are Gilbertine houses, but the list also includes Nun Cotham and Stixwould in Lincolnshire, and Hampole and Wykeham in Yorkshire. In addition, Catesby in Northamptonshire is described explicitly in the *Mappa* as a community of nuns of Sempringham.[152] There is no corroborative evidence that Catesby was ever a member of the Gilbertine order, although it is clear that it had a resident community of brothers and canons.[153] It could be argued that these other nunneries merely reflect the influence of St Gilbert. An alternative possibility is that the forms of organization which he adopted as solutions to the needs of the nuns were already operating in other convents—again in response to the practicalities of the situation. Was he an innovator as the Chronicler of Walden claimed? This author stressed the novelty of the double Gilbertine communities and stated that in the houses of his order men and women lived together in a new and unheard-of manner.[154] But this statement was made in the context of an attempt to denigrate St Gilbert's foundations and deplore the action of their patron in burying his wife in one of them rather than within the unsullied walls of Walden.

It was probably the deliberate organization of both men and women, lay and clerical, into an order which was novel.[155] This is suggested in the picture of Gilbert's achievement drawn by the *Vita*. This stresses the fourfold aspect of the order which is likened to a chariot with four wheels—clerical and laymen on one side and literate and illiterate women on the other.[156] Archbishop Roger of York, in a letter written jointly with Bishop Hugh of Durham, suggested that the nunnery of Watton was unique in his diocese.[157] It is probable that this statement relates to the order of Sempringham, with the archbishop distinguishing it from Malton Priory, also in the York diocese, which was for canons only. It is unfortunate that the

---

[151] *Gervase of Canterbury*, ii, 429, 432, 439, 441.

[152] Ibid. 431.

[153] For the presence of men at Catesby see above, n. 107. In VCH *Northants.*, ii, 121, n. 3 it is mistakenly suggested that Catesby was unusual in having canons at the nunnery.

[154] The text of this 12th-cent. chronicle is only preserved in transcripts dating from the late 16th cent.: see BL Arundel MS xxix, fo. 14 and BL Cotton MS Vesp. E. vi, fo. 60ᵛ. The extract referred to is printed in *MA*, vi [ii], 975, no. 2.

[155] The originality of the Gilbertine order as set against a brief survey of Continental movements is discussed in *Book of St Gilbert*, pp. xlii–liv.

[156] *Book of St Gilbert*, 50–3. For the use of fourfold symbols to describe the order see Elkins, 'The Gilbertines', 175–6.

[157] 'Unica quippe domus est in Eboracensi diocesi in qua canonici et conversi cum monialibus, infra eadem septa que quidem ampla sunt, sed seorsum, ut fama publica est, honeste habitant', *Book of St Gilbert*, 150.

chronology of the foundations is not clear, and it is not possible to ascertain with any degree of certainty whether the houses, such as Swine, which apparently had canons as part of their community were in existence before St Gilbert took the step of adding canons to his order.[158] The nunnery of Stixwould may have been founded as early as the reign of Henry I and it was certainly in existence by 1139 × 1142, but specific evidence for the presence of canons comes from the second half of the century. The priories of Swine, Greenfield, Wykeham, and Legbourne were apparently founded in the mid-twelfth century[159] at precisely the time of the main expansion of the order of Sempringham. It would appear that in the twelfth century several houses of women apparently had men forming part of their community. Both their existence and the development of the Gilbertine order reflect the exigencies of the women's dependence, and their need for continuing and structured support from male religious. In the words of the saint's biographer: 'as is laid down in the decrees of the fathers it is essential that communities of maidens be controlled through the support and administration of monks and clerks.'[160] Some form of double organization provided a practical answer to the problem of the *cura monialium,* and explains both the popularity of the order of Sempringham and, in view of the increasing unease about such association between the sexes, its limitations and the subsequent modification of the founder's ideal.

[158] The probable date of this was some time after Oct.–Nov. 1148, after Gilbert's return from Clairvaux. For the possible dates see ibid., p. xli and n. 5.

[159] For the dates of these foundations see Appendix A.

[160] *Book of St Gilbert,* 47.

II
The New Continental Orders and the
Foundation of English Nunneries

5 The Order of Cluny

THE Norman Conquest intensified the links between England and Continental monasteries and reform movements. Norman monasteries were granted land in England,[1] and several small religious houses were founded as dependent on a European mother house.[2] Many monastic foundations in England were linked with the great reform movements which originated on the Continent—emanating from centres such as Cluny, Cîteaux, Fontevrault, Arrouaise, and Prémontré. A sizeable number of English nunneries have been classified as belonging to one or other of the new Continental orders.[3] In the case of houses of monks and canons, links with particular Continental monasteries and lines of affiliation to particular orders are generally clear-cut and well established. This is far less true of nunneries. The circumstances of their foundation are often obscure and there is little indication as to which order they belonged. Several of the new orders were reluctant to associate themselves with women. The reformers of Cluny and Cîteaux were primarily concerned with the renewal of the monastic ideal for men, and only later came to take cognizance of feminine vocation. By contrast, the Arrouaisian and Premonstratensian canons seem at first to have welcomed women converts, while later attempting to exclude them.[4] Links with men's communities and the establishment of double houses were an important aspect of the early history of several of the new orders—echoing themes raised by the study of the Benedictine and Augustinian nunneries in the first section of this book. This

[1] For a study of these holdings see D. Matthew, *The Norman Monasteries and their English Possessions* (Oxford, 1962).

[2] The houses whose foundation was linked with the spread of the new orders are studied in this and the following chapters. Apart from these, only two nunneries appear to have been founded in England as daughter houses of individual European convents. Roger de Montgomery, Earl of Shrewsbury, granted an estate at Lyminster to Almenêches, which he had rebuilt in c.1060 × 1070. It is not clear when Lyminster had resident nuns and developed into a priory; KH suggests c.1082 (KH, 254 and 260–1); a later date of –1178 is proposed in Power, 635–6. Clear evidence of the existence of a priory only dates from c.1201: see Appendix A. Lillechurch (Higham) was a daughter house of St Sulpice, and its foundation can be linked with the order of Fontevrault: see pp. 131–2.

[3] The total number is at least forty—the bulk of them classified as Cistercian, i.e.: two Cluniac, three of the order of Fontevrault, three Arrouaisian, three Premonstratensian, two of the order of the Hospitallers, and twenty-seven Cistercian.

[4] For a general study of the new orders as they related to women see M. Fontette, *Les Religieuses a l'âge classique du droit canon. Recherches sur les structures juridiques des branches féminines des ordres* (Bibliothèque de la Société d'Histoire Écclésiastique de la France 28; Paris, 1967).

section studies the women's convents founded in England apparently as part of the expansion of the orders of Cluny, Cîteaux, Fontevrault, Arrouaise, Prémontré, and the Hospital of St John of Jerusalem, and attempts to evaluate their links with these Continental movements.

The great house of Cluny, founded in 909 near Mâcon in Burgundy, came to be a centre of major reform.[5] These reforms at first had little direct effect on nuns.[6] But in *c*.1055 the priory of Marcigny was founded by Abbot Hugh to enable women to partake in the strict monastic vocation of Cluny.[7] This step was taken, at least in part, to provide for influential relatives such as the mother and sister of the abbot. The priory was established on lands belonging to the Semur family, and clearly involved close cooperation between Hugh and his brother, Geoffrey II of Semur. Geoffrey's sister and his daughter became nuns at Marcigny, and he himself eventually received the Cluniac habit.[8] The first recorded prioress of Marcigny was another sister of St Hugh, and his niece was the third.[9] The establishment of a community of women linked with the abbey of Cluny solved many family problems. Geoffrey III of Semur entered the religious life there together with one son, his wife, and two or three daughters.[10] Evidence from the reconstructed cartulary of Marcigny provides several other examples of husband and wife taking vows together under the auspices of Cluny,[11] and even more striking is the record of Count Guy, who took the religious habit there together with

---

[5] There is a large literature on the Cluniac order. For a bibliography see N. Hunt, *Cluny under St Hugh 1049–1109* (London, 1967), 214–23. A useful survey of the order is given in *DHGE*, xiii (1956), 35–174, s.v. 'Cluny'.

[6] For some isolated examples where individual nunneries or abbesses were influenced at an early date by Cluniac reforms see Hunt, *St Hugh*, 186–7.

[7] A modern history of Marcigny has yet to be published and the whole question of Cluniac nuns on the Continent needs further research. A general survey is given in a chapter on Cluniac nuns in Hunt, *St Hugh*, 186–94. See also the appendix in G. de Valous, *Le Monachisme clunisien des origines au xv*[e] *siècle*, 2 vols. (Archives de la France Monastique 39, Paris, 1935), i, 379–90. A major source for the history of the priory is the reconstruction of the lost cartulary: see J. Richard, *Le Cartulaire de Marcigny-sur-Loire (1045–1144). Essai de reconstitution d'un manuscrit disparu* (Dijon, 1957). The motives behind the foundation are given in a charter of Abbot Hugh which states: 'Bonum etenim nobis visum est ut, sicut per sanctorum patrum nostrorum fundationem peccatores viri apud Cluniacum portum salutis habebant, si seculo et ponpis ejus abrenuntiare vellent, ita et peccatricibus feminis de mundi laqueis ad locum hunc fugientibus, et pro commissis suis ex corde gementibus, divina clementia regni celestis non clauderet introitum' (ibid. 166, no. 288). The abbot also refers to his aims in founding the priory in a letter about Marcigny directed to his successors (*PL*, clix [1854], 949–50).

[8] *Cartl. Marcigny*, 2, no. 2; 159–60, no. 280; 8, no. 6; 17, no. 16; 12, no. 11.

[9] The list of prioresses is given in F. Cucherat, *Cluny au onzième siècle* (2nd edn.; Autun, 1850), 229–32.

[10] *Cartl. Marcigny*, 15–17, no. 15.

[11] Ibid. 20, no. 20 and n. 2; 84–5, no. 115. See also an example of husband and wife taking

members of his family and thirty of his knights. It seems that all the dependent women were provided for at Marcigny.[12]

It has been suggested that the desire of several members of a family to enter religion could be the motive behind the foundation of a double house.[13] Marcigny has often been excluded from such a description because it was situated at some distance from Cluny. Although clearly dependent on the abbey and forming one organizational unit, there was no bond of geographical proximity.[14] Some evidence indicates, however, that in the early period of its history, Marcigny was regarded in a real sense as forming a double foundation with Cluny. As suggested in the previous chapter, association between the sexes in the pursuit of a religious vocation could take many forms and should not be obscured by later developments or over-strict definitions as to what constituted a double house. It has been shown that a necrology containing some ten thousand names, and previously thought to derive from the priory of Villars-Les-Moines, originated at Marcigny.[15] Many of the early entries, dating from no later than the beginning of the twelfth century, were written by a nun. More than one hundred and fifty nuns are listed as 'members of our community' together with monks. No distinction seems to be made between the sexes in terms of status, and the descriptions 'nun of Cluny' and 'nun of Marcigny' appear to be interchangeable.[16] Evidence from the reconstructed cartulary confirms the suggestion that brothers and sisters were regarded as members of the community at Cluny. Some references are to 'fratres et sorores monasterii Cluniacensis', while other charters refer to the brothers and sisters of Marcigny.[17]

These men would presumably have belonged to the small

religious vows in a charter preserved in *Recueil des chartes de l'Abbaye de Cluny. Collections de documents inédits*, ed. A. Bernard and A. Bruel, 6 vols. (Paris, 1876–1903), v, 34–7, no. 3,681, versions i and ii.

[12] Count Guy's epitaph telling of the mass conversion is recorded in *Bibliotheca Cluniacensis*, ed. A. Quercetanus and M. Marrier (Paris, 1614), 1,647. The number of followers is remarkably similar to those brought by St Bernard to Cîteaux.

[13] E. de Moreau, 'Les Monastères doubles. Leur histoire, surtout en Belgique', *Nouvelle Revue théologique* 66 (Louvain, 1939), 790–1.

[14] For maps showing the situation of Cluny and Marcigny see G. Charvin, *Statuts, chapîtres généraux et visites de l'ordre de Cluny*, 9 vols. (Paris, 1965–), vi; Annexe, *Atlas des monastères de l'Ordre de Cluny au Moyen Âge* (Paris, 1977), 10 and 11. Moreau stresses the importance of both a geographical and a juristic bond: see Moreau, 787–8; and Berlière omits Marcigny from his discussion of double houses because of its distance from Cluny: see Berlière, 'Les Monastères doubles', 3.

[15] J. Wollasch, 'A Cluniac Necrology from the time of Abbot Hugh', in *Cluniac Monasticism in the Central Middle Ages*, ed. N. Hunt (London, 1971), 143–90.

[16] Ibid., esp. 166–8.

[17] *Cartl. Marcigny*, 73, no. 102 (1095); 29, no. 31; 54, no. 72; 97, no. 164.

community of monks established at the priory to look after the nuns. There seem to have been at least twelve monks,[18] who were probably housed in separate buildings.[19] Initially at least, they were apparently still regarded as monks of Cluny, and several important members of the abbey held office as prior of Marcigny.[20] Geoffrey III of Semur was prior from 1109–22, and the position was also held by Reinard of Semur, nephew of Saint Hugh. In addition, Hugh, later Abbot of Cluny, was claustral prior of the nuns from 1109–22.[21] The suggestion of frequent interchange between Marcigny and the abbey is reinforced by the career of Seguin de Paray. He seems to have been prior of Marcigny from 1095–1111, was then recalled to Cluny where he continued to act for the priory, and subsequently took up the full duties of prior again when he relinquished his office of chamberlain to the abbot.[22] It is possible that the position of this masculine community at Marcigny underwent some modification during the course of the twelfth century. Early evidence seems to confirm the interlocking of the two communities. A charter of Geoffrey III of Semur, dating from before 1088, referred to the brothers of Cluny who lived at Marcigny.[23] Several early charters reveal men making grants to Marcigny as they entered the religious life, without making it clear whether they were becoming members of the community there rather than at Cluny.[24] Some charters, however, dating from the first decades of the twelfth century, indicate that men were entering Marcigny itself.[25] It may be that this reflects a greater degree of separation between the two communities, with the earlier flexibility of membership becoming more formalized and a distinct group of brothers being associated with the nuns.[26]

Abbot Hugh appears to have controlled the community at Marcigny during his abbacy. The Blessed Virgin was regarded as

[18] This is the number given in *Bibl. Cluniacensis*, 1,751. Evidence from the visitation returns shows that in the 13th cent. the number varied from fourteen to twenty: see Charvin, i, 273, no. 54 (1262); 304, no. 69 (1269); 322, no. 74 (1272); 405, no. 105 (1281); ii, 2, no. 131 (1290); 82, no. 147 (1295). This entry suggests that fourteen was the accustomed number.

[19] It has been suggested that they shared the same church: see R. Graham, *English Ecclesiastical Studies* (London, 1929), 19. The wording of a charter of Abbot Hugh, dated 1102, indicates that there were two churches: see *Cartl. Marcigny*, 166, no. 288.

[20] Abbot Hugh appears to have established two priors: one who was in charge of the temporal administration at Marcigny, and the other who had particular responsibility for the spiritual direction of the nuns: see Hunt, *St Hugh*, 189.

[21] A list of priors is given in Cucherat, 221–8. For a note on this index of priors and its value as a source see *Cartl. Marcigny*, pp. xvi–xviii.

[22] Ibid., p. xvii. See also Hunt, *St Hugh*, 192–3.

[23] *Cartl. Marcigny*, 13, no. 13.

[24] Ibid. 53–4, nos. 70–2; 58, no. 78; 67, no. 92.

[25] Ibid. 117–18, nos. 201–3; 137–8, no. 258; 172–3, no. 291.

[26] The 13th-cent. visitation returns suggest that Marcigny, with its small community of brothers, was regarded as a separate priory: see above, n. 18.

perpetual abbess while the abbot appointed the priors and prioresses as mortal representatives of her authority.[27] A charter which mentions the profession of a nun shows that the abbot himself presided.[28] Hugh seems to have had particular care for his community of dependent women. In a letter addressed to his successors, he made a special plea for the priory of Marcigny.[29] The *Vitae* of the saint record his foundation of the community as a matter of pride,[30] and it is clear that the impact of the establishment of a feminine community as a branch of the abbey of Cluny was considerable. Contemporaries marvelled at the strictness of the religious life followed there by the women. Abbot Hugh seems to have taken particular measures to ensure their dedication. In contrast to the practices at the abbey of Cluny, no one under the age of 20 was to be admitted.[31] The community seems to have consisted of two groups: one strictly enclosed as anchoresses, the others, still strictly enclosed, but leading a more cenobitic life.[32] At Marcigny, as at several English convents, there were close links between anchoress and nun.[33] The prestige of Marcigny was still high during the abbacy of Peter the Venerable (1122–56). His own mother had taken the veil there, together with his nieces, and he described the community in glowing terms as a sepulchre or prison, housing those who had gloriously died to the world before their physical death.[34]

It has been suggested by one historian of Cluny that Marcigny provided the model for other houses of Cluniac nuns in that they were all linked with a community of monks,[35] and that the only exception was the Italian house of Cantu. The general argument is strengthened as it seems probable that Cantu itself was initially founded as a double establishment, with both monks and nuns forming the community.[36] But then attitudes seem to have changed. During the abbacy of Peter the Venerable, it was agreed that houses

[27] Hunt, *St Hugh*, 191.

[28] *Recueil des chartes de Cluny*, v, 182, no. 3,285. Later statutes suggest that the priors of women's houses came to receive new entrants even though it was made clear that the right was delegated by the abbot: see Valous, i, 381.

[29] *PL*, clix (1854), 949–52.

[30] Ibid. 868 (*Vita auct. Hildeberto*); *Vie de S. Hugues Abbé de Cluny 1024–1109*, by A. L'Huillier (Solesmes, 1888), 586 (*Vita auct. Gilone*).

[31] *PL*, clix (1854), 951.

[32] Hunt, *St Hugh*, 187–9; *PL*, clix (1854), 900. The existence of these two communities within the priory would seem further to illustrate the hypothesis that in the 12th cent. there was no sharp demarcation between nun and anchoress.

[33] See Chapter 2, esp. p. 31.

[34] *The Letters of Peter the Venerable*, ed. G. Constable, 2 vols. (Cambridge, Mass., 1967), i, 270, no. 107; 427–34, no. 185; see also ii, 238–9.

[35] Valous, i, 382–6.

[36] Hunt, *St Hugh*, 193.

of women were not to be closer than two miles to a Cluniac monastery.[37] Implicit in this decree is the fear that trouble might be caused by the close proximity of the sexes. A later edict of Hugh V of Cluny, dating from 1200, expressed such unease more plainly. It is stated that in future women were not to be received as nuns, sisters, or almswomen, unless they were on the point of death. In places where they were already received, they were to be strictly separate from the monks.[38] By the thirteenth century, it would seem that the inclusion of women in the Cluniac order was not altogether welcome. In the twelfth century, however, the prestige of Marcigny was undoubtedly considerable, and the community of nuns was highly regarded in England. Archbishop Anselm visited the priory and attempted to obtain the entrance of his sister there.[39] Matilda, the widow of King Stephen, Adela his mother, and possibly other members of the family, took the veil at Marcigny.[40] Archbishop Thurstan of York, impressed by the virtues of Christina of Markyate, suggested that she should follow her vocation at this famous priory.[41] Two nunneries founded in England during the twelfth century are usually described as Cluniac—the abbey of Delapré, Northampton, and the priory of Arthington in Yorkshire. It has to be decided whether they, like Marcigny, were in some sense double communities, and what was the nature and extent of their links with the order of Cluny.

The first Cluniac monastery in England was established at Lewes in 1077, and by the mid-twelfth century there were some thirty Cluniac foundations for men.[42] The strength of their links with the order and a continental mother house varied. While some were clearly daughter houses of Cluny, or another Cluniac monastery such as La Charité-sur-Loire, the monasteries of Reading and Faversham, although following Cluniac customs, appear not to have had institutional links with the order on the continent.[43] The two English

---

[37] Charvin, i, 32, no. 47 (1132 × 1146).

[38] Ibid. i, 43, no. 9.

[39] Hunt, *St Hugh*, 191.

[40] Cucherat, 238 and 235. It has been pointed out, however, that this list of nuns at Marcigny has to be treated with caution: see *Cartl. Marcigny*, pp. xiv–xvi and 102–3, n. 2.

[41] Talbot, *Life of Christina*, 126. She might well have felt somewhat out of place. An analysis of sixty-five consecrations of nuns at Marcigny reveals that the majority of women entering there had been married: see J. Verdon, 'Les Moniales dans la France de l'Ouest aux xie et xiie siècles. Étude d'histoire sociale', *Cahiers de civilisation médiévale*, 19 (Univ. de Poitiers, 1976), 253–4.

[42] The Cluniac houses are listed in KH, 96–8. For an article on the establishment of the men's houses in England, see B. Golding, 'The Coming of the Cluniacs', in R. A. Brown (ed.), *Proceedings of the Battle Conference on Anglo-Norman Studies, III, 1980* (Woodbridge, 1981), 65–77. See also L. Guilloreau, 'Les Prieurés Anglais de l'Ordre de Cluny', *Revue Mabillon* 8 (Paris, 1912–13), 1–42, 159–88.

[43] KH, 74, 65.

nunneries were both founded in the middle of the twelfth century.[44] There seems to be no evidence that they were ever visited by Cluniac houses on the continent as members of the order.[45] Nor do the sources provide any hint of a connection beween Marcigny and the houses of Delapré or Arthington.[46] As in the case of Reading and Faversham, this would not necessarily preclude some form of link with the Cluniacs at their foundation. The main source for the classification of the nunneries as belonging to the order seems to be Dugdale.[47] Tanner follows in suggesting that Delapré was Cluniac, but expressed a hint of reserve, and described Arthington as Cluniac or Benedictine.[48] The thirteenth-century registers of bishops and archbishops make no reference to the order of either house.[49] The documents which Dugdale cites for the nunneries do not appear to provide evidence that they were Cluniac. Nevertheless, it is possible that the *Monasticon* embodies a genuine tradition of an early association with the order.

The study of the priory of Marcigny suggested the possibility of some form of double organization, and so the proximity of the nuns of Delapré to the Cluniac monastery of St Andrew, Northampton, is suggestive.[50] St Andrew was founded in 1093 × 1100 as a daughter house of La Charité-sur-Loire.[51] The founder was Simon de Senlis, Earl of Northampton, who was buried at La Charité,[52] and it is clear that the house retained its right of visitation over the English monks.[53] The visitation records make no reference to nuns, and there is little to suggest that the monastery was concerned with the

[44] For details of dating see Appendix A.

[45] For 13th-cent. visitations of the men's houses in England see Charvin, i, 275–7, no. 55 (1263); 351–3, no. 86 (1276); 381–90, no. 99 (1279). The two English houses are not included in the list of Cluniac nunneries given in Charvin, vi, 317.

[46] It is stated in *Bibl. Cluniacensis*, 1,710, that Marcigny had a dependent priory in England. The nunnery did possess some English lands, namely the manors of Welby and Navenby in Lincolnshire, and Allington, Slaughterford, and Broome in Wiltshire. But these were administered by the men's house of Monkton Farleigh: see *Cartl. Marcigny*, 102–3, n. 2, and this seems to be the house referred to. There seems to be no question of the lands providing endowments for new nunneries. It has been pointed out that gifts of English land to Norman monasteries were often not intended to be the focus of new cells, but merely to swell existing endowments: see Matthew, *Norm. Monasteries*, partic. 28–65.

[47] *MA*, v, 207 (Delapré); ibid., iv, 518 (Arthington). They are also listed as Cluniac in the first edition of the *Monasticon*: see *Monasticon Anglicanum* (1st edn.), ed. R. Dodsworth and W. Dugdale, 3 vols. (London, 1655–73), i, 1,011, 691.

[48] T. Tanner, *Notitia Monastica*, revised edn., J. Nasmith (London, 1787). Northampton xxiv (3) (Delapré); Yorks. v (Arthington).

[49] KH, 270 suggests that Arthington was described as Benedictine in *MA* and Cluniac in the later archbishops' registers; VCH *Yorks.*, iii, 187 also suggests that the registers show that the priory was Cluniac, but I can find no evidence for this in the 13th cent.

[50] It was situated by the north gate of Northampton, while the nunnery was outside the south gate.

[51] KH, 97, 101.

[52] *Complete Peerage*, vi, 640–1.

[53] Charvin, i, 276 (1263), 352 (1276), 383 (1279).

vocation of women. But an entry in the cartulary of the house, dating from c.1130 × 1147, records an agreement between Matilda de Monville, daughter and heiress of Nigel de Monville, and the Cluniac monks. It is stated that in return for a grant to St Andrew's she could receive the habit of religion there, and have with her one nun (*sanctimonialis*) of her own choosing, in addition to servants. Careful provision is made for the nun, who is to stay in the event of Matilda's prior death, and for the lady herself to choose another companion if the first should pre-decease her. The monks promised that if any other lady retired to the monastery, one of the brothers was to attend her and perform those services due to a sister.[54] The purpose of the agreement was presumably to provide for Matilda in her old age. The second Lateran Council in 1139 condemned the practice of women who lived in private dwellings in religious houses, and whilst not living strictly under a rule, wished to be called nuns.[55] It is interesting that the next decree legislated against nuns who joined with monks or canons in the choir.[56] It is probable that Matilda de Monville was culpable under all these counts. It is not impossible that attempts to regularize the life of such ladies could sometimes be a factor in the development of a nunnery.

The house of Delapré was apparently founded c.1145 × 1153 by Earl Simon, son of the founder of the house of monks.[57] The original endowment of the nunnery came from lands in Hardingstone which had been granted at an early date to St Andrew's. A charter of Prior Arnulf records the transfer of this land from the monks to provide for the site of the nunnery.[58] Earl Simon gave money in return, and the grant was probably made at his instigation, but it does suggest the possibility of a link between the two houses. Other factors, however, seem to militate against the suggestion that the conveyance of land might reflect a common origin, rather than a mere business transaction. The first is the tradition recorded in Leland, that the

[54] BL Cotton MS Vesp. E. xvii, fos. 199–199ᵛ. Matilda's husband died in 1130 × 1134, see I. J. Sanders, *English Baronies. A Study of their Origin and Descent 1086–1327* (Oxford, 1960), 45. Her grant to Northampton was confirmed by her son in a deed dated 1147: see *MA*, v, 190, nos. 3 and 4. Her daughter was a nun at Elstow.

[55] *Conciliorum Oecumenicorum Decreta*, ed. J. Alberigo et al., 3rd edn. (Bologna, 1973), 203, canon 26.

[56] Ibid., canon 27. 'Simili modo prohibemus, ne sanctimoniales simul cum canonicis vel monachis in ecclesia in uno choro conveniant ad psallendum.' This has sometimes been interpreted as a general decree against double houses, but it probably represents a more specific prohibition.

[57] For Delapré see VCH *Northants.*, ii, 114–16; R. A. Serjeantson, *A History of Delapré Abbey Northampton* (Northampton, 1909). See also J. Wake and W. A. Pantin, 'Delapré Abbey, its History and Architecture', *Northants. Past and Present* (Northants. Rec. Soc. 2; 1954–9), 225–41. For the probable date of the foundation of Delapré see Appendix A.

[58] *Facsimiles of Early Charters from Northamptonshire Collections*, ed. F. M. Stenton (Northants. Rec. Soc. 4; 1930), 144, no. 55 (c.1145).

nunnery was moved to Northampton from Fotheringay.[59] Another factor is the status of Delapré as an abbey. Prior Arnulf referred to the new foundation merely as *monasterium*,[60] and a charter of King Stephen confirming the grants made to the nuns gives no precise indication of whether it was an abbey or a priory.[61] But Azelina, who held office in the time of Stephen, is described as abbess in a later confirmation of Delapré's endowments, and so too are her successors.[62] It would seem very unlikely that the daughter house of a priory would be accorded the status of an abbey at its foundation or shortly after. Cluniac houses generally ranked as priories, partly as a result of the strongly monarchical form of organization within that order.[63] A possible explanation is that the nunnery should be regarded as similar to Reading and Faversham, both of which were abbeys. These seem to have been founded with help from Cluny, but without implications of institutional dependence. Another possibility is that Delapré made use of the Cluniac liturgy. The prestige of Marcigny, the refuge of aristocratic ladies,[64] might well give an added reason for the claim by the Earl of Northampton's foundation to be associated with the order of Cluny. Perhaps some support, as well as land, came from the nearby Cluniac monastery, but no evidence exists in the meagre surviving sources to show the monks undertaking the *cura monialium*. The foundation of Delapré was noted in the cartulary of St Andrew's,[65] and the possibility that the house of women was originally linked with the Cluniac monks, and that some of the nuns had previously been associated with the monastery cannot be ruled out. It is interesting that the house of Cantu in Italy seems to have become an abbey of nuns in the twelfth century after apparently being founded as a double house.[66] The movement away from forms of double organization would, as already suggested, probably lessen the likelihood of any surviving sources preserving details of such association.

The small priory of Arthington in Yorkshire was founded

[59] Leland, *Itin.*, i, 4. It is clear that the nuns did possess the church of Fotheringay which was confirmed to them by Malcolm of Scotland 1157 × 1165: see *Reg. Regum Scot.*, i, 279, no. 274.

[60] *Northants. Charts.*, 144, no. 55.

[61] *Reg. Regum*, iii, 226, no. 614.

[62] *MA*, v, 208, no. 1.

[63] For a discussion of this aspect of Cluniac organization see B. K. Lackner, *The Eleventh Century Background of Cîteaux* (Cistercian Studies ser., 8; Washington, 1972), 40–166, partic. 88–9.

[64] The aristocratic status of many of the nuns of Marcigny is a striking feature: see Cucherat, 87–91 and Verdon, 'Les Moniales', 254.

[65] BL Cotton MS Vesp. E. xvii, fo. 4, printed in *MA*, v, 190, no. 1. An agreement dated 1259 between the prior and monks of St Andrew's and the abbey of nuns, gives no indication of a particular link between the houses: see BL Addit. chart. 47,072.

[66] Hunt, *St Hugh*, 193.

c.1150 × 1158 by Peter de Arthington and his son, Serlo.[67] Early charters relating to the nunnery provide no evidence as to its order.[68] In 1312 a nun of the house was transferred to Yedingham, generally held to be a Benedictine community, because, according to the bishop, it was of the same order.[69] Later evidence suggests that at some point Arthington claimed to be Cistercian, and in the sixteenth century the priory was included in a list of houses to be visited by Cistercian abbots.[70] Confusion as regards the order of a house of nuns was not unprecedented in the later Middle Ages. In 1408 the ecclesiastical visitors of the women situated near the cathedral of Paderborn in Germany found that they wore the habit of Cîteaux, were following the rule of Cluny, and did not know to which order they belonged.[71]

In the fourteenth and fifteenth centuries, the episcopal and archiepiscopal registers record visitations of both nunneries.[72] Such episcopal intervention has been interpreted as reflecting the distance of England from the central organization of the order.[73] Yet in an entry of 1432, Delapré is described as belonging to the Benedictines,[74] and earlier entries contain nothing to suggest that the convents were linked with Cluny. This contrasts with the position for the men's houses. For example, in 1271, the register of Bishop Gravesend records collaboration with the prior of Charité-sur-Loire over the appointment of the prior of St Andrew, Northampton.[75] It is quite clear that the monks belonged to the Cluniac order. No such firm statement can be made of the nuns. It is not surprising, therefore, that when the English lands of the order were seized during the French wars, Arthington and Delapré were not affected.[76] It may be that uncertainties as to the order of the house were a later

[67] For a background history of the priory see KH, 270 and VCH *Yorks.*, iii, 187–90. For the date of the foundation see Appendix A.

[68] W. T. Lancaster, 'Four Early Charters of Arthington Nunnery' *Miscellanea VI* (Thoresby Soc., 22; Leeds, 1915), 118–28. Lancaster, however, assumes it was Cluniac.

[69] *The Register of William Greenfield, Lord Archbishop of York, 1306–15*, transcr. W. Brown, ed. A. H. Thompson, 5 vols. (Surtees Soc. 145, 149, 151, 152, 153; 1931–40), iii, 69.

[70] J. M. Canivez, *Statuta Capitulorum Generalium Ordinis Cisterciensis ab anno 1116 ad annum 1786*, 8 vols. (Louvain, 1933–41), vi, 719, cap. 46.

[71] Valous, i, 389.

[72] Lincolnshire Archives Office, Episcopal Register III John Dalderby (1300–20). Memoranda, printed in Serjeantson, *Delapré*, 7–8; *Reg. Greenfield*, ii, 31–2 (1307) and 227 (1315) (Arthington).

[73] Valous, i, 388.

[74] *Lincoln Visitations*, i, 1420–36, 44.

[75] *Rotuli Ricardi Gravesend, diocesis Lincolniensis*, ed. F. N. Davis, additions by C. W. Foster and A. H. Thompson (Cant. and York Soc. 31; 1925), 117 (1271). See also *Reg. Sutton*, ii, pp. xviii and 104–7.

[76] The omission of Delapré is noted in A. K. McHardy, 'The Alien Priories and the Expulsion of Aliens from England in 1378', in D. Baker (ed.), *Church Society and Politics, Studies in Church History* 12 (Oxford, 1975), 134, n. 8.

development, and do not preclude an earlier allegiance to Cluny with the nunnery following its observances, and influenced by the prestige of Marcigny, even if not in a formal sense integrated into the order. It is a distinct possibility that the nuns of Northampton may initially have been linked with the nearby priory of Cluniac monks. If no firm conclusion can be reached about the order of Delapré in the early years of its history, the designation of Arthington as Cluniac seems to rest on a very slender basis, and probably derives from an error. The *Bibliotheca Cluniacensis* listed the priory of *Arenthona* as a Cluniac house subject to La Charité.[77] This clearly refers to the priory of St Andrew, Northampton. But confusion was possible, and the mistake was made by Duckett in 1888 when he transcribed the name as Arthington and included it in his list of Cluniac priories.[78] Further possibilities exist for confusion with the endowment of Delapré including lands in Hardingstone, a name which in its Latin form resembles that of Arthington. It would seem safer to conclude that the Yorkshire priory, rather than being a foundation of the order of Cluny, illustrates the uncertainty of order which surrounds so many nunneries.

[77] *Bibl. Cluniacensis*, 1,749. This was published in 1614 and so is an earlier source than the first edition of the *Monasticon*.

[78] G. F. Duckett, *Monasticon Cluniacense Anglicanum, or Charters and Records Illustrative of the English Foundations of the Ancient Abbey of Cluny from 1077 to 1534*, 2 vols. (privately printed, Lewes, 1888), i, 32 and 37; ii, 211. Compare id., *Visitations of English Cluniac Foundations* (London, 1890), 41, where *Arenthona* is translated as Northampton.

6 The Order of Cîteaux

THE early Cistercians were remarkable for their hostility to women.[1] The whole tenor of several of the first statutes is that women were to be avoided at all costs. No Cistercian abbot or monk was to bless a nun—a decree which originally was probably intended to stop the Cistercians concerning themselves with women religious.[2] It was not until 1213 that a decree of the General Chapter specifically dealt with communities of nuns. But by the middle of the thirteenth century a large number of European nunneries had been formally accepted into the order, and this is reflected by the number of decrees dealing with women and their convents. In 1241, twenty of the seventy-five statutes of that year were concerned with the needs and demands of religious ladies.[3] Such a development clearly caused problems, and in 1220 and again in 1228 decrees were passed ordering that no more convents of women were to be received into the order. As with other strict tenets advocated by the Cistercian reformers, such as the rejection of all feudal and ecclesiastical revenues, peremptory legislation may have been softened by indulgent execution. It was recognised that the Cistercian monks could not prevent nuns imitating their customs, but it was clearly laid down that the monks should not accept responsibility for any more houses or accept the task of visiting them. The suggestion that such a wise prohibition was meant to be taken seriously is reinforced by the specification of penalties for disobedience—an erring monk or lay brother was to be expelled from his community and the punishment could only be revoked by a decision of the General Chapter itself.[4] The pressures proved too great, and Cistercians, who at first seem to have thought a Cistercian nun was a contradiction in terms, eventually sheltered and organized a large number of nunneries, even

[1] Some of the research embodied in this chapter was published in article form in 1978 see S. P. Thompson, 'The Problem of the Cistercian Nuns in the Twelfth and Early Thirteenth Centuries', in *Medieval Women*, 227–52. This article concentrates on the European aspects of the question, whereas in this chapter the evidence for the English nunneries is set out in greater detail.

[2] Ibid. 227–8.

[3] Ibid. 228.

[4] Ibid. 238. For a discussion of the strict rules embodied in early Cistercian legislation, their repetition, and their infringement, see L. J. Lekai, 'Ideals and Reality in Early Cistercian Life and Legislation', in J. R. Sommerfeldt (ed.), *Cistercian Ideals and Reality* (Kalamazoo, 1978), 4–29.

if such links with women caused problems and they subsequently tried to limit their number.

A study of European 'Cistercian' nunneries in the twelfth century shows that a few, such as Tart, Coiroux, and Las Huelgas in Spain, had particular links with the order. Tart was established by dissident nuns from Jully with the help of Stephen Harding; Coiroux was closely dependent on Obazine which joined the Cistercian order in 1147; and Las Huelgas, founded by Alfonso VIII of Castille in 1187, seems from its foundation to have put forward vigorous claims to be Cistercian.[5] Many other convents probably simply imitated Cistercian customs. For those lacking official status, it could be argued that the strength of their claims to belong to the order would depend on the reality of their links with a Cistercian monastery, and the degree of their adherence to the Cistercian tenets—questions which are difficult to answer in the absence of detailed local studies. In the thirteenth century the success of a nunnery in gaining admittance to the order, particularly in the years immediately following the prohibition of 1228, seems to have depended on papal intervention or the power and persuasion of a patron or founder.[6] The claims of English nunneries to be Cistercian in the twelfth and thirteenth centuries have to be set against this background of initial rejection and uncertainty.

Twenty-seven English nunneries are classified by Knowles and Hadcock as Cistercian, and it is noted that sixteen of these were at some point in their history recorded as belonging to another order.[7] In addition to these twenty-seven convents, the house of Stamford in Northamptonshire, apparently claimed to be Cistercian for some part of the thirteenth century,[8] and Langley in Leicestershire put forward similar claims in the twelfth.[9] The white habits of the ladies at the nunnery of Brewood in Shropshire led to them also being

---

[5] For a fuller discussion of the links between these houses and Cîteaux see Thompson, 'Cistercian Nuns', 229–32, 237–8.

[6] Ibid. 241–2.

[7] The nunneries classified in KH as Cistercian are: Baysdale, Catesby,* Cook Hill, Ellerton, Esholt, Fosse,* Gokewell,* Greenfield,* Hampole,* Handale,* Heynings,* Keldholme, Kirklees,* Legbourne,* Marham, Nun Appleton,* Nun Cotham,* Pinley,* Rosedale,* Sewardsley,* Sinningthwaite, Stixwould,* Swine, Tarrant, Whistones, Wintney, and Wykeham*. The sixteen houses for which other orders are recorded are marked with an asterisk (KH, 272).

[8] KH, 266. The old county boundary is used, rather than the modern one.

[9] A letter of Alexander III, dating from 1170 × 1180, referred to Langley as Cistercian: see P. Jaffé, *Regesta Pontificum Romanorum ab condita ecclesia ad annum 1198*, 2 vols. (Leipzig), 1885–8, repr. Graz, 1958), ii, no. 13,528, printed in *MA*, iv, 221, no. 2. For a discussion of these claims see p. 106 of this Chapter. Farewell, the mother house of Langley, is described as Cistercian in what appears to be an isolated reference in a 15th-cent. episcopal register: see VCH *Staffs.*, iii, 222, n. 1.

classified as Cistercian by some antiquaries,[10] and the dedication of
the nunnery of Lacock to St Bernard, even though the house
belonged to the Augustinian order, would suggest that it too may
have aspired to follow at least some of the Cistercian ideals and
traditions. The order of the nunneries is often not easy to establish
for the evidence is scanty and difficult to interpret. Charters,
including foundation charters, rarely make reference to it, and later
descriptions in royal or episcopal records of a house being Cistercian
may reflect the nuns' attempts to gain the privileges of the order
rather than the realities of close links with Cîteaux.

Of all these convents which have sometimes been described by
antiquaries or historians as Cistercian, only Marham in Norfolk and
Tarrant in Dorset appear to have been fully incorporated into the
order at an early stage in their history. Marham was unique in that it
was founded as a Cistercian abbey. It was established in 1249, and a
statute of the General Chapter of 1250 refers to its inspection by two
Cistercian abbots.[11] The *Annals of Waverley* record how, in 1252,
the foundress Isabel, widow of Hugh d'Aubigny, consulted the abbot of
Waverley, and the house was received into the society of the order.[12]
The wording of the *Annals* suggests that papal permission was
received for the countess to go to Waverley. It may be that the
support of the Supreme Pontiff also aided the reception of the
nunnery into the Cistercian order, but by 1250 such incorporations
were frequent,[13] and Isabel herself, as the child of William de
Warenne and Maud, daughter of William Marshall, was an
influential patroness. In her foundation charter the countess specifically referred to her nunnery as an abbey of the Cistercian order.[14]
She donated four marks and a cask of wine to the monks of
Waverley, presumably in gratitude for their support and to ensure
that it continued.[15]

Apart from this mid-thirteenth-century foundation, only one other
nunnery, Tarrant, is mentioned in the thirteenth-century statutes of
the Cistercian order. A decree of 1243 entrusted the correction and
reform of the nuns of Tarrant to the Cistercian abbots of Boxley and
Robertsbridge.[16] The convent is again mentioned in decrees promulgated in 1257.[17] The earliest specific reference to the house as

[10] VCH *Salop*, ii, 84.   [11] Canivez, ii, 355, cap. 43.
[12] *Annales Monastici*, ed. H. Luard, 5 vols. (Rolls ser. 36; London, 1864–9), ii, *Ann. de Waverley*, 344–5.
[13] Thompson, 'Cistercian Nuns', 241.
[14] *MA*, v, 744, no. 1.
[15] *Ann. Waverley*, 344–5.
[16] Canivez, ii, 271, cap. 62.
[17] Ibid., ii, 434, cap. 50.

Cistercian occurs in an oath taken by Claricia to Richard Poore, Bishop of Salisbury, at her installation as abbess of Tarrant some time before 1228.[18] Tarrant is also described as Cistercian in the close rolls of 1233, when the nuns were declared exempt from the payment of a tax.[19] The original founder of the nunnery was Ralph de Kahaines, and the foundation probably took place before 1176.[20] An examination of the evidence, fragmentary as it is, suggests that it may originally have been a traditional Benedictine house, only later developing links with the Cistercians. A confirmation charter of Henry III, dated 1235, refers to Ralph's grant and the donations of his son William, and suggests the early dedication of the convent was to All Saints rather than the usual Cistercian dedication to St Mary.[21] Both this and references in early charters to grants of tithes, suggest characteristics of a traditional Benedictine house. There is no trace of any links with a Cistercian abbey or that Ralph de Kahaines favoured the Cistercians.[22] In the absence of evidence it would seem unwise to assume that Tarrant was founded as a Cistercian house at a date when the existence of any nunneries belonging to the order is highly questionable.

It may well be that the links with the Cistercians were forged or strengthened under the patronage of Bishop Richard Poore in the early years of the thirteenth century. When Ralph's son William died in *c.*1221, his heir was left a minor, and the wardship was granted to the bishop, who appears to have taken considerable interest in the nunnery.[23] According to tradition, Tarrant Keynes was his birthplace, and the church was confirmed to him by the canons of Merton.[24] Bishop Richard is sometimes described as the founder of

---

[18] The declaration of Abbess Claricia to Bishop Richard is preserved in the Salisbury Diocesan Record Office, Chapter records, press 2, box 1.

[19] *Cal. Close Rolls* 1231–34, 295. The nunnery is also described as Cistercian in a charter of 1265, printed in *MA*, v, 620, no. 1. It is possible that the nunnery had adopted Cistercian customs at an earlier date. If the nunnery 'Camesturne' in Dorset listed in the *Mappa Mundi* (*Gervase of Canterbury*, ii, 422) can be identified with Tarrant (? [Tarrant] Keynston) the nuns there are described as *moniales albae*. For a discussion of the use of white habits by the Cistercians and other reformed orders of the 12th century see pp. 100–1.

[20] Evidence from the pipe rolls suggests Ralph de Kahaines was dead by 1175 × 1176. See *PR 21 Henry II*, 23 and *PR 22 Henry II*, 155. The date suggested in KH for Tarrant is *c.*1186 (KH, 272, 276).

[21] *MA*, v, 621, no. 6. Dedication to the Virgin was obligatory for Cistercian houses (Canivez, i, 17, cap. 18), and it does occur in later Tarrant charters: see *MA*, v, 620, nos. 2 and 3.

[22] Ralph appears to have made grants to the Augustinian canons of Merton: see *MA*, vi (i), 247, no. 2.

[23] *Cal. Pat. Rolls* 1232–47, 174.

[24] *Charters and Documents illustrating the History of the Cathedral, City, and Diocese of Salisbury in the Twelfth and Thirteenth Centuries*, ed. W. R. Jones and W. D. Macray (Rolls ser. 97; London, 1891), 169.

Tarrant.[25] An entry in the Cistercian statutes of the year 1223 referred to the incorporation of an abbey requested by the Bishop of Salisbury.[26] The house is simply described as an abbey, with no reference to it being a community of nuns, but the next decree in the statutes does refer to women,[27] so it is conceivable that the reference to nuns was omitted in error, or even because it was more politic to do so. It is possible that this decree could mark the official incorporation of Tarrant into the Cistercian order in spite of the 1220 decree prohibiting the reception of any more nunneries.[28] Richard Poore was clearly an able and forceful man, and the Cistercians viewed him with favour, making it more likely that he could obtain their official recognition for a community of nuns.[29]

If there is doubt as to when Tarrant was accepted into the order, the position of the other so-called Cistercian nunneries is considerably more ambiguous. A decree of the General Chapter of 1535 lists seventeen houses which are to be visited by Cistercian abbots, and so presumably by this date belonged to the order, but the list is puzzling. It includes the nunneries of Arthington—traditionally regarded as a Cluniac house—and Newcastle and Wallingwells, both usually classified by historians as Benedictine.[30] There seems to be no evidence from the previous history of these three convents to indicate that they were Cistercian or had aspirations to belong to the order. The fact that there is no mention in earlier statutes of any of the listed houses—apart from Marham and Tarrant—being incorporated into the order, does not necessarily mean that they were not: it may simply not have been recorded. But later evidence suggesting a house was Cistercian cannot be taken to prove that it had always belonged to the order. For the centuries following the Norman Conquest such claims need close scrutiny.

Some general indications suggest that no official recognition was given by the order to the majority of English 'Cistercian' nunneries in the twelfth and thirteenth centuries. With the exception of Marham

[25] Matthew Paris described Tarrant as 'domum scilicet sanctimonialium quam venerabilis episcopus R. Dunelmensis a fundamentis construxerat', *Matthaei Parisiensis Chronica Majora*, ed. H. R. Luard, 7 vols. (Rolls. ser. 57; London, 1872–84), iii, 479. Richard Poore, who became Bishop of Durham in 1228, was also described as founder of the nunnery in a confirmation charter of Henry III: see *Cal. Chart. Rolls 1226–57*, 232. For a discussion of the role of bishops as founders and patrons of nunneries see Chap. 10.
[26] 'Petitio Cantuariensis et Domini Sarisberiensis de abbatia iterum Ordini incorporanda exauditur' (Canivez, ii, 29, cap. 30). The use of the word *iterum* is surprising, as there seems to be no earlier mention of the petition in the statutes.
[27] Ibid., cap. 31.
[28] Ibid., i, 517, cap. 4.
[29] In 1237 the General Chapter decreed a mass for his soul: see ibid., ii, 170, cap. 11.
[30] The houses listed are: Arthington, (Nun) Appleton, Cook Hill, Ellerton, Esholt, Gokewell, Greenfield, Hampole, Kirklees, Marham, Newcastle, Nun Cotham, Sinningthwaite, Stixwould, Swine, Tarrant, and Wallingwells: see Canivez, vi, 719, caps. 45 and 46.

and Tarrant they are all priories, whereas Cistercian monasteries had the status of abbeys.[31] The general emphasis of the order was to give individual houses a considerable degree of autonomy, and in the statutes of the General Chapter the word abbey is used.[32] In 1233, however, a decree of the General Chapter provides an isolated example of a priory of nuns being incorporated into the order,[33] and there is no suggestion that the status of the house was regarded as an obstacle. In the twelfth century there sometimes appears to have been a lack of clear distinction, with the early charters of some convents describing the house as an abbey, while other evidence makes it clear it was a priory, headed by a prioress.[34] It would seem hazardous to argue that any community designated a priory, and so implicitly of lesser status than an abbey, could never be Cistercian. As has been suggested in previous chapters of this book, women's convents were frequently dependent on a community of male religious, and within the Cistercian order a priory of nuns may have seemed less of an anomaly than a priory of monks because of the women's need for male chaplains and masculine support. But it is significant that the only convents with the status of abbey were Marham and Tarrant, the two nunneries which were incorporated into the order in the thirteenth century. Furthermore, in Wales the Cistercian nunneries, although small and poor, were apparently designated as abbeys.[35] The fact that these English 'Cistercian' houses were priories probably indicates their lack of formal status within the order. Such lack of official recognition given to the nunneries by the Cistercian order in the twelfth and early thirteenth centuries would also explain their omission from medieval lists of Cistercian foundations. For example, a list of Cistercian abbeys, probably written in the early thirteenth century, makes no mention of women's convents.[36] If the group of priories which at some time appear to have claimed to be Cistercian,

[31] For the argument that all Cistercian houses were abbeys see Fontette, 34.

[32] There are no priories among the Cistercian houses for men listed in KH, 112–15. In the 15th cent. the statutes of the order reveal occasional examples of Cistercian priories: see Canivez, iv, 655, cap. 78 and 660, cap. 22.

[33] Canivez, ii, 117, cap. 31.

[34] For example at Nuneaton in Warwickshire the house is described as an abbey in the Earl of Leicester's foundation charter printed in *Calendar of Documents Preserved in France Illustrative of the History of Great Britain and Ireland*, i, AD 918–1206, ed. J. H. Round, PRO texts and calendars; London, 1899), 376, no. 1,062, although most charters refer to it as a priory and its head as a prioress. Similarly some early charters of Stixwould priory refer to it as an abbey (BL Addit. MS 46,701, fo. 1); this is also true of Langley Priory: see *Acta I Lincoln 1067–1185*, 88–9, no. 142.

[35] See D. H. Williams, 'Cistercian Nunneries in Medieval Wales,' *Cîteaux. Commentarii Cistercienses* 26 (Westmalle, 1975), 155–74. Cf. KH, 272 where they are listed as priories. These Welsh nunneries clearly had close links with particular Cistercian monasteries.

[36] BL Cotton MS Faust. B vii, fo. 36, printed in W. Birch, 'On the Date of Foundation ascribed to Cistercian Abbeys of Great Britain', *Journal British Archaeol. Assoc.*, 26 (London, 1870), 281–99 and 352–69.

or have been classified by historians as belonging to the order, were
not fully incorporated, their claims to be Cistercian are harder to
assess—did they depend on links with Cistercian monks, or have
validity because the nuns followed Cistercian customs, or were such
claims based on a desire to avoid taxation?

The *Mappa Mundi*, which dates from the beginning of the
thirteenth century, is unique in providing a contemporary list of
women's convents which gives some indication of the order of the
communities it catalogues. But the classification is simply in terms of
colour, with the nuns being described as white or black. Seven
nunneries are described as communities of *moniales albae*.[37] It is
tempting to take this description as meaning that they were
Cistercian. White habits certainly came to be regarded as a mark of
the order. Orderic Vitalis noted that white was favoured by the
monks following the new practices emanating from Cîteaux, and
that they wore no dyed garments. Further evidence is provided by the
author of the *Vita Aelredi*, who compared the new white monks to
flocks of seagulls, and regarded the whiteness of their habits as a sign
of the purity of their souls.[38] But it is not clear how far the clothing
of the Cistercians was uniformly white. The ruling of St Benedict, as
cited in the early statutes of the order, stressed the importance of
simple clothing, but made no reference to colour. A Cistercian
manuscript of the early twelfth century shows monks wearing habits
of brown and grey as well as white,[39] and they are described as grey
monks in the *Dialogue between a Cistercian and a Cluniac* written in
the second half of the twelfth century.[40]

It is probable that in the twelfth century there was considerable
variety in the nuns' clothing. This is suggested by attempts in the
thirteenth century to introduce some measure of uniformity. A decree
of the General Chapter in 1235 demanded that a cowl should be
worn, or a cloak, but not both. It is clearly stated that the nuns' veils
must be black, but there is no reference to the colour of the rest of
their habit.[41] It is also not clear how far the clothes of the Cistercian
nuns were distinct from the other reformed orders of the twelfth

[37] *Gervase of Canterbury*, ii, 418–49. The houses are: Amesbury (420), Camesturne
(? Tarrant) (422), Shouldham (428), Brewood (438), Duva (Keldholme), Rosedale and
Sinningthwaite (440). For the *Mappa Mundi* as a source see Chap. 2, n. 91.

[38] *Orderic Vitalis*, iv, 310–27; Walter Daniel, *Life of Ailred of Rievaulx*, ed. and trans.
F. M. Powicke (London, 1950, repr. 1963), 10.

[39] Canivez, i, 13, cap. iv; C. N. L. Brooke, *The Monastic World 1000–1300* (London,
1974), 28, 139. A feature of unbleached material is that it can take a variety of muted colours,
with whiteness eventually predominating after washing.

[40] 'Dialogus inter Cluniacensem Monachum et Cisterciensem', E. Martène and U. Durand,
Thesaurus Novus Anecdotorum, v (Paris, 1717), 1,645. For the dating of the 'Dialogue' see W.
Williams, 'A Dialogue between a Cluniac and a Cistercian', *Journal of Theological Studies* 31
(1930), 167.

[41] Canivez, ii, 139, cap. 3.

century. As has already been noted, houses of the Gilbertine order were described in the *Mappa Mundi* as having white canons and nuns, and Shouldham in Norfolk, a Gilbertine convent, is described as a house of white nuns.[42] The nuns of the Sempringham order are generally thought to have worn a black Benedictine habit with the addition of a white cowl.[43] The statutes of the order stress the colour of the cloth only in relation to the veils and head-dresses,[44] and St Gilbert's biographer records that the founder of the order favoured the use of 'grey' materials and avoided dyed clothing.[45] This would reflect the links between his order and the Cistercians.[46] St Gilbert had hoped that his nuns would be allowed to affiliate to the followers of St Bernard, and the rejection of his request did not destroy his admiration for the reformers. The *Mappa* also lists Amesbury in Wiltshire as having white nuns.[47] Amesbury was refounded in 1177 as a priory of the order of Fontevrault.[48] The ladies of this order wore white habits—long robes of white wool covered with a sleeveless surplice. Their veils were black, and the clothing was of rough material.[49] Other orders besides these adopted habits of unbleached wool as a sign of their return to simplicity. The Premonstratensian sisters wore habits of undyed wool, but with a black tunic as well as a black veil. Over the tunic was worn a white alb probably covering the dark material beneath. Their cloaks were of undyed wool and so of a nondescript or whitish colour.[50] White habits, therefore, were not necessarily a distinguishing mark of the Cistercians, although nuns wishing to emulate the customs of the order would be more likely to wear white rather than black. Apart from Amesbury and Shouldham, one other house not generally regarded as Cistercian is listed in the *Mappa* as being a community of white nuns—Brewood in Shropshire.[51] Other evidence confirms that the nuns of Brewood wore white.[52] But by the fourteenth century, if

[42] For the description of Shouldham see *Gervase of Canterbury*, ii, 428.

[43] Graham, *St Gilbert*, 70–1.

[44] *MA*, vi (ii), lxxix. The *Mappa Mundi*'s description of white canons and nuns ('canonici albi et moniales') would seem to imply that the nuns wore white as well as the canons.

[45] *Book of St Gilbert*, 66–7.

[46] Ibid., pp. xix–xxii. For a discussion of the question of Cistercian influence see also Golding, 'St Bernard and St Gilbert'.

[47] *Gervase of Canterbury*, ii, 420.

[48] For the foundation of this house as a priory of the order of Fontevrault see Chap. 7, pp. 121–3.

[49] Fontette, 76, n. 78.

[50] F. Petit, 'Les Vêtements des Prémontrés au 12ᵉ siècle', *Analecta Praemonstratensia* (Tongerloo / Averbode, 1925–), xv (1939), 23.

[51] *Gervase of Canterbury*, ii, 438 (listed under Staffordshire but distinguished from Brewood Black Ladies, Staffordshire, which is also listed).

[52] They are described as the white nuns of Brewood in a charter of c.1180 × 1186 (*The Cartulary of Haughmond Abbey*, ed. U. Rees (Shropshire Archaeol. Soc., Cardiff, 1985), 48, no. 149; see also no. 151. Leland also refers to their white habits: see Leland, *Itin.*, v, 15.

not earlier, they were following the Augustinian rule.[53] It is possible that the colour of the nuns' habits reflects some emulation of the Cistercian order at an early period of the nunnery's history, but there is no definitive evidence of a link with the Cistercians, and an alternative possibility is that their links were with a reformed order of canonesses such as the Premonstratensians.

On the other hand, several houses described by historians as Cistercian are listed in the *Mappa Mundi* as communities of black nuns. According to this the women at Cook Hill, Farewell, Greenfield, Sewardsley, and Ellerton wore black.[54] Although the colour of the ladies' habits is by no means conclusive, it does seem unlikely that nuns ardently wishing to follow the Cistercians would choose this colour rather than following the reformers' tradition of undyed cloth. Other evidence also suggests that some of these convents were probably originally Benedictine foundations. At Cook Hill in Worcestershire, the earliest evidence of the priory's existence dates from 1155 × 1156.[55] According to a fifteenth-century account, the nuns were originally at Spernall and of the Benedictine order before they changed site and settled at Cook Hill some two miles away.[56] The probability of a Benedictine origin is strengthened by the entry in a bishop's register which shows that in 1288 the Bishop of Worcester confirmed the election of a new prioress and asked the abbot of Alcester, a Benedictine monastery, to install her.[57] It appears that the earliest evidence of the house being Cistercian is an entry in the statutes of the order of 1491, confirming the election and installation of a prioress. In the fourteenth century an entry in the *Liber Albus* of Worcester refers to it as Benedictine,[58] and so the nunnery's adoption of Cistercian customs may have been relatively late in its history. This may also be true of Ellerton and Sewardsley as there seems to be no twelfth- or thirteenth-century evidence to indicate that they were Cistercian.[59]

---

[53] The house is described as Augustinian in 1310: see *Registrum Ricardi de Swinfield episcopi Herefordensis MCCLXXXIII–MCCCXVII*, ed. W. Capes (Cantilupe Soc., and Cant. and York Soc.; 1909), 458. It may have been originally established as an Augustinian house: see VCH *Salop*, ii, 83.

[54] *Gervase of Canterbury*, ii, 435, 438, 430, 431, 441.

[55] *PR 2–4 Henry II* (1155 × 1156), 62, 156.

[56] *Cal. Pap. Lett:*, v, 405.

[57] Hereford and Worcs. Record Office MS b.716.093-BA 2648/1(i), fo. 294ᵛ. See also T. R. Nash, *Collections for the History of Worcestershire*, 2 vols. (Oxford, 1781–2), ii, 16.

[58] Canivez, vi, 22, cap. 49. It is interesting that this decree reveals some confusion as to whether the house was an abbey or a priory. For a discussion of the significance of this see p. 99. *Liber Albus of the Priory of Worcester Parts I and II, Priors John de Wyke 1301–17 and Wulstan de Bransford 1317–39*, ed. J. M. Wilson (Worcs. Hist. Soc.; 1919), 87, no. 1,188.

[59] There is very little evidence about the early history of either Ellerton or Sewardsley. None of the surviving 12th- and 13th-cent. Sewardsley charters make any reference to its order, but a

An examination of the early history of several other nunneries later described as Cistercian suggests that at their foundation they were not linked with this order. Handale in Yorkshire, which is classified as Cistercian in Knowles and Hadcock, was probably founded in the first half of the twelfth century. The first mention of its existence occurs in the cartulary of Whitby Abbey with the date of 1133.[60] If this date is correct,[61] it seems an unlikely time for a Cistercian nunnery to be established so soon after the coming of the Cistercians to the north and at a time when the order was apparently antagonistic to women. Apart from the mention in the cartulary, there is other evidence to suggest that in the twelfth and thirteenth centuries Handale was linked with the Benedictine abbey of Whitby. A monk of Whitby acted as proctor for the nuns in 1220,[62] and in 1267 Archbishop Giffard appointed another member of this monastery as the guardian of Handale.[63] It seems first to have been described as Cistercian in the sixteenth century[64] and it would seem probable that at its foundation and for the twelfth and first half of the thirteenth centuries at least it should be classified as Benedictine. At Nun Appleton, another Yorkshire house classified as Cistercian in Knowles and Hadcock, the early charters relating to its foundation in the middle of the twelfth century, do not refer to the order of the house.[65] An interesting charter of Eustace de Merc, the husband of the foundress Alice de St Quentin, referred to the grant of a church to found a convent of nuns of the same congregation, profession and order of the nuns of Appleton.[66] No mention is made of the Cistercians. The earliest record of any claim to belong to this order is in 1270 when the nunnery, together with Stamford and Nun Cotham, sought to gain exemption from taxation.[67]

Several nunneries seem to have put forward claims to be Cistercian in an attempt to gain the privileges of the order, particularly

document transcribed in the Canons Ashby cartulary (BL Egerton MS 3033, fo. 8) suggests that Sewardsley was demanding exemption from taxation which may indicate that the nuns were at this date claiming to be Cistercian: see above. According to Tanner, Sewardsley is described as Cistercian in the Lincolnshire registers (Tanner, *Northants.*, xxxiii) but I have found no record of this, and in the mid-15th cent. attempts were made to link it to the nunnery of Delapré, Northampton, probably a Cluniac house (KH, 275–6). Ellerton's claims to be Cistercian seem to be documented in the 16th cent. see Canivez, vi, 719, cap. 46, and Leland's statement that the nuns there wore white clothes (Leland, *Itin.*, iv, 29).

[60] *EYC*, ii, 240, no. 897.
[61] Farrer argues for a later date of *c.*1150 × *c.*1170, see ibid. 240 and 301.
[62] BL Cotton MS Nero D. iii, fo. 62 (Cartulary of St Leonard's York).
[63] *Reg. Walter Giffard*, 54. He was also *custos* of Baysdale, another 'Cistercian' nunnery.
[64] KH, 273.
[65] *EYC*, i, 419–20, no. 541; 425–6, no. 545; ibid., xi, 114, no. 100.
[66] BL Cotton MS Nero C. iii, fo. 227, printed in *EYC*, i, 426, no. 546, where the name of the church granted for the new foundation is wrongly transcribed as Covenham.
[67] PRO E326/11,356 printed in Sturman, 'Stamford', app. iv, 391–2.

exemption from tithes and the tenth of 1266. This is comparatively well documented in the case of Nun Cotham. There is little in the earliest documents to suggest a link with the Cistercian order. In a charter dating from the middle of the twelfth century, the founder of the house stated that the nuns followed the Benedictine order, making no mention of Cistercian customs.[68] Furthermore, a bull of Pope Alexander III addressed to Nun Cotham, and again describing it as Benedictine, contains a clause permitting the religious there to transfer to a stricter monastery—a provision not generally included in bulls relating to Cistercian houses.[69] But in a letter of Pope Alexander III dating from 1177 a reference is made to the nuns following the institutions of the Cistercian brothers, and the phrase is linked with claims for exemption from tithes.[70] As if to reinforce this claim, the pope wrote to the Archbishop of York and the Bishop of Lincoln about the nunnery and that of Swine, referring to the Cistercian brothers' exemption from tithes and claiming the same privilege for the nuns.[71] Links between claims to be Cistercian and exemption from taxation are also apparent at Stamford. In its early years it was closely controlled by the Benedictine monks of Peterborough, the founding house. But there is extant an *inspeximus* of a group of documents dating from 1269–73 which stated that Stamford was Cistercian and so exempt from the payment of a tenth.[72] Some of the claims of these documents are puzzling. It is argued that the nuns of St Michael, Stamford, came from the Yorkshire nunnery of Nun Appleton and were instructed by them in the ways of the Cistercians.[73] It is not clear if this refers to an original colonization of Stamford by Nun Appleton, or a later development. As already noted, there seems little evidence to support the claims of Nun Appleton to be a Cistercian foundation. What is clear is that there was some collaboration between nunneries in an attempt to

---

[68] Oxford, Bodleian MS Top Lincs. d 1, fo. 12ᵛ.

[69] *MA*, v, 677, no. 4. The dating clause of this bull is omitted, and it is described in *PUE*, iii, 31 as a bull of Alexander IV. But it apparently dates from *c.*1168 × 1177; cf. the bull of Alexander III printed in *PUE*, iii, 366–7, no. 236.

[70] *PUE*, iii, 370–1, no. 241. As Professor Holdsworth has pointed out, references to the institutes of the Cistercian brothers are comparatively rare in papal bulls confirming possessions pre-Alexander III. For example, a bull of 1156 referred to the monks of Rufford as following the Benedictine rule, while a bull of Alexander III dated 1160 referred to Cistercian customs: see *Rufford Charters*, ed. C. Holdsworth, 4 vols. (Thoroton Soc. Rec. ser. 29, 30, 32, 34; Nottingham, 1972–81), ii, 364, 366–8. For a detailed study of the links between the claims of Nun Cotham and the other Lincolnshire houses to be Cistercian and the demands for payment of a tenth, see C. Graves, 'English Cistercian Nuns in Lincolnshire', *Speculum* 54 (1979), 492–9.

[71] *MA*, v, 494, no. 2.

[72] PRO, E326/11, 356, transcribed in Sturman, 'Stamford', app. iv, 391–2.

[73] Ibid. See also Sturman, 'Stamford', 40–2.

avoid taxation. In the Nun Cotham cartulary there is a copy of a charter of Henry III declaring that the nuns of Stixwould were exempt from the levy of the tenth as they were of the Cistercian order.[74] It is quite possible that Stamford also copied these nunneries in seeking to gain exemption from the tax on the grounds of being Cistercian. But Stamford seems to have later abandoned its claims to belong to the order, and tried to obtain exemption from taxes on the grounds that it was poor rather than because it was Cistercian.[75]

Claims to be Cistercian made in the context of avoiding taxation did not necessarily reflect the views of the Cistercian abbots or the General Chapter. An entry on the close rolls of Henry III reveals the abbot of Cîteaux complaining to the dean of Lincoln that, although six 'abbesses' wore the Cistercian habit, they did not belong to the order and had no right to claim its privileges.[76] The houses listed were Stixwould, Greenfield, Nun Cotham, Legbourne, Gokewell, and Stamford. As has already been shown, the five Lincolnshire convents clearly numbered canons as well as nuns among their community, and Stamford was a dependent foundation of the great Benedictine abbey of Peterborough and closely controlled by it.[77] There is little evidence from the early documents of any of the houses to suggest links with Cistercian monks. The foundation charters of Stixwould, transcribed in the cartulary of the house, make no mention of the order of Cîteaux or its customs. An early charter of the foundress was witnessed by the Cluniac prior of Pontefract and the Benedictine prior of Spalding.[78] At Greenfield, the foundation charter was witnessed by the Cistercian abbot of Louth Park, but another witness was the Augustinian head of Grimsby. At Gokewell, an early charter recording the foundation was witnessed by the Cistercian abbot and chapter of Kirkstall although other charters are testified by the Augustinian canons of Thornholme.[79] The abbot of Cîteaux was probably right in denying the official validity of the claims of these nunneries to be Cistercian. But his rejection did not put an end to such claims. In 1294 an entry on the patent rolls referred to Legbourne, Nun Cotham, and Nun Appleton as Cistercian, and in the sixteenth century four of these nunneries— Gokewell, Greenfield, Nun Cotham, and Stixwould—are included in

[74] Oxford, Bodleian MS Top Lincs. d 1, fo. 44.

[75] Sturman, 'Stamford', 205–6.

[76] *Cal. Close Rolls 1268–72*, 301. These houses were in fact priories.

[77] See pp. 61–2.

[78] BL Addit. MS 46,701, fo. 1.

[79] BL Harl. chart. 50 I 30, printed in *MA*, v, 580, no. 2 (Greenfield); *EYC*, vi, 202, no. 103; 204, no. 105 (BL Egerton chart. 622); and 206, no. 107 (Gokewell).

a list of houses to be visited by Cistercian abbots, suggesting that by this date they had won recognition from the General Chapter.[80]

Another example of a house which appears to have claimed to be Cistercian in an attempt to gain privileges is Langley in Leicestershire. An account of a dispute over the payment of tithes which took place between these nuns and the canons of Breedon at the end of the twelfth century, refers to a letter from Pope Alexander III which stated that the nuns had professed the Cistercian order and were exempt from the payment of certain tithes.[81] Papal judges delegate were ordered to try to obtain an agreement. Unless it could be proved that the nuns had been paying the tithes for thirty years, the pope decreed that the canons should be ordered to cease from troubling the women. Part of the prior of Breedon's defence was that the nuns did not belong to the Cistercian order and so were not exempt. After two years of dispute, the judges appear to have decided for the nuns. But a later decision ordered the nuns of Langley to pay some tithes to Breedon Priory. This agreement, which dates from 1183 × 1188 made no mention of the order of the house or its claims to be Cistercian.[82] Later references describe the nunnery as Benedictine,[83] and it would seem that the nuns eventually abandoned their claims to belong to the order of Cîteaux.

It appears, therefore, that several nunneries put forward claims to be Cistercian in an attempt to obtain the privileges of the order in relation to tithes and certain taxes, although at Langley and Stamford claims to belong to the order were probably soon abandoned. In view of the poverty of many of the women's houses, such efforts to lessen fiscal burdens are not surprising. But to see the whole question of attempts to maintain links with the order in these terms would be a distortion. Herman of Laon's account of the ladies of Montreuil-les-Dames toiling in the fields[84] revealed a dedication and zeal on the part of religious ladies which should not be underestimated. It is probable that some English nunneries adopted Cistercian customs because they were attracted by the austerity and fervour of the new order. According to the account in the Cistercian annals of Manrique, women and virgins flocked to hear Gilbert of Hoyland, and follow the Cistercian rule under the auspices of the

---

[80] *Cal. Pat. Rolls 1292–1301*, 90. Swine is also described as Cistercian in this entry; Canivez, vi, 719, cap. 46. Legbourne, Heynings, and Nun Cotham are called Cistercian in the Alnwick visitation returns: see *Lincoln Visitations*, ii (i), 183–7, 132–5; ii (ii), 248–52.

[81] *MA*, iv, 221, no. 2.

[82] T. Madox, *Form. Ang.* 23.

[83] It is described as a Benedictine house in the Alnwick visitations: see *Lincoln Visitations*, ii (i), 173.

[84] 'Hermanni monachi, De miraculis S. Marie Laudunensis', *PL*, clvi (1880), 1,001–2.

blessed abbot of Swineshead.[85] This statement is entered in the annals under the year 1163, but Manrique admits that he has not been able to identify any particular nunnery housing these women. Gilbert was abbot from *c.*1153–72 and it is clear that he wrote for nuns.[86] But it is not possible to establish whether any particular community of women followed the Cistercian rule under his direction. The nearest houses to Swineshead were the Gilbertine establishments of Haverholme, Sempringham, and Catley, all founded before 1163. There is a fragment of evidence showing contact between Gilbert of Hoyland and Stixwould, as the abbot and Simon of Stixwould together witness a charter of the Cistercian house of Kirkstead.[87] But Manrique's description could well be more significant in reflecting the renown of the abbot and the zeal of some nearby nuns, rather than providing evidence for the existence of one particular Cistercian nunnery.

At Sinningthwaite in Yorkshire there is evidence to suggest imitation by the nuns of Cistercian customs. The founders of the nunnery certainly favoured the order. Bertram Haget gave valuable grants to Fountains,[88] and one of his sons, Ralph, became abbot first of Kirkstall and then of Fountains.[89] The *Mappa Mundi* describes the house as having white nuns.[90] A letter of Pope Alexander III of 1172 refers to the nunnery as following the Benedictine rule and the institutes of the Cistercian brothers, and several subsequent papal bulls refer to the house as being Cistercian and so exempt from tithes.[91] There are, however, some divergences from what might be expected of a Cistercian house. At the end of the twelfth century, Archbishop Geoffrey took the nuns under his protection, and his charter made no reference to the Cistercian order.[92] By 1276 the women apparently found this archiepiscopal interest irksome and vigorously appealed to the pope against the right of the archbishop to visit them, claiming the exemption of the Cistercian order and referring to the authority of the abbot of Fountains. But they seem to have lost this appeal, for the nunnery was visited and disciplined by

---

[85] A. Manrique, *Cisterciensium seu verius ecclesiasticorum annalium a condito Cistercio*, 4 vols. (Lyons, 1642–59), ii, 376.

[86] For Gilbert's sermons see *The Works of Gilbert of Hoyland. Sermons on the Song of Songs*, ed. and trans. L. C. Braceland, 3 vols. (Cistercian Fathers, ser. 14, 20, 26; Kalamazoo, 1978–9). Sermons nos. 15–21 are clearly addressed to nuns: see ibid., vol. ii.

[87] *Danelaw Docs.*, 108, no. 161.

[88] *Memorials of the Abbey of St Mary of Fountains*, ed. J. Walbran, 3 vols. (Surtees Soc. 42, 67, 130; 1863–1918), i, 123, n. 6.

[89] *HRH*, 136 (Kirkstall), and 133 (Fountains).

[90] *Gervase of Canterbury*, ii, 440.

[91] *EYC*, i, 167–8, no. 200; *MA*, v, 465–7, nos. 6, 7, 9, and 10.

[92] *MA*, v, 464, no. 2.

subsequent archbishops.[93] This failure to establish their independence from the archbishop at the end of the thirteenth century would
not preclude the possibility—indeed the likelihood—that the
nunnery had aspired to have links with the Cistercian order from an
early date. At the time of the Dissolution it was reported that the
nunnery possessed a tunic of St Bernard—tangible evidence of their
devotion to the Cistercian cause.[94]

At Wintney in Hampshire, there is a suggestion of a particular link
between the nunnery and the Cistercian abbey of Waverley. Wintney
was founded before 1154 × 1161 by a Geoffrey fitz Peter.[95] The
foundation charters are only preserved in an *inspeximus* copy of
Edward III, and have some features which raise doubts as to their
authenticity.[96] The charter of Geoffrey fitz Peter claimed that the
convent was founded by Waverley, and he invoked the whole weight
of the monks' authority to bind the nuns to an agreement about the
number of masses to be performed by the women for his soul.[97] It is
difficult to assess this claim that the nunnery was founded under the
auspices of this Cistercian abbey. The abbot and prior witnessed one
of Wintney's charters,[98] but there seems no other evidence of any
link between the houses. No mention of the nunnery was made in the
Waverley annals. The late thirteenth-century obituary roll of the
nunnery recorded the death of six abbots of Reading, but mentioned
only one abbot of Waverley.[99] But the nuns are described as white in
entries on the pipe rolls in the twelfth century, and an episcopal
register in the late thirteenth century describes the house as
Cistercian.[100] The fragmentary nature of the evidence makes firm
conclusions difficult.[101] The founder of Wintney, Geoffrey fitz Peter,

[93] *MA*, v, 464–5. For later visitations see *Reg. Greenfield*, ii, 204–6 (1314–15); see also
VCH *Yorks.*, iii, 176–7. For the role of bishops at English 'Cistercian' nunneries see J. Nichols,
'Medieval Cistercian Nunneries and English Bishops' in *Distant Echoes*, 237–47.

[94] *Letters and Papers Foreign and Domestic of Reign of Henry VIII*, x, ed. J. Gairdner,
(London, 1887), 141.

[95] He cannot be identified with the justiciar of the same name. Apart from the early date, the
names of his wife and mother differ from those of the justiciar: see *Cal. Chart. Rolls 1327–41*,
392. There is further evidence of an earlier Geoffrey fitz Peter in *PR 7 Henry II* (1160 × 1161), 57.

[96] For example, a confirmation charter of Henry II has the addition of a 13th-cent. dating
clause (*Cal. Chart. Rolls 1327–41, 391*).

[97] Ibid. 392.

[98] Ibid.

[99] BL Cotton MS Claud. D. iii, fos. 140ᵛ–162ᵛ. This is printed in *Johannis de Trokelowe,
Annales Edwardi II Henrici de Blaneford Chronica et Edwardi II Vita*, ed. T. Hearne (Oxford,
1729), 384–93. The Abbot of Waverley is Adam: see ibid. 387. This could either refer to Adam
I (1216–19) or Adam II (1219–36).

[100] *PR 31 Henry II* (1184 × 1185), 214 and *PR 32 Henry II* (1185 × 1186), 177;
Registrum Johannis de Pontissara, Episcopi Wyntoniensis AD MCCLXXXII–MCCCIV, ed.
and trans. C. Deedes, 2 vols. (Cant. and York Soc. 19, 30; 1915–24), i, 98 and ii, 509.

[101] The first edition of the *Monasticon* listed Wintney as Benedictine, see *Monasticon*, 1st
edn. i, 483.

may well have wished his nunnery to be supported by the white monks of Waverley. What actual part they took in the foundation and subsequent care of the convent remains obscure. As at Sinningthwaite, and Whistones near Worcester, described as a priory of white nuns,[102] the women may well have imitated customs of the Cistercians and regarded themselves as belonging to the order— aspirations which were probably not supported by any organizational framework.

A study of the English Cistercian nunneries in the twelfth and first half of the thirteenth century reveals a web of uncertainties. Of the twenty-seven houses classified as Cistercian in Knowles and Hadcock only two were clearly formally incorporated into the order: Marham was founded in the mid-thirteenth century as a Cistercian nunnery, and Tarrant, an earlier foundation, was probably formally incorporated into the order by *c*.1233. Other houses, such as Wintney and Sinningthwaite, may have had particular links with the Cistercian abbeys in the twelfth century. At least for some periods of their history their claims to be Cistercian probably had some validity, although their lack of formal status within the order meant that they were under the jurisdiction of archbishop and bishop. The five Lincolnshire houses which put forward vigorous claims to be Cistercian in the thirteenth century in the context of obtaining exemption from taxation were not recognized by the abbot of Cîteaux because of their lack of formal status within the order. But his statement confirms that they wore the Cistercian habit, and in the saga of claim and counter-claim the Bishop of Lincoln testified that they followed Cistercian customs.[103] For other nunneries evidence as to the order of house remains confused. Hampole in Yorkshire clearly had resident brothers. No evidence survives of links with a Cistercian abbey, or with the order of Sempringham, but the nuns apparently wore white and the house's claims to be Cistercian were endorsed by Pope Innocent III and referred to by Archbishop Walter Giffard.[104] In 1276 the archbishop ordered Hampole and Nun

---

[102] For the foundation of Whistones, possibly by Bishop Walter de Cantilupe, see pp. 198–9. The nuns are described as the white sisters or nuns of Worcester in entries on the Close Rolls: see *Cal. Close Rolls 1237–42*, 310 (1241) and ibid. *1264–8*, 331. They were described as the White Nuns of Whistones of the order of St Benedict at various points in the 15th cent.: see Nash, *Worcs.* i, 220–2; while an entry in a 14th-cent. episcopal register specifically refers to them as Cistercian: see *Calendar of the Register of Adam de Orleton, Bishop of Worcester 1327–1333*, ed. R. M. Haines (Worcs. Hist. Soc., N.S. 10; London, 1979), 47, no. 34.

[103] Oxford, Bodleian MS Top Lincs. d 1, fo. 43ᵛ. The bishop makes it clear, however, that the nuns are under his jurisdiction.

[104] Hampole is described as a community of white canons and nuns—the description used for Gilbertine houses—in the *Mappa Mundi*; see *Gervase of Canterbury*, ii, 441; a letter of Pope Innocent III of 1204 referring to the nunnery as Cistercian is calendared in *Letters of Pope*

Appleton to have friars minor as their confessors in spite of the prohibition of the Cistercian abbots, who, stated the Archbishop firmly, had no jurisdiction over them. But, despite this denial of Cistercian authority, his statement implies that he regarded the nuns as belonging to their order. Such lack of organizational support and official links with the order must have caused problems and blurred distinctions. The resulting ambiguity is reflected in the Suppression Papers, where Hampole is described as 'ordinis Sancti Augustini et de regula Sancti Benedicti Cistercien'.[105]

At Catesby in Northamptonshire, founded in *c.*1150 × 1176, a papal bull of Innocent IV describes it as Cistercian, and the nunnery was favoured by Archbishop Edmund Rich, who was a supporter of the white monks. It is called Cistercian in the fifteenth-century visitation of Bishop William Alnwick.[106] But in *c.*1231 a papal bull of Gregory IX had referred to the house as Benedictine;[107] there were apparently resident canons at the nunnery, some of whom were linked with the Augustinian house of Canons Ashby, and it has already been noted that Catesby is described as belonging to the order of Sempringham in the *Mappa Mundi*.[108] Both Catesby and Swine were apparently organized like the Gilbertine establishments as double houses. Swine Priory in Yorkshire may well have been founded, like Sempringham itself, by a priest who gathered nuns round him and ministered to them. The community numbered canons, lay brothers, and sisters as well as nuns.[109] What fragmentary evidence there is suggests that, in the thirteenth century, one at least of the *magistri* of the house was a canon from the Augustinian house of Healaugh Park, with a subsequent one being recruited from the Premonstratensian house of Croxton.[110] According to the *Mappa*

Innocent III, 100, no. 602; for the archbishop's reference to their order see *Reg. Walter Giffard*, 295. It is interesting that Sinningthwaite is also included in the ruling, but the name is interlined in the text. It was at this time that the nuns of Sinningthwaite were claiming exemption from the archbishop's jurisdiction: see pp. 107–8.

[105] *VCH Yorks.*, iii, 165, n. 28.

[106] Oxford, Bodleian MS Dodsworth, lxiii, fo. 79. Edmund became a *confrater* of the Cistercian house of Pontigny, and was in exile there: see C. H. Lawrence, *St Edmund of Abingdon. A Study in Hagiography and History* (Oxford, 1960), 263–4; *Lincoln Visitations*, ii (i), 46–53.

[107] See the bull printed in *MA*, iv, 637–8, no. 3. Although ascribed here to Gregory VIII, this appears to be a bull of Pope Gregory IX dated 1231.

[108] In the 13th cent. a canon of Ashby acted (apparently somewhat unwillingly as the bishop had to order him to resume his duties at the convent) as *magister* of the nuns: see *Reg. Sutton*, iv, 123–4. For the possible connection between Canons Ashby and the Arrouaisian order see p. 151. As these wore white habits it could help explain the *Mappa Mundi*'s description of the nuns as 'moniales de Simplingeham' (*Gervase of Canterbury*, ii, 431).

[109] See pp. 69–70.

[110] The account of a dispute between the abbey of Meaux and the nuns of Swine indicates that Hamo, *magister* of the nuns, came from Healaugh Park: see *Chron. Meaux*, ii, 13; for the

Mundi it was a community of black nuns. Swine's classification as Cistercian would seem to depend on claims put forward in the twelfth and thirteenth centuries to obtain taxation privileges, but a measure of recognition seems to have been obtained, for it is described as of the order of St Bernard at the Dissolution.[111] The success of the order of Sempringham, with its imitation of many of the Cistercian ideals and practices, and the practical solution of resident brothers and canons, may be a factor in explaining why so few English nunneries were officially Cistercian and incorporated into the order.

There seems to be some evidence for the view that the Gilbertines, for a large part of the twelfth century, were thought to provide women with the nearest possible approach to the sanctity of the Cistercians. In his foundation charter for the nunnery of Haverholme, Bishop Alexander of Lincoln stated that the Gilbertine nuns seized on the narrow life of the Cistercian order so far as they were able.[112] Close textual study of the sermons of the Cistercian abbot Gilbert of Hoyland suggest that some were preached to double communities of monks and nuns, possibly the nearby Gilbertine houses of Sempringham, Haverholme, and Catley. It is also interesting that the Cistercian archbishop, Henry Murdac, placed the small girl who was to become the subject of a saga of scandal and edification at the Gilbertine house of Watton.[113] The *Mappa Mundi*'s difficulty in distinguishing between Cistercian and Gilbertine communities, with its description of Nun Cotham, Stixwould, Hampole, and Catesby in the same terms as the Gilbertine houses, while Shouldham is classified as a community of white nuns, may reflect a real confusion.

Most of the English 'Cistercian' nunneries were priories, founded at a time when the Cistercians did not recognize nuns, and the presence of several canons and resident brothers did not harmonize with the organization demanded by the General Chapter as more European nunneries came to be incorporated in the second half of the thirteenth century. Moreover, most of the houses were small, poor, and without powerful patrons—factors which again lessened their

appointment of the canon of Croxton see *The Register of John le Romeyn, Lord Archbishop of York 1286–96*, i, ed. W. Brown (Surtees Soc. 123; 1913), 203. Subsequently a *magister* was appointed from the Trinitarian house of Knaresborough (VCH *Yorks.*, iii, 180).

[111] VCH *Yorks.*, iii, 181.

[112] *Acta I Lincoln 1067–1185*, 24–5, no. 37. See also Golding, 'St Bernard and St Gilbert', 44–8.

[113] The possibility that Gilbert preached to a double community of monks and nuns was suggested in a paper given by Father Braceland at the 6th Annual Conference of Cistercian Studies: see *Cistercian Studies* 11 (1976), 151. See also *Gilbert of Hoyland. Sermons*, i, 11–12. For the story of the nun of Watton see Chap. 4, pp. 74–5.

chances of official recognition and support from the Cistercian monks. A further example of the difficulty of obtaining formal incorporation into the order in the early years of the thirteenth century is provided by Lacock. It was an abbey and its foundress Ela, Countess of Salisbury, was a powerful lady and a great admirer of the white monks. Her nunnery was dedicated to the Virgin and Saint Bernard, and she obtained a grant of confraternity with the Cistercians—granted because of the great devotion which she had for the order.[114] But Lacock, founded as it was only a year after the prohibition of the General Chapter in 1228, had to be content with adopting the Augustinian rule.

[114] VCH *Wilts.*, iii, 303 and n. 8.

7 The Order of Fontevrault

THE Cluniac and the Cistercian orders were both founded for men, and the incorporation of women caused problems. The order of Fontevrault, however, was from its origins concerned with female vocation. Robert of Arbrissel was notable for his success in attracting women converts to his call to repentance and the apostolic life.[1] Fontevrault, founded by him, developed as an order for women, with men included within the framework of the organization in a subservient capacity.[2] The strangeness of a double establishment dominated by women has puzzled historians. In the eighteenth century, Hélyot wrote that some regarded Fontevrault as having reversed the natural order in giving positions of authority to those who ought to obey.[3] But medieval writers were apparently not concerned with this feature. William of Malmesbury noted that a remarkable convent of nuns existed at Fontevrault, but it was the strict observance of the rule of silence which he found distinctive, and he made no mention of the subordinate position of the brothers of the order.[4] Similarly Jacques de Vitry (c.1160–1240) commented on the rigour of the rule of life rather than on the role of the men.[5] A theme of this book is that in the early years of the twelfth century, communities in which men and women followed the religious life in association may have been more widespread than has hitherto been supposed. A study of the origins and development of the order of Fontevrault helps to elucidate such forms of double organization. It also has particular relevance to England, as the order was greatly favoured by the English royal house.[6] Three nunneries were founded

---

[1] For an article concentrating on the impact of Robert of Arbrissel's career on women see J. Smith, 'Robert of Arbrissel: *Procurator Mulierum*', in *Medieval Women*, 175–84. See also J. Bienvenu, 'Aux origines d'un ordre religieux. Robert d'Arbrissel et la fondation de Fontevraud (1101)', *Cahiers d'Histoire* 20 (1975), 226–51 and idem, *L'Étonnant Fondateur de Fontevraud, Robert d'Arbrissel* (Paris, 1981).

[2] For general studies of the order see L. Picard, *L'Ordre de Fontevrault de 1115 a 1207* (Saumur, 1933); R. Niderst, *Robert d'Arbrissel et les origines de l'Ordre de Fontrevrault* (Rodez, 1952). See also H. Niquet, *Histoire de l'Ordre de Font Evraud* (Paris, 1642). For a summary of the history of the order see *DHGE* 17 (1971), s.v. *Fontevrault*. A useful bibliography is also given in *The Historia Occidentalis of Jacques de Vitry*, ed. J. F. Hinnebusch (Spicilegium Friburgense 17; Fribourg, 1972).

[3] P. Hélyot and M. Bullot, *Histoires des ordres monastiques religieux et militaires et des congregations séculières de l'un et de l'autre sexe*, 8 vols. (2nd edn., Paris, 1721), vi, 83.

[4] William commented sagely on the wisdom of a strict observance of silence: 'quia semel laxato silentio feminae pronae sunt ad mussitandum frivola', *Willelmi Malmesbiriensis monachi, De Gestis Regum Anglorum*, ed. W. Stubbs, 2 vols. (Rolls ser. 90; 1887–9), ii, 512.

[5] Hinnebusch, *Jacques de Vitry*, 130.

[6] Fontevrault provided the burial place for Henry II and Eleanor of Aquitaine as well as Richard I: see Hallam, 'Monastic Patronage', 102–6. A charter expressing Eleanor's particular

in England as members of the order—Westwood, Nuneaton, and Amesbury;[7] the latter a re-foundation established by Henry II himself.

Robert of Arbrissel probably did not set out to found an order of nuns. The evidence of his life given in the two contemporary accounts, one by Baudry, Archbishop of Dol, and the other by Brother Andrew, a monk of Fontevrault, indicate a restless man whose main vocation was preaching.[8] There seems little doubt as to his success. His eloquence and personality attracted large numbers of followers, both men and women.[9] His first foundation, in c.1096, was for canons at La Roë, but he seems to have taken little subsequent interest in them.[10] Marbod, Archbishop of Rennes, wrote to reproach him for abandoning the canons and for favouring the female converts.[11] The significance and nature of Robert of Arbrissel's concern for women has been interpreted in different ways. He has been described as playing a crucial role in elevating the whole status and position of the female sex[12] and as regarding women with particular compassion and tenderness.[13] The chronicle of William of Newburgh suggested that Robert took a conscious decision to concern himself with female converts, while other leaders, such as Bernard of Tiron and Vitalis of Savigny, devoted their energies to the needs of the male disciples.[14] Yet Robert's regard for women should not be glamorized as deriving from an elevated concept of female status. It has been shown that his practice of syneisactism—of consorting with women to demonstrate and prove his death to physical desires—has to be set in the context of his goals of self-

affection for this nunnery is printed in *Cal. Docs. France*, 375–6. For other grants by her to Fontevrault see ibid. 388–9, 390–1. It has, however, recently been pointed our that her support for the nunnery did not develop until 1185 × 1186 and that although she retired there in 1194 she only took the habit of Fontevrault on her death bed: see J. M. Bienvenu, 'Aliénor d'Aquitaine et Fontevraud', *Cahiers de civilisation médiévale* 29 (1986), 15–27. For a general discussion of royal patronage see Chap. 9.

    7 In addition to these three nunneries, two other houses had links with the order: Grovebury, a community of brothers: see p. 129, and the nunnery of Lillechurch (Higham) which had links with followers of Robert of Arbrissel: see pp. 131–2.

    8 'Vita B. Roberti auctore Baldrico episc. Dolensi', *AASS*, Feb., iii, 603–8; 'Alia Vita B. Roberti sive extrema conversatio et transitus eius, auctore monacho Fontis Ebraldi Andrea', ibid. 609–16. For the Vitae see Bienvenu, *Robert d'Arbrissel*, 161–4.

    9 'Multi confluebant homines cuiuslibet conditionis: conveniebant mulieres, pauperes et nobiles, viduae et virgines, senes et adolescentes, meretrices et masculorum aspernatrices', 'Vita auctore Baldrico', *AASS*, Feb., iii, 606.

    10 Bienvenu, 'Aux origines d'un ordre religieux', 235–6. Robert did, however, return to La Roë at least once when a new abbot was installed in 1101: see Niderst, 41.

    11 *PL*, clxxi (1893), 1480–6.

    12 J. Michelet, *Histoire de France*, 17 vols. (2nd edn., Paris, 1835–67), ii, 298–301.

    13 J. Petigny, 'Robert d'Arbrissel et Geoffroi de Vendôme', *Bibl. École des Chartes*, 3rd ser. 15 (1853–4), 14.

    14 *Chron. Newburgh*, 51–2, cap. 15.

discipline and austerity,[15] and relates to his own penitential progress rather than simply to the welfare of his women followers. Similarly his ministry to women may in part reflect his personal search for humility and discipline.

Robert seems to have had special concern for the humble and despised. He welcomed prostitutes and lepers, the outcasts of society.[16] Such concern was based on Christ's teaching,[17] and was a mark of the hermit's struggles to follow the apostolic life. Indeed it could be argued that, far from elevating women, the preacher's concern for them derived from his general sympathy for the destitute and the inferior. It is evident that Robert was particularly concerned with ladies of doubtful virtue—those in greatest need of repentance. Geoffrey of Vendôme wrote to him about some of the scandalous rumours resulting from his association with women, and indicated that Robert was favouring the repentant prostitutes rather than the high-born ladies who wished to follow him.[18] If leading a group of female followers, preferably poor and outcast, appealed to Robert, taking the step of submitting to and serving the weaker sex may also have been linked with the same goal of self-mortification and penitence.[19] According to the account of Brother Andrew, Robert himself indicated this in stating that he and his disciples took the step of serving women as a further measure aimed to provide for the safety of their own souls.[20] Robert may well have seen the caring and subordinate role of the men as an indication of their sanctity, rather than their subservience. In describing the end of Robert of Arbrissel's life, Andrew also recorded that the ailing leader offered the brothers of Fontevrault the option of leaving if they did not wish to remain subject to women.[21] The writer, himself one of their number, clearly regarded it as a mark of virtue that they chose to remain.

Apart from such considerations of motivation, the development of Fontevrault as an establishment for women may have partly resulted

---

[15] D. Iogna-Prat, 'La Femme dans la perspective pénitentielle des ermites du Bas-Maine (fin XIe debut XIIe siècle)', *Revue d'histoire de la spiritualité*, 53 (1977), 54–64. See also Bienvenu, *Robert d'Arbrissel*, 65–8.

[16] 'Vita auctore Baldrico', 607.

[17] e.g. the precepts enshrined in the Matthew 21: 31–2, and 25: 31–40.

[18] This letter is printed in *PL*, clvii (1898), 181–4. I agree with the view that the group Robert favoured was not the ladies of high rank as sometimes assumed: see Bienvenu, 'Aux origines d'un ordre religieux', 242.

[19] This interpretation was also held by some historians. Abbé Édouard, writing in the 19th cent., regarded Robert's submission to Abbess Petronilla as an act of supreme humility: see J. Édouard, *Fontevrault et ses monuments, ou histoire de cette royale abbaye*, 2 vols. in one, (Paris, 1873–4), i, 67.

[20] 'Et quod his maius est, et me et meos discipulos, pro animarum nostrarum salute, earum servitio submisi', 'Vita auctore Andrea', 609.

[21] Ibid. 608–9.

from practical considerations. For Robert was a practical man. His choice of a widow to rule the house, and his rejection of virginity as a necessary attribute for an abbess, seem to have been justified on pragmatic grounds.[22] Initially the organization of the men and women at Fontevrault into separate buildings represented a practical development, the result of Robert's success in attracting followers of both sexes.[23] Although there is clear evidence for the presence of men at Fontevrault,[24] it is the women who dominate the early documents. Papal bulls taking the order under the protection of Rome make no mention of men.[25] Most of the early grants were made to Robert and the nuns of Fontevrault.[26] Occasionally brothers of the order witnessed charters, but there is little to suggest that they were regarded as important members of the new community.[27] William of Newburgh described Fontevrault as a *monasterium feminarum*.[28] This probably reflects both the numerical superiority of the women and the fact that the purpose of the foundation was for them.[29] This would also help explain why Robert chose women as leaders of the developing order. Petronilla, the first to have been given the title of abbess, and Hersende, her predecessor, clearly possessed consider-able ability.[30] Both were able to provide the organization and qualities of leadership necessary to free Robert, and possibly other male followers, to continue their lives as wandering preachers and seekers after salvation.

If the dominance of women in the order of Fontevrault can in part be explained by practical as well as theoretical considerations, the degree and extent of feminine supremacy was nevertheless notable. Regulations for the brothers of Fontevrault stressed their subordinate position. They were to serve the nuns 'sub vinculo obedientiae usque

[22] 'Sed quomodo poterit quaelibet claustrensis virgo exteriora nostra convenienter dispensare quae non novit nisi psalmos cantare?', ibid. 609.

[23] J. von Walter, 'Die ersten wanderprediger Frankreichs', in N. Bonwetsch and R. Seeberg (eds.), *Studien zur geschichte der Theologie und der Kirche* (Leipzig, 1903), 147–51.

[24] See e.g. 'Vita auctore Baudrico', 606.

[25] e.g. a bull of Paschall II, dated 1106 (*PL*, clxiii (1893), 164–5), and another of 1112 (ibid. 296–7). These are calendared in Jaffé, i, 721, no. 6,034 and 746, no. 6,315.

[26] Some sixty-three early charters are printed in *PL*, clxii (1889), 1,095–1,118. It has been noted, however, that the texts are not above criticism: see R. I. Moore, 'The Reconstruction of the Cartulary of Fontevrault', *BIHR* 41 (1968), 89, n. 7.

[27] e.g. *PL*, clxii (1889), 1,114, no. 48; 1,106, no. 25. It is noted in Walter, '*Wanderprediger*', 169 that brothers are mentioned in these deeds only six times.

[28] *Chron. Newburgh*, 52.

[29] For the importance of Fontevrault being primarily a community for women, see also P. S. Gold, 'Male/Female Co-operation: The Example of Fontevrault', *Distant Echoes*, esp. 156–8.

[30] For accounts of these ladies see Picard, partic. 1–5, and for the choice of Petronilla and Robert's hesitations see Bienvenu, *Robert d'Arbrissel*, 132–5. It is possible that the compilation of the Fontevrault cartulary reflects the ability of Petronilla: see Moore, 'Cartl. Fontevrault', 94–5.

ad mortem . . . et cum debitae subjectionis reverentia'.[31] The second clause of their rule enjoined them to be content with what the nuns gave them.[32] Petronilla, as abbess, had full power to rule the church of Fontevrault, and this power seems to have extended to spiritual as well as to temporal matters.[33] The power of the abbess was probably in part a reflection of her aristocratic status. For a significant group of the early women followers were strikingly aristocratic. Hersende and Petronilla were both of noble birth, and even at an early date their influence was considerable. The ensuing predominance of high-born women within the order was hardly in accordance with the views of their founder, concerned as he was with the poor and outcasts of society. Nevertheless, it was a powerful force which not even Robert could withstand. Fontevrault was showered with gifts from noble families.[34] The convent of Boulauc, a Fontevraldine house in Gascony, eventually required a special authorization from the abbess of Fontevrault to receive a girl who was not of noble birth.[35]

It has been suggested that the inferior position of the men reflected their lower social status or their lack of ability.[36] Evidence indicates, however, that in some cases the entrants were from the same family, with fathers and sons joining with their wives and daughters in taking religious vows at the same community.[37] If the subservience of the male members of the order was initially a deliberate mortification on the part of Robert and the men following him, the status of the brothers may have been subtly modified after the death of their leader. During his lifetime the personal dominance of Robert could not be belied by humility. Although he did not rule the order in any constitutional sense, or have any formal title, his prestige and

---

[31] This passage comes from the prologue to the brothers' rule and is printed in *PL*, clxii (1889), 1,081–2. For a description of the three versions of the surviving rules see Gold, 'Fontevrault', 154–5.

[32] *PL*, clxii (1899), 1,081–2.

[33] Fontette, 69, n. 22; see also *PL*, clxii (1899), 1,083–4.

[34] e.g. by the counts of Anjou: see J. Chartrou, *L'Anjou de 1109 à 1151. Foulque de Jerusalem et Geffroi Plantegenet* (Paris, 1928), esp. 258–63, 325–6.

[35] F. Cassassoles, *Monographie du couvent de Boulauc dans le Canton de Saramon* (Auch, 1859), 26. This study also shows that aristocratic dominance began early in the history of the nunnery: ibid. 23–6.

[36] Knowles, *Monastic Order*, 204. Another suggestion put forward is that Robert gave control to the women as none of the men had sufficient ability or character to undertake the responsibility: see A. Jubien, *L'Abbesse Marie de Bretagne et la réforme de l'Ordre de Fontevrault d'après des documents inédits* (Angers / Paris, 1872), 9–10.

[37] For example a noble lady and her son entered Boulauc: see Cassassoles, 58. At the priory of La Madeleine-lès-Orléans, a certain Odo entered the community together with his wife, his three sons, and two daughters: see L. Vauzelles, *Histoire du prieuré de la Magdeleine-Lez-Orléans de l'Ordre de Fontevraud* (Paris, 1873), 30 and 213, no. ix. For examples of families entering Cluny see pp. 84–5.

charisma must have meant that he was a dominant presence, a powerful figure despite his renunciation of power. Early grants to Fontevrault referred to him as *dominus*, and it was not until nearly two years before his death that Petronilla received the title of abbess—a title given to her by Robert himself.[38] His ambivalent position as both a servant and a leader of the order is illustrated by his death-bed request to Agnes, prioress of Orsan, that he should be buried at Fontevrault. According to the account of Brother Andrew, his words were a mixture of command and entreaty.[39] Robert's position and prestige must have reflected on his male followers. The subservient role of the men at Fontevrault may have been tempered by the example and sanctity of their leader. His death increased the power and authority of the abbess and probably modified the position of brothers in the order.[40]

The humble position of the men, particularly if they were not fired by the desire for penitence and self-sacrifice, was likely to cause problems. Some rose to meet this challenge. Aimeric, prior of the house of Bragayrac in the diocese of Toulouse, and all the members of his house, placed themselves under the authority of the abbess of Fontevrault in 1122, and promised their service and obedience to her and to her successors.[41] Yet there are hints of discontent. As early as 1118 a bull of Gelasius II forbade heads of other religious houses to receive brothers from Fontevrault.[42] In 1144 another bull, promulgated by Lucius II, contained an exhortation to the men of Fontevrault to be faithful to their vocation and urged bishops to force those who had left to return.[43] As the order developed and grew, the subservient role of the brothers may have become harder to maintain.

After the initial foundation at Fontevrault in *c.*1101, the expansion of the order was rapid. Some of the new establishments seem to have resulted from the success of Robert's preaching. He probably played an important part in the founding of the priories of La Puye, Gaine, and many others.[44] The order spread to Normandy with the

---

[38] Gold, 'Fontevrault', 153.

[39] 'Impero tibi obsecrando et obsecro imperando, sicuti Domine meae filiae atque discipulae', 'Vita auctore Andrea', 615. For the death and burial of Robert see Bienvenu, *Robert d'Arbrissel*, 149–59.

[40] For the implicit suggestion that he may have forseen this and questioned whether the brothers would remain after his death see p. 115 of this chapter.

[41] Niquet, 262–4. The house had previously belonged to the congregation of Gerard de Sales.

[42] *PL*, clxiii (1893), 504; Jaffé, i, 778, no. 6,662.

[43] *PL*, clxxix (1899), 865. For further evidence of these difficulties see Fontette, 78–9 and n. 8.

[44] For the priories founded by Robert's death (with map), see Bienvenu, *Robert d'Arbrissel*, 109.

foundation of the house of Clairrussel in the diocese of Rouen and the priory of Chaise Dieu in the diocese of Evreux.[45] Early in the twelfth century, Alfonso of Castille confirmed the monastery of Vega to the abbess of Fontevrault, and in less than ten years the house was said to have two hundred nuns.[46] Apart from the personality of Robert, this rapid spread may in part reflect the renown in which the order was held. Additional statutes further restricted contact between men and women, regulated clothing, and spelt out stricter discipline.[47] A vivid picture of austerity and dedication is revealed in the account of the nuns of Fontevrault who were fired to shame by an eloquent sermon, and cutting off their curls made the considerable sacrifice of a shorn head to illustrate their death to the vanities of this world.[48]

The spread of the order raises the question of how far control remained centrally at Fontevrault. Initially at least, Fontevrault appears to have kept close control over the expansion. Abbess Petronilla seems to have followed the example of Robert himself and travelled widely.[49] Apart from the personal energy of Robert and subsequently of the abbess of Fontevrault, the General Chapter was a further organ of centralization. The first, held in 1149, was presided over by Hugh de Fosse, abbot of Prémontré.[50] No *acta* are extant for this meeting, and little is known about any subsequent chapters in the twelfth century. But in *c.*1189 Matilda of Flanders wrote to the heads of the Fontevraldine houses stating that the General Chapter had to be postponed because of difficulties caused by war and famine.[51] This would suggest that such assemblies were held quite regularly. The wording of the letter, with its instruction that the document should be kept for only one night before being sent on to other houses, indicates that there was a considerable degree of contact between the priories of the order.

Theoretically at least, the abbess of Fontevrault appears to have

---

[45] For the main houses of the order, with a note of the date of their foundation see *DHGE*, xvii (1971), 965–6. Chaise Dieu had particular links with the English house of Nuneaton, see pp. 124–5 of this chapter.

[46] Picard, 76–8.

[47] The rule is printed in *PL*, clxii (1889), 1,079–82. See also Fontette 75–7 and Gold, 'Fontevrault', 154–5.

[48] 'Vita B. Giraldi de Salis', printed in E. Martène and U. Durand, *Veterum scriptorum et monumentorum historicorum dogmaticorum, moralium amplissima collectio*, vol. vi (Paris, 1729), 996–7.

[49] Evidence for Robert's travels is given in 'Vita auctore Andrea', 610. Abbess Petronilla was visiting a priory when called back by the dying founder (ibid. 613–14). In 1123 she was at Hautes Bruyères, in 1124 at Tours, and in 1140 she visited Boulauc (Picard, 59, 62, and 113).

[50] Petronilla must have been old by this date, but it may also have been considered that only a man would have the necessary authority. The choice of Hugh is not surprising as Prémontré was a double house: see Chap. 8.

[51] Niquet, 421–2.

remained the principal permanent symbol of central authority within the order. She had to approve the election of prioresses to hold office for three years. She also sent confessors to direct the brothers at the priories.[52] Yet the extent in practice of the power of the prioress and how far she actually was dependent on the abbess is by no means clear. When a great lady such as the widow of the Count of Astarac was prioress of Boulauc and head of a nunnery founded on lands granted by her own family,[53] it would seem likely that she enjoyed considerable powers. It is also clear that the priories could possess lands in their own right.[54]

If the degree of control exercised by the abbess of Fontevrault over the priories is open to question, so too is the position of the brothers at the daughter houses. According to the rule, the men were to act in a subservient capacity, not only at Fontevrault, but also in all the dependent priories.[55] Clause nine of the men's rule decreed uniformity among the brothers, ordering that the men everywhere should follow the regulations laid down at Fontevrault about eating and sleeping.[56] The *Vita Andrea* suggested that the men were originally sent to the priories from the mother house.[57] Evidence from the priory of La Madeleine-lès-Orléans supports this, as the prior, Odo Ruffinus, and twelve brothers appear to have come from Fontevrault.[58] But with the expansion of the order it would seem unlikely that this degree of centralization could continue. It has already been noted that papal bulls suggest difficulties in recruiting, or at least in retaining, brothers willing to serve the Fontevraldine nuns, and with the position of the brothers probably undergoing some modification at the death of Robert, the tensions inherent in their status and organization may have become more apparent.[59] Whether the priors and brothers retained strong links with Fontevrault and the abbess as they served nuns in distant priories, is far from clear. The relationship between the prior and the prioress also needs clarifi-

[52] For the abbess's theoretical powers see Fontette, 68–72 and Gold, 'Fontevrault', 154.

[53] Cassassoles, 5–6.

[54] For example Orsan possessed considerable endowments which seem to have been granted to the priory rather than to Fontevrault itself: see F. Deshoulières, 'Le Prieuré d'Orsan en Berri', *Mémoires de la Société des Antiquaires du Centre* 25 (1901), 70. For evidence from English houses of the order see pp. 125–6 of this chapter.

[55] *PL*, clxii (1889), 1,081–2. For a discussion of the role of the men see Gold, 'Fontevrault', 156–60.

[56] *PL*, clxii (1889), 1,083.

[57] 'Vita auctore Andrea', 610.

[58] Vauzelles, 15.

[59] See pp. 117–18 of this chapter. In his study of Marie of Bretagne's reforms in the 15th cent. Jubien declared that it was the bizarre organization of the order, so contrary to the laws of nature, which later led the brothers to revolt against the abbess (Jubien, *Marie de Bretagne*, 10).

cation: how far did the priors have authority within the dependent houses, how far were they subject only to the abbess rather than to the head of their particular priory? A study of the English houses provides no clear answer to these questions, but fragments of evidence gleaned from them give some insight into the organization of the order of Fontevrault in the second half of the twelfth century as it expanded beyond the sea to England.

The English houses of the order of Fontevrault have received little attention from historians.[60] All three of the English foundations had aristocratic founders, thereby reflecting the traditions of the order as it developed on the Continent. Westwood in Worcestershire was established in the middle of the twelfth century by Eustacia de Say and her son. Her parentage is not known, but the fact that her children adopted her name suggests that she was of high rank.[61] Nuneaton was founded by Robert, Earl of Leicester and his countess Amicia at about the same date, and Amesbury's re-foundation in 1177 as a member of the order was at the initiative of Henry II. Apart from the founders themselves, the aristocratic status of many of the patrons of these three nunneries is striking. It was noted by Stenton in connection with the series of thirty Nuneaton charters which he edited.[62] The other charters relating to the house which are preserved in the British Library confirm the impression of aristocratic domin-ance.[63] Westwood too had important patrons such as Ida of Boulogne, daughter of Count Matthew and Mary of Blois.[64] At Amesbury, royal patronage was reflected in the connections of some of the inhabitants. Alpesia, a cousin of Henry III, was a nun there, and in *c.* 1192 Amicia Pantulf, one of Queen Eleanor's ladies, made a grant to the nunnery clearly intending to take the veil and end her

[60] This was apparent in a discussion following M. Bienvenu's paper on Fontevrault—two of the names given for the English houses are inaccurate, as was the suggestion that Henry I founded a convent of the order in England: see Bienvenu, 'Aux origines d'un ordre religieux', 244–5. General studies of the order virtually ignore the English houses, and H. F. Chettle, 'The English houses of the Order of Fontevraud', *Downside Review*, N.S. 61 (1942), 33–55, contains little about the 12th cent. A recent paper by Dr Chibnall has greatly helped to remedy the situation: see M. Chibnall, 'L'Ordre de Fontevraud en Angleterre au xiie siècle', *Cahiers de civilisation médiévale*, 29 (1986), 41–7.

[61] For Eustacia and her son Osbert see Chibnall, 'L'Ordre de Fontevraud en Angleterre', 43–4. For the hypothesis that she could possibly be identified with Eustacia, Countess of Essex, see pp. 172–3 of this chapter.

[62] *Danelaw Docs.*, 237.

[63] The Aston charters include some 184 relating to Nuneaton which date from the 12th and early 13th cents. The authenticity of some of these relating to the church of Catherington are open to question: see *HRH*, 217, n. 2. Nevertheless, this large group of charters provides valuable evidence for the priory. There are only isolated examples of names of donors which do not suggest an aristocratic pedigree; e.g. *Danelaw Docs.*, 247, 248, nos. 329–30.

[64] BL Cotton MS Vesp. E. ix, fos. 5 and 6 (Westwood cartl.); printed in *MA*, vi (ii), 1,006, no. 18 and 1,007, no. 22.

days in the convent.[65] In the thirteenth century the links with the royal house were continued. In 1285 Mary, daughter of Edward I, took the veil at Amesbury, together with thirteen other girls of noble birth, and the queen mother, Eleanor of Provence, also became a nun there.[66]

For Westwood, Nuneaton, and Amesbury, the order of Fontevrault seems to have been an important factor in their foundation. The earliest evidence for the foundation of the nunnery of Westwood is contained in a confirmation charter of Henry II. The wording makes it quite clear that the grants were made to Fontevrault and that the new house was founded as a member of this order.[67] Charters recording donations to all three nunneries make frequent allusion to their being Fontevraldine.[68] This is in interesting contrast to the majority of other English nunneries where the order of the house is often not mentioned in the charters. It suggests that there was a considerable sense of identity within the order. Evidence also exists of specific links with the mother house. Amesbury was colonized with nuns from Fontevrault, and the prioress herself came from the Continent.[69] The re-founding of Amesbury and the choice of the order was clearly due to Henry II. Before this the king had shown considerable interest in the other English houses linked with Fontevrault. He had granted the church of Chalton, Hampshire, and the right to hold a fair to the priory of Nuneaton.[70] His confirmation charter to the nunnery of Westwood included wide privileges, for example that the nuns were not to be impleaded for any of their possessions unless before the king himself.[71] In 1164 he granted the manor of Leighton Buzzard, later to develop into the priory of Grovebury, to the nuns of Fontevrault.[72]

---

[65] *Cal. Lib. Rolls* 1226–40, 195 (Alpesia); *Cal. Docs. France*, 387 (Amicia).

[66] *Ann. Mon.*, iv, 491 (*Ann. Worcs.*) and iii, 326 (*Ann. Dunstable*). For the private income reserved to these noble ladies see S. Wood, *English Monasteries and their Patrons in the Thirteenth Century* (Oxford, 1955), 122.

[67] *Recueil des Actes de Henri II, Roi d'Angleterre et Duc de Normandie concernant les provinces françaises et les affaires de France*, ed. L. Delisle and E. Berger, 4 vols. (Paris, 1909–27), i, 175–6 (1155 × 1158).

[68] *Cal. Docs. France*, 376, no. 1062, *Danelaw Docs.*, 239–40, no. 319 (Nuneaton); *Recueil Henri II*, i, 175–6 (Westwood); *MA*, vi (ii), 1005, nos. 10 and 11; *Cal. Chart. Rolls 1257–1300*, 157–9 (Amesbury).

[69] For the history of Amesbury see VCH *Wilts.*, iii, 242–59.

[70] *Monasticon* (1st edn.), i, 519. For the fair see *Recueil Henri II*, i, 394–5, no. 247. For Henry's patronage of Fontevrault see E. M. Hallam-Smith, 'Henry II as a Founder of Monasteries', *Journal of Ecclesiastical History* 28 (1977), 117–18.

[71] *Recueil Henri II*, i, 176, no. 73. It is possible that the king had personal links with the foundress Eustacia's son Osbert. According to tradition Osbert's wife was daughter of Walter de Clifford, and so sister to Rosamund, Henry II's mistress: see Nash, *Worcs.*, i, 240–1.

[72] *Recueil Henri II*, i, 385–6, no. 238. From 1164 on the pipe rolls record grants of £48. 8s. to the nuns of Fontevrault: see Hallam, 'Henry II', 118. For the development of the community of Grovebury at Leighton Buzzard see pp. 129–30 of this chapter.

However, the most important manifestation in England of his patronage of Fontevrault was the re-foundation of the Wiltshire convent. Whether or not this was part of his penance for Becket's murder,[73] or a logical extension of his support for the order, Amesbury was to become the most important of the English houses, eventually almost rivalling the mother house itself. Twenty-one nuns, under the former sub-prioress of Fontevrault, were sent to England to form the nucleus of the new convent. In 1186 the nuns were installed in their new buildings in the presence of the king and the abbess of Fontevrault.[74]

It is possible that the foundation of Nuneaton and Westwood may initially have been encouraged and planned by Abbess Matilda, Henry II's aunt.[75] The tradition is recorded that she died in 1155 at the moment when she was about to plant the standard of the order in England.[76] Both Westwood and Nuneaton were founded at about this time. The first site of Nuneaton was at Kintbury in Berkshire, and a charter recording the earl's grants to establish the convent there can be dated some time after 1147.[77] The community was still there in 1153, and the move to Nuneaton had taken place by c.1157.[78] Perhaps the death of Matilda slightly delayed the formalities of the new foundation. Abbess Matilda may have known the Countess of Leicester. Amicia was the daughter of Ralph, lord of Gael and Montfort in Brittany. She had been betrothed to Richard, the illegitimate son of Henry I who had died in the wreck of the white ship in 1120.[79] The abbess of Fontevrault had been widowed in the same disaster.[80] Her successor, Audeburga, was probably present at the dedication of Nuneaton, and the suggestion that it was this foundation which Abbess Matilda had planned to visit is further strengthened by the endorsement on the back of a charter of Audeburga confirming a grant made by Nuneaton. This endorsement, written in a twelfth-century hand, extolled the virtues of

---

[73] For a discussion of this question see *Councils and Synods with Other Documents Relating to the English Church I AD 871–1204*, 2 vols., ed. D. Whitelock, M. Brett, and C. N. L. Brooke, pt. ii, 1066–1204 (Oxford, 1981), 947–8.

[74] *Gesta Henrici II*, i, 354. See also VCH *Wilts.*, iii, 244. For a further discussion about the role of the king in this foundation see p. 167.

[75] For evidence of her close relationship with Henry see *Reg. Regum*, iii, 125, nos. 329–31.

[76] Edouard, i, 213.

[77] BL Addit. chart. 47,384.

[78] BL Addit. chart. 47,423. This is witnessed by Isabel, former Countess of Northampton, as the wife of the grantor, Gervase Paynell and so cannot be before 1153. The community was at Nuneaton by the issue of the charter printed in *Cal. Docs. France*, 376, no. 1,062. The editor suggests the dates of 1155–9, but a terminal date of c.1157 seems more accurate: see Le Neve, *Fasti*, rev. edn., iii, *Lincoln*, ed. D. Greenway (London, 1977), 33, and n. 2.

[79] *Complete Peerage*, vii, 529–30.

[80] According to Niquet, Matilda then retired to Fontevrault, aged only 14 (Niquet, 407).

Matilda and lamented her death.[81] It is interesting, however, that the nunnery of Westwood also appears to have been founded at about this time. Henry II's confirmation charter to the Worcestershire nunnery dates from 1155 × 1158,[82] and the wording of the charter, in which the king agreed that a convent of nuns of the church of Fontevrault should be founded at Westwood, suggests that the grant was made at an early stage in the process of foundation.[83] The visit of the abbess may well have been the occasion for the issuing of the royal charter to Westwood and the completion of the formalities of the establishment of the new community.

Apart from Fontevrault itself, another priory of the order, Chaise Dieu in Breteuil, may well have played a part in the foundation of Nuneaton. In 1125 Robert and his wife, Amicia, made grants to a certain hermit called Hugh. Subsequently, in c.1132, a lord of the area built the house of Chaise Dieu for Hugh and his followers.[84] Towards the middle of the twelfth century, the hermit gave himself and his brothers to the service of the nuns of Fontevrault,[85] and women as well as men subsequently served God at the priory of Chaise Dieu.[86] This step would have strengthened links between the Leicesters and the order of Fontevrault. According to one account, a group of nuns under the leadership of Albreda de Beaumont was sent from Chaise Dieu to found Nuneaton in England.[87] The details of the account are clearly inaccurate, but other evidence confirms that there were links between the Warwickshire priory and the Norman house. Robert of Chaise Dieu witnessed charters to Nuneaton,[88] and

[81] *Danelaw Docs.*, 248–9.

[82] *Recueil Henri II*, i, 175–6.

[83] It is possible that the process of founding the nunnery had started earlier. Nash stated that Osbern fitz Richard and Hugh fitz Osbern, Eustacia's father-in-law and husband, had contributed to the endowment of Westwood (Nash, *Worcs.*, i, 350). He cited no authority for this. The founding of monasteries probably often took many years: see Galbraith, 'Foundation Charters', esp. 214–15.

[84] A. J. Devoisins, *Histoire de Notre-Dame du Désert, L'Ermitage (460–1125), Le Prieuré (1125–1675), La Chapelle (1675–1900)* (Paris, 1901), 99–118. For the history of Chaise Dieu see also J. F. Vaugeois, *Histoire des antiquités de La Ville de l'Aigle et de ses environs* (L'Aigle, 1841), 271–5.

[85] For a similar action on the part of the prior of Bragayrac and his community see p.118 of this chapter.

[86] Devoisins suggested that women joined the community as a result of the link with Fontevrault (Devoisins, 117), but a group of hermits sometimes included both sexes: see above p. 196.

[87] Devoisins, 118. Audeburga was abbess of Fontevrault, not Chaise Dieu. Devoisins seems to base his account on documentary evidence, but the reference to a charter witnessed by Becket as chancellor and Robert of Chaise Dieu, suggests that the charter may have been BL Addit. chart. 53,108 (printed *Monasticon* [1st edn.], i, 520). This makes clear the close link with Fontevrault, but does not suggest that Nuneaton was a daughter house of Chaise Dieu. For the question of the authenticity of this charter see p. 125, n. 93.

[88] BL Addit. chart. 53,108; see also the reference to him in *Danelaw Docs.*, 248–9, no. 331.

in 1286 a charter of the prioress of Chaise Dieu acknowledged the receipt of a sum of twelve marks due every year from the prior and prioress of Nuneaton.[89] It is difficult to assess the claim that Albreda de Beaumont, a nun of Chaise Dieu, was the first prioress of the English house. The first known prioress who held office was probably Agnes,[90] but she may not have been the first to head the new community. Robert of Leicester had five sisters, and one is said to have been called Albreda, and to have married Hugh of Châteauneuf.[91] It remains a possibility that she entered Chaise Dieu as a widow and subsequently became prioress of a daughter house founded by her brother. It would help to explain why Amicia, who herself took the veil at Nuneaton,[92] does not seem to have held the office of prioress there. But the existence of Albreda as first prioress of Nuneaton must remain in doubt.

Once the nunneries were established as members of the order, there is the question of their continuing relationship with Fontevrault. An interesting charter of Abbess Audeburga, probably dating from her visit to England in c.1155, granted to Nuneaton the right to receive nuns, brethren, and sisters into the priory and to retain money offerings made to the convent. The charter states that this was a practical measure necessitated by the remoteness of the priory from Fontevrault and the difficulties of travelling.[93] Other evidence suggests that the house of Nuneaton was accorded some independent status. Many grants were made to it with no explicit reference being made to the rights of Fontevrault.[94] The same is true of the other

A charter of the Earl of Leicester recorded an exchange whereby the nuns of Chaise Dieu held land in Nuneaton (BL Addit. chart. 47,382). It is also clear that Amicia made grants to Chaise Dieu: see BL Addit. chart. 47,381.

[89] BL Addit. chart. 47,389.

[90] *HRH*, 217. She held office c.1160, but there are possibilities of confusion with her (?) successor Alice. As some of the charters refer simply to the prioress as 'A' (see Appendix B), the possibility that Amicia came to hold the office is not completely ruled out.

[91] *Complete Peerage*, vii, 526, n. c. Evidence for the marriage of these ladies comes from Orderic Vitalis, but he does not give the names of the sisters: see *Orderic Vitalis*, vi, 20–1 and 332–3.

[92] See pp. 173–4. The date when she entered the nunnery is not established, but it was probably c.1155 × 1168. Ladies who had founded convents not infrequently took the veil in their foundation. For other examples see Chap. 9.

[93] BL Addit. chart. 53,108, printed in *Monasticon* (1st edn.), i, 520. The authenticity of this document could be questioned, particularly as there are curious features about some of the Nuneaton charters (see above n. 63). This charter has no seal or seal tag, but it is written in a 12th-cent. hand, and the witnesses seem plausible. The fact that the nunnery possessed a considerable degree of autonomy would probably argue for its acceptance as valid evidence.

[94] e.g. the majority of charters printed in *Danelaw Docs.*, 237–60. Some donors made grants to Fontevrault for the use of Nuneaton, e.g. a donation of Hawise, Countess of Gloucester, printed in *Earldom of Gloucester Charters. The Charters and Scribes of the Earls and Countesses of Gloucester to AD 1217*, ed. R. B. Patterson (Oxford, 1973), 82–3, no. 78.

English houses of the order.[95] A puzzling feature of some early Nuneaton charters is that the foundation is described as an abbey.[96] Technically all the dependent houses of the order were priories, and there is no evidence that Nuneaton was ever ruled by an abbess. It is possible that the description reflects the founders' intention to establish an abbey—a course of action not possible within the structure of the order. It may be that the Earl and Countess of Leicester, though content with a priory, ensured that their foundation was given status and independence.

In spite of this measure of autonomy, there was considerable contact between the priories in England and the mother house. At Nuneaton, Gila, prioress of Fontevrault, ratified an agreement made by a certain Eilieva about her illness and possible reception into the community. The sick lady is careful to ensure that she would have the protection of the nunnery while ill, and yet retain the freedom to decide whether to return to the world or take the veil in the event of recovery.[97] The presence of the prioress suggests that she was visiting Nuneaton. John, prior of Fontaines, a French priory of the order, also witnessed the charter, as did the prioress of Amesbury. In 1227, Abbess Bertha of Fontevrault confirmed a decree of the prior and prioress of Nuneaton, probably also indicating a visit from the head of the mother house.[98] At Amesbury in 1221, the abbess of Fontevrault corroborated with her seal a gift made by the convent.[99] Other examples show the abbess supporting the English houses in some of their claims to property. Audeburga wrote on behalf of Westwood to Bishop Roger about a dispute over the church of Dodderhill.[100] Earlier, Abbess Matilda of Flanders seems to have encouraged her niece, Ida of Boulogne, to make a grant of land to Westwood.[101]

Contact with the mother house may well have become increasingly difficult in the thirteenth century. The English loss of Anjou after 1204 must have intensified the difficulties of communication with Fontevrault, and may have been a factor in the development in importance of Amesbury. Fortified by the prestige of being a royal

---

[95] For example the Westwood charters preserved in BL Cotton MS Vesp. E. ix, fos. 2ᵛ–9ᵛ and printed in *MA*, vi (ii), 1,004–10. For examples where Fontevrault is mentioned see n. 68 of this chapter.

[96] e.g. the Earl of Leicester's foundation charter printed in *Cal. Doc. France*, 376, no. 1,062 and a charter of his daughter Isabel, printed *Danelaw Docs.*, 251, no. 334. For other examples where a priory of nuns is described as an abbey see Chap. 6, n. 34.

[97] *Danelaw Docs.*, 247, no. 329.

[98] BL Addit. chart. 48,490. This is a 14th-cent. copy.

[99] VCH *Wilts.*, iii, 246.

[100] *The Cartulary of Worcester Cathedral Priory (Register 1)*, ed. R. R. Darlington (Pipe Roll Soc., N.S. 38; 1968 for 1962–3), 88–9, no. 162 (1175 × 1178).

[101] BL Cotton Vesp. E. ix, fo. 6; printed in *MA*, vi (ii), 1,007, no. 22.

foundation, it appears to have become the most dominant of the English houses, possibly exercising a supervisory role over the other priories. Prioress Joan of Amesbury witnessed a Nuneaton charter,[102] and the suggestion that Amesbury came to hold a dominant position, is further supported by entries in the margin of the surviving fragment of the Westwood cartulary which note that the prior of Amesbury had agreed to certain grants.[103] Amesbury also became important within the order as a whole. Abbess Joan (1265–76) experiencing opposition to her rule at Fontevrault, was said to have withdrawn to Amesbury with her two nieces and another nun and to have attempted to govern the whole order from there.[104] Earlier, Adela of Brittany, who became abbess of the order in 1228, seems to have been brought up in the court of Henry III and to have retained a special affection for Amesbury.[105]

There is little evidence to suggest that Amesbury, or the other English priories, attempted to break their links with the mother house of Fontevrault.[106] Such apparent contentment is in marked contrast to developments within other orders, where English nunneries seem sometimes to have deliberately worked to end their subjection to a continental mother house.[107] This relative lack of discontent may reflect the degree of autonomy given to the priories. It may also be a consequence of the aristocratic and international outlook of the high-born ladies of the order. Princess Mary did not become prioress of Amesbury, but she acted as agent for the abbess of Fontevrault, and together with the king, persuaded her English convent to accept a prioress sent from the mother house rather than one of their own choice.[108] It is also possible that the comparative stability of the order resulted from the presence of brothers who served the Fontevraldine nuns, and that, as at Sempringham, the existence of the double order solved some problems caused by the need of the nuns for masculine support.[109]

---

[102] *Danelaw Docs.*, 247, no. 329.

[103] BL Cotton MS Vesp. E. ix, fos. 3, 6ᵛ, and 8ᵛ.

[104] VCH *Wilts.*, iii, 248.

[105] *Edouard*, i, 255–6.

[106] The reverence in which the founder Robert of Arbrissel and the order continued to be held is indicated by a prayer inserted in a book which probably belonged to Amesbury: see Chibnall, 'L'Ordre de Fontevraud', 45–6.

[107] This was the case with Harrold in Bedfordshire: see pp. 152–5. See also above, pp. 131–2 for indications of problems in the relationship between Lillechurch and the mother house of St Sulpice.

[108] VCH *Wilts.*, iii, 248. In a later election dispute, Mary, now officially appointed vice-gerent of the abbess of Fontevrault in England, acted with the prioress in securing the local English candidate rather than that of the abbess of Fontevrault (ibid. 249).

[109] The success of Fontevrault is stressed in Gold, 'Fontevrault', 160–2. She suggests this may in part have been due to the sizeable number of men attached to the nunneries, thereby ensuring the availability of a large 'staff'.

Little is known about the numbers and organization of the brothers attached to the English houses of the order of Fontevrault. As with the mother house, references to the nuns predominate, and evidence about the men has to be gleaned from witness lists and the occasional reference. Clearly all three nunneries had a prior whose role was not unimportant.[110] The prior of Amesbury acted with the bishop and the chancellor of Salisbury to enforce papal edicts in the case of a disputed election at Shaftesbury.[111] A case about tithes was conducted in front of John, prior of Amesbury, in 1221.[112] Apart from such hints of independent status, the priors of the houses appear to have granted land jointly with the prioress of the nunnery.[113] They also acted for the prioress in law suits.[114] It is difficult to say how far they were subject to the authority of the prioress. It has been noted that the priors of several of the European houses increased their power and position, and came to have complete control of temporal administration.[115] In the mid-fourteenth century the priors rather than the prioresses seem to have gone to Fontevrault for the General Chapter,[116] suggesting a similar development may have taken place at the English houses.

The status and number of the other brothers is also difficult to determine. At Amesbury in 1256 there were said to be six chaplains in addition to the prior, a clerk, and sixteen lay brothers, to serve a community of some seventy-six nuns.[117] In the twelfth century, the evidence of the Nuneaton charters suggests the presence of at least eight men.[118] The impression given is that the masculine community, though small, was important. Two of the chaplains were described as

---

[110] At Nuneaton, references to prior occur soon after the foundation of the house: see *HRH*, 217. At Amesbury and Westwood the first known priors date from the end of the 12th and beginning of the 13th cent. (ibid. 207 and 221). This could merely reflect the greater amount of evidence extant for Nuneaton.

[111] *Cal. Pap. Lett.*, i, 61–2 (1219).

[112] *Sarum Charts.*, 114. The reference to a prior of Amesbury nonplussed the editor.

[113] For Amesbury see the references in VCH *Wilts.*, iii, 245, where it is noted that the arrangement did not persist. At Nuneaton, priors feature with prioresses in some 14th-cent. charters, e.g. BL Addit. charts. 47,604, and 47,627. Fifteenth-cent. charters usually just refer to the prioress.

[114] For example *Rotuli Curiae Regis. Rolls and Records of the Court held before the King's Justiciars or Justices. 6 Richard I–1 John*, ed. F. Palgrave (Record Commission; London, 1835), 144; *Curia Regis Rolls*, v, 58 (1207).

[115] F. Grelier, 'Le Temporel de l'Abbaye de Fontevrault dans le Haut-Poitou des origines à la réforme du xvᵉ siècle', *École des Chartes. Positions des Thèses* (Paris, 1960), 37.

[116] *Cal. Close Rolls 1343–46*, 383.

[117] VCH *Wilts.*, iii, 246–7. For a discussion of the terminology *fratres* and *conversi* see pp. 71–2.

[118] A chirograph dating from *c*.1160 × *c*.1180, is witnessed by two priests and six brothers (*fratres*), and refers to the brothers and sisters of the house (BL Addit. chart. 47,854). This is one of the Catherington charters, written in a 13th-cent. hand and apparently a later copy: see above n. 63. Another witness list of similar date names the prior, four priests, a reeve, a deacon,

dominus in a charter dating from the end of the twelfth century witnessed by all the brothers of Nuneaton,[119] and in 1268 a royal gift to Amesbury specifically stated that it was given for the support of the brethren of the house as well as for the sisters.[120]

It is probable that the brothers retained some links with Fontevrault. According to tradition, some accompanied the nuns initially sent from the mother house at the foundation of Amesbury in 1177.[121] This would seem to have been the practice in the first years of the expansion of the order on the Continent, and some men from Chaise Dieu Priory may also have helped to colonize Nuneaton. Yet, as stated in Audeburga's charter to the Warwickshire house, the prioress could recruit without reference to Fontevrault.[122] It is possible that brothers of the order in England came to be given some centralized support from the priory of Leighton or Grovebury, the name which came to be used in the second half of the thirteenth century. After Henry II had granted the manor of Leighton Buzzard to Fontevrault in 1164, payments resulting from this gift continued to be made to the mother house rather than to the English nunneries.[123] The cell of brothers established there probably consisted of a proctor and some companions administering the estate for Fontevrault. It does not seem to have become conventual, although the distinction between such cells and a priory was by no means clear, with the head of a cell sometimes being given the title of prior.[124] The evidence suggests that there may have been some interchange between brothers at Leighton and those serving in the nunneries. Vitalis, described as prior of Leighton (Grovebury) in 1196, was probably the same man as Brother Vitalis who was prior of Nuneaton at the end of the twelfth century.[125] Earlier, in c.1160 × 1180, he had witnessed a Nuneaton charter as Vitalis the priest.[126] A Brother Nicholas, once prior of Westwood, was put in

and three other men who may also have been linked with the nunnery (BL Addit. chart. 53,109). Early 14th-cent. evidence suggests a similar number of seven men including the prior: see VCH *Warwicks.*, ii, 66. The author of the VCH article assumes that they were secular chaplains.

[119] *Danelaw Docs.*, 247, no. 329.
[120] *Cal. Chart. Rolls 1257–1300*, 100.
[121] VCH *Wilts.*, iii, 245.
[122] BL Addit. chart. 53,108. For this charter see above, p. 125.
[123] See above, p. 122.
[124] Grelier, 'Le Temporel de Fontevrault', 36. For Grovebury (the name used by late in the reign of Henry III) see Chibnall, 'L'Ordre de Fontevraud', 44. For a note on excavations there with a provisional plan of the buildings see S. Youngs, and J. Clark, 'Medieval Britain in 1981', *Medieval Archaeology* 26 (1982), 171–2.
[125] *HRH*, 103 and 217. For a similar possibility of exchanges of brothers and central support from an all male community within the Gilbertine order see p. 75.
[126] BL Addit. chart. 47,854.

charge of the manor at Grovebury.[127] William de Verney appears to
have been prior of Nuneaton in 1256 × 1257, before becoming prior
of Grovebury.[128] It is interesting that a letter of 1287 from the abbess
of Fontevrault indicates that William had links with all the English
priories. The abbess decreed that on his death his moveables at
Nuneaton and Westwood were to go to those houses, with all his
possessions at Amesbury and Leighton reverting to Fontevrault
itself.[129] The community at Leighton probably retained close links
with the mother house at Fontevrault, and was the only one of the
houses in England which seems to have been regarded as an alien
priory.[130] Charters dating from the mid-thirteenth century show that
grants were made to the brothers of the order there.[131] It is possible
that the community as a whole came to act in a supporting role to the
priories of nuns. In the early thirteenth century the prioress of
Nuneaton used brothers of Leighton as her attorneys,[132] and they
also acted as witnesses to charters concerning the nunnery.[133] Such
use of the community at Grovebury may have developed during the
thirteenth century, possibly reflecting difficulties in recruiting men to
serve the nuns at the individual houses.

For the convents of the order of Fontevrault, as with the other
double houses, reliance on men following the religious life together
with the nuns did not provide a lasting solution to the problem of the
women's need for masculine support. Nevertheless, for the twelfth
and at least part of the thirteenth century, the attachment of men to
the order was probably a stabilizing factor. As with the Gilbertines,[134] the nunneries seem to have stayed within the framework of
the order, enjoying a resulting sense of identity. Some historians of
Fontevrault have attributed the later difficulties of the order to
Robert of Arbrissel's folly in making the brothers submit to the
nuns.[135] There may have been particular problems inherent in the stress
on the men's subservience, but to view the organization of the order
as an unmitigated disaster would seem to reflect prejudice rather than
historical accuracy. It may well be that the role of the men was

[127] *Cal. Close Rolls 1259–61*, 212 (1260). He caused considerable problems as he was
accused of murder and outlawed.

[128] BL Addit. charts. 47,594 and 48,498.

[129] BL Addit. chart. 47,418.

[130] KH, 104.

[131] PRO, E210/139 (dated 1248 × 1249), E210/331 (1257).

[132] *Curia Regis Rolls*, vii, 66 (1214).

[133] e.g. BL Addit. charts. 48,027 and 48,000 (B).

[134] It is sometimes suggested that Fontevrault provided the inspiration for Sempringham:
see e.g. Knowles, *Monastic Order*, 204; but this is to imply that double houses were a rare
phenomenon. There is some evidence of contact in England between the two orders. Gilbert of
Sempringham and another Gilbertine brother witnessed an agreement between Nuneaton and
Kenilworth: see BL Addit. chart. 53,102.

[135] e.g. Jubien, *Marie de Bretagne*, 10.

modified in the priories and that some form of balance was achieved between the prior and the prioress and their individual spheres of influence. In 1274, Mathilda de Clare planned to found a convent of nuns at Sandleford in Berkshire. They were to be served by a separate community of ten priests of the order of Fontevrault.[136] Although the plans never materialized, they indicate that even in the last quarter of the thirteenth century, the brothers of Fontevrault were still thought to provide one possible solution to the *cura monialium*.

One other English community was founded by a continental mother house linked with Robert of Arbrissel. The nunnery of Lillechurch, or Higham[137] in Kent was an offshoot of St Sulpice des Bois, a community situated in the diocese of Rennes and originally founded by Raoul de la Fuyate, a disciple of Robert.[138] Mary, daughter of King Stephen, was a nun in this community which was also a double foundation. When her father gained the crown of England, she, together with other companions from St Sulpice, were settled into the nunnery of Stratford in Middlesex.[139] The customs of the princess and her associates were clearly different from those of the nuns of Stratford. Discord arose, and the issue was eventually settled by the foundation of a new house for the princess at Lillechurch in Kent.[140] The nuns of Stratford renounced all claims to grants given when Mary joined their community, and the wording of the charter recording the settlement suggests their relief at the departure of the alien group.[141] It is clear that the mother house of St Sulpice retained links with the new foundation in Kent. The manor of Lillechurch and other grants were confirmed to the abbey of St Sulpice.[142] A charter preserved in the archives of St John's College, Cambridge, records the settlement of a controversy between the mother and daughter house.[143] It appears that the English nuns had complained to the pope that St Sulpice had damaged their possessions.

---

[136] *Cal. Pap. Lett.*, i, 448 (1274).

[137] Early documents refer to the house as Lillechurch, with the name Higham coming into use increasingly from *c.*1239 onwards.

[138] L. H. Cottineau, *Répertoire topo-bibliographique des Abbayes et Prieurés*, 3 vols.: i–ii (Mâcon, 1935–7), iii, ed. G. Poras (Mâcon, 1970), ii, 2,896–7. For the cartulary of the house see *Cartulaire de l'Abbaye de Saint-Sulpice-La-Forêt*, ed. P. Anger (Extrait du Bulletin Archéologique d'Ille-et-Vilaine, 1911).

[139] This house was in existence by 1122. For a background history see VCH *Middlesex*, i, 156–9; KH, 266.

[140] For the background see VCH *Kent*, ii, 145–6.

[141] SJC archives, D46.98. This is printed, from a later transcript, in A. Saltman, *Theobald, Archbishop of Canterbury* (London, 1956), 379–80, no. 155.

[142] e.g. the confirmation charter of King John preserved in SJC archives D98.29. A charter of Mary's brother, William, refers to the grant being made to St Sulpice (SJC archives, D46.6, printed, from a later transcript, in *MA*, iv, 382, no. 3).

[143] SJC archives, D10.29. The document is dated 1238.

In response, the abbey claimed that the church and manor of Lillechurch had been granted to it, and that the prioress there was wont to come to St Sulpice to receive her charge, promising obedience and making her profession at the mother house. Lillechurch denied this claim, but it was eventually agreed that the prioress, freely elected by the Kent community, should go to St Sulpice, and be received there with honour. The abbey was to have the right to make an annual visitation, and to send two nuns to be received into the community of Lillechurch. The agreement also contains interesting provisions about the chaplains. Both the abbess and the prioress of St Sulpice had the right to choose a chaplain from their community to go to the English house. One of these was to be English and able to hear the confessions of the English nuns. Should there be any problem over discipline or suitability, the man was to be recalled and the abbey to send a substitute.[144]

This evidence from Lillechurch suggests a degree of tension in the relations between the Continental abbey and its daughter house in England. At the same time, St Sulpice probably provided a structure of visitation and support. The clause in the agreement about the return of an unsuitable chaplain suggests both the possibility of problems and a way of dealing with them. Within the order of Fontevrault, later evidence shows considerable friction between nuns and brothers. At Amesbury in 1400 the prioress, together with some of her sisters, was imprisoned apparently at the incitement of the prior, who had been expelled. The measures taken by the prioress to improve the situation are interesting and imply the demise of the double order: she apparently reduced the number of canons at the house from twelve to four and appointed secular chaplains instead.[145] The difficulties inherent in the position of the men, pointed out by Robert of Arbrissel when on his death-bed, had thus finally come to fruition.

[144] The chaplains were to be chosen 'de capellanis simplicibus gestantibus habitum' provided that they were not the prior or the procurator of the abbey (SJC archives, D10.29, line 34).

[145] VCH *Wilts.*, iii, 252.

8   The Canonical Orders of the Twelfth Century

THE brothers of the order of Fontevrault were initially regarded as canons, although later, in the fifteenth century, they adopted the Benedictine rule.[1] The development of the canonical order and the adoption of the Augustinian rule by regular canons was a slow and complex process.[2] The *ordo canonicus* is not easy to define. The twelfth-century *Book of Different Orders and Callings in the Church* distinguished three main groups of canons: those cut off from men, those who dwelt near men, and those whose vocation was amongst mankind.[3] Although in the twelfth century the order of canons included a more contemplative strain, with little to distinguish its followers from the more austere Benedictine monks and the Cistercians, other groups had a more practical orientation.[4] It is not surprising that the brothers of both Fontevrault and Sempringham, men whose vocation was concerned with the care of women, should follow the canonical rule of St Augustine.[5]

Most Augustinian communities had no official bond between them, but in the twelfth century there developed reformed congregations of canons, with their houses linked and under some form of centralized authority. Two of the most important of these—the Premonstratensian and Arrouaisian orders—initially welcomed female converts and established double houses for men and women. But unease at such close association of the sexes became increasingly apparent. In England three convents of women were founded following the Premonstratensian customs—Orford (Irford) in Lincolnshire, Broadholme in Nottinghamshire, and Guyzance (Brainshaugh) in Northumberland. Whatever their links with the canons initially, all were established as separate communities by the end of the twelfth century. Harrold, in Bedfordshire, was originally founded as a

---

[1] Fontette, 73, n. 57. They seem to have adopted the Benedictine rule in 1474. In the charters and early statutes the men are described as *fratres* rather than monks or canons: see Bienvenu, *Robert d'Arbrissel*, 143–4.

[2] A general study of the development of the order of canons and their adoption of the Augustinian rule is given in Dickinson, *Austin Canons*, 7–90. For detailed work on the rule see L. Verheijen, *La Règle de Saint Augustin*, 2 vols. (Paris, 1967).

[3] *Libellus de diversis ordinibus*, 56. For this treatise see also Chap. 4, n. 1.

[4] Dickinson, *Austin Canons*, 74. For an account of the order which emphasizes its practical versatility see R. W. Southern, *Western Society and the Church in the Middle Ages* (Harmondsworth, 1970), 241–50.

[5] It has already been noted that men attached to independent communities of Benedictine nuns were sometimes described as canons: see pp. 70–1.

daughter house of Arrouaise, but subsequently achieved independence from the Arrouaisian canons. It is possible that other nunneries were also linked at an early date with the reformed canons, with such links becoming subsequently obscured as the canons became increasingly reluctant to accept responsibility for women. The establishment of female communities linked with the Premonstratensian and Arrouaisian canons gives further evidence of the existence of double houses in the first half of the twelfth century, and the ensuing attempts to move away from such forms of organization.

In the early years of its history, the Premonstratensian order was remarkable for the way in which it embraced the religious needs of women as well as men.[6] Herman of Laon talked of one thousand sisters at Prémontré itself and ten thousand within the whole order.[7] Even if allowance is made for a little exaggeration, it is clear that, as with Robert of Arbrissel, St Norbert's followers numbered many women. At Prémontré, the house was initially organized in the form of a double monastery, with communities of men and women functioning side by side in separate but adjacent buildings, and forming a unity under the rule of the abbot. A similar form of organization was adopted by other houses, and Jacques de Vitry gives a detailed description of Premonstratensian double monasteries.[8] The earliest-known statutes of the order, probably dating from the first half of the twelfth century, contain decrees relating to the communities of women. These show that they were under the authority of a prioress and suggest that their work was partly concerned with the care of the canons and brothers.[9]

It is generally argued that this situation changed in about 1140 with the Premonstratensian abbots admitting the failure of the

[6] A brief history of the life of St Norbert and the development of the order is given in H. M. Colvin, *The White Canons in England* (Oxford, 1951), 1–25. A useful general survey is to be found in the *Dictionnaire de théologie catholique*, ed. A. Vacant, xiii (Paris, 1936), s.v. *Prémontrés*, 2–31. For the individual houses of the order see N. Backmund, *Monasticon Praemonstratense*, 3 vols. (Straubing, 1949–56; idem., 2nd edn. i (2 parts), Berlin/New York, 1983). Bibliographies are given in Colvin, *The White Canons*, 369–76 and in H. Lamy, *L'Abbaye de Tongerloo depuis sa fondation jusqu'en 1263* (Louvain/Paris, 1914), pp. xxxiii–xl. For the needs of religious women and their attachment to itinerant leaders see B. M. Bolton, 'Mulieres sanctae', in D. Baker (ed.), *Sanctity and Secularity: The Church and the World*, *Studies in Church History* 10 (Oxford, 1973), 77–95.

[7] 'Ex libro iii Hermanni monachi de miraculis S. Marie Laudunen', *AASS*, Jun., i, 865, 866. St Norbert's mission to women is singled out for particular praise (ibid. 866).

[8] Hinnebusch, *Jacques de Vitry*, 134–5.

[9] These early statutes are edited in R. Van Waefelghem, 'Les Premiers Statuts de l'Ordre de Prémontré,' *Analectes de L'Ordre de Prémontré* 9 (1913), 1–74. The date suggested for them by the editor is 1135 × 1143. It has subsequently been proposed that these statutes may derive from an earlier lost version and date from 1140 × c.1161. For a recent discussion of the problems of their dating see P. Lefèvre, *Les Statuts de Prémontré au milieu du XIIe siècle* (Bibliotheca Analectorum Praemonstratensium, fasc. xii; Averbode, 1978), pp. xxiii–xxxiv.

double monastery, and taking the decision to exclude sisters from the houses of canons.[10] Jacques de Vitry indicates disquiet about situations in which men and women lived in close proximity in the Premonstratensian double houses, when he tells of increasing moral danger as the original fervour lessened and narrow communicating windows were widened into doors.[11] But the chronology of the changed attitude to women and the move away from double foundations is not clear. Some historians have suggested that the decision to have no more double houses was taken earlier, in 1137.[12] From c.1141 the sisters at Prémontré were on the move, first to Fontanelle, a nearby grange, and eventually to Bonneuil, a site some distance from the parent abbey.[13] A charter of Bishop Bartholomew of Laon, recording the initial moves of the sisters to buildings he had established at Fontanelle, seems to suggest a personal initiative on the part of Abbot Hugh of Prémontré.[14] Moreover, the continued moves of the sisters indicate a developing policy rather than a clear-cut implementation. Some of the other abbots may have been consulted and have agreed with the decision to remove the sisters, but it is not clear that this was a general decree binding on all.[15]

The early Premonstratensian abbots seem to have enjoyed a considerable amount of autonomy within the structure of the order,[16] and information from individual houses suggests that the sisters were moved to separate sites at different times. At Tongerloo, where the first abbot seems to have accepted women as members of the community, evidence of the existence of sisters at Eewen, a separate site, comes from the time of Abbot Hubert (c.1157–67).[17] At the abbeys of Park and Floreffe, both double houses, it is not clear when and how far the women were moved.[18] At Marchtall, in the

[10] See A. Erens, 'Les Sœurs dans l'ordre de Prémontré,' *Analecta Praemonstratensia* 5 (1929), 8. See also Lamy, *L'Abbaye de Tongerloo*, 97 and Colvin, *The White Canons*, 327–8.

[11] Hinnebusch, *Jacques de Vitry*, 135. See also the warnings expressed by St Bernard to the abbot of Cuissy (*PL*, clxxxii (1879), 199–201, no. 79).

[12] 1137 is the date given in Lamy, *L'Abbaye de Tongerloo*, 97, who notes the absence of evidence. According to an unpublished thesis on Prémontré, 1137 rather than 1141 is the correct date for the decision to move the sisters: see G. Richou, 'Essai sur la vie claustrale et l'administration intérieure dans l'Ordre et l'Abbaye de Prémontré au XIIe et au XIIIe siècles', *École Nationale des Chartes, Positions des thèses des élèves* (Paris, 1875), 28.

[13] For Bonneuil and the moves of the sisters see Backmund, ii, 484 and 589 (map).

[14] This charter is printed in C. L. Hugo, *Sacri et canonici ordinis Praemonstratensis Annales*, 2 vols. (Nancy, 1734–6), i (*Probationes*), pp. cccxviii–cccxix.

[15] No decree is extant referring to the separation of the sisters from the canons, although edicts have been preserved prohibiting the reception of sisters: see pp. 136–7. It is often assumed that there was a general decree of separation: see Hugo, *Annales*, i, 391.

[16] *Dict. de théol. catholique*, xiii, 7.

[17] Lamy, *L'Abbaye de Tongerloo*, 99–101.

[18] For Park and Floreffe see Backmund, ii, 317–22 and 373–8; see also V. and J. Barbier, *Histoire de l'Abbaye de Floreffe de l'Ordre de Prémontré* (Namur, 1880).

diocese of Constance, which adopted the Premonstratensian rule in
c.1170, sisters seem to have remained close to and part of the
community until some hundred years later.[19] It is not surprising that
any decision to move the women away from the parent abbey would
take some time to implement. This may well have been the case at
Prémontré itself. In 1138 a bull of Innocent II confirming the
possessions of the abbey referred to the necessity of securing
adequate endowment for the sisters from the monastery's resources,
pointing out that some of the grants had been donated because the
women were there.[20] This would suggest that measures were being
taken to separate the communities by this date, and thus supports the
view that any decision had been taken before 1140. The sisters from
Prémontré were only established at Fontanelle in *c*.1140, and did not
settle at Bonneuil till *c*.1148.[21] The papal clause attempting to
safeguard the women's endowment was repeated in 1143, 1147, and
with a slightly different wording again in 1154.[22] This series would
seem to indicate further that efforts to achieve greater separation
between the canons and the sisters were taking place throughout the
period and formed a continuous process rather than a single event.

The significance of these moves of the women is not clear. Some
historians have assumed that their removal was linked with the
decision not to admit any more sisters into the order.[23] Others have
argued that separating the communities did not necessarily imply a
rejection of the women.[24] As there is no actual decree extant
referring to the separation of the sexes in the Premonstratensian
houses, it is not easy to ascertain the position and intentions of Abbot
Hugh. It is clear that the General Chapter promulgated decrees
ordering that no more women should be received into the order, but
it is not possible to date them. In 1198 a bull of Innocent III referred
to such a decree having been passed by the Chapter some time before
and subsequently repeated.[25] The second redaction of the Premonstratensian statutes, which probably dates from the second half of the

---

[19] Backmund, 2nd edn., i (i), 61–4.

[20] This bull is printed in J. Le Paige, *Bibliotheca Praemonstratensis Ordinis* (Paris, 1633),
426–8; calendared in Jaffé, i, no. 7,926.

[21] Backmund, ii, 484.

[22] For the other bulls see Le Paige, *Bibliotheca Praemonstratensis*, 428–9. See also Fontette,
19, n. 40. In 1154 Pope Adrian IV ordered that the sisters should receive suitable sustinence
from the canons.

[23] See P. Lefèvre, *Les Statuts de Prémontré reformés sur les ordres de Gregoire IX et
d'Innocent IV au XIIIᵉ siècle* (Louvain, 1946), p. xi. The earliest sources, e.g. Le Paige,
Bibliotheca Praemonstratensis, 421–2, and Hugo, *Annales*, i, 7, just imply a decision to
separate the women from the canons.

[24] Lamy, *L'Abbaye de Tongerloo*, 97–8.

[25] *Die Register Innocenz' III*, ed. O. Hageneder and A. Haidacher, 2 vols. in 4 (Graz-Köln,
1964–79), i, 286–7, no. 198.

twelfth century, makes no reference to women in the order,[26] although additions to these regulations, presumably of later date, include an edict that no more sisters were to be received.[27] It has been suggested that the silence with regard to women in this second codification was because the decision had already been taken to exclude the sisters,[28] but apart from later mentions of women in statutes of the order, this argument is weakened by the fact that there are also no decrees in the codification relating to lay brothers, and there is no doubt that they remained within the order. It has been argued that this omission may indicate difficulties in enforcing rules on these brothers, as well as the general problems facing the Church during the period of schism under anti-Pope Victor IV.[29] It is certainly clear that lay brothers could be a troublesome element,[30] and it may have been that the women were regarded in the same light. While it would seem unwise to conclude that sisters were excluded from the Premonstratensian order by the date of the second codification of the statutes, the lack of any reference to them could certainly indicate difficulties, or that they were being marginalized to the fringes of the order, with the status of both the brothers and the women being more clearly differentiated from that of the canons.

The decrees which are extant relating to the sisters are frequently difficult to interpret. One, incorporated in the first collection of statutes, states that an altar involving the cure of souls can be accepted at a church where there is a cloister of sisters.[31] Another early decree regulates the number of sisters, stating that if any church had too many, no less than ten were to be sent out to form a new grouping.[32] If the word church—*ecclesia*—here refers to a community of Premonstratensian canons, these decrees could still indicate the existence of double houses. If, however, it refers to a church granted to a Premonstratensian abbey, this would suggest that the women were grouped in particular places, presumably apart from the community of canons. Another decree, printed by Martène as an

[26] For a recent discussion of the problems of dating these statutes see Lefèvre, *Les Statuts de Prémontré . . . XIIᵉ siècle*, pp. xxiv–xxvii.

[27] These additions are printed in E. Martène, *De antiquis Ecclesiae ritibus*, 3 vols. (2nd edn., Antwerp, 1736–7), iii, 925–6. These follow his edition of a version of the second codification.

[28] This suggestion is made in Erens, 'Sœurs de Prémontré', 9–10, and Fontette, 19.

[29] This is the hypothesis put forward in Lefèvre, *Les Statuts de Prémontré . . . XIIᵉ siècle*, pp. xiii–xxvii.

[30] For the revolt of the lay brothers at Sempringham see p. 74. There was also trouble with the brothers at Grandmont: see J. Becquet, 'La Première Crise de l'Ordre de Grandmont', *Bulletin de la Société Archéologique et Historique du Limousin* 87 (Limoges, 1960), esp. 298–313.

[31] Van Waefelghem, 'Les Premiers Statuts', 45. This is in the context of a general prohibition against the acceptance of such altars.

[32] Ibid. 66.

addition to the second codification of statutes, forbade the sisters to leave their cloister, 'nisi forte mittantur de claustro ad claustrum ejusdem abbatiae ad commanendum'.[33] This would certainly seem to suggest that the women were close to the parent abbey, if not part of the same complex.

Decrees concerning the women are more precise in the statutes of 1236 × 1238. One, again prohibiting the reception of sisters, had the additional clause: 'nisi in locis illis qui sunt ab antiquo recipiendis cantantibus sororibus in perpetuum deputata.'[34] This would seem to mean that no new communities of women were to be set up, but that the existing ones might continue. In this thirteenth-century codification of the statutes there is one clause which echoes the phrasing of the earlier decree restricting the movement of the women, without the previous ambiguity. It states that 'sorores nostrae non egrediantur nec evagentur, nisi forte mittantur de claustro ad claustrum morature ad minus per annum'.[35] This time it is clear that the permitted movement would seem to apply to a transfer to another community of sisters.

It would seem that changes in the policy of the Premonstratensian canons towards the women in their order developed slowly and were difficult to enforce. Even when the sisters were transferred to buildings geographically separate from the canons, the idea of a single community could still perpetuate.[36] At Floreffe, a house founded by St Norbert, a charter dating from c.1175 refers to a rent given when the daughter of the donor took the veil amongst the sisters of the monastery.[37] These women, although housed separately from the abbey in the nearby church of St Martin, seem to have been regarded as members of the single community.[38] This may also have been the case at other Premonstratensian houses.[39] The example of Prémontré, with its removal of the sisters to ever more distant sites,

---

[33] Martène, *De ritibus*, iii, 925.

[34] Lefèvre, *Les Statuts réformés . . . au XIIIe siècle*, 114–15. For the significance of the description 'sorores cantantes' see p. 147 of this chapter.

[35] Lefèvre, *Les Statuts réformés . . . au XIIIe siècle*, 113.

[36] For evidence from the English houses see pp. 140–3 of this chapter.

[37] Barbier, *L'Abbaye de Floreffe*, 55. Unfortunately the *pièces justificatives* cited as evidence, were not included in the book, so it is not possible to check the charter.

[38] Similarly at Rivreulle, the community dependent on the Premonstratensian abbey of Bonne Esperance, an act of 1182 referred to women being received at the parent abbey. See U. Berlière, 'L'Ancien Monastère des Norbertines de Rivreulle', *Messager des sciences historiques ou archives des arts et de la bibliographie de Belgique* (Gand, 1893), 389. See also above p. 85 for the relationship between Cluny and Marcigny.

[39] More detailed research is needed to establish the position of the dependent communities of women in relation to the parent abbeys, and the degree of their independence. Some seem to have been sited close by: see Barbier, *L'Abbaye de Floreffe*, 30–1. For the English houses see pp. 140–3 of this chapter.

may not have been followed by all communities. Repeated prohibitions about the reception of women, reinforced by Innocent III in 1198, did not solve the problem. In 1270 yet more decisive measures appear to have been attempted, with a decree that the suppression of nuns should be undertaken with vigour and that those already admitted should be allowed to move to another order.[40] A violent antipathy to the presence of women linked with their community was apparently expressed by the abbot and canons of Marchtall in 1273. They declared that the wickedness of women surpassed all, and that they would in no way endanger their souls by receiving any more.[41] The authenticity of this letter can be questioned, but it suggests that difficulties over the reception of women were still a factor even at this late date.

In the twelfth and the first part of the thirteenth century, therefore, several Premonstratensian monasteries apparently had dependent communities of women linked to them. This may reflect the determination of the sisters rather than the inclination of the abbots. In 1241 it was agreed that women should still be received at Bonneuil. The numbers were to be strictly limited, and the reception of the sisters was to be controlled by the abbot of Prémontré. It was also decided that the female head of the community was to be called *magistra*, as it was felt that the title *priorissa* might imply that she had jurisdiction over the cure of souls.[42] It would appear that the abbot was attempting to resolve problems arising from the reception of sisters by tightening his control. A further indication that the Premonstratensians opposed tendencies towards independence on the part of the women's communities, appears in a decree forbidding the heads of these communities to accept the profession of canons in their houses.[43] Presumably they were to be received at the parent abbey. The existence of men at the women's houses is confirmed by charter evidence.[44] It is an over-simplification to regard either 1137 or 1140 as marking the decisive abandonment of any concept of double houses. The Premonstratensian abbots may well have wished to exclude women as their order developed, but they found, as did the Cistercians, that this was not easy to achieve.

A study of the English Premonstratensian nunneries indicates that the initial expansion of the order in this country involved the

[40] Hugo, *Annales*, i, 83.

[41] Ibid., ii, 147–8. For a note doubting the authenticity of this letter see Backmund, i, 85.

[42] Hugo, *Annales*, i (*Probationes*), cccxx.

[43] Erens, 'Sœurs de Prémontré', 22 and n. 17 (the correct reference to the statute is Le Paige, *Bibliotheca Praemonstratensis*, 854).

[44] See Hugo, *Annales*, i (*Probationes*), cccxix. For brothers at the English houses of the order see p. 143.

reception of women. Newhouse, the first Premonstratensian monastery established in England, had two nunneries linked with it, Orford
in Lincolnshire, and Broadholme in Nottinghamshire. The second
foundation for men, Alnwick in Northumberland, had a dependent
community of women at Guyzance. By contrast there appears to be
no evidence that the later houses were concerned with female
followers. Newhouse was founded in *c.*1143 as a daughter house of
Licques.[45] As an offshoot of one of St Norbert's original foundations, this abbey was clearly linked with the continental centres of the
Premonstratensian order. It has been argued that it could not have
been a double foundation as the Premonstratensian order had ceased
to have double houses before this date,[46] but in view of the
continental developments discussed above such an interpretation
may be an over-simplification. The first reference to sisters associated
with Newhouse occurs in a confirmation charter of Bishop Robert of
Lincoln drawn up in 1153 × *c.*1156. This mentions a *cimiterium
sororum* in connection with the church of St Michael, Orford, which
had been granted to the abbey.[47] A confirmation charter of Henry II,
dating from 1156 × 1162, took the abbey of Newhouse under his
protection and referred to the canons, brothers, and sisters of the
community.[48]

The sisters attached to the abbey may from an early date have been
associated with the church of Orford. This was situated some
thirteen miles away from the parent abbey and had been granted to
Newhouse by December 1148 × 1154.[49] An alternative possibility,
however, is that the women were moved to Orford from Newhouse,
for they seem to have been regarded as an integral part of the abbey's
community. Apart from the reference to sisters in the royal
confirmations, two Newhouse charters dating from middle of the
twelfth century refer to Brother Ralph of Orford, presumably the
canon in charge of the sisters, in terms which suggest that he was still
regarded as a member of Newhouse.[50] It is a charter of Ralph
d'Aubigny, drawn up not long before 1189, which first gives the

---

[45] For Newhouse see Colvin, *The White Canons*, 39–52, and for the later history of the
abbey see VCH *Lincs.*, ii, 199–202.

[46] Colvin, *The White Canons*, 328. See also H. M. Colvin, 'A Twelfth-Century Grant to
Irford Priory', *Lincs. Archit. and Archaeol. Soc. Reports and Papers* 5 (2) (1953), 83, where he
reiterates that there can have been no possibility of double houses in England although the
charter indicates the presence of men and women.

[47] *Acta I Lincoln 1067–1185*, 108, no. 179.

[48] *Recueil Henri II*, i, 342, no. 205. See also ibid., i, 340, no. 204. See also the reference to
sisters in a later confirmation charter: *Danelaw Docs.*, 178–9, no. 243 (*c.*1175 × 1179).

[49] *Acta I Lincoln 1067–1185*, 106, no. 178.

[50] *Danelaw Docs.*, 186, no. 249, and 185, no. 248. The charters are witnessed by brother
Ralph 'and the whole convent'. As Colvin pointed out, this must refer to the community at
Newhouse: see Colvin, *The White Canons*, 49, n. 6.

impression that Orford was a distinct institution. This records gifts to the Premonstratensian nuns and to the brethren serving God in the church of St Mary, Orford.[51] No representative from the canons of Newhouse witnesses the charter. The list of witnesses was headed by the Premonstratensian abbot of Barlings, together with canons from the Gilbertine houses of Ormsby and Watton.

It is probable that Ralph d'Aubigny, as lay patron, played a vital part in the establishment of the nunnery of Orford.[52] His wife, Sybil de Valoignes, was the widow of William de Percy, the probable founder of Stainfield Priory in Lincolnshire.[53] She is explicitly associated with Ralph in the confirmation charter to Orford, and it is perhaps not fanciful to imagine that her influence played some part in the establishment of a convent which was not a mere appendage of Newhouse. The suggestion that at the end of the twelfth century Orford developed as an independent nunnery from a double community associated with Newhouse would explain some of the somewhat ambiguous wording of the charters.[54] Ralph's charter referred to a grant of the church of St Michael to the church of St Mary, Orford—wording which suggests that they were two different churches. Other evidence, however, indicates that there was only one church which, being conventual, was suppressed at the Dissolution.[55] The dedication to St Mary could reflect the establishment of a nunnery, with its own buildings and endowment, round the church of St Michael, as a development from a church which housed sisters attached to the abbey of Newhouse.

As at Orford, the land in Broadholme which came to provide the site for a nunnery was originally granted to Newhouse.[56] A charter of Edward II confirmed the donations made to the community of women at Broadholme, and referred to grants made by Peter de Goxhill and Agnes his wife, the founders of the abbey of Newhouse.[57]

---

[51] Colvin, *The White Canons*, 351–2. For the original document see Colvin, 'Irford Priory', 83–6. It is interesting that the word *moniales* rather than *sorores* is used in this charter. For a discussion of the implications of this terminology see pp. 147–8.

[52] Ralph was the younger brother of William d'Aubigny and Robert de Tosny, recorded as the original donors of the church to Newhouse: see Colvin, *The White Canons*, 329.

[53] *EYC*, xi, 3–4.

[54] The wording has puzzled some historians: see Colvin, *The White Canons*, 329–30.

[55] Ibid. 330.

[56] *Acta I Lincoln 1067–1185*, 105, no. 178 (1148 × 1154), and 107, no. 179 (1153 × c.1156).

[57] This is printed in *MA*, vi (ii), 919–20, calendared in *Cal. Pat. Rolls, 1317–21*, 253. For Peter of Goxhill, who died in 1166 × 1167, and his grants to Newhouse, see Colvin, *The White Canons*, 40–8. It is interesting that these grants were apparently made to Newhouse on the day when Peter's overlord, Rannulf of Bayeux, was separated from his wife, who took a vow of chastity, presumably as a prelude to entering a religious community. See *MA*, vi (ii), 865, no. 1.

Their names are probably the justification for the claim that Broadholme was an earlier foundation than Orford.[58] But it is not possible to ascertain from such a late source whether the grants were originally made to the Premonstratensian abbey and subsequently transferred to Broadholme, or whether they indicate that Broadholme housed sisters in the time of the abbey's founders. Leland records that the foundress of the community there was Agnes de Goxhill.[59] It is a possibility that she and her husband were responsible for a double community of men and women at Newhouse, with the sisters subsequently being removed to a more distant site. Broadholme is situated some thirty miles away from Newhouse, and so further away from the parent abbey than the other two dependencies of women.[60] Unlike Orford, the early charters make no reference to a church there.[61] It may be that the establishment of sisters at Broadholme occurred at a later stage in the efforts of the Premonstratensian canons to deal with their female followers. While there is no firm evidence to date the presence of sisters there, Edward II's charter contains a reference to a concession granted by 'A', abbot of Newhouse, to the sisters, concerning grants which had been made to them.[62] This seems to refer to an earlier concession, and the only abbot pre-dating the charter whose name started with that initial was Adam, who was abbot of Newhouse at the end of the twelfth century.[63] This could suggest either a separation of endowment necessitated by a move of the sisters to Broadholme, or indicate that the community already established there was being given a more separate status. Whatever the correct interpretation, it is clear that the abbey of Newhouse continued to exercise a considerable measure of control over Broadholme. In 1354 ordinances were drawn up which strengthened the authority of the prioress, but the abbot retained the right to hear confessions four times a year, and to visit the house annually for two days.[64]

The history of the nunnery of Guyzance (Brainshaugh), is even more obscure than that of the other two women's convents. The

[58] This claim is made in R. E. Cole, 'The Priory, or House of Nuns, of St Mary of Brodholme of the Order of Prémontré', *Associated Archaeol. Soc. Reports and Papers* 28 (1) (1905), 49. He cites no evidence.

[59] Leland, *Coll.*, i (i), 94; cf. Colvin, *The White Canons*, 331, where it is noted that there is no evidence for this in medieval records.

[60] For a map showing the position of the Premonstratensian communities, see Colvin, *The White Canons*, 461.

[61] There is, however, reference to a cemetery at Broadholme (as at Orford): see *Acta I Lincoln 1067–1185*, 112, no. 181 (c.1156 × 1166).

[62] *MA*, vi (ii), 919, no. 1.

[63] *HRH*, 197.

[64] This agreement was apparently at the request of Queen Isabella, and was confirmed by Pope Alexander V; see *Cal. Pap. Lett.*, vi (1404–15), 159–60.

community was little known even to contemporaries. A letter of Gervase, abbot of Prémontré, written to the abbot of Newhouse in the early thirteenth century, declared that he had never heard of the house at Guyzance.[65] The church of Guyzance was granted to the abbey of Alnwick by Richard Tyson some time before 1152.[66] Alnwick itself was founded in 1147 as a daughter of Newhouse. The founder, Eustace fitz John, was also the founder of the two Gilbertine houses of Watton and Malton.[67] The foundation date for the house of Guyzance is given in the chronicle of Alnwick as the year 1000. This chronicle survives only in a sixteenth-century transcript,[68] and the date is clearly wrong. Women seem to have been at Guyzance by 1152 × 1167.[69] It is situated some ten miles from the abbey, and the dependence of the women on the canons is reflected in deeds such as that of 1219 in which a half carucate of land in Guyzance was acknowledged to belong to the abbot, canons, and nuns, and the women were described as being in the ward of the abbot of Alnwick.[70] It is perhaps no coincidence that the house, which presents no evidence of any independent life, did not survive till the end of the Middle Ages. The community of women came to an end, and the chapel and buildings were occupied by the canons of Alnwick.[71]

At all three nunneries, charters refer to the presence of brothers as well as sisters.[72] In the case of Broadholme and Guyzance there is evidence that some, at least, were canons of the parent abbey. In the fourteenth century it was agreed that only one canon of Newhouse

[65] 'Domus illa de Ghines nobis est omnino ignota'; see C. L. Hugo, *Sacrae antiquitatis monumenta historica dogmatica diplomatica* (Stivagii, 1725), 63, no. 69; see also no. 70. This confession of ignorance was in response to a request from the abbot of Alnwick about the reception of his widowed mother as a nun. For an article on the letters of Gervase see C. R. Cheney, 'Gervase, Abbot of Prémontré: a medieval letter writer', *Medieval Texts and Studies* (Oxford, 1973), 242–76.

[66] *MA*, vi (ii), 868. See also Colvin, *The White Canons*, 332–3. For Richard Tyson see *EYC*, xii, 14–15.

[67] Colvin, *The White Canons*, 53–6.

[68] Ibid. 385.

[69] These are the dates of Abbot Patrick of Alnwick, who was said in a later source to have made an agreement concerning the advowson of the nuns of Guyzance: see *Northumberland Pleas from the Curia Regis and Assize Rolls 1198–1272*, ed. A. H. Thompson (Newcastle upon Tyne Record Series 2; 1922), 217, no. 655.

[70] *Feet of Fines, Northumberland and Durham*, ed. A. M. Oliver and C. Johnson (Newcastle upon Tyne Record Series 10; 1931 [1933]), 26, no. 54.

[71] Colvin, *The White Canons*, 333–4. Some of the communities of women attached to Premonstratensian abbeys on the continent also probably did not survive: see Fontette, 19.

[72] For references to brothers at Orford see above p. 141. Colvin argues that the brothers mentioned in Ralph d'Aubigny's charter must be canons of Newhouse (Colvin, 'Irford Priory', 84), but it seems more likely that they were resident at Orford. Reference is made to brothers at Broadholme in BL Harl. chart. 58 G. 40. For brothers at Guyzance see *Cal. Chart. Rolls 1300–1326*, 87.

would be resident at Broadholme, to help prevent the impoverish-
ment of the house.[73] The title *magister*, given to one of the canons
who stayed at Guyzance after the disappearance of the nuns,
probably reflects the office of a predecessor who was in charge of the
women.[74] At Orford, however, there is little to suggest continuing
links with the canons of Newhouse. It may be that some links were
maintained with the abbey, and that the canons acted as chaplains
for the nuns. But this is not clear, and Orford appears to have had a
measure of independence from Newhouse. The community was
apparently governed by a prioress and a prior in the thirteenth
century,[75] and land seems to have been granted to Orford without
any reference to the abbey of canons.[76] Evidence from the early
fourteenth century, however, indicates that Newhouse exercised
some financial control over the nuns through a *provisor*.[77] But this
was at a time when several nunneries were being placed under the
control of a male official, often called a *custos*, in an attempt to
improve their financial situation,[78] and may not reflect similar
control by the abbey in earlier years.

It has been suggested that other nunneries, founded independently
of any particular community of canons, subsequently became
associated with the Premonstratensian order, linked to it by an
informal bond rather than by ties of strict dependence.[79] The English
houses of Swine and Stixwould have been named as communities
which may have been associated with the order.[80] A fragment of an
obituary for Newhouse is extant and contains an obscure reference
to one Countess Agnes, who is described as the foundress of the
church of St Mary in 'Seyna'.[81] The identification of this with Swine
is not clear.[82] The Yorkshire house certainly included canons within
its community, but no evidence connects them at an early date with
the Premonstratensian order.[83] Rather it is Stainfield, founded as a

---

[73] *Cal. Pap. Lett.*, vi (1404–15), 160.

[74] Colvin, *The White Canons*, 334.

[75] *HRH*, 218 and see Appendix B.

[76] See e.g. BL Harl. chart. 54 C. 47 (*c.*1186 × *c.*1218).

[77] BL Harl. chart. 55 E. 20 (1316).

[78] In the 14th cent. bishops' registers reveal that a male official or *custos* was frequently
appointed to help with a nunnery's finances.

[79] Erens, 'Sœurs de Prémontré', 12.　　　　[80] Backmund, ii, 72–3, 90, 596.

[81] *Report on the Manuscripts of the Earl of Ancaster Preserved at Grimsthorpe* (Historical
Manuscripts Commission 66; 1907), 483.

[82] There appears to be no Countess Agnes associated with the foundation of Swine, a
community whose probable founder was Robert de Verli: see p. 69.

[83] In 1287 the Archbishop of York asked if a canon of the Premonstratensian house of
Croxton could hold office as master of Swine but there is no hint of a permanent link with the
order, and the next *magister*, apparently appointed because of the financial difficulties of the
nuns, was a canon of the Trinitarian house of Knaresborough: see pp. 110–11, n. 110.

Benedictine convent, whose prioress, together with several nuns of the house, features in the Newhouse obituary.[84] This probably reflects the links between Sybil de Valoignes and the Premonstratensian order through her marriage with Ralph d'Aubigny. It is not known whether the nuns of Stainfield ever adopted the customs and usages of the canons, but Stainfield, in association with Stixwould, was re-founded as a Premonstratensian community in 1537.[85] In England, therefore, any subsequent association of an established convent with the order remains shadowy. The history of the Premonstratensian nunneries is more clearly seen in the context of their origins as double houses, with the communities of women developing in close association with the communities of canons.

In the twelfth century the Arrouaisian canons, like the Premonstratensians, admitted women to their order.[86] In origin an eremitical foundation, there is no evidence that the layman Roger, who first sought solitude in the deserted forest near Arras, had any particular concern for the needs of religious women. Under his successor Conan, the group at Arrouaise became less solitary in emphasis, and with Abbot Gervase (1121–47), the expansion of the community clearly included the reception of women.[87] It was stated in an account of the order, written in c.1186, that this abbot admitted them freely.[88] It may be that he had a particular concern for women who were seeking to follow a religious vocation.[89] Under him the grange at Margère seems to have developed in part at least to shelter the Arrouaisian sisters. The earliest mention of their presence which can be dated occurs in 1142, but another reference implies that women were there at an earlier date.[90] Margère was not the only Arrouaisian house where sisters were present. In 1137 the Bishop of Thérouanne gave permission to Abbot Gervase to build a house for the sisters of the order, with a chapel, cemetery, garden, and farm

[84] *HMC Ancaster*, 483, 485.

[85] In 1536 the nuns of Stainfield were allowed to take over the buildings at Stixwould, and in 1537 the house was briefly re-founded as a community of Premonstratensian canonesses. See VCH *Lincs.*, ii, 147. This could be a further hint of a link between Stainfield (rather than Stixwould) and the order.

[86] For a study of the order see L. M. Milis, *L'Ordre des chanoines réguliers d'Arrouaise. Son histoire et son organisation de la fondation de l'Abbaye-Mère (vers 1090) à la fin des chapîtres annuels (1471)*, 2 vols. (Bruges, 1969). A full bibliography is given in ibid. 15–55.

[87] Ibid. 114–17.

[88] This is in the chronicle of Abbot Walter drawn up in the form of an introduction to the cartulary of Arrouaise. For a description of this important source see ibid. 62–5. The abbot's historical account is printed in *MGH Scriptores*, xv (2), 1,117–25. For a summary of the contents of the cartulary see H. Michel, 'Inventaire sommaire du cartulaire d'Arrouaise', *Bulletin de la Société des Antiquaires de Picardie* 28 (Amiens, 1917–18), 251–73.

[89] A study of the foundation of Harrold Priory in England suggests a particular interest on the part of Abbot Gervase: see pp. 150–2.

[90] Milis, 117, and n. 2.

buildings. This developed into the grange at Beaulieu.[91] By 1151 there were women at St Vorles, and when the Bishop of Cambrai confirmed the grange of Belaise to the abbot of Arrouaise, his charter referred to the sisters there.[92] There is also evidence of communities of women at several other houses, for example Hénin Liétard, St Nicholas de Pré, and St Crépin-en-Chaye.[93]

It is not clear how these communities, consisting of brothers as well as sisters, were organized. At Margère grants were made to the men and women serving God there, and the prior of the house seems to have been helped by two *prepositi*, one for the canons and one for the lay brothers.[94] Similarly at Beaurepaire, a dependent community of the abbey of Cysoing,[95] it seems that the sisters lived side by side with the canons and lay brothers. A charter dating from *c*.1200 × 1206 implies the existence of two groups under a prior and a prioress.[96] It is not possible to establish how many men were there and how many were canons. But the charter stated that two parts of a donation would go to the sisters of Beaurepaire, whilst the third was reserved for the use of the canons and brothers.[97] This, combined with the existence of two *prepositi* at Margère for canons and lay brothers, would seem to indicate the presence of a sizeable number of men.

These establishments for brothers and sisters seem to have been regarded as granges, with the unit closely dependent on the parent abbey.[98] The purpose of such cells was in part at least to provide material resources for the mother house, and the presence of the sisters there suggests that the main emphasis of their religious life may have been on practical work rather than on contemplation. It has been argued that the women should be classified as lay sisters, not nuns.[99] This view has also been propounded for the Norbertine

[91] Milis, 119. The text of this charter is printed in A. Gosse, *Histoire de l'abbaye et de l'ancienne congrégation des chanoines réguliers d'Arrouaise* (Lille, 1786), 51–2.

[92] Ibid. 170, n. 5 and 520, n. 4.

[93] Ibid. 507–8. For maps showing the position of these Arrouaisian communities see ibid., vol. ii.

[94] Ibid. 117, n. 4.

[95] For the earlier history of this abbey and its adoption of Arrouaisian customs see ibid. 146–7.

[96] *Cartulaire de l'Abbaye de Cysoing et de ses dépendances*, ed. I. de Coussemaker (Lille, 1883), 87, no. 66.

[97] Ibid. The editor suggested in his heading to this charter that the brothers referred to were at Cysoing, but the wording indicates that they were at Beaurepaire.

[98] Milis, 518–22.

[99] Gosse discussed this question, noting that some sisters seemed to be little more than servants while others were aristocratic. He could find no obvious demarcation between them, and concluded that they must have followed the same rule: see Gosse, 191–2. Compare the view in Milis, 502–6, where it is argued that a distinction was made between canonesses and lay sisters.

sisters.[100] It is true that the early sources rarely describe the women of either order as nuns, using rather the terminology *sorores* or *conversae*.[101] But in the early years of the twelfth century the distinction between a nun and a lay sister probably had little meaning. The Premonstratensian sisters seem at first to have been concerned with the care of the canons, performing tasks such as the washing and mending.[102] Practical work seems generally to have been part of the reforming programme of the twelfth century.[103] The women as well as the men were concerned with dispensing charity. A hospital was established at Prémontré,[104] and evidence from other houses of the order suggests that the sisters may have been particularly concerned with hospital care.[105]

The word *conversus* initially referred to the fact of conversion rather than the convert's status. The change of meaning, to describe a layman following a religious vocation in a subordinate capacity, probably took some time to evolve. Moreover, with women there could be no distinction between lay and clerical. It would seem premature to interpret *conversae* in the first part of the twelfth century as referring to lay sisters rather than to fully professed nuns, and so imply a demarcation which was probably a later development. By the end of the century there probably was some distinction. The two words *sorores* and *conversae* seem to refer to different categories in Innocent III's bull of 1198 forbidding the reception of women,[106] and the development seems to have been towards a more contemplative life for the sisters. In the statutes of 1236 × 1238 it was agreed that *sorores cantantes* could be received at places where they had long been accepted.[107] This description would suggest a vocation centred on the liturgy. The increasing stress on educated women who could sing the office is made clearer in a fragmentary visitation return for the English community of Guyzance. This states that no nun—*monialis*—was to be received into the community there unless she was like those at Broadholme and Orford, that is able to read and sing.[108] A similar development probably took place

[100] Fontette, 16–17.

[101] Milis, 502–3.

[102] This is made clear in the letter of the abbot of Park to St Hildegarde of Bingen: see *AASS*, Jun., i, 818.

[103] It has already been suggested that the vocation of many women may have originally been linked with hospitals and practical charity: see Chap. 3.

[104] Colvin, *The White Canons*, 309. For a general study of the practical aspects of the Premonstratensian vocation see ibid. 306–14.

[105] e.g. at Eewen and Floreffe: see Backmund, ii, 283 and Barbier, *L'Abbaye de Floreffe*, 33–5.

[106] *Reg. Inn. III*, i, 286–7, no. 198.

[107] Lefèvre, *Les Statuts réformés . . . au XIIIᵉ siècle*, 114.

[108] *Collectanea Anglo-Premonstratensia*, ed. F. A. Gasquet, 3 vols. (Camden 3rd ser., 6,

within the Arrouaisian order. Roger, Abbot of Cysoing, writing towards the end of the twelfth century, described the devotion of the devout inhabitants of Beaurepaire in terms of women who, having put aside the cares of Martha, chose the best part with Mary.[109] This would suggest a move towards a greater stress on contemplation.

It has been argued that the status of the women affects the question as to whether they formed double establishments with the canons of the order, and that the first Premonstratensian establishments should not be classed as double monasteries because the women were not fully professed nuns.[110] Similarly, it has been suggested that the women at Arrouaise were moved out to Margère and other granges and formed a third group within the order.[111] If the *sorores* and *conversae* of the early documents are not the equivalent of the later lay sisters, this lessens the force of such an argument. There clearly came to be lay women on the fringes of the order. A document of 1249 referred to the *mulieres illiteratae* who lived by the wall of the monastery of St Nicholas de Pré and looked after the animals.[112] But this cannot be taken to prove that the women within the order were all of this status. It is hard to believe that such a description would be applicable to the daughters of noble families who were entering Arrouaisian communities by the end of the twelfth century.[113] It is also not clear that all the women were moved out from Arrouaise. In c.1154 a grant was made by a Ralph de Dena when his daughter entered the community there.[114] It is possible that she lived at the priory of Margère nearby, with the wording of the grant merely indicating that granges were regarded as an integral part of the abbey. But another grant of 1199 gave one thousand eels to the sisters of Arrouaise, Margère, and Beaulieu, suggesting that they were indeed different establishments.[115] It thus seems that women were sometimes attached to an abbey, rather than always being housed at outlying granges.[116]

It may be that a development towards an increased stress on a

---

10, and 12; 1904–6), ii, 104. Colvin notes that there seems to be no evidence for the date he suggests of 1478, and that the entry refers to Guyzance rather than Broadholme: Colvin, *The White Canons*, 390.

[109] *Cartl. Cysoing*, 69, no. 52. For the biblical allusion see Chap. 3, n. 73.

[110] Fontette, 16–17.

[111] Milis, 371–4.

[112] Ibid. 249.

[113] A bull of Innocent III, seeking to restrict admission to Beaurepaire, refers to pressure from noble families to gain admittance for their female relatives: see *PL*, ccxv (1855), 1,330, no. 221. Milis notes examples of aristocratic recruits and argues for the existence of canonesses at some houses: Milis, 509 and 513.

[114] Milis, 278–9.   [115] Ibid. 506.

[116] For example there seem to have been women attached to the abbeys of Hénin Liétard, Boulogne, and Marœuil.

contemplative rather than a practical role for women resulted in lay sisters—women of lesser social status—coming to do the menial tasks, and that this development was linked with the greater separation of the sisters from the canons. In both the Premonstratensian and Arrouaisian orders the existence of enclosed nuns following a religious life centred on liturgy and contemplation may have been in part a result of the wish to isolate the women. But even at the dependent granges there seem to have been resident canons and brothers. It has been argued that only in Ireland were there double houses, and that these had evolved from native origins rather than reflecting the customs of the order.[117] Gerald of Wales talked of the scandal of the order in Ireland, with abbeys where canons and nuns lived in dangerous proximity.[118] But this may not mean that the Irish houses were unique.[119] With the status of the women in Arrouaisian houses on the Continent being by no means clear, and with evidence suggesting a close association of men and women following the religious life within the order, the argument that the Arrouaisian communities were not double houses because the women were not nuns would seem to be open to question.

The Arrouaisian canons soon found, like their Norbertine brothers, that the reception of women caused problems. From the end of the twelfth century there is evidence of attempts to limit the number of sisters. In 1197 it was agreed that there should be no more than six at Hénin Liétard.[120] In 1209 the Bishop of Arras ordered that the number of women at Beaurepaire should be limited to twelve, with the stipulation that any new recruit must be at least 50 years old.[121] This presumably was to lessen the chances of both moral lapses and the sisters being a long-term burden on the house. The stipulated numbers probably represented a drastic curtailment.[122] The discontent which led to such a measure is set out in a letter of Innocent III to the bishop. The pope declared that the house of Beaurepaire, besides having canons and brothers, was burdened with a multitude of women whom they were unable to support and whom, it is implied, they never wanted.[123] The female community was eventually suppressed in favour of the canons. Besides limiting the number of

---

[117] Milis, 371–4.

[118] *Giraldi Cambrensis*, iv, 183.

[119] Studies of the Irish church do not suggest that double houses were unique to Ireland: see J. A. Watt, *The Church in Medieval Ireland* . . . (The Gill History of Ireland 5; Dublin, 1972), partic. 21–2. See also P. J. Dunning, 'The Arroaisian Order in Medieval Ireland', *Irish Historical Studies*, 4 (1945), 297–315.

[120] Milis, 507.

[121] *Cartl. Cysoing*, 89–90, no. 68.

[122] The numbers of sisters were apparently sizeable, for example thirty to thirty-five at Margère and Beaurepaire and about forty-eight at Hénin Liétard: see Milis, 507.

[123] *Cartl. Cysoing*, 89–90, no. 68; *PL*, ccxv (1855), 1,330, no. 221.

sisters, the bishop decreed that the number of canons should be increased, and in 1255 it was ordered that canons should be substituted for sisters as the women died. The grange was to be ruled by a prior under the jurisdiction of the abbot of Cysoing.[124] No more is heard of the ladies of Beaurepaire.

A general concern about the sisters of the order is reflected in a bull of Pope Honorius III. Dated 1222, this decreed that the women within the order, scattered as they were in different houses, should be collected together in one cell.[125] This probably in part reflects the decline in the number of sisters. It also shows anxiety about the association of the sexes, and the desire to have the women more strictly segregated from the canons and brothers. In 1233 it was agreed that no woman should be received as a *conversa* without the assent of the General Chapter.[126] This implies both a reluctance to receive female converts and, at the same time, hints at pressure to do so. The Arrouaisian canons, like the Premonstratensians, had difficulties in dealing with the importunities of religious women.

From its origins the Arrouaisian order had links with England. It is possible that Conan and Heldémare, early leaders of the community at Arrouaise, had been at Waltham.[127] Two twelfth-century abbots of Arrouaise were apparently of English origin.[128] The main expansion of the order across the channel took place in the time of Abbot Gervase (1121–47). It is perhaps no coincidence that he was associated with the counts of Boulogne. Before he entered Arrouaise he had been a clerk at the court of Eustace III,[129] and a charter of the count's daughter, Matilda, the future queen of England, referred to him as a beloved friend.[130] Early contacts between the order and England seem to have come from Boulogne. In 1121 the canons of the Arrouaisian house of St Wulmer were granted the right of free crossing to England, and Missenden, the first monastery of the order in this country, was colonized from Ruisseauville in the diocese of Thérouanne.[131]

Abbot Gervase seems to have played an important part in the foundation of the main English nunnery of the Arrouaisian order, the

[124] *Cartl. Cysoing*, 183–4, no. 141.
[125] *Regesta Honorii Papae III*, ed. P. Pressutti, 2 vols. (Rome, 1895), ii, 80, no. 4042. For a similar gathering-together of the English sisters of the order of the Hospitallers see p. 156.
[126] Milis, 248.
[127] Dickinson, *Austin Canons*, 106.
[128] These were Fulbert (1151–61) and Robert (1197–1209): Milis, 126, 134.
[129] Ibid. 114–15.
[130] J. C. Dickinson, 'English Regular Canons and the Continent in the Twelfth Century', *TRHS*, 5th ser. 1 (1951), 81.
[131] Milis, 277–9.

priory of Harrold.[132] The original grant of Sampson le Fort, the lay founder, was made to Gervase as abbot of Arrouaise.[133] This may simply reflect the general dependence of daughter foundations on the mother house,[134] but some evidence suggests that Gervase had a personal interest in the development of the Bedfordshire nunnery. An account of the early history of the house is given in a charter of Robert de Braose, the stepson of Sampson le Fort. According to this, Gervase sent his sisters to Harrold. The terminology used is *sorores carnales*, implying that they were relatives of the abbot, not simply members of his flock.[135] The abbot certainly seems to have visited England, possibly for the foundation of the priory, and the church of Stevington was granted to Harrold in his presence.[136] Gervase also witnessed the foundation charter of Canons Ashby in Northampton- shire.[137] In this charter he is described as the former abbot of Arrouaise. In view of his links with Queen Matilda, it is possible that he retired to England.

It is difficult to date the foundation of Harrold Priory with any precision. Sampson le Fort was a vassal of the Earl of Huntingdon, and a charter of Malcolm of Scotland refers to alms given in the time of David, who was Earl of Huntingdon from 1113–36; this suggests a date of before 1136.[138] The abbey of Arrouaise clearly played a significant part in the foundation. According to the account of Robert de Braose, the first to receive and care for the church of Harrold was Hilbert Pélice, a canon of Arrouaise and a kinsman of Sampson.[139] Guy, the first to be given the title of prior of Harrold,

---

[132] The main sources for Harrold, including the 15th-cent. cartulary (BL Landsowne MS 391) are printed in *Records of Harrold Priory*, ed. G. H. Fowler (Beds. Hist. Rec. Soc. 17; 1935).

[133] *Records of Harrold Priory*, 16, no. 2 (i). See also the confirmation charter of Earl Simon printed in G. H. Fowler, 'Early Records of Turvey and its Neighbourhood' (Beds. Hist. Rec. Soc. 11; 1927), 48–9, no. 1B.

[134] Early grants to the monastery of Bourne, another English house of the Arrouaisian order, were also made to Gervase: see *MA*, vi (i), 370, no. 1.

[135] This charter, which relates to Harrold's struggle for independence, is enrolled in the Missenden cartulary: see *The Cartulary of Missenden Abbey*, ed. J. G. Jenkins, 3 vols. (Bucks. Rec. Soc. 2, 10, 12; 1938–62), iii, 182, no. 809. Sampson held the land by right of his wife, Albreda de Blosseville. Robert de Braose was her son by her first husband. For a family tree see Fowler, 'Turvey Records', 138, no. 2. Earl Simon's confirmation also seems to refer to the abbot's sisters stating that the grant was made to Gervase 'ad sustentacionem sororum suarum sanctimonialium' (ibid. 49, no. 1B).

[136] For the grant of the church of Stevington to the priory, and the subsequent disputes over ownership see C. R. Cheney, 'Harrold Priory: a Twelfth-Century Dispute', *Medieval Texts and Studies* (Oxford, 1973), 285–313.

[137] This charter is preserved in the Canons Ashby cartulary, BL Egerton MS 3033, fo. 1. The number of Arrouaisian witnesses would suggest early links with the order.

[138] *Reg. Regum Scot.*, i, 199, no. 139. Fowler suggests a foundation date of 1136 × 1138: see *Records of Harrold Priory*, 8.

[139] *Cartl. Missenden*, iii, 182, no. 809. Hilbert is described in the charter as a kinsman of Sampson not Gervase as the editor suggests.

also came from the mother house and may have been the brother of Abbot Gervase.[140] It is not clear when Gervase sent his sisters, but they were accompanied by a brother 'B' from Arrouaise.[141] As at the other houses of the order, brothers seem to have formed part of the community. A confirmation of Malcolm of Scotland referred to the nuns serving God and the brothers who, by the grace of God, cared for the women according to the institutions of Arrouaise.[142] Similar references to the brothers occur in other charters.[143] Sampson le Fort confirmed the grant of a virgate to the brothers and sisters of Harrold.[144] An earlier charter of Malcolm of Scotland confirmed the donation made to the prior and canons of Harrold, with the sisters being mentioned as if in a subsidiary position.[145] There is a reference to canons of Harrold in the pipe roll of 1162 × 1163,[146] and another charter of King Malcolm refers to an agreement made between the brothers of Harrold and Robert de Braose.[147] The impression given by these fragmentary references is of an important community of men which included canons.

Such male dominance would reflect the control of the mother house. In his charter Robert de Braose stated that the prior of Harrold had always been nominated by the mother house, and that he had authority over the nuns and the endowments of the community. This account of Robert de Braose is itself an indication of attempts on the part of the priory of Harrold to gain a greater degree of independence from Arrouaise. It declares that Gila and Jelita, two women who had come to England from the Arrouaisian abbeys of Margère and Boulogne, were merely guests and had no right to stay in the English house.[148] This would seem to suggest that they were regarded as subversive elements. The status of Gila and

[140] It is possible that Guy was the brother of Gervase as he is described as 'frater Gervasii', wording suggesting more than a spiritual bond: see ibid. and *Records of Harrold Priory*, 9 and 58–9. Prior Guy witnessed the foundation charter of Canons Ashby (BL Egerton MS 3033, fo. 1) together with Gervase who is described as former abbot of Arrouaise, and also a charter of Malcolm of Scotland (*Reg. Regum Scot.*, i, 238, no. 204 [1161 × 1164]).

[141] Fowler suggests a date of *c.*1145 (*Records of Harrold Priory*, 9). The charter merely indicates it was after the grant of Harrold to Arrouaise. If 'Brother B' is the same as the one acting for the nuns in 1179 × 1185 (*Cartl. Missenden*, iii, 189, no. 818) it could indicate a later date.

[142] *Reg. Regum Scot.*, i, 222, no. 180 (1160 × 1161).

[143] See *Records of Harrold Priory*, 115, no. 178 (*c.*1160 × 1180), and *Reg. Regum Scot.*, ii, 158–9, no. 56 (1165 × 1170).

[144] *Records of Harrold Priory*, 47, nos. 54 and 55. This charter mentions a croft near the ditch of the canons. It is possible this refers to canons at Harrold.

[145] *Reg. Regum Scot.*, i, 199, no. 139 (1157 × 1158). 'Confirmasse ecclesie beati Petri apostoli de Harewoldia et priori et canonicis et sororibus ibidem Deo servientibus. . . .'

[146] *PR 9 Henry II* (1162 × 1163), 20.

[147] *Reg. Regum Scot.*, i, 204, no. 149 (1157 × 1162).

[148] *Cartl. Missenden*, iii, 182, no. 809.

Jelita is not clear, for they are described in the charter as both *conversae* and *moniales*. This has been taken to indicate that the community at Harrold initially consisted of lay sisters and brothers, and that the two women may have been lay sisters at their continental houses, subsequently becoming nuns at Harrold.[149] It would seem more likely that the description *conversae* merely reflected the continental usage and does not imply a lowly status on the part of the visitors.[150] Both became prioresses of Harrold,[151] and it is probable that they were the first to hold this office; and both played a part in the struggle of the community to gain more independence. By the end of the century Harrold had broken its ties with the abbey of Arrouaise. Such a development is hardly surprising. The strict control implied in the charter of Robert de Braose was firmly stated as policy by Abbot Walter of Arrouaise in his introduction to the cartulary of the abbey. He declared that Arrouaise did not have or wish to have independent priories.[152] Such control would not have been easy to maintain. With the resignation of Gervase in 1147 the order had been ruled by a series of weak abbots.[153] A firm yet flexible organization would have been needed to achieve stable control over a daughter house situated so far away.[154] The order of Arrouaise had no such organization.[155]

The stages by which the priory of Harrold achieved independence are not clear, but it would seem that initially an attempt was made to subject the community to the abbey of Missenden.[156] This explains why Robert de Braose's charter setting out the history of Harrold's

[149] Fowler suggests that by 1158 there was a prior and canons and professed nuns rather than lay sisters at the house (*Records of Harrold Priory*, 9–10); see also Milis, 505.

In her discussion of the foundation of Harrold, Sharon Elkins argues that Harrold was unusual within the order in being founded for nuns (Elkins, *Holy Women*, 55–6). But women formed part of the Arrouaisian expansion, and it would certainly seem that both men and women originally formed the community at Harrold. I do not think it can be assumed that the number of men increased later.

[150] Early charters of the Scottish kings refer to the women of Harrold as nuns (*sanctimoniales*), e.g. *Reg. Regum Scot.*, i, 222, no. 180 (1160 × 1161); compare the terminology *sorores* used by Abbot Walter (*Cartl. Missenden*, iii, 189, no. 818).

[151] *HRH*, 213.

[152] 'Neque enim liberos vel emancipatos prioratus habemus, vel habere volumus, sed in omnibus locis nostris tam possessores quam possessiones, semper in abbatis Arroasiensis dispositione consistere et claustralium debent usibus deservire' (Milis, 292). For the chronicle, see above, n. 88.

[153] Ibid. 126–8. Fulbert was the only possible exception, and his vigour may have caused his resignation.

[154] It is interesting to compare the agreements apparently reached for Nuneaton and Higham: see pp. 125, 132.

[155] Several English houses left the order at the end of the 12th cent.: see Milis, 297. For examples of weakness in the central organization which, particularly when coupled with claims of stringent control, may have led to such desertion, see ibid., chap. 7, partic. 225–32.

[156] For the foundation of this Arrouaisian abbey in *c.*1133 see ibid. 279–80.

foundation as a dependency of Arrouaise came to be enrolled in the
Missenden cartulary. The Missenden solution is indicated in a
charter of Abbot James of Arrouaise (1170–80) in which he ceded
the churches of Harrold and Brayfield to the Buckinghamshire abbey
for an annual payment of thirty shillings.[157] No mention is made of
the women. The document simply states that the grant of the
churches was being made by Arrouaise to the brothers of Missenden
on account of their proximity. Representatives of four English houses
of the order witnessed this charter, but there is no reference to any
member of the community at Harrold. The probability is that the
priory did not wish to be taken under the direction of Missenden. An
attempt was made to persuade Abbot Walter that this abbey's claims
to control Harrold had no validity. But Abbot Walter eventually
declared that he had been misled, and ordered the sisters of Harrold
to be obedient to Missenden as they had been from the time of Abbot
James.[158] Further steps towards independence are recorded in the
Missenden cartulary. It was agreed that the nuns would pay half a
mark to Arrouaise, and the abbot of Missenden would try to get the
settlement accepted at the mother house.[159] Another document,
dated 18 October 1188, records the final settlement, apparently
obtained through the good offices of the Bishop of Lincoln, whereby
the abbot of Missenden freed the nuns and the churches of Harrold
and Brayfield from all subjection, while the nuns agreed to pay half a
mark to the Buckinghamshire abbey.[160] But enrolled in the Harrold
cartulary is a charter of Abbot Gervase, stating that the priory was in
no way subject to the abbey of Arrouaise.[161] This puzzled the
compiler of the cartulary who noted that if it had been produced in
the dispute, no money payment would have been imposed on
Harrold. Some historians have dismissed the charter as a forgery.[162]
In the absence of any original document any assessment of its
authenticity has to be tentative. The nuns certainly had a motive for
producing such a charter, and it is very difficult to reconcile its
content with the witness of Robert de Braose and the views of Abbot

---

[157] This charter is printed in ibid. app. II, 599, and can be dated *c.*1179. The church of Cold
Brayfield in Bucks. had been part of the original endowment of Harrold: see *Records of
Harrold Priory*, 16, no. 2.

[158] *Cartl. Missenden*, iii, 189, no. 818. The probable date of this letter is 1179 × 1185.

[159] Ibid., iii, 182–3, no. 810 (18 June 1188).

[160] *Records of Harrold Priory*, 57, no. 69*** from the original at Bedford County Record
Office. My interpretation of the breaking of ties between Harrold and Arrouaise differs from
that of Sharon Elkins who suggests that Arrouaise wished to divest itself of responsibility, while
the nuns wanted to maintain the link (Elkins, *Holy Women*, 121). Although Arrouaise
certainly found the women within their order caused them problems and may have preferred
the Missenden solution, I doubt if, given the autocratic ethos of the order, they would have
instigated Harrold's moves to independence.

[161] *Records of Harrold Priory*, 58, no. 70 (BL Lansdowne MS 391, fos. 18ᵛ–19).

[162] For this view see Milis, 291.

Walter about the undesirability of independent priories. But it may be significant that this was the abbot who struggled to reassert centralized control from Arrouaise.[163] There is some evidence that Abbot Gervase may have thought differently. When the house of Ruisseauville in the diocese of Thérouanne was initially planned as a cell of Arrouaise, Gervase apparently argued that it should be given the status of an abbey, as he was not sure how it could be controlled from the mother house.[164] It is conceivable that Gervase was willing to allow Harrold a measure of independence, and that the charter embodies a genuine tradition. Nevertheless, doubt remains.[165]

It is possible that Harrold was not the only community of women in England which followed the customs of Arrouaise. The early history of Wothorpe near Stamford is obscure, and there may have been a community of nuns there at an early date linked with Crowland.[166] In c.1160, however, the abbot of Bourne granted the church of Wothorpe to the nuns there. It is not clear by what right he made this grant, and although the community of women was declared to be free from paying all dues, some element of control by the abbot is implicit in the decree that the number of nuns there should not exceed thirteen. The witness list of the charter is badly mutilated, but it seems that the abbot of Stirling and a member of Harrold Priory attested it.[167] It is also possible that the Gervase named as another witness, and whose title is illegible, is the former abbot of Arrouaise. Bourne was an early foundation,[168] and it is possible that the establishment of nuns at Wothorpe involved the settlement of women linked with the Arrouaisian abbey. There seems to be no further evidence of links between Wothorpe and the order of Arrouaise, although it is interesting that two early historians of the nunnery thought that it was Augustinian.[169] Several monasteries were linked with Arrouaise for a short period of their history, with the links subsequently being broken.[170] It is possible that two houses

---

[163] Ibid. 129–33, 232–5.

[164] Ibid. 143.

[165] The charter seems to refer to the sisters of Gervase as members of Harrold, a claim made in other sources (see p. 151), and so a possible indication of the charter being genuine. But the phrase 'sororibus meis sanctimonialibus' is ambiguous, and could just refer to members of his community. See also n. 135.

[166] For this possibility, and the unreliability of the source which suggests it, see p. 65.

[167] *The Registrum Antiquissimum of the Cathedral Church of Lincoln*, ed. C. W. Foster and K. Major, 10 vols. (Linc. Rec. Soc. 27–9, 32, 34, 41, 42, 46, 51, 62, 67; 1931–73), ii, 39, no. 347. Stirling was later known as Cambuskenneth.

[168] It was founded in 1138: see KH, 138 and 149.

[169] *The History and Antiquities of Northamptonshire, Compiled from the Manuscript Collections of John Bridges*, ed. P. Whalley, 2 vols. (Oxford, 1791), ii, 593. See also J. Drakard, *The History of Stamford* (Stamford, 1822), 591.

[170] e.g. Warter in Yorkshire, Arbury in Warwickshire, and possibly St James's, Northampton. See Milis, 281–2, 285–6, and 293, n. 4.

of English sisters, not just one, were lost to the abbey of Arrouaise in the course of the twelfth century.

The women attached to the order of St John of Jerusalem also followed the Augustinian rule. The history of these sisters in England reflects developments similar to those experienced by the Premonstratensian and Arrouaisian *sorores*. At first apparently welcomed to the order, they seemed originally to have followed a practical vocation, caring for travellers and for the sick.[171] But by the end of the twelfth century measures were taken to remove them from the houses of brothers and to place them in a separate community. A charter of Henry II, dating from *c.*1186 × 1188, ordered that Buckland in Somerset should be granted to the Hospitallers for the purpose of housing all the sisters of the order in one place.[172] The women had apparently previously been attached in twos and threes to different preceptories.[173] The small number of them associated with the men at these houses would suggest that their function was still in part to help with practical charity. The establishment of the sisters in one community may have modified their vocation. Although they are frequently described as sisters (*sorores*)[174] the word nun is sometimes used, and some of the recruits were evidently aristocratic.[175]

The move did not entirely separate them from the brothers of the order, for there are references to both brothers and sisters at Buckland.[176] Some evidence suggests that husband and wife may sometimes have entered the community together.[177] But, as with other orders of canons, there clearly came to be discord between the

[171] For the development of the order, and the association of the convent of Aconbury with the Hospitallers, see pp. 50–3.

[172] This charter is transcribed in the 15th-cent. cartulary of Buckland, preserved in the Taunton Record Office. It is calendared in *Cartulary of Buckland Priory in the County of Somerset*, ed. F. W. Weaver (Somerset Rec. Soc. 25; 1909), 5–6, no. 7. The motive of placing the sisters together in one community is also stressed in the episcopal charters ratifying the grant: see ibid. 7–8, no. 11, and 8–9, no. 12. For a history of Buckland see VCH *Somerset*, ii, 148–50, and T. Hugo, *The Medieval Nunneries of the County of Somerset* (London, 1867) (Buckland), 1–248.

[173] A list of these preceptories and the names of the women are given in the account written by a Brother John Stillingflete in 1434: see VCH *Somerset*, ii, 148. A manuscript of this, written on paper in a 16th cent. hand, is preserved in the College of Arms (MS L 17, fos. 141–62). See M. Gervers, 'A History of the Cartulary of the Order of the Hospital of St John of Jerusalem in England (BM Cott. MS Nero E VI)', *Scriptorium* 28 (1974), 266–7 and n. 25.

[174] e.g. in the early 13th-cent. grants to the house: see *Cal. Pat. Rolls 1225–32*, 266 (1229), and *Cal. Chart. Rolls 1226–57*, 52 (1227).

[175] Agnes, daughter of William, Earl of Arundel, became a nun—*sanctimonialis*—there: see *Cal. Close Rolls 1231–34*, 165, and *Cal. Lib. Rolls 1226–40*, 205 (1233).

[176] *Cal. Pat. Rolls 1232–47*, 91 (1235).

[177] *Cartl. Buckland*, 161, no. 291. See also *Curia Regis Rolls*, xi, 175–6, no. 870, where a case is recorded of a woman apparently forced to enter Buckland with her husband, and who subsequently claimed that she was not professed (1223).

men and the women. Ordinances of Roger de Vere, prior of the order in England, in the second half of the thirteenth century, refer to trouble between the two groups.[178] It was agreed that the sisters were to have a brother as steward, and maintenance to provide for a secular priest. The prioress was to have some authority over the steward, but he could only be dismissed from his office with the assent of the prior. These ordinances probably represent a restriction on the degree of involvement of the brothers, with a corresponding recognition of the role of the prioress. Fourteenth-century evidence, however, reveals continuing discontent, with the brothers of the order unhappy at a situation where they had to provide help for the sisters at their expense, while gaining nothing but trouble in return.[179] According to this account, the community of sisters at Buckland numbered fifty. As with the other orders there was probably pressure to accept women. Some statutes of 1262 imply the rescinding of an earlier decree against the reception of women into the order because of the financial benefits linked with their entry.[180] Eventually, however, in 1500, it was decided to close the preceptory of brothers at Buckland,[181] and in England, links between women following a religious vocation and the order of St John of Jerusalem were brought to an end.

Evidence from the Hospitallers, therefore, as well as from the Arrouaisian and the Premonstratensian canons, suggests that the association of women with the new orders did not provide stability. The religious fervour of the twelfth century and its manifestation in the new orders of the time must have been a factor behind the foundation of several of the nunneries founded after the Conquest. Many were linked with masculine communities and formed double houses. Yet the association of women wishing to follow a religious vocation with the canonical orders did not provide a permanent solution to the problems of providing support for the nunneries. Support of a different kind was also sought from both lay and episcopal patrons.

[178] *Cartl. Buckland*, 14–16, nos. 19 and 20. The dating of these priors is not easy, as the list given in the Hospitaller cartulary, BL Cotton MS Nero E. vi (ii), fo. 467ᵛ, is not accurate. Roger occurred in 1265 and 1272: see *The Cartulary of the Knights of St John of Jerusalem in England. Secunda Camera Essex*, ed. M. Gervers (Records of Social and Economic Hist., N.S. 6; London, 1982), 278–9, no. 489, and 518, no. 888. It is stated in the list that Roger died in 1270: see ibid. 571, no. 961.

[179] This account of Buckland is printed in *The Knights Hospitallers in England, being the Report of Prior Philip de Thame to the Grand Master Elyan de Villanova for AD 1338*, ed. L. Larking (Camden Soc., 65; 1857), 19–20.

[180] E. J. King, *The Rule, Statutes, and Customs of the Hospitallers 1099–1310* (London, 1934), 59, no. 22.

[181] VCH *Somerset*, ii, 149–50.

III
Founders and Patrons

9 The Role of Lay Founders and Patrons in the Foundation of the Nunneries

LAY founders clearly played a vital role in the establishment of religious communities. For monasteries to survive, sufficient endowments had to be granted to provide an economic base. But the relationship between a founding family and a religious house was more than an economic transaction. Studies of individual monasteries have shown how they could be the favoured object of the benevolence of a powerful patron, and that the importance of the interplay of family and feudal relationships in the establishment and growth of such communities cannot be overestimated.[1] The Norman lords who came over to England at the Conquest were already founders and patrons of monasteries. Houses such as Holy Trinité de Caen, Almenèches, Saint-Amand de Rouen in Normandy, and later Fontevrault on the border of Poitou and Anjou, continued to provide for the Norman aristocracy well into the twelfth century, attracting sizeable gifts and receiving noble postulants. In England, the Anglo-Saxon foundations such as Shaftesbury, Wilton, and Barking, established in the seventh to the ninth centuries by kings, queens, and saints,[2] enjoyed the patronage of the new as well as the old nobility and received their ladies into the religious life.

For many post-Conquest English foundations the situation was different. As has been suggested in the first part of this book, several convents probably developed slowly from a nucleus formed round an anchoress, or propagated from another religious institution. A few, particularly the nunneries of the order of Fontevrault, were founded by the king and others of high rank, and came, like the older foundations, to be supported by lords and to provide a home for aristocratic ladies desiring to follow a religious life. The founding and support of such English houses can be seen as part of the movement whereby Norman families became established in England and severed links with their Continental patrimonies. But many nunneries established in the twelfth century apparently lacked a noble founder or wealthy patron. A study of their problems has to be

[1] D. Baker, 'Patronage in the Early Twelfth-Century Church: Walter Espec, Kirkham and Rievaulx', in Traditio-Krisis-Renovatio aus Theologischer sicht. Festschrift Winifried Zeller (Marburg, 1976), 98.
[2] Amesbury, Minster in Sheppey, and Wherwell were founded by royal widows, Polesworth, Romsey, Shaftesbury, and Winchester by kings and queens. Even those with ecclesiastical founders (Barking and Chatteris) were established by no less than a saint and a bishop (KH, 104, 261, 267, 263, 264, 265, 268, 256, 257).

set against the background of the continuing patronage by the aristocracy of the pre-Conquest English foundations and the great Norman houses.

The establishment of a monastery was a slow and complex process, although foundation charters, in recording the grant of land and other initial endowments, often conceal this and present an over-simplification of the foundation process.[3] Buildings took time to erect, and the dedication of the church, the symbolical expression of the new community, could take place several years after the first steps towards founding the house.[4] If the foundation of a religious house cannot be seen as a single event, the concept of a single founder can also be misleading. There are examples where all the evidence suggests that a particular individual, or husband and wife acting together, took the initiative and provided the lands and endowment for the setting-up of a new religious community. Rannulf de Glanville was in a very real sense the founder of Leiston. Besides granting the abbey site and sufficient lands to give a base for economic survival, he apparently helped to choose the abbot who was to head the new community.[5] Examples of similar vigorous and decisive acts of foundation also exist for the nunneries. Lacock Abbey in Wiltshire can be seen as the creation of Ela, Countess of Salisbury, while Lillechurch, or Higham as it came to be called, was founded in Kent by King Stephen and his Queen Matilda.[6] Many nunneries, however, have no clear founder.[7] This can in part be explained by the general lack of sources for the early history of women's convents, as well as possibly reflecting the slow growth of a community from diverse origins. In some cases it may also indicate the probability that the nunneries were corporate foundations, with several families contributing to their initial endowment. This was true of the Gilbertine house of Alvingham and possibly also of Sixhills, and Sempringham itself probably only survived because of the endowments of several benefactors.[8] Another example may well be Fosse, where tradition records that it was founded by local inhabitants.[9] To search for a single founder may distort the reality of a more corporate initiative.

---

[3] Galbraith, 'Foundation Charters', 205–22. Detailed research into particular houses further illustrates the complexity of the foundation process; e.g. for Leiston see *Leiston Abbey Cartulary and Butley Priory Charters*, ed. R. Mortimer (Suffolk Rec. Soc.; 1979).

[4] Binns, *Dedications*, 9–10.

[5] *Cartl. Leiston*, 2–3.

[6] For the foundation of Lacock and Higham see pp. 169–70 and 166 of this chapter.

[7] The founders of the nunneries are listed in Appendix A. At least eighteen have unknown or uncertain founders.

[8] For Alvingham see Golding, 'Alvingham and Bullington', 7-11 and for Sempringham see VCH *Lincs.*, ii, 181.

[9] KH, 273.

Combined action to establish a nunnery may have been necessitated in part by the social and economic status of many of the founders, for the majority of them seem to have been of middle rank. It would seem that over seventy of the nunneries founded after the Conquest were established by local lords who held neither title nor high office.[10] In Yorkshire, William de Percy was the only representative of the baronial class to feature in the list of founders of the women's convents. The others, like William de Arches and his family, though important men locally, were of lesser rank.[11] It is not possible, however, to give a detailed and accurate analysis of the social standing of the founders of the English nunneries established after the Conquest. Apart from the difficulties of assessing their status, there is often not the evidence to establish with any certainty who was the founder. The description of a man or woman as the *fundator* of a religious community is ambiguous. The word is sometimes used for a later patron. The obituary list for the priory of Wintney in Hampshire describes three different people, all of whom lived at different times, as *fundator*.[12] One, a Geoffrey fitz Peter, who lived early in the second half of the twelfth century, was probably the original founder in the sense that he granted the site and some of the initial endowments of the community.[13] Richard de Heriard, who lived in the early thirteenth century, is described as benefactor and founder of the stone church, and Richard Holte and his wife Christine, who seem to have lived in the fifteenth century, are also called founders.[14] A lack of any clear distinction between founder and patron is not surprising, for a founder of a new community would become its patron in the sense of having particular responsibilities and rights in relation to the nunnery. Moreover, in England these duties and benefits, as other aspects of feudal lordship, generally passed to the founder's heirs or his feudal lord.[15] Such possibilities of confusion increase the difficulties of identifying the founder.

A further problem in the way of discovering the founder of a new religious community and assessing his role, is the tendency for later

---

[10] See Appendix A.

[11] Burton, *Yorks. Nunneries*, 24.

[12] BL Cotton MS Claud. D. iii, fos. 146ᵛ, 147ᵛ, 157ᵛ, printed in Trokelowe, *Annales*, 387, 391.

[13] For this Geoffrey fitz Peter see Chap. 6, n. 95. He was also described as the founder of Wintney in a response to an enquiry of 1295: see *Reg. Pontissara*, ii, 509.

[14] For Richard de Heriard see *Cal. Chart. Rolls 1327–41*, 393, 397. For Richard Holte and Christina see VCH *Hants.*, ii, 503. Similarly Roger IV de Tosny is described in a charter as the founder of Flamstead when the nunnery was probably established by his grandfather see p. 28.

[15] The role of patrons in the 13th cent. is studied in Wood, *Patrons*; see particularly Chap. II.

tradition to elevate to this position a person whose rank or prestige had caused their help to be sought. The most obvious candidate for such elevation was the king.[16] Indeed, there are occasions when the monarch seems to have deliberately sought the description of founder.[17] Broomhall in Berkshire was said to have been founded by King John, but a pipe roll entry shows that the nuns were already there in 1157 × 1158.[18] At Armathwaite in Cumberland, a long and involved charter stated that the nunnery had been founded by Willliam Rufus. The extensive grants and privileges, apparently donated by royal munificence, invite scepticism, and there is little doubt that it is a forgery.[19] William the Conqueror was described as the founder of Hinchingbrooke nunnery.[20] This may reflect a confusion with William of Scotland, as this king apparently granted the site to the nuns there, but other charters indicate that the community had been founded earlier at a different site.[21] The suggestion that Empress Matilda was the foundress of the priory of Kington in Wiltshire also seems to have little basis.[22] It is possible that she issued a confirmation charter or made a grant,[23] but the earliest benefactor who appears to have donated the site was Robert, son of Wayfer of Brinton. Both he and Adam of Brinton, probably his brother, seem to have made important initial grants to the community.[24] Claims of a royal founder may conceal the more important or earlier donations of a less prestigious benefactor.

[16] For the role of kings as founders and patrons of monasteries see Hallam, 'Monastic Patronage', and idem 'Henry II'.

[17] Henry I was 'founder' of several small houses, even though his donations to them may not have been large; see C. N. L. Brooke, 'Princes and Kings as Patrons of Monasteries, Normandy and England', in *II Monachesimo e la Riforma Ecclesiastica 1049–1122* (Miscellanea del Centro di Studi Medievali, 6, Milan, 1971), 125–44.

[18] *PR 2–4 Henry II*, 151. An enquiry at the time of the Suppression stated that the house was founded by the king's ancestors: see VCH *Berks.*, ii, 81. John did make grants to the nuns (*Rot. Chart.*, 48b).

[19] *Cal. Pat. Rolls 1476–85*, 208 (1480), printed in *MA*, iii, 271, no. 1.

[20] *Valor Eccl.*, iv, 256. This is followed in *MA*, iv, 388 and in *Joannis Lelandi antiquarii de rebus Britannicis Collectanea.*, ed. T. Hearne, 6 vols. (London, 1770), i (i), 48.

[21] According to a confirmation charter of Bishop Hugh of Lincoln, William of Scotland had granted the site to the nuns: *Acta IV. Lincoln 1186–1206*, 52–3, no. 72. See also *Reg. Regum Scot.*, ii, 474, no. 539 (1165 × 1174). Other charters show that Roger de Cundy, steward of Roger de Mowbray, was an important early benefactor if not the founder of the original community at Eltisley: see *Charters of the Honour of Mowbray 1107–91*, ed. D. E. Greenway (London, 1972), 123–4, nos. 168–9. A change of site could result in a community having more than one 'founder'.

[22] *MA*, iv, 397. The claim appears to involve hearsay and be based on the views of John Aubrey who had access to a cartulary of the house which is now lost.

[23] The empress did found the Cistercian house of Loxwell (Stanley) in Wiltshire, and also helped the hermits of Red Moor (KH, 125 and 124).

[24] For the grants of Robert and Adam see *MA*, iv, 398–400, nos. 10, 13 and 3. These suggest Robert was the founder. Adam is described as son of Wayfer in the late 15th-cent. obituary of the house, Cambridge University Lib. MS Dd viii 2, art. 1. This is printed in part in J. E. Jackson, 'Kington St Michael', *Wilts. Archaeol. Magazine* 4 (1858), 60–7.

Similarly, the confirmation of an overlord could lead to subsequent claims that he was the founder. For example, the statement that Conan, Earl of Richmond, founded the convent of Rowney in Hertfordshire in the second half of the twelfth century has to be treated with caution. Evidence that he established Rowney comes from the patent roll of 1459. According to this, Conan granted land to the yearly value of 10 marks—a small sum for a foundation.[25] Similarly, there is little to support the tradition that the Earl of Chester was the original founder of St Mary's nunnery, Chester.[26] The charter, preserved on the patent rolls, which refers to the foundation of the nunnery, appears to be merely a confirmation of crofts given by Hugh, son of Oliver, a citizen of Chester. The purpose of these gifts was to build a church, suggesting Hugh was the founder.[27] Earl Rannulf made some small grants to the nuns, as did several of his successors who subsequently exercised rights of patronage over the community,[28] but the description of him as founder probably reflects his prestige as overlord of Chester rather than any major grant or action on his part. Certainly the poverty and difficulties of the nuns of Chester contrasts with the wealth of the house of Savigniac monks at Basingwerk, an undisputed foundation of the earl.[29]

Not surprisingly, there appears to be some correlation between the status of the founder, when he is known, and the size of the endowment provided for the new foundation. The priory of Nuneaton in Warwickshire was founded by Robert, Earl of Leicester and his countess Amicia. The early endowment included the manor of Eton, and land paying £25 of rent in Kintbury. His daughter Isabel and her son also made sizeable grants of two carucates of land and pasture for 300 sheep.[30] Figures given in the taxation returns for Pope Nicholas IV in 1291 indicate that the income of the house was

---

[25] *Cal. Pat. Rolls 1452–61*, 503–4. It is clear that Conan made grants to Rowney: see a charter transcribed in PRO, E132/2/19. For the possibility that the origin of Rowney may have been linked with the grant of a hermitage by the earl see pp. 27–8. This would give further justification for the claim he was the community's 'founder', but the identification of the hermitage with the community at Rowney is not clear.

[26] It is implied he is founder in KH, 257 and he is called founder in Power, 686, and this is the view of Sharon Elkins: see Elkins, *Holy Women*, 72, although she notes that he may have been restoring an earlier settlement. Other historians have suggested that he was not really the founder: see VCH *Cheshire*, iii, 146 and W. F. Irvine, 'Notes on the History of St Mary's Nunnery Chester', *Journal of the Chester and North Wales Archit., Archaeol. and Hist. Soc.*, N.S. 13 (1906), 67–109, esp. 71.

[27] *MA*, iv, 313–14, no. 1; calendared *Cal. Pat. Rolls 1399–1401*, 297.

[28] *Cal. Pat. Rolls 1399–1401*, 297–303. For the grant of the nunnery to Clerkenwell by the Earl of Chester see p. 215.

[29] KH, 115. For the poverty of the nuns of Chester and their statement in a letter to Queen Eleanor (*c.*1253) that they were reduced to begging for food, see Power, 172.

[30] *Cal. Docs. France*, 376–7, no. 1,062.

in excess of £105, and at the Dissolution the house was valued at over £253.[31] By contrast, Pinley in the same county, founded by Robert de Pillarton, a tenant of the Earl of Warwick, was apparently initially only given the site of the house in Pinley.[32] It has been calculated that in 1291 the temporal income of the house was under £4.[33] Other nunneries were apparently poverty-stricken at their origins. At Haliwell in London, an eloquent letter from Bishop Gilbert Foliot asked the Bishop of Lincoln to confirm the grant of a church to the nunnery, and described the site and endowments of the house as so restricted that they were more suitable for a cemetery than to provide for the community's sustenance.[34] The poverty of the nunneries generally is marked. In Yorkshire, the *Valor Ecclesiasticus* indicates that at the Dissolution all but one of the nunneries were valued at below £100 per annum, and all but seven below £40.[35]

For those nunneries founded in England after the Conquest, only three have strong claims to a royal founder. Lillechurch in Kent was established by King Stephen and Matilda of Boulogne to provide a suitable community for their daughter, Mary.[36] She was first placed in the nunnery of Stratford, Middlesex, together with other nuns from her former home of Saint Sulpice. But this placement of the princess clearly caused discord, and the transfer of grants from Stratford to a new community at Lillechurch can be traced in the charters.[37] Confirmation was granted by Mary's brother William, as well as by the king and queen, and some of the charters reflect the princess's importance by stating that the grants were made to her.[38] The initiative of her parents, particularly the queen, and their personal motive for founding Lillechurch are clear.[39]

[31] VCH *Warwicks.*, ii, 68; KH, 104.

[32] *MA*, iv, 115, no. 1.

[33] KH, 275. At the Dissolution Pinley's net income was £23 (ibid. 272). At the end of the 12th cent. an indulgence granted by Archbishop Hubert to visitors to the priory referred to the nuns' poverty: see *English Episcopal Acta III Canterbury 1193–1205*, ed. C. R. Cheney and E. John (London, 1986), 228–9, no. 575.

[34] *Foliot Letters and Charters*, 245, no. 172.

[35] Burton, *Yorks. Nunneries*, 11–17.

[36] Mary subsequently became abbess of Romsey, a pre-Conquest foundation: see *HRH*, 219.

[37] For the establishment of Lillechurch as a daughter house of St Sulpice see p. 131. Lillechurch had previously been held by the monks of St John Colchester. Matilda granted East Donyland to them in exchange: see *Reg. Regum*, iii, 79–80, no. 221 (1148 × 1152). There was still some dispute over ownership: see the settlement negotiated by Gilbert Foliot in *c.*1179 × 1180 (SJC archives MS D 46.138, printed in *Foliot Letters and Charters*, 409, no. 360).

[38] William's confirmation is preserved in SJC archives MS D 46.6, printed in *MA*, iv, 382, no. 3. The confirmation charter of Bishop Walter of Rochester records the release of Lillechurch by Abbot Hugh of Colchester to Mary and the nuns (SJC archives MS D 46.21).

[39] Another charter of Abbot Hugh referred to the transfer of land at the request of Matilda 'gratia filiae suae Marie' (SJC archives MS D 46.22; printed in *MA*, iv, 382, no. 4).

Amesbury in Wiltshire, though a re-foundation of an existing pre-Conquest community, was in a large measure the creation of Henry II. The papal bull issued at the foundation emphasized the desire of the king to institute the order of Fontevrault, and to increase the size of the nunnery and its endowments.[40] The pipe rolls record an expenditure of some £881. Although it has been suggested that this was not a large amount for a major foundation,[41] it still represents a sizeable amount to be spent on a convent of women. If one of the royal post-Conquest foundations was to provide a suitable religious community for a royal princess, and the other was a re-foundation, the third—the foundation of the abbey of Burnham in Buckinghamshire by Richard, King of the Romans, Earl of Cornwall, and brother to King Henry III—seems to have benefited little from its illustrious founder. Established in 1266, Richard granted the community of Augustinian canonesses only a small endowment, and the earl and his family seem to have shown the community far less interest and favour than their foundation of Cistercian monks at Hailes.[42]

A larger group of nunneries were founded by wealthy widows of aristocratic status, sometimes with royal support. The earliest was Elstow in Bedfordshire, established by Judith, niece of the Conqueror and widow of Waltheof, Earl of Huntingdon, who was executed in 1076. She may have founded the nunnery as an act of reparation for the betrayal of her husband.[43] It was a wealthy house and an abbey.[44] Another major foundation was the abbey of Godstow. The history of this house illustrates the difficulties of deciding who has the most valid claim to be described as founder, even where the foundation process is relatively well documented. The initial impetus was given by Edith, widow of William Lancelene.[45] She apparently lived a solitary life for some time before a vision guided her to

[40] *Cal. Docs. France*, 378–9, no. 1,069. For the refoundation of Amesbury as a priory of the order of Fontevrault see p. 123.

[41] Hallam, 'Monastic Patronage', 105–6.

[42] For Earl Richard see *Complete Peerage*, iii, 430–2, and for Burnham see VCH *Bucks.*, i, 382–4. Earl Richard was buried at Hailes and this monastery was worth over £120 in 1291, and £357 at the Dissolution (KH, 120, 113). Burnham was assessed at over £63 in 1291, and £51 in 1535 (KH, 279, 278).

[43] S. R. Wigram, *Chronicles of the Abbey of Elstow . . . with Some Notes of the Architecture of the Church by M. J. C. Buckley* (Oxford, 1885), 1. See also VCH *Beds.*, i, 353. The saga of his imprisonment and execution is described by Orderic Vitalis: see *Orderic Vitalis*, ii, 320–3.

[44] It has been calculated that by 1160 Elstow held over forty-eight properties (I am grateful to Sister Maura O'Carroll, who is working on Elstow, for this information). At the Dissolution its value of £284 made it one of the wealthiest of the women's houses.

[45] An account of Edith and her actions in originating the community of Godstow is preserved in the cartulary of the house: see the Latin version (PRO, E164/20, fo. 1) and the English translation (*Cartl. Godstow*, 26–7). Apparently she was a widow of status and enjoyed the support of Henry I.

found a community at Godstow. A confirmation charter of Bishop Alexander of Lincoln, probably issued at the time of the dedication of the church in 1138, underlined the importance of her role. It stated that the nunnery was founded through her generosity and under her direction and that she built the church and helped to gather the endowments.[46] She entered the community and ruled it as its head for many years.[47] The site of Godstow was held by John de St John, a local lord. He witnessed a charter of the bishop granting ecclesiastical immunities to the new foundation, and he made small grants of a meadow and a mill in Wolvercote.[48] It is not clear whether he gave the site or whether it was purchased from him by Edith. The editors of the *Monasticon* argued that as the lord of the site, he, rather than Edith, must be regarded as the founder.[49] His charter confirming the land at Godstow to the nuns suggests that he was regarded as having some rights over the house, for he agreed that after Edith's death the new head (*gubernatrix*) was to be a member of the community.[50] But he was soon overshadowed by members of the St Valéry family, and subsequently by Henry II who became patron of the abbey.[51] Reginald de St Valéry appears to have been overlord of the site. He made donations to Godstow at its foundation and also confirmed the initial grant of land there.[52] The confirmation charter of Bishop Alexander shows that powerful benefactors such as King Stephen and his family made sizeable grants to the nuns of Godstow when the church was dedicated.[53] The abbey was one of the wealthiest of the post-Conquest foundations.[54] To describe John de St John as the founder of this community would seem to inflate his importance.[55]

Whatever grants were made by kings and lay lords such as John de St John and Reginald de St Valéry, it is clear that the main initiative for the foundation of Godstow, as at Elstow, came from a widow of

---

[46] 'Sub providentia et regimine memorabilis matrone deo devote Edithe que loci illius ecclesiam proprio sumptu et labore collatisque fidelium elemosinis in honorem sancte dei genitricis virginis Marie et beati Iohannis Baptiste a primo lapide prudenter edificavit, ac deo co-operante ad finem usque perduxit', *Acta I Lincoln 1067–1185*, 20, no. 33.

[47] The exact number of years is in doubt: see *HRH*, 211–12.

[48] *Acta I Lincoln 1067–1185*, 23, no. 34 and 21, no. 33.

[49] *MA*, iv, 357–8 and note.

[50] PRO E164/20, fo. 1, printed in *MA*, iv, 363, no. 4; *Cartl. Godstow*, 27, no. 3.

[51] For the family see G. H. Fowler, 'De St Walery', *The Genealogist*, N.S. 30 (London, 1914), 1–17. John de St John seems to have been enfeoffed with St Valéry lands in *c*.1143, and was succeeded by Reginald in *c*.1150: see *Foliot Letters and Charters*, 512.

[52] *Acta I Lincoln 1067–1185*, 21, no. 33.

[53] Ibid.

[54] Its value was estimated at nearly £200 in 1291 and £275 in *c*.1535 (KH, 259, 253).

[55] It is pointed out in VCH *Oxon.*, ii, 72 that King Stephen's grants seem to have been considerably more valuable than those of John de St John.

noble rank. At least four other houses of nuns were established by widowed ladies of aristocratic status. The house of Stixwould in Lincolnshire was founded c.1139 × 1142 by Lucy, dowager Countess of Chester, the widow of Ivo de Taillebois, Roger fitz Gerold, and Rannulf I, Earl of Chester.[56] After the latter's death in c.1129, she paid five hundred marks to be allowed to remain unmarried for five years.[57] A charter of Lucy, addressed to her sons, granted all her land in Stixwould, Thorp, and Honington to the nuns. There is no explicit claim that she is the foundress, but the charter is witnessed by the priors of two religious houses, and in an interesting phrase the countess asked her sons to protect the nunnery, 'nam utillimum erit mihi et vobis ante Deum'.[58] This may refer to general spiritual benefits resulting from the prayers of the nuns, but, together with Lucy's action to avoid another husband, could indicate that she, like Edith, became a nun at her own foundation. A prioress of Stixwould called Lucy is mentioned in charters transcribed in the cartulary and dated 1160 and 1168.[59] The countess's first husband died c.1094,[60] and if she married young it is just possible, though unlikely, that she might still have been alive at that date. But a prioress with the initial 'L' also occurs as late as 1184.[61] If this also refers to a Lucy, it would clearly overstretch the possible longevity of the countess. There are interesting similarities with Godstow, where the foundress seems to have lived to a remarkable age, and where a second Edith apparently succeeded her as head of the community.[62] The account of the early history of the house stated that two daughters entered Godstow and both became prioresses.[63] It is a possibility, though this is mere speculation, that a daughter of the dowager Countess Lucy, similarly named, also entered Stixwould.[64]

The abbey of Lacock in Wiltshire, founded in 1229, was

[56] *Complete Peerage*, vii, 743–6, app. J. This article discusses the difficult question of Lucy's parentage. For the background history of Stixwould see VCH *Lincs.*, ii, 146–9.

[57] *PR 31 Henry I*, 110.

[58] This charter is transcribed in the Stixwould cartulary, BL Addit. MS 46,701, fo. 1. For a description of the cartulary see Davis, *Med. Cartls.*, 106, no. 931.

[59] BL Addit. MS 46,701, fos. 1ᵛ and 104.

[60] *Complete Peerage*, vii, 743.

[61] *HRH*, 220.

[62] Ibid. 211–12. A confirmation that there were two Ediths is given in a papal decretal of 1158 × 1181: *Papal Decretals Relating to the Diocese of Lincoln in the Twelfth Century*, ed. W. Holtzmann and E. Kemp (Linc. Rec. Soc. 47; 1954), 34–5, no. 14. The title 'abbess' means this must refer to Godstow.

[63] *Cartl. Godstow*, 27. The names given for these daughters are Emma and Hawise, not Edith. They may have held the office of prioress while their mother was abbess. For the ambiguities of the initial status of Godstow, although it clearly became an abbey, see p. 182.

[64] For other examples where the name of an early prioress is the same as that of the foundress see p. 180.

established by a widow who, without doubt, subsequently entered the convent and became abbess.[65] Born at Amesbury, Ela, Countess of Salisbury, was engaged as a young girl to William Longespée, an illegitimate son of Henry II.[66] It is possible that she began to plan her foundation shortly after her husband's death in 1226, but delayed its completion as her son was still a minor.[67] In 1229 a charter of Ela recorded the grant of her manor and the advowson of the church of Lacock to found a nunnery.[68] Although there was some difficulty in obtaining the whole advowson, Lacock was fortunate in having a secure endowment. The manor and vill provided a nucleus, with the manor of Hatherop being added soon after.[69] Ela may always have intended to enter the house. This is suggested by the fact that no abbess seems to have been appointed, and the community was initially headed by a prioress.[70] But a phrase in two of the charters recording the foundation process suggests that she was keeping her options open. In an agreement between Ela and her son drawn up on 22 July 1236, William confirmed the grant of the manor of Chitterne for her support for the rest of her life whether or not she became a nun.[71] This proviso is echoed in another charter which records the donation of the manor to the nuns,[72] although in a previous document William promised to grant Chitterne to Lacock to provide for his mother, who by then would have taken the religious habit.[73] By 1238, however, the countess had clearly committed herself to a renunciation of the world, for an entry on the liberate rolls refers to her as the former countess, now a nun.[74] A year later she was abbess elect,[75] and she held office for some eighteen years before resigning after designating her successor. She died in 1261 when she was said to be 74 years old,[76] and so she, like Edith and possibly Countess

---

[65] For Lacock see the article by Helena Chew in VCH *Wilts.*, iii, 303–16.

[66] *Complete Peerage*, xi, 379–82.

[67] This is suggested in VCH *Wilts.*, iii, 303; see also W. G. Clark-Maxwell, 'The Earliest Charters of the Abbey of Lacock', *Wilts. Archaeol. Magazine* 35 (1907–8), 191. He calculates that William was 18 in 1229.

[68] PRO E40/9350, calendared in *Lacock Abbey Charters*, ed. K. H. Rogers (Wilts. Rec. Soc. 34; Devizes, 1979), 10, no. 1 and printed, Clark-Maxwell, 'Earliest Charts.', 200–1, no. 1.

[69] Clark-Maxwell, 'Earliest Charts.', 202, no. 5; calendared in *Lacock Charts.*, 11, no. 6 (1231 × 1232).

[70] She was called Wymarca and her name occurs in 1233 (*Lacock Charts.*, 93, no. 375). Abbess Ela reiterated a grant made by her as prioress (ibid. 30, nos. 80–1).

[71] 'Utrum religionem subierit necne.' This charter is calendared in *Lacock Charts.*, 12–13, no. 12, and printed in Clark-Maxwell, 'Earliest Charts.', 204–5, no. 10.

[72] *Lacock Charts.*, 69, no. 263; printed, Clark-Maxwell, 'Earliest Charts.', 208, no. 17.

[73] *Lacock Charts.*, 68, no. 262.

[74] 'E. quondam Comitisse Sarr' moniali de Lacock', PRO C62/12, membrane 9, calendared in *Cal. Lib. Rolls 1226–40*, 322.

[75] *Sarum Charts.*, 251–2, no. 222.

[76] W. L. Bowles and J. G. Nichols, *Annals and Antiquities of Lacock Abbey in the County*

Lucy, had lived to a considerable age. Having a lady of such distinction as foundress and abbess was of considerable benefit to the convent. The king made grants to her of 50 marks and a weekly cartload of wood for her hearth. In 1260, after her resignation as abbess, she petitioned for it to be increased to a daily provision— instead Henry III granted her forty acres of forest as a better gift.[77]

As has already been noted, the Countess of Salisbury did not succeed in her desire to have her foundation officially affiliated to the Cistercian order, and the abbess and nuns of Lacock had to be content with following the Augustinian rule. But twenty years later another powerful widow, Isabel, Countess of Arundel, succeeded in founding a convent of Cistercian nuns at Marham in Norfolk.[78] Her husband, Hugh d'Aubigny, died on 7 May 1243,[79] and twenty-two days later her marriage was granted to Peter, son of the Count of Geneva. There is the suggestion that she preferred to remain free of such ties, for the entry on the patent roll contains the clause that alternatively the count was to be the recipient of any money she might pay to retain her freedom of choice,[80] and in the event she appears not to have remarried. The nunnery was situated on land inherited through her father, and was unique in that it was founded as an abbey of the Cistercian order. Confirmation charters from John de Warenne, brother of the countess, from the Bishop of Norwich and from Henry III, were obtained and transcribed in the Marham cartulary.[81] It has been shown that by far the most valuable endowments were given to the house at an early stage, with the foundress herself making eleven individual grants which in themselves were sufficient to provide a viable economic base for the community. Isabel died in 1279 and was buried in her abbey.[82] There is no evidence, apart from her reluctance to remarry, to suggest that she entered the religious life and lived as a nun at Marham.

Later in the thirteenth century another widow, Matilda, Countess of Gloucester and Hertford, re-founded a priory of canons as an abbey of nuns for the soul of her dead husband. The number of canons had apparently dwindled to three, and in 1284 the countess

---

of Wilts with Memorials of the Foundress Ela, Countess of Salisbury (London, 1835), app. 1, p. v. For the suggestion that she was some years younger than this, see Clark-Maxwell, 'Earliest Charts.', 199.

[77] Calendared in *Lacock Charts.*, 16, no. 22 (1260).

[78] For the foundation of this house and the links between Lacock and the Cistercian order see pp. 96 and 112.

[79] *Complete Peerage*, i. 238.

[80] *Cal. Pat. Rolls 1232–47*, 377 (1243). He was probably a relative of the queen's uncle, Peter of Savoy.

[81] Nichols, 'Marham Abbey', 224–5, 235.

[82] Ibid. 30, 15–22, 3, 21.

obtained papal permission to establish in their stead a community of forty Augustinian canonesses.[83] An earlier attempt on the part of Matilda to establish a community of women at Sandleford in Berkshire had apparently been abandoned,[84] and it may be that a refoundation at Canonsleigh seemed the better option. The countess agreed to endow the community with £200 per annum, but unfortunately for the nuns she died within four years. By this date only two of the promised five manors had been transferred to the canonesses, and the endowment was only completed by her grandson some thirty years later. Even the advance of 600 marks paid by the countess as security seems to have been lost—seized by Edward I to advance his wars.[85] It is possible that a second nunnery in the southwest was established by a noble widow. It has been suggested that the house of Cornworthy in Devon may have been founded by Eva, daughter of William Marshall, Earl of Pembroke. According to tradition she was widowed when her husband, William de Braose, was hanged in 1230.[86] But no charter evidence survives to confirm this hypothesis and the house seems to have remained poor and obscure.

Only nine of the nunneries founded after the Conquest were abbeys, and five of these—Elstow, Godstow, Lacock, Marham, and Canonsleigh were established by widows of noble rank.[87] In addition the dowager Countess Lucy's foundation of Stixwould is referred to as an abbey in some early charters, as is the prestigious foundation of Nuneaton, although both subsequently developed as priories.[88] It is possible that Westwood in Worcestershire was also founded by an aristocratic lady who, though not a widow, was in matrimonial difficulties. The foundress, Eustacia de Say, has not been clearly identified, and her parentage is unknown.[89] One of the wives of Geoffrey de Mandeville, second Earl of Essex, was called Eustacia.[90]

---

[83] *Cartl. Canonsleigh*, pp. ix–xii.

[84] *Cal. Pap. Lett.*, i, 448 (1274). Cf. ibid. i, 478 where the foundation is at Canonsleigh for the same number of nuns (forty) and with the same value (£200 p.a.)

[85] *Cartl. Canonsleigh*, p. xii.

[86] H. R. Watkin and E. W. Windeatt, *The Priory for Nuns of St Mary, Cornworthy, Devon*, issued as an appendix to *Devon and Cornwall Notes and Queries* (1921), 4–5. See also *Complete Peerage*, i, 22.

[87] The others were Malling founded by Bishop Gundulf, Northampton founded by Simon de Senlis, and Burnham founded by Richard Earl of Cornwall. Tarrant developed as an abbey under the patronage of Bishop Richard Poore.

[88] Stixwould is referred to as an abbey in the confirmation charter of the foundress's son Rannulf (BL Addit. MS 46,701, fo. 1) and of the Bishop of Lincoln (*Acta I Lincoln 1067–1185*, 161, no. 257 [1154 × 1166]). For the early description of Nuneaton as an abbey see p. 126.

[89] For a note on Hugh fitz Osbern and his wife Eustacia see *Cartl. Worc.*, p. xxxiv.

[90] She witnesses some charters as Eustacia *comitissa*: see BL Sloane chart. xxxii, 64. This probably dates from 1157 × 1188: see J. H. Round, *Geoffrey de Mandeville* (London, 1892),

Apparently the earl refused to live with her as his wife and the marriage was annulled.[91] The earl's father had formed a close alliance with William de Say I who had married his sister Beatrice.[92] It is a possibility that a further cementing of this alliance could have been the marriage of his son, Geoffrey, with another member of the Say family. Such an identification of the countess with Eustacia de Say, the foundress of Westwood, is hypothetical, but it would seem to accord with the fragmentary evidence. As an older woman, one who had previously been married to Hugh fitz Osbern, it might in part explain the earl's rejection of her. The foundation of the nunnery seems to have taken placed at about the time of the annulment of Earl Geoffrey's marriage with Eustacia, and could represent an attempt by her to increase the security of her position.

Westwood was a priory, not an abbey. As with Nuneaton and Amesbury, although aristocratic foundations, the status of the house was dictated by the custom of the order whereby all daughter houses were priories dependent on the abbey of Fontevrault.[93] Nuneaton provides an example of a prestigious foundation established by an earl and countess where the role of the wife was clearly of great importance and she subsequently herself entered the nunnery. It has already been suggested that Amicia, Countess of Leicester, may have had personal contact with Abbess Matilda of Fontevrault and played an important part in the establishment of the priory of Chaise Dieu in Breteuil, which became a member of the order.[94] Amicia witnessed several of the charters recording grants to Nuneaton.[95] Moreover, it is clear that she entered the nunnery. A charter witnessed by Gilbert of Sempringham and Earl Robert, and dating from *c.*1156 × 1168, refers to a grant given by the prior of Kenilworth to Nuneaton at the request of Amicia, now a nun there.[96] Letters are extant from Bishop Gilbert Foliot of London to the countess. One refers to the virtues of the life of the cloister, and it is probable that she had already embraced the religious life, while another episcopal letter reveals that

228–9. Eustacia and the earl made a grant to Clerkenwell nunnery: see *The Cartulary of St Mary Clerkenwell*, ed. W. O. Hassall (Camden 3rd ser. 71; 1949), 3, no. 2. For the foundation of Westwood as a priory of the order of Fontevrault see pp. 123–4.

[91] *Complete Peerage*, v, 117. She was said to have subsequently married the Count of St Pol.

[92] For William de Say see ibid., xi, 464–5. There is no record of a sister of William with the name Eustacia, but as evidence for the female branches of a family tree is often scanty this would not necessarily rule out the possibility of the existence of such a lady.

[93] See pp. 119–20, 126.

[94] See pp. 123–5.

[95] BL Addit. chart. 47,384. This refers to land initially granted at Kintbury, the earliest site of the house. See also BL Addit. charts. 47,871, and 48,488 and *Danelaw Docs.*, 251, no. 334 (–1158). Amicia is described as the foundress of Nuneaton in Leland, *Coll.*, i, (i), 50.

[96] 'Petitione pie recordationis Amicie quondam Comitisse Leircestr' tunc vero monialis de Eatona' (BL Addit. chart. 53,102).

she had been ill, possibly indicating a factor in her conversion to the life of a nun.[97] Tradition records that Amicia's husband also took the religious habit, becoming a canon at St Mary's, Leicester, an abbey founded by him in 1143.[98] He seems to have acted as justiciar until his death in 1168, so the date of 1153 sometimes given for his renunciation of the world must be inaccurate.[99] It would seem that his wife was the first to enter a religious community. She may have become a nun soon after the establishment of the convent at Nuneaton, and her desire for the religious life could have been a motive behind the nunnery's foundation.

The great majority of nunneries founded in England after the Conquest were priories and less prestigious than the three nunneries of the order of Fontevrault. Their founders were generally of lesser rank, and it is clear that a number of them were established by widows. At Neasham in County Durham, a confirmation charter of Henry II and a papal bull of Adrian IV reveal that the site and initial endowments of the nunnery were given by Emma de Teise, described as daughter of Waldef, and her sister Engeleise.[100] It is probable that she made the endowment after the death of her husband. In the first decades of the thirteenth century, Grace Dieu in Leicestershire was founded by Rose de Verdon.[101] A charter recording her grants to the house indicates that she was a widow and had been married more than once.[102] Later in the thirteenth century the house of Flixton was also founded by a widow. Margery, widow of Bartholomew de Crek, obtained a licence from her overlord to found a religious house.[103] A charter recording the foundation stated, following a common formula, that it was established for the salvation of the soul of relatives—her mother, her father, and her late husband.[104] There is no evidence that Margery herself became a nun at Flixton although the closeness of her links with the community is witnessed by her will, dating from 1282, with its provision that she was to be buried there and that the prioress, together with the Bishop of Norwich, were to be executors.[105]

---

[97] *Foliot Letters and Charters*, 266–7, no. 195, dated by the editor as 1163 × 1168; 159–60, no. 120. (1148 × 1163).

[98] KH, 163.

[99] *Complete Peerage*, vii, 529.

[100] *PUE*, i, 317–19, no. 67 (1157), and *EYC*, i, 311–12, no. 400. It is suggested in KH, 262 that the founder was an early baron of Greystoke.

[101] For Grace Dieu see KH, 280 and VCH *Leics.*, ii, 27–8. See also *DHGE*, 21 (1985), 1,016–17.

[102] Her foundation charter referred to the souls of her husbands, indicating she had more than one (*MA*, vi, 567, no. 1).

[103] BL Campbell chart. xii, 20 (c.1258).

[104] BL Stowe chart. 291. For other provisions of the charter see p. 185.

[105] BL Campbell chart. iii, 1 (1282).

Other nunneries were founded by widows who subsequently remarried. In Yorkshire, Agnes de Arches probably started the foundation of Nunkeeling as the widow of Herbert de St Quentin, and then married successively Peter de Fauconberg and William Foliot.[106] Yedingham in the same county was established by Helewise de Clere. She was probably the wife of Roger de Clere I,[107] and it seems that the nunnery was founded after his death and before her remarriage to Jocelin d'Arci. Alice de St Quentin, daughter of Agnes de Arches, was the foundress of the Yorkshire house of Nun Appleton. After the death of her first husband in c.1150, Alice eventually married Eustace de Merc.[108] He is sometimes described as the founder of the nunnery together with his wife.[109] He was clearly a benefactor to Nun Appleton, but the charter referring to his grants is almost certainly later than that of Alice.[110] An interesting charter of Eustace reveals the intention of establishing a daughter house of Nun Appleton at Coddenham in Suffolk. The charter states that this grant was made by concession of his wife in whose dowry the church was sited.[111] But the attempt to found another nunnery proved abortive, and Coddenham was eventually granted by Eustace to his house of Augustinian canons at Royston.[112] It is probable that this transfer took place after the death of Alice de St Quentin. She was without doubt the main benefactress of Nun Appleton, and the loss of Coddenham may provide further evidence of her importance, and the insecurity of the nuns after the death of their foundress.[113]

The predominant role of a married woman is further illustrated in the founding of the nunnery of Bungay in Suffolk, and in this case there may have been particular reasons why a wife sought to obtain additional security by establishing a convent. Countess Gundreda, daughter of Roger, Earl of Warwick, and wife of Roger de Glanville, appears to have played a major part in the foundation of the house,

---

[106] Her earliest charter makes no reference to her later husbands, and was presumably drawn up after the death of Herbert in c.1129 and before her remarriage (*EYC*, iii, 53, no. 1,331). This would indicate a date of c.1129–30. For Agnes and her husbands see *Early Yorkshire Families*, ed. C. Clay and D. Greenway (Yorks. Archaeol. Soc., Record ser. 135; 1973), 79, 26–7.

[107] C. Clay, *Notes on the Family of Clere with a Bibliography of the Writings of Sir Charles Clay* (privately printed, 1975), 15–16.

[108] *EYC*, xi, 94–5. The Arches family were responsible for the foundation of Nun Monkton priory as well as Nunkeeling and Nun Appleton: see Burton, *Yorks. Nunneries*, 18.

[109] VCH *Yorks.*, iii, 170.

[110] *EYC*, i, 422, no. 543 (c.1163); compare ibid. 419, no. 541 (1144 × 1150).

[111] BL Cotton MS Nero C. iii, fo. 227, printed in *EYC*, i, 426, no. 546. Farrer wrongly identified the church as Covenham.

[112] The church was granted by Eustace to Royston before 1184: see VCH *Yorks.*, iii, 171.

[113] Alice granted a further carucate of land with her body for burial (*Rot. Chart.*, 143b). The date of her death is not known.

which was dedicated to the Holy Cross.[114] The nunnery was established by 1183, when its foundation is recorded in the *Chronicle of John de Oxenedes*.[115] A charter of Henry II, which probably dates from 1188 and confirms grants to the nunnery, makes it clear that most of them came through Gundreda.[116] Roger was a crusader and probably died in the Holy Land.[117] In 1198 Gundreda paid £100 not to be forced to marry against her will.[118] There is no evidence to show whether she entered the house as a widow, but it would seem a possibility, and the foundation of the priory may have reflected both her rank as a countess and the need to provide for the wife of a crusader.[119]

A similar motive linked with the crusades may have been behind the foundation of Wroxall, in Warwickshire. An account of the origins of the priory, probably written in the fifteenth century, tells of the vision of the founder, Hugh fitz Richard, who was taken prisoner while on a crusade. After a long imprisonment he was miraculously transported back to his home by the intervention of St Leonard and, according to the account, he founded the nunnery as a thanks-offering. It appears that his wife and his two daughters subsequently became nuns at Wroxall.[120] Leaving aside the question of Hugh fitz Richard's rapid transportation from captivity, some of the details in the account can be verified. Both his wife and his sons are accurately named, and Margaret's son by a previous marriage was Robert, prior of Monmouth. The chapel of Wroxall and grants in Hatton had originally been given to this community, and their transfer to the nuns may reflect Robert's involvement and that of his mother.[121] The earliest evidence for the existence of Wroxall dates from 1123 × 1153,[122] so it is possible it was founded after Hugh escaped from being captured on the Second Crusade. As at Bungay, the foundation

---

[114] She had previously been married to Hugh Bigod and there is some doubt about her parentage (*Complete Peerage*, ix, 585, n. e and 586). Roger was the uncle of Rannulf de Glanville: see R. Mortimer, 'The Family of Rannulf de Glanville', *BIHR* 54 (1981), 4–5.

[115] *Chron. Oxenedes*, 69.

[116] *Cal. Chart. Rolls 1327–41*, 225–6. It is suggested that the date for this charter was 1176, but Hugh Bigod did not die until 1177 and the date suggested by Eyton is 1188: R. Eyton, *Court, Household and Itinerary of King Henry II* (London, 1878), 285.

[117] Mortimer, 'Glanville', 5.

[118] *PR 10 Richard I*, 94.

[119] For the grants of five churches and other lands from her *maritagium* see S. J. Bailey, 'The Countess Gundred's Lands', *Cambridge Law Journal*, 10 (1948–50), partic. 89–90.

[120] The account is taken from a MS now apparently lost. A version is printed in *MA*, iv, 90–2. See also J. W. Ryland, *Records of Wroxall Abbey and Manor* (London, 1903), pp. xii, 214–17. The author seems to have used as a source an obituary list for the priory, and also refers accurately to an entry in a bishop's register (*Reg. Godfrey Giffard*, ii, 256).

[121] *Cal. Docs. France*, 414, no. 1,148. For names of the family see ibid. 412, no. 1,146.

[122] See the confirmation charter of Roger, Earl of Warwick, PRO E210/7431.

of the nunnery may have been linked with the insecurities of a having a crusading husband.[123]

The evidence from Nun Appleton and Bungay, as well as Nuneaton, suggests that when a nunnery was founded by a husband and wife the significance of the woman's role can be obscured. In several cases it is clear that a convent was sited on land which had formed part of the wife's marriage portion or her dowry.[124] This is true of Baysdale, Bungay, Clerkenwell, Harrold, Little Marlow, Redlingfield, and Tarrant as well as Nun Appleton.[125] The lack of power and rights possessed by women in relation to the holding of land[126] provides an explanation both of the hidden nature of the women's role in any foundation established by husband and wife, and also the number of widows among female founders. Only when her husband had died could she exercise any control over her dower. The establishing of a nunnery by a widow suggests that a motive may have been a desire for security, and other foundresses may have taken religious vows beside Edith, Ela, and Amicia at Godstow, Lacock, and Nuneaton. Even for those who stayed in the world, founding a nunnery may well have seemed the best way of crystallizing a measure of independence.

Apart from the possibility of providing security for widows or wives, another purpose in founding a nunnery may have been to provide for a member of the founder's family. It seems clear that both Margaret and her daughters became nuns at Wroxall. Making provision for Mary was clearly the reason for the establishment of Lillechurch by King Stephen and his queen, and several of Abbot

[123] The use of a nunnery to provide security for a crusader's dependants is further illustrated by the actions of a Robert Damas who, when leaving for Jerusalem in 1106, made a grant to Marcigny with the proviso that if he died his wife and daughter would be received into the religious life if they so wished (*Cartl. Marcigny*, 79–80, no. 109).

[124] The technical distinction between *maritagium* (generally given by the bride's father) and *dos* (assigned to his new wife by the husband) seems often to have been imprecise. *Dos* is defined as 'Id quod cum muliere datur viro, quod vulgariter dicitur maritagium': see *Dictionary of Medieval Latin from British Sources*, i, fasc. iii, *D–E*, ed. R. E. Latham and D. R. Howlett, with assist. A. H. Powell and M. A. Sharpe (London, 1986), s.v. *dos*. See also A. W. B. Simpson, *A History of the Land Law* (2nd edn., Oxford, 1986), 68, n. 49.

[125] The first site of Baysdale was at Hutton, which formed part of the dowry of Ralph de Neville's wife, Hawise (*MA*, v, 508, no. 1). Harrold was situated on land inherited through Albreda de Blosseville, wife of Sampson le Fort (*Records of Harrold Priory*, 182). Tarrant seems to have been inherited by the founder of the nunnery through his wife, the daughter of Hugh Maminot: J. Hutchins, *History and Antiquities of . . . Dorset*, 3rd edn. by W. Shipp and J. W. Hodson, 4 vols. (London, 1861–70), i, 319. For Little Marlow see *Rot. Lit. Claus.*, 325b. Redlingfield was established on a site inherited through the foundress (*MA*, iv, 26, no. 1), as was Clerkenwell: see p. 189.

[126] For a study of the very limited rights of women in relation to land see J. des Longrais, 'Le Statut de la femme en Angleterre dans le droit commun médiéval', in *La Femme*. (ii), *Recueils de la Société Jean Bodin pour l'histoire comparative des institutions* 12 (Brussels, 1962), 135–241.

Gervase's relatives seem to have formed the nucleus of the new community at Harrold. At Campsey Ash in Suffolk, a royal confirmation charter confirming the grants of the founder, Theobald de Valoignes II, stated that the grants were made by Theobald to his sisters to found a house of nuns for them and for others who wished to serve God with them.[127] The causal link is not generally so clearly stated, but it seems evident that daughters and other relatives of the founders frequently entered new foundations. A royal example had been set by the Conqueror at Holy Trinity, Caen, where Cecilia, daughter of William and Matilda, the founders of the abbey, became a child oblate.[128] Lower in the social scale, at least two of the Yorkshire nunneries were probably founded, in part at least, to enable daughters to follow the religious life. Matilda de Arches, child of William and Juetta, the founders of Nun Monkton, clearly entered the convent and became the first prioress.[129] At Marrick, the charter of the founder, Roger de Aske, notifying the archbishop of his grants to the priory, made no mention of his daughters entering the community. But charters confirming the grant reveal that at least two of Roger's children became nuns at Marrick at the time of its foundation, and it is possible one held the office of first prioress.[130]

In the case of Marrick Priory, the entrance of members of the founding family into the house is not at first apparent. A close examination of the surviving charters for other Yorkshire houses shows that Nun Monkton and Marrick were not the only examples. At Sinningthwaite a daughter of Bertram Haget, the founder, entered the nunnery. This is revealed by a phrase in a confirmation charter of Roger de Mowbray which refers to a grant being made with the sister of Geoffrey Haget, son of Bertram.[131]

On occasion, older members of the founding family entered the convent. At Wilberfoss it is not clear who was the founder of the

---

[127] 'Ad fundandam ibidem domum religiosam sanctimonialium in honore Dei et gloriose Virginis Marie matris ejus ad opus ipsarum et aliarum que eis adherebunt in servicio Dei comorantium' (*Rot. Chart.*, 116b [1204]).

[128] *Charters and Custumals of the Abbey of Holy Trinity Caen*, ed. M. Chibnall (Oxford, 1982), p. xxi, n. 2.

[129] *HRH*, 218, n. 1 suggests that she was prioress, and she (M.) is given this title in a charter of Bishop Hugh of Durham: see *Feodarium Prioratus Dunelmensis*, ed. W. Greenwell (Surtees Soc. 58; 1871), 163. References to Prioress Matilda also occur in some original charters preserved in the Duke of Northumberland's MSS Alnwick Castle, X series, div. 6 (I am indebted to Dr Burton for these references).

[130] *EYC*, v, 76–8, nos. 173–5. For the suggestion that a daughter, Isabella de Aske, was the first prioress, see Marshal General Plantagenet Harrison, *The History of Yorkshire* (London, 1835), 218–19. Unfortunately he provides no evidence to justify such a statement.

[131] *Mowbray Charts.*, 179, no. 265. For a family tree of the Haget family see *The Chartulary of . . . Healaugh Park*, ed. J. S. Purvis (Yorks. Archaeol. Soc., Record ser. 92; 1936 for 1935), 2.

community. An *inspeximus* charter of George, Duke of Clarence, shows that important early grants were made to the nunnery by Alan, son of Elias, and Jordan fitz Gilbert.[132] It is probable that Alan was one of the founders,[133] and a close reading of the charter shows that some of the grants were made when his mother entered the community. Examples of female relatives of the founding family entering the new establishment are not confined to Yorkshire. At Littlemore, Oxfordshire, the little daughter of the founder, Robert de Sandford, seems to have been received into the house,[134] and in Hertfordshire a child of Henry d'Aubigny, who made some early grants to the cell of Sopwell in Hertfordshire, and is sometimes described as its founder, entered the developing community.[135] At Kington in Wiltshire, charters indicate that the sister of the founder's wife entered the convent.[136] Legbourne in Lincolnshire appears to owe its foundation to two brothers, Berengar Falconer and Robert fitz Gilbert.[137] The community may first have been initiated at Hallington by Berengar before changing site and, with grants from Robert, developing as a priory at Legbourne.[138] Two daughters of Berengar apparently became nuns, and one charter refers to the possibility that Matilda, wife of Robert fitz Gilbert, might also enter the religious life.[139]

Both Joan and Agnes, sisters of the founder of Campsey Ash, came to hold the office of prioress,[140] as had Edith's daughters at Godstow and Princess Mary at Lillechurch. At other nunneries there are hints that early prioresses may have been younger members of the founding family. Redlingfield in Suffolk was established in *c*.1120 by

---

[132] *MA*, iv, 356, no. 5.

[133] Alan is described as the founder in ibid. 354. He is listed as a founder in Burton, *Yorks. Nunneries*, 39, and in KH, 267 where the claims of Jordan fitz Gilbert are also noted.

[134] Oxford, Bodleian MS Oxon. chart. a8 no. 4 (*c*.1150 × 1160).

[135] BL Cotton MS Tib. E. vi (ii), fo. 204, printed in *MA*, iii, 365, nos. 3 and 4. Henry is called the founder in VCH *Beds*., i, 351, n. 4. For his grants and the possible anchoretic origin of Sopwell see pp. 23–40.

[136] *MA*, iv, 400, nos. 10 and 13.

[137] For the fitz Gilbert family see W. O. Massingberd, 'Lincoln Cathedral Charters' *Associated Societies Reports and Papers* 26 [2] (1902) 323–5. For the grants made by the brothers, transcribed from the cartulary now lost, see Oxford, Bodleian MS Dodsworth, lxxv, fos. 23–7, and *MA*, v, 634–5.

[138] They are also described in some charters as the nuns of Keddington, and Robert fitz Gilbert granted them land in Karledale and Hallington (*MA*, v, 635, no. 3). The community of Gilbertine nuns at Alvingham had a grange at Keddington, but the nature of the link, if there was one, between the two communities is not clear. A possibility might be that the nuns of Alvingham took over the buildings as the nuns of Keddington changed site. Another charter of Robert refers to the nuns of Karledale (Oxford, Bodleian MS Dodsworth, lxxv, fo. 23). The only safe conclusion seems to be that the nuns settled at Legbourne after changes of site.

[139] Oxford, Bodleian MS Dodsworth, lxxv, fo. 27; *Acta I Lincoln 1067–1185*, 45–6, no. 70.

[140] *HRH*, 210.

Manasses, Count of Guisnes, and his wife Emma, the daughter of William de Arques, on land she had inherited.[141] Emma and her husband also founded the nunnery of St Leonard at Guisnes. According to one account, after the death of her husband she completed the endowment of this house, and herself became a nun there.[142] It is interesting that the name of an early prioress of Redlingfield was Emma.[143] There are other examples of nunneries where the name of an early prioress reflects that of a foundress. At Ickleton in Cambridgeshire, the manor had been granted by King Stephen with Euphemia as the second wife of Aubrey de Vere, first Earl of Oxford.[144] It is not clear who were the founders of the priory but the de Veres have a strong claim,[145] and the name of a prioress, alive some fifty years after the foundation of the house, was Euphemia.[146] At Castle Hedingham in Essex it is possible that the prioress Lucy, whose death was mourned in the beautifully illustrated mortuary roll, was a daughter of the de Vere family, the probable founders of the nunnery. Leland stated that she was the wife of the first Earl of Oxford, but there seems to be no evidence that he had a wife of this name.[147] It is clear from the mortuary roll that she was a lady of high rank. In this, Lucy was described as the foundress of the nunnery, and as Castle Hedingham was the head of the barony of the de Vere family it would seem probable that she was a relation. The dating of the roll as some forty years after the foundation of the priory, coupled with the fact that the eulogy of the

[141] For the background history of the nunnery see VCH *Suffolk*, ii, 83–5. Emma had previously been married to Nigel de Monville: see Round, *Geoff. de Mandeville*, app. v, 397.

[142] A. Du Chesne, *Histoire généalogique des maisons de Guines, d'Ardres, de Gand, et de Coucy*, 2 parts (Paris, 1631), ii, 41–2. See also T. Stapleton, 'Observations upon the Succession to the Barony of William of Arques, in the County of Kent during the Period between the Conquest of England and the Reign of King John', *Archaeologia* 31 (1846), 216–37, partic. 224–8.

[143] *HRH*, 218 points out that evidence for the names of Redlingfield prioresses is based on a modern list which carries little weight, but a surviving charter (BL Addit. chart. 10,640) confirms the existence of a prioress called Emma.

[144] *Complete Peerage*, x, 202, 205. Euphemia died in 1153. The priory was in existence by 1158 and may have been founded earlier.

[145] An alternative suggestion is that Ickleton was founded by the de Valoignes: see VCH *Cambs.*, ii, 223, and ibid. vi, 233; cf. ibid. ii, 146. It may be that this house too was founded by more than one family.

[146] *HRH*, 213. Another prioress of a later generation with an unusual name which reflects that of a lady who clearly played a part in the foundation of the nunnery is Burgia, head of the community of Langley in Leicestershire. She was elected prioress in 1229 × 1230 (*Rot. Wells*, ii, 312). The founders of the priory, established in the middle of the 12th cent., were William Pantulf and his wife Burgia (Appendix A).

[147] Leland, *Coll.*, i (i) 63. This is followed by other historians: see KH, 257 and VCH *Essex*, ii, 122. But see *Complete Peerage*, x, 207, n. b.

dead lady refers to the virtues of virginity, suggests the possibility that she may have been a daughter of the first Earl of Oxford.[148]

It appears, therefore, that a significant number of women entered a nunnery founded by a member of their family, and it is probable that the sources obscure the frequency of such links.[149] Detailed study has shown that all the founders of Alvingham and Bullington entered the communities themselves, or placed relatives there.[150] There may sometimes have been particular reasons for establishing a nunnery as a possible retreat for women relatives, making it a significant factor behind the foundation. But practical considerations of providing a refuge for a widow or unmarried daughters should not be dismissed as irreligious, nor may they always have been the main motive for founding a nunnery. The entrance of family members into the new community could be an illustration of the link between the nunnery and its founder, and a further testimony to the spiritual purpose of the foundation as a retreat from the world and a focus of prayer for the living and the dead. The establishment of monasteries and nunneries may often have had a practical as well as a religious motivation, but a dual purpose would not necessarily involve tension between the spiritual and the secular.[151]

Whatever the motive, the entrance of members of the founding family would have deepened the relationship between founder and nunnery. Evidence of the continuance of such links is provided by the occasional charters which reveal later generations of the founding family entering the nunnery. Granddaughters of the founder became nuns at Wykeham in Yorkshire, Lacock in Wiltshire, Aconbury in Herefordshire, and Clerkenwell in London.[152] A continuing link with a lay patron, usually the founder's heir, was recognized in canon law and was an important aspect of the monastery's later history.

[148] Weever in his *Funeral Monuments* made the more cautious statement that Lucy, the foundress and first prioress, was probably one of the de Vere family (*MA*, iv, 436, n. 1). For the roll, BL Egerton MS 2849, see p. 11.

[149] A particular reason for obscuring the link between the reception of a nun and the donation of a grant by the members of her family was the suggestion that such practices were simoniacal. For a discussion of this question see pp. 187–9. My view that a significant number of female relatives may have entered houses founded by their kinsmen differs from that of Sharon Elkins who suggests that this was infrequent (Elkins, *Holy Women*, 69).

[150] Golding, 'Alvingham and Bullington', 336.

[151] For a study of motives involved in the foundation of monasteries, see R. Mortimer, 'Religious and Secular Motives for some English Monastic Foundations', in D. Baker (ed.), *Religious Motivation: Biographical and Sociological Problems for the Church Historian*, Studies in Church History 15 (Oxford, 1978), 77–85.

[152] *MA*, v, 670, no. 3 (Wykeham); ibid., vi, (i) 501 (Lacock); *Cartl. Clerkenwell*, 50, no. 72. Daughters from a later generation of the Lacy family also entered Aconbury (*MA*, vi, (i) 136).

Sometimes, as at Cook Hill in Worcestershire, early difficulties were remedied by a later patron. The house was in existence by 1155 × 1156,[153] though no 'founder' is known. The community then obtained a powerful patroness in Isabel de Mauduit, Countess of Warwick. She made several grants to Cook Hill, and was sometimes described as foundress of the nunnery.[154] Similarly, Godstow benefited from the acquisition of a new patron, Henry II. After the death of Henry's mistress Rosamund Clifford, and her burial at Godstow, Bernard de St Valéry granted that the nunnery, together with its demesne and right of advowson, should be held in chief of the king who became its patron.[155] Such a grant of patronage away from the heirs of the founder was unusual, reflecting the prestige of the king, and in this case it undoubtedly conferred benefits. The status of Godstow, which clearly became an abbey, was raised. According to Roger of Howden, Henry conferred many benefits on the nunnery for the sake of Rosamund, and sizeable amounts of money were granted to the nuns for building-work after her death in 1176.[156] With the initial endowment of the nunneries often being small, the continued provision of grants and support from patrons and benefactors was vital. The heirs of the founders were frequently involved in the establishment of the new community and subsequently themselves made grants to the nuns. An emotional scene portraying this transfer of responsibility at the death of a founder is described in a charter of Legbourne Priory in Lincolnshire. At the burial of his father in the priory, William, son of Robert fitz Gilbert, promised his support to the community, confirmed the grants of his father, and added grants of his own.[157]

In return for such protection and support, patrons and benefactors were entitled to the spiritual benefits of the community's prayers, and to certain rights and privileges. The general spiritual benefit expected from a donation to a religious community features in many of the charters. Standard formulae, as in the foundation charter for Flixton, record that the foundation or the grant was made for the

[153] There is a reference to it in *PR 2–4 Henry II*, 62, 156. The house seems to have moved to Cook Hill from Spernall in War.: see *Cal. Pap. Lett.*, v, 405 (1400).

[154] T. Habington, *A Survey of Worcestershire*, ed. J. Amphlett, 2 vols. (Worcs. Hist. Soc.; Oxford, 1895–9), i, 311. For a discussion of her claims to be the foundress see VCH *Worcs.*, ii, 156–7.

[155] The original charter recording this agreement is preserved in the Bodleian Library: Oxford, Bodleian MS chart. Oxon. 2740 (1180); see also *Cartl. Godstow*, 30–1, no. 5.

[156] *Chronica Rogeri de Hovedene*, ed. W. Stubbs, 4 vols. (Rolls ser. 51; 1868–71), iii, 167. He relates how Bishop Hugh of Lincoln ordered the removal of her tomb from near the altar. The royal grants are listed in *The History of the Kings' Works*, ed. H. M. Colvin, 6 vols. (London, 1963–82), i, 90.

[157] *MA*, v, 634, no. 1.

salvation of the grantor's soul and the souls of his ancestors and others named in the charter. Specific rights and privileges claimed by patrons as the founders' heir and the feudal lord of the religious house were clearly defined by the thirteenth century, and related chiefly to custody in vacancies and licence and assent in elections.[158] In the twelfth century, in the absence of episcopal registers to provide information about elections, the exact role of the patron is less clear.

Some benefits, in addition to the prayers of the community, could be claimed by patrons and benefactors. One such was the right of burial at the convent. As the description of Robert fitz Gilbert's funeral shows, it could be an occasion for further donations. It is probable that founders were often buried in the house they had established, although there is not the evidence to establish the frequency of this or whether it was regarded as a right for them and their heirs as patrons. It is interesting that Alice de St Quentin, foundress of Nun Appleton, made special provision for her burial at the convent, granting an additional carucate of land to the nuns.[159] Numerous charters of benefactors testify to the provision of grants in return for the promise of burial. Hawise, Countess of Gloucester, granted 100 shillings worth of land to Nuneaton together with her body at her death.[160] The burial of Rosamund at Godstow was the reason for Henry II's particular support of the nunnery, and it was the wish of Geoffrey fitz Peter, Earl of Essex, to provide a fit burial-place for his wife, Beatrice de Say, which was one of the motives for the foundation of the Gilbertine priory of Shouldham. When he died in 1212 he was buried by his lady's side, and this burial requirement is stated in the foundation charter of the priory when he made the initial endowment for the nunnery.[161]

Lower in the social scale there are numerous examples of benefactors making grants in return for the right of burial in the priory.[162] The importance of obtaining the earthly remains of a powerful lord is shown clearly by the saga at the Gilbertine nunnery of Chicksands, where Rose de Beauchamp, the foundress, made valiant if unsuccessful attempts to obtain the body of her eldest son so that he could be buried at her foundation. All she managed to secure, however, were the hangings and furniture from his private

---

[158] Wood, *Patrons*, 11.

[159] *Rot. Chart.*, 143b.

[160] *Glos. Charts.*, 72–3, no. 67.

[161] *MA*, vi (ii), 974, no. 1.

[162] e.g. Amicia de Crast granted half a mill to Nuneaton, with the right to bury her body (BL Addit. chart. 47,615 [1216]). Examples of burial grants in the Nun Cotham cartulary are those of Richard de Scures and his wife, and Agnes de Cotun (Oxford, Bodleian MS Top Lincs. d 1, fos. 14ᵛ, 67).

chapel.[163] A common burial ground, uniting the community in death as in life, would be important for any religious community. It may be that the value of such burial grants and the possibility of providing this service for patrons and benefactors is a further explanation as to why the provision of a cemetery seems sometimes to have been a factor in the early development of a convent. At Orford it is the reference to the cemetery of the sisters which is the first indication of the existence of a community separate from the parent abbey.[164] At Bungay, grants of the foundress were made to enlarge the cemetery of the church.[165] At Sopwell, the account in the *Gesta Abbatum* records the actions of Abbot Geoffrey in establishing the community and places high priority on his assigning to them a cemetery. But this was done with the clear provision that only nuns—no one else either lay or clerical—was to be buried there. Presumably this was to prevent the nuns from attracting burial grants at the expense of the abbey of St Albans.[166]

Apart from rights claimed in death, it seems that patrons and benefactors may have claimed and exercised rights for the living— that of placing women in the community to follow the religious life. This was apparently demanded by the patrons of Westwood, for a charter of William de Stuteville renounced the right he thought he held from his ancestor, Hugh de Say, always to have a nun in the priory.[167] The foundress of Bungay granted as a concession that she would not place inmates in the community without the assent of the prioress and convent.[168] Other benefactors may sometimes have demanded rights of placement. At Arthington in Yorkshire, Alice de Romeli's grants to the nuns were confirmed by Warin fitz Gerold and William de Curci her son, and it was stated that she had the right—a right her heir would inherit—always to have a nun nominated by her in the convent.[169]

As well as possibly exercising rights to nominate nuns, it is probable that the patrons of a nunnery exercised some control over the choice of the prioress. Rights in relation to elections came to be clearly formulated, and were one of the most important aspects of

[163] Graham, *St Gilbert*, 38–9.

[164] *Acta 1 Lincoln 1067–1185*, 108, no. 179 (1153 × c.1156).

[165] *MA*, iv, 338, no. 2.

[166] *Gesta Abbatum*, i, 81–2. Similarly the assigning of a cemetery and regulations about its use was an important part of the foundation of Baysdale nunnery, with care being taken not to infringe the rights of the parish church (*EYC*, i, 443–4, no. 564). For men's houses, too, the need for a cemetery could cause problems. The attempt of the monks of Battle to establish a conventual settlement at the church of St Olave in Exeter caused great problems with the cathedral chapter, who denied the monks the right to have a cemetery for their benefactors (Brett, *English Church*, 93).

[167] *MA*, vi, 1,006, no. 15; BL Cotton MS Vesp. E. ix, fo. 5.

[168] Ibid. iv, 338, no. 2.

[169] *EYC*, iii, 472.

patronage. The patron's licence was needed to elect, and his agreement required for the final choice.[170] This is set out in a thirteenth-century charter of the prioress of Grace Dieu.[171] In the twelfth century, the picture is less clear. Sometimes early charters relating to the foundation of the nunnery explicitly state that the election of the prioress should be free,[172] or the more specific right, as at Godstow, that the nuns would be free to choose a member of their own community.[173] An agreement is set out in a charter of Flamstead nunnery dating from *c.*1162 × 1209. In this the patron, Roger de Tosny, confirms the grants made to the house and then refers to the agreement made with the nuns that a new prioress would only be elected with his consent.[174] Similarly, a thirteenth-century charter of the Bishop of Lincoln confirmed that the new prioress had been canonically elected at Stainfield and approved by the patron and that the latter's assent should in future be required at the election of a prioress.[175] It is not easy to ascertain how much control was in fact exercised by the patrons. In the twelfth century, prioresses are generally known only by their first names, making it impossible to identify their family. But there are some examples in the early thirteenth century of such heads having the same name as known patrons. A relative of Bertram Haget became prioress of Sinningthwaite, and at Blackborough a later prioress, Katherine de Scales, was presumably of the same family as the founder Roger de Scales and his wife Muriel.[176] Similarly, at Little Marlow in Buckinghamshire a member of the d'Auvers family, patrons of the house, was prioress in the first part of the thirteenth century.[177] The right to a free election generally became accepted. Rights over the election of a new prioress and to custody in a vacancy were renounced by Margery de Crek in her foundation charter for Flixton.[178] Nevertheless, the possibilities of subtle influence over the choice of a new head would remain.

[170] Wood, *Patrons*, chap. IV, partic. pp. 40–1. For the formalities of elections and the influence of patrons in the later history of the nunneries, see Power, 42–56.

[171] *Ecclesiastical Documents viz I. A Brief History of the Bishoprick of Somerset from its Foundation to the Year 1174, II. Charters from the Library of Dr Cox Macro*, ed. J. Hunter (Camden Soc., o.s. 8; 1840), 66–7.

[172] This is the case in a charter for the priory of Legbourne: see *MA*, v, 635, no. 2.

[173] *Acta I Lincoln 1067–1185*, 23, no. 34.

[174] *MA*, iv, 300, no. 1; *Cartl. Beauchamp*, 210, no. 370.

[175] *Acta IV Lincoln 1186–1206*, 183–4, no. 291 (1203 × 1206).

[176] *HRH*, 219. She was the daughter of Alice Haget and Jordan; Katherine de Scales occurs in 1238: see BL Egerton MS 3137, fo. 62 and *MA*, iv, 204. Similarly two 13th-cent. prioresses of Littlemore in Oxfordshire, Amabilia and Amice de Sandford, were probably members of the founding family (*Reg. Gravesend*, 226).

[177] *Rot. Wells*, ii, 33.

[178] BL Stowe chart. 291. For the development of claims for free elections see Wood, *Patrons*, chapter IV, esp. 41–5.

The suggestion that some patrons of nunneries may have exercised considerable control is implicit in a charter, which probably dates from the first decades of the thirteenth century, of the little-known nunnery of Foukeholme in Yorkshire. This states that the prioress and convent entrust themselves and all their goods to William de Coleville, their patron. It is confirmed that on the death of the prioress another shall be elected with the agreement of William or his heirs, and that no *magister* or *custos* shall be given authority without the patron's consent. Furthermore it is agreed that no nun, or sister, or secular person male or female, would be received into the house without the instruction and agreement of William and his heirs.[179] It would seem that this agreement was to settle previous disputes between the nuns and Philip de Coleville, William's father. A similar reference to the founder having control over the reception of nuns occurs in a charter for the small house of Sewardsley, Northamptonshire, established by Richard de Lestre. He granted the nuns land and allowed them to have three oxen, ten cows, and 200 sheep in his pasture. In return the nuns promised that they would not receive any new members except through him.[180] A more limited measure of control is specified in the charter of Roger de Tosny, in which it is agreed that at the nunnery of Flamstead nuns in excess of the agreed number of thirteen should only be admitted with his, the patron's, consent, or that of his heirs.[181] When Archbishop Pecham tried to place a nun in the abbey of Burnham, the nuns objected on the grounds that the Earl of Cornwall, their founder, forbade the reception of new nuns without his licence. The episcopal retort was to deny that the earl would have any such right, but the nuns' claim may not have been entirely fictitious.[182]

Such concern over the number of inmates at a nunnery is not surprising. There is evidence to suggest that there was pressure to receive inhabitants, and for financial stability a balance had to be maintained between endowments and the number of nuns the community had to support. Papal sources hint that lords sometimes exerted pressure to obtain the admission of their candidates. A papal

---

[179] This charter is preserved in the Yorkshire Record Office, Mauleverer Brown Archives FL 8; printed in Brown, 'Thimbleby', 335. The date of the charter is sometimes given as later 13th cent. (see ibid. and Wood, *Patrons*, 146), or *c.*1240 (Burton, *Yorks. Nunneries*, 23), but the witnesses suggest it may have been earlier in the 13th cent.: see *EYC*, i, 357, no. 465; ii, 57, no. 710 and *Three Yorkshire Assize Rolls for the Reigns of King John and Henry III*, ed. C. T. Clay (Yorks. Archaeol. Soc., Record ser. 44; 1911), 6–7.

[180] PRO E326/3229. See also VCH *Northants.*, ii, 125 where the reference to the deed is given wrongly.

[181] *MA*, iv, 300, no. 1. See also p. 185.

[182] *Registrum epistolarum Fratris Johannis Peckham Archiepiscopi Cantuariensis*, ed. C. T. Martin, 3 vols. (Rolls ser., 77; 1882–5), i, 189–90.

bull issued at the request of the nuns of Carrow in Norfolk in 1229 attempted to stop lords from using their influence to force the community to receive more inmates than they could maintain.[183] Attempts to stop nunneries receiving more inhabitants than they could afford to maintain were also made by the king acting as patron. In 1276, Henry III forbade Aconbury to receive new nuns without his consent because of their dire financial position. He claimed that the house had been founded by his ancestors, and warned of the trouble he would cause the nuns if they disobeyed his edict.[184] At Flixton, founded in 1258, early charters reveal strenuous attempts by the foundress and the Bishop of Norwich to tackle the problem at the outset by limiting the number of nuns in the convent and ensuring that there was adequate provision for them. Additional nuns were only to be received if there was an increase in revenues of the house by 50 shillings per annum. It is clearly stated that the reason for these measures is to avoid the poverty which is often a damaging feature of nunneries.[185]

Many of the early grants to the nunneries seem to have been made when a member of the grantor's family entered the community. For example, at Elstow a confirmation charter of Henry I shows that three at least of the benefactors made grants when their daughters became nuns there.[186] The usual formula to indicate any association between a grant and the reception into the nunnery of a relative is the wording *cum filia mea* or *cum matre mea* in parenthesis to the stated grant. But the absence of any such phrase in a charter recording a donation does not necessarily mean that the grant was unconnected with the reception of a nun. The phrase may simply have been omitted for brevity or for reasons of caution. This is probably increasingly true of charters dating from the later twelfth and early thirteenth centuries, when canonists had come to apply the stigma of simony to grants linked with the reception of novices. The doctrine, developed in the second half of the twelfth century, that the provision of such dowries was simoniacal,[187] probably led in many cases to the obscuring of any association of grant and admission. It would appear, however, that the practice of requiring gifts on entry was widespread. In the thirteenth century, critics of such simoniacal

---

[183] BL Harl. chart. 43 A 34, printed in *MA*, iv, 71, no. 5 and wrongly dated in VCH *Norfolk*, ii, 352, n. 4 as 1273.

[184] *Cal. Pat. Rolls* 1266–72, 109.

[185] BL Stowe chart. 294 (1262 × 1263). See also Stowe chart. 293.

[186] This is printed in *MA*, iii, 413, no. 3, where it is wrongly attributed to Henry II, and calendared in *Reg. Regum*, ii, *1100–1135*, 240, no. 1,654.

[187] J. H. Lynch, *Simoniacal Entry into Religious Life from 1000–1260: A Social, Economic and Legal Study* (Ohio, 1976), *passim* and esp. 98 and 116.

practices suddenly shifted the stress of their concern from entry into religion in general, to the malpractices of the nuns. Canon 64 of the Lateran Council of 1215 was outspoken:

Since the simoniacal stain has infected so many nuns to such a degree that they receive scarcely any as sisters without a price, and they wish by pretext of poverty to palliate a crime of this sort, we prohibit entirely that this be done from henceforth.[188]

The suggestion that gifts were frequently demanded from entrants to nunneries is endorsed by the report that when Archbishop Edmund Rich wished to find places for his two sisters at a nunnery, Catesby was the convent chosen by the saintly prelate, apparently because it did not demand a gift as a condition of entry.[189] Where cartularies are extant they provide numerous examples of grants being made when a member of the family entered the house. At Stixwould in Lincolnshire, William and Alan fitz Ketell made a grant with their two daughters, Gilbert de Neville with his two daughters, Eustace, son of Hugh le Fleming with his wife and his daughter, and John de Hesel granted a mill when his three daughters became nuns.[190] The Godstow cartulary reveals at least twenty-four examples of a grant being made when a member of the grantor's family became a nun.[191] It is interesting that one entry in the Nun Cotham cartulary, recording that two of the daughters of Robert de Croxton entered the community with a possible option on a third, has apparently been rubbed, possibly in an attempt to erase it.[192] The linking of endowments to entrants is a striking feature of the nunneries.[193] It is hardly surprising that the economic insecurity of many of the women's convents, with their small initial endowments, necessitated grants on entry. But if grants were linked with the reception of a new nun, they may well have done little to increase the community's resources. In some cases such dowry grants were part of a series of benefactions made by the donor, and the entrance of a daughter may have cemented an existing link with a benefactor

---

[188] Lynch, *Simoniacal Entry* 193–4; for the text of the decree see *Constitutiones Concilii Quarti Lateranensis una cum commentariis glossatorum. Monumenta Iuris Canonici*, series A, *Corpus Glossatorum*, ii, ed. A. Garcia y Garcia (Vatican, 1981), 104–5 and 376.

[189] Lawrence, *St Edmund*, 107–8, 222, 250. Extant charters, however, reveal the Rich family making grants to Catesby (ibid. 316–17). Presumably these were made freely without any previous pact or promise, and so were acceptable as a voluntary offering.

[190] BL Addit. MS 46,701, fos. 4, 9ᵛ, 43ᵛ, and 44.

[191] e.g. *Cartl. Godstow* (i) 158, no. 193; 178, no. 232; (ii) 570, no. 767. For examples from Yorkshire houses see Burton, *Yorks. Nunneries*, 20–1.

[192] Oxford, Bodleian MS Top Lincs. d 1, fo. 23ᵛ.

[193] This is also pointed out by Dr Burton in her study of the Yorkshire nunneries: see Burton, *Yorks. Nunneries*, 20–1.

rather than creating it.[194] It is also possible that other grants, apparently simply donations to the nunnery, were associated with the entrance of a new member, thereby putting an added strain on the convent's finances, despite the accompanying grant.[195]

A study of Clerkenwell in London, a house where the survival of the cartulary and some original charters means that there is a relative wealth of evidence, provides a summary of some of the points raised in this chapter about the foundation of nunneries and their subsequent links with patrons and benefactors. The founder, Jordan de Bricett, was of middle rank. He was the younger son of Ralph fitz Brian, who had established monastic communities at Great Bricett, Suffolk, and Stansgate in Essex.[196] The nunnery was founded on land inherited through his wife, Muriel de Munteni.[197] Charters show that the original grant was made to a Robert who is described simply as *capellanus*. He was to found a house of prayer, and seems to have been entrusted with some choice as to the nature of the foundation. In another charter, Jordan notified the Bishop of London of his agreement to the foundation and stated that the land had been given to Robert on condition that he should endow a community of grey monks or nuns.[198] The land was to be held from Robert during his lifetime and subsequently from Jordan and his heirs.

A cleric, as well as a lay founder, clearly played an important part in the establishment of Clerkenwell. Jordan's role was probably that of an entrepreneur. He was also the founder of the priory of the Hospital of St John of Jerusalem,[199] and his contribution was probably to grant the site for the new foundation. The wholesale establishing of two major monasteries would have been beyond the means of Jordan de Bricett. The foundation of the nunnery was a family affair, with several of the founder's children making grants to

[194] This point is illustrated by evidence from some of the Gilbertine nunneries: see Golding, 'Alvingham and Bullington', partic. 336–7.

[195] In France the visitation returns of Archbishop Rigaud, dating from the first half of the 13th cent., reveal the prelate's attempts to limit the numbers to achieve greater financial stability, and show that the nuns were frequently tempted to accept such dowries and receive a new member. For these returns see Power, app. 11 particularly 658. For the role of the English bishops in attempting such regulation see Chap. 10, esp. pp. 205–6.

[196] KH, 181, 102.

[197] As a younger son, Jordan probably inherited his land through his wife: see J. H. Round, 'The Foundation of the Priories of St Mary and of St John Clerkenwell', *Archaeologia* 56 (1899), ii, 225–6.

[198] 'Hec Rodberto concessi quatinus super easdem acras domum orationis edificare et religionem quam placuerit ad serviendum deo atque supplicandum inponat', *Cartl. Clerkenwell*, 31, no. 40, 31–2, no. 42.

[199] This was established at about the same time and on an adjacent site. For a discussion of the dates of the foundations see Round, 'Clerkenwell', 223–8.

the new community.[200] Even if the desire of members of the family to enter the religious life was not a factor behind the genesis of the nunnery, it is clear that a daughter of Jordan and Muriel became a nun at Clerkenwell.[201] Similarly, grants made by benefactors were frequently linked with the entrance of members of their family into the community.[202] There are hints of the significance of Muriel de Munteni,[203] and her role should not be obscured by that of her husband. After the death of Jordan, Muriel remarried and she and her husband, Maurice de Tottenham, made further grants to the nuns.[204] Subsequent generations of the Munteni family also became nuns.[205] The original endowment granted to Clerkenwell was merely ten acres and the site for a mill. Subsequent grants by the founding family and many others meant that the nunnery came to hold land in eleven different counties. As with the other London houses, Clerkenwell was able to benefit from numerous small grants from wealthy citizens, and eventually obtained a reasonable income.[206] To regard the house as established by one lay founder would be a distortion. Though seminal in providing the site for the community, the contribution of such a founder was frequently minimal, and did not provide a secure economic or organizational base for the future development of the community. For this many nunneries relied on the continuing support of the founding family acting as patrons, and on the support of other benefactors. They also needed help from spiritual patrons, and as links with monks and canons became weaker, sought help from the secular church and its leaders, the bishops.

[200] e.g. their daughter Emma and her husband (*Cartl. Clerkenwell*, 39–40, no. 55; 54, no. 79; 60, no. 88); another daugher Lecia and her husband Henry Foliot (ibid. 29, no. 39; 43, nos. 61–2). Henry apparently entered a religious house during her lifetime (ibid. 33, no. 44).

[201] A charter records an additional grant made to the community by Jordan to enable one of his daughters to enter the house if she so wished (ibid. 51, no. 74 [1156 × 1162]). Subsequent charters refer to grants for a daughter Rose's clothing, apparently indicating that she did enter the house (ibid. 61, no. 90; 33, no. 44). It is also possible that Lecia entered: see ibid. 50, no. 72.

[202] e.g. *Cartl. Clerkenwell*, 19–20, no. 22; 20–1, no. 24; 27, no. 35 and 28, no. 37; 117, no. 185; 167–8, no. 258.

[203] She is described as 'domina donationis' in one charter (ibid. 33, no. 43).

[204] Ibid. 37–8, no. 52. Maurice also made grants on his own, with no mention of his wife: see ibid. 36–7, nos. 49–51.

[205] Ibid. 50, no. 72.

[206] It is noted that the London houses were able to build up their resources, and obtain a higher level of income than many other nunneries: see C. N. L. Brooke and G. Keir, *London 800–1216: The Shaping of a City* (London, 1975), 329–30.

10   The Role of Episcopal Founders and Patrons in the Foundation of the Nunneries

NUNNERIES were founded by prelates of the church as well as by laymen.[1] But claims of an episcopal founder have to be treated with caution. There were several reasons why a bishop might be involved in the process of establishing a new religious community. In theoretical terms episcopal intervention would need little justification. Theologically the bishop was regarded as the figure of Christ for his flock,[2] and specific duties were outlined in canon law. Gratian cited several early authorities which demonstrated the bishop's responsibility for safeguarding the religious life.[3] The need for prelates to protect the possessions of the religious is often stressed,[4] and many early charters recording the foundation of nunneries are in the form of a notification to the bishop or a confirmation charter issued by him. The consecration of a new church or chapel would be performed by a bishop, raising the possibility that he might subsequently be claimed as a founder of the community. In the course of the twelfth and thirteenth centuries the duty and work of the bishops in overseeing religious houses increased.[5] It is difficult to distinguish a bishop's role as founder or patron from his duties of pastoral and spiritual care for men and women religious.

Changes in the role and functions of a bishop from the eleventh to the thirteenth centuries are illustrated by the fact that it was probably

[1] For bishops as patrons and founders of monasteries in the reign of Henry I see Brett, *English Church*, 137–40. Some work has been done on the role of particular prelates as patrons: see A. G. Dyson, 'The Monastic Patronage of Bishop Alexander of Lincoln', *Journal of Ecclesiastical History* 26 (1975), 1–24. As more episcopal *acta* are edited, sources for the study of 12th cent. bishops will be more available. For the current project in this field see Smith, *Acta I Lincoln 1067–1185*, p. xxix. Bishops played an important part in the foundation of several men's houses, and in the case of the Augustinian order seem to have provided the main initiative behind the refoundation of at least twelve houses of canons. On this point I am grateful for the help of Miss Jane Herbert, who, before her tragic death, was working on the Augustinian houses. In her book Sharon Elkins stresses the early initiative of the bishops in founding nunneries after the Norman Conquest. This is certainly true for Malling and Clementhorpe, and may have been for others, but the evidence of episcopal founders for St Sepulchre Canterbury, Ivinghoe, Stratford, and Brewood Black Ladies is not clear.

[2] This is discussed in Brett, *English Church*, 114.

[3] *Corpus Iuris Canonici editio Lipsiensis secunda post Aemilii Ludovici Richteri curas . . . recognovit . . . Aemilius Friedberg*, 2 vols., i, *Decretrum Magistri Gratiani* (Lipsiae, 1879), e.g. 832–3.

[4] Brett, *English Church*, 136–7.

[5] For a study of episcopal involvement with nunneries in the 13th cent. and later see Nichols, 'Cistercian Nunneries and Bishops', 237–47. For the development of bishops' chanceries which both enabled and reflected the increasing work load see C. R. Cheney, *English Bishops' Chanceries 1100–1500* (Manchester, 1950).

only in the early period that nunneries were actually founded by a prelate. Malling was established in c.1095 by Gundulf, Bishop of Rochester.[6] Gundulf, a monk who had received the religious habit at Bec, was a close friend of both Lanfranc and Anselm.[7] He went with Lanfranc to St Stephen's, Caen, and assisted him there as prior of the new foundation. His mother became a nun at the sister house of Holy Trinity, and according to his biographer Gundulf played an important part in her commitment to the religious life.[8] When he became Bishop of Rochester, amongst his many other activities[9] he continued to promote the monastic vocation. Monks were established in the church of Rochester, and by the bishop's death in 1108, the community was said to number sixty.[10]

The *Life* of Gundulf states that he was beloved by both sexes, and took care to promote the welfare of both.[11] An extant letter from Archbishop Lanfranc, ruling on questions relating to nuns, suggests that Gundulf had been concerned with questions of female vocation early in his episcopate.[12] Towards the end of the eleventh century the bishop built a convent for nuns at Malling, providing both buildings and endowment.[13] The account of the foundation in the *Vita* suggests that Archbishop Anselm provided support and help.[14] It also links the establishment of the community of women at Malling with the establishment of the monks at Rochester.[15] The tithes and churches which provided the initial endowment for the abbey were

[6] For the date of the foundation see Appendix A. The history of the abbey is outlined in VCH *Kent*, ii, 146–8. See also F. H. Fairweather, 'The Abbey of St Mary Malling, Kent', *Archaeological Journal* 88 (1931), 175–92.

[7] The *Vita Gundulphi*, which was probably written by a monk of Rochester, is an important source, even if its main purpose is to edify rather than to inform: see *The Life of Gundulf, Bishop of Rochester*, ed. R. Thomson (Toronto, 1977). See also R. A. L. Smith, 'The Place of Gundulf in the Anglo-Norman Church', *EHR* 58 (1943), 257–72. For his co-operation with Lanfranc, see particularly M. Gibson, *Lanfranc of Bec* (Oxford, 1978), 155–6. Letters witnessing to this close relationship with Anselm are printed in *PL*, clviii (1853), cols. 1,071–2, 1,079–80, 1,086, 1,089, 1,119–20, 1,139–40, and 1,150–1.

[8] *Life of Gundulf*, 31. The two houses at Caen were founded by Duke William and Matilda: see *Orderic Vitalis*, ii, 190. For the entrance of their daughter there see above, p. 178.

[9] For his work as a builder see Colvin, *King's Works*, i, 28–31.

[10] KH, 74.

[11] 'Amabilis enim utrique sexui ad religionis pietatem prodesse studuit et utrique sexui', *Life of Gundulf*, 58.

[12] *The Letters of Lanfranc, Archbishop of Canterbury*, ed. H. Clover and M. Gibson (Oxford, 1979), 167, no. 53 (1077 × 1089).

[13] Grants to the nunnery are specified in a confirmation charter of Archbishop Theobald: see Saltman, *Archbishop Theobald*, 395–6, no. 173. In 1291 the temporalities of the house were valued at a total of £83.9s. 11d., of which some £45 came from the diocese of Rochester (VCH *Kent*, ii, 147).

[14] *Life of Gundulf*, 58. Archbishop Anselm was clearly concerned with the vocation of women: see above, p. 36.

[15] 'Sicut in civitate Rofensi construxerat virorum, ita et feminarum coenobium in possessione sua quam Mellingas dicunt vir Dei aedificare curavit', *Life of Gundulf*, 58.

confirmed to the nuns by the prior and convent of St Andrew, Rochester.[16] This confirmation probably dates from an early stage in the foundation.[17] It may merely reflect the wish to base the grants on as firm a title as possible, but it might also suggest that the monks, as well as the bishop, were concerned in the granting of the endowment. There is no evidence that the monks of Rochester acted as chaplains for the nuns, but it is probable that Bishop Gundulf himself provided a link between the two communities. The *Vita* emphasizes the strength of his monastic vocation.[18] This may in part reflect the author's viewpoint, but it is interesting that the bishop seems to have retained close personal control over the nuns. It is recorded that he preferred not to appoint an abbess but to rule the community himself.[19] According to the account, it was only when on his deathbed that the bishop agreed to choose a lady to head the community.

Charter evidence confirms the subjection of the nuns to the authority of their episcopal founder. The new abbess had to swear fealty and subjection, and to promise that without licence from the bishop she would not appoint or depose a prioress, receive a nun, or grant away land. The occasion of this charter, which is preserved in an early Rochester register, may well have been when Gundulf was dying. The witnesses, who include a *medicus*, indicate a date between 1107 and the bishop's death on 7 March 1108.[20] Malling, in a spiritual as well as a temporal sense, was Gundulf's own foundation. Apart from providing endowments, he seems to have recruited ladies of known vocation from other monasteries to join his community, and he acted as their spiritual father. The *Vita* states that it was the piety of the bishop, as well as the practical provision made by him, which attracted recruits to the abbey and that it was through his sanctity that mere women, despite their own frailty, sought to achieve holiness.[21]

Archbishop Thurstan of York was another prelate who was

[16] *Registrum Roffense*, ed. J. Thorpe (London, 1769), 481.

[17] Only the initial of the prior 'R' is given. This probably refers to Ralph who held office till 1107 (see *HRH*, 63).

[18] *Life of Gundulf*, 64.

[19] 'Abbatissam tamen eis primum praeficere noluit, sed eas (moniales) per plures annos propria cura regere curavit', ibid. 58.

[20] The register in which this charter is transcribed dates from the early 12th cent.: see *Textus Roffensis*, ed. P. Sawyer, *Early English MSS in Facsimile* 11 [2] (Copenhagen, 1962), fo. 198. See also *Life of Gundulf*, 82–3. The word I have translated as prioress is *prior*. It is possible this refers to a male official, but in the context a prioress would seem more likely and it appears that the word *priorissa* came into usage later, towards the end of the 12th cent.: see R. Latham, *Revised Medieval Latin Word List* (London, 1965), 372.

[21] *Life of Gundulf*, 58.

concerned with the monastic vocation of both women and men.[22] Born in Normandy, he may well have received his schooling at Caen, the town dominated by the two great monasteries founded by the Conqueror for monks and for nuns. After his consecration in 1119, he helped with the foundation of the priory of St Bees, and acted as a vigorous patron for Hexham and Nostell, as well as giving his support to Prior Richard and the other dissident monks of St Mary's, York, in the saga of their establishment of a new community at Fountains.[23] He was described as the 'promoter of holy vocations'.[24] In 1119 he stayed with Adela of Blois and eventually accompanied her to Marcigny when she took the veil there.[25] The *Life of Christina of Markyate* tells how the hermit Roger enlisted Thurstan's help in securing support for his young protégée.[26] He must have been impressed by the dedication and virtue of the recluse, for the *Life* records that he attempted to persuade her to follow her vocation as head of the new community of nuns which he had established at Clementhorpe, York.[27]

The earliest datable reference to the nunnery of Clementhorpe is a charter of *c.*1125 × 1133 in which Archbishop Thurstan notified the dean and chapter and all his tenants that he had granted to the nuns at St Clement the site on which their buildings had been constructed, two carucates of land, 20 shillings from an annual fair, and other specified tithes and grants of land from the archiepiscopal demesne.[28] The dean and chapter, who witnessed this document, subsequently confirmed these grants to the nuns in a separate charter.[29] It would seem that Thurstan, supported by the chapter, played a major part in providing the site and the initial endowment for the nunnery. But very little is known about the circumstances surrounding the foundation of the nunnery of Clementhorpe. The church of St Clement, the nunnery church, seems by the fifteenth

[22] For a study of Thurstan see D. Nicholl, *Thurstan, Archbishop of York, 1114–40* (York, 1964).

[23] Ibid. 143, 127–36, 151–91.

[24] Ibid. 192–212 from Talbot, *Life of Christina*, 110; cf. *Gesta Abbatum*, i, 100.

[25] Nicholl, *Thurstan*, 194.

[26] Talbot, *Life of Christina*, 110–16. The cleric to whom the archbishop commended Christina unfortunately proved unworthy of his trust. For the account of his vigorous attempts to seduce the virgin see ibid. 112–16. It is difficult to explain by what right the Archbishop of York became involved in Christina's case.

[27] Ibid. 126.

[28] *Acta V York 1070–1154*, 60–1, no. 74. See also Burton, *Yorks. Nunneries*, 47, n. 19. For a background history of the priory see VCH *Yorks.*, iii, 129–31.

[29] *EYC*, i, 279, no. 358. For a note on the interest of these charters as reflecting both the common interest of bishop and chapter, and the concept of the chapter as being in some measure distinct, see Brett, *English Church*, 197–8.

century at least to have been used for parochial purposes as well as for the nuns.[30] It is possible that this reflects an earlier situation, with the first nuns, as at Sempringham, being attached to an existing parish church, and subsequently being provided with buildings and endowment. The donations made by the archbishop probably only provided a starting point. A confirmation charter of Henry II, dating from 1175, made merely a passing reference to Thurstan before proceeding to itemize donations given by others.[31] Archbishop Roger may also have given practical support to the nuns,[32] but by the end of the twelfth century, links with the prelate were clearly causing problems. In 1192, Archbishop Geoffrey attempted to grant the priory of Clementhorpe to the abbey of Godstow. The nuns appealed to the pope, stating that from their foundation they had been free from any such dependence.[33] They seem to have won their case, as there is no subsequent evidence of a link between Godstow and Clementhorpe. The reasons behind the archbishop's action can only be surmised. Perhaps Geoffrey of York wished to devolve the responsibility which fell on him as the successor of Thurstan and ensure that others provided the necessary oversight for the convent.

Both Malling and Clementhorpe clearly owed their foundation in a large measure to the initiative of a prelate of the church. The same is true of the Gilbertine nunnery of Haverholme, although the original intention of Bishop Alexander of Lincoln was to grant the site to the Cistercian monks of Fountains.[34] It was only when they moved to Louth Park that the marshy island was granted to the women. The claims of other nunneries to have been founded by a member of the episcopate are supported by less evidence. The house of Farewell in Staffordshire is usually described as a foundation of Bishop Roger de Clinton (1129–48).[35] Roger seems to have taken a considerable interest in religious foundations, probably playing a major part in the establishment of the Savigniac house of Buildwas, and St John's

---

[30] VCH *City of York*, 377.

[31] *EYC*, i, 279–81, no. 359. Charters recording grants to Clementhorpe are transcribed in the Dodsworth manuscripts: see Oxford, Bodleian MS Dodsworth viii, fos. 102ᵛ, 108ᵛ, 109, 110, 141–2. Some of these are printed in *EYC*, ii, 352–4, nos. 1,037–9.

[32] *Rot. Chart.*, 40b.

[33] The story is recorded in several chronicles. The fullest account is by Roger of Howden; see *Gesta Henrici II*, ii, 240, and *Chron. Howden*, iii, 188; see also *Memoriale Fratris Walteri de Coventria. The Historical Collections of Walter of Coventry*, ed. W. Stubbs, 2 vols. (Rolls ser., 58; London, 1872–3), ii, 22. For other attempts by the ecclesiastical authorities to link small nunneries with larger convents see p. 215.

[34] *Acta 1 Lincoln 1067–1185*, 24–5, no. 37. For Haverholme see also *Book of St Gilbert*, p. xxxi.

[35] For the background history of this house see VCH *Staffs.*, iii, 222–5.

Hospital, Lichfield.[36] Farewell developed from a hermit community,[37] and it is probable that the role of the bishop was more to
regularize the position of the community of women than to initiate a
new foundation. It is a possibility that bishops may have regarded
hermits as a somewhat disturbing element in the church and have
attempted to control them.[38] Bishop Roger certainly had contact
with several eremitical communities. He issued a charter to the
hermits of Blithbury, Staffordshire, as well as witnessing another
recording grants to the community as it developed into a nunnery.[39]
He also granted a charter to the hermits of Red Moor, the group
which subsequently formed the nucleus of the Cistercian abbey of
Stoneleigh.[40] In this charter he specifically referred to the possibility
of women following the religious life in association with the hermits,
and gave such a development his blessing.[41] At Farewell he granted
the site and land to assart to the hermits at the church of St Mary,
and subsequently transferred the endowment, at the brothers'
request, to the community of women there. His charter to the nuns
stated that he granted the church of St Mary, with a mill, wood,
pannage, and six villeins who had formerly been his tenants. As at
Malling and Clementhorpe there is a suggestion of corporate
responsibility. Some land and services were granted by the bishop at
the request of Hugh, his chaplain and the canons of Lichfield. The
charter was witnessed by the dean, treasurer, and four archdeacons.
It concludes with the bishop urging all parishioners to make grants to
the house and support it.[42]

It would certainly seem that episcopal support, including the
provision of some of the endowment, was a factor in the development of a community of nuns at Farewell.[43] But it is not clear that
the site was originally granted by Roger de Clinton. Royal
confirmation charters obtained by the nunnery make no reference to
the bishop having played a particular role in the foundation, but
make it clear that the site was in the royal forest.[44] In the fourteenth

---

[36] KH, 116, 370.

[37] See above p. 27.

[38] Holdsworth, 'Christina', 189.

[39] For these charters and the question of the eremitical origin of Blithbury see above,
pp. 26–7.

[40] KH, 124, 125–6.

[41] 'Si quas mulieres Deo devotas religiosas, et regularem vitam professas ad Dei cultum
necessarias praedicti fratres congregare, Deo propitio, aliquando potuerint in divina doctrina
eas suscipiant, et nostra licentia et concessione eas regulariter doceant et regant', MA, v, 446,
no. 2.

[42] MA, iv, 111, no. 1.

[43] Bishop Walter, Roger's successor, confirmed this charter and added a grant of his own
(MA, iv, 111, no. 1).

[44] Cal. Pat. Rolls 1374–77, 182. See also MA, iv, 111–12, nos. 3 and 4.

century it was alleged that the crown was patron of the house.[45] To ascribe the foundation of Farewell to Bishop Roger de Clinton would be an oversimplification.

The bishop was also reputed to have established the nearby nunnery of Brewood Black Ladies.[46] There is no direct evidence to support this, but the manor of Brewood was among the episcopal possessions, and it is probable that the site was granted by Roger.[47] A bull of Gregory IX relating to the nunnery is transcribed in one of the Lichfield registers—the *Magnum Registrum Album*. It has interesting references to the bishop, mentioning future acquisitions which might be obtained by episcopal grant as well as from royal gifts and offerings of the faithful. It also states that the bishop was to confer benediction of the nuns and ordination of the chaplains without hint of corruption. Other provisions of the bull imply a desire to safeguard the community's freedom, both in the election of a prioress and the reception of new converts.[48] It is possible that this represents an attempt by the nuns to safeguard their position against the bishop as well as against lay patrons. Bishop Roger may have had a particular concern to help women seeking to follow a religious vocation. The grant of Oldbury, Warwickshire, to the group of nuns who eventually settled at Polesworth, was made in his presence and ratified by him.[49] But the nature of his role in the foundation of these nunneries is not easy to establish.

Several other houses of nuns were said to have been founded by a bishop. According to the fourteenth-century chronicler, William Thorne, the house of St Sepulchre, Canterbury, was founded by Archbishop Anselm. This is a late source for such a claim, but it is possible that Thorne derived his information from an earlier chronicle.[50] The archbishop was clearly concerned with the religious vocation of women, but it is unlikely that his was the sole initiative in the establishment of nuns there, and more probable that he

[45] *Cal. Pat. Rolls 1396–99*, 293 (1398).

[46] VCH Staffs., iii, 220–2. See also G. P. Mander, 'The Priory of Black Ladies of Brewood co. Stafford. Some Charters and Records and Notes on the Same', *Staffs. Hist. Collections* (Staffs. Record Soc; 1940) 175–220.

[47] VCH *Staffs.*, v, 25 and 36.

[48] *Magnum Registrum Album. The Great Register of Lichfield Cathedral*, ed. H. E. Savage *Staffs. Historical Collections*; (1926 for 1924), 336–7, no. 703. The register, which dates from the early 14th cent., is described in *Fourteenth Report of the Royal Commission of Historical Manuscripts* (London, 1895), app. viii, (1895), 206–26. See also Davis, *Med. Cartls.*, 64, no. 563.

[49] *MA*, ii, 367, nos. 8 and 9. For a further discussion of the role of bishops in ratifying foundations see pp. 203–4.

[50] *Chron. Will. Thorne*, 215. For notes on Thorne's Chronicle and his probable use of earlier sources see *Councils and Synods I* (ii), *1066–1204*, 807, n. 3.

facilitated the regularization of a community which had developed round an anchoress.[51]

Another nunnery, Ivinghoe, was reputed to have been founded by Bishop William Giffard of Winchester (1107–29). Ivinghoe was a small and poor priory situated in Hertfordshire.[52] The manor was part of the endowment of the see of Winchester from before the Conquest,[53] and a confirmation charter of Thomas of Canterbury referred to the possessions granted to the house by Bishop William.[54] The bishop was probably a member of the same family as Walter Giffard, Earl of Buckingham.[55] He was a friend of Anselm, and was clearly concerned with monastic vocation. He founded the abbey of Waverley, the first Cistercian house in England, in 1128, and also the priory of Augustinian canons at Taunton in c.1120. In addition he played a part in the establishment of canons at Southwark.[56] He seems to have quarrelled violently with the monks at Winchester, but became reconciled, and eventually died vested as one of their community.[57] Archbishop Thomas's charter gives no details about the grants made by Bishop William, and the general poverty and obscurity of the house does not suggest a major episcopal initiative. It certainly presents a contrast to the bishop's foundations for men at Waverley and Taunton.

Another small house said to have been founded by a bishop was the nunnery of Whistones near Worcester.[58] According to Nash it was founded by Walter de Cantilupe (1237–66).[59] Bishop Walter had a reputation for vigorous action. He promulgated statutes for monks and canons, and worked to ensure their observance.[60] One decree hints at a concern for the vocation of nuns with the demand that clerics were not to frequent nuns' churches without reasonable

---

[51] See pp. 36–7.

[52] It was formerly within the boundary of Buckinghamshire. Very little is known about the house: see VCH Bucks., i, 353.

[53] Ibid. 233.

[54] English Episcopal Acta II Canterbury 1162–1190, ed. C. R. Cheney and B. A. Jones (London, 1986), 9–10, no. 16.

[55] For a note on the bishop's parentage see J. H. Round, Feudal England (London, 1895), 469–70. Walter founded the Augustinian house of Notley, Bucks. (KH, 169).

[56] KH, 127–8, 175, and 174.

[57] Ann. Mon. ii (Ann. Winchester), 46–9.

[58] The nunnery was situated to the north of the city: see note in KH, 276, where it is pointed out that the map in VCH Worcs., ii, 90 shows it wrongly as five miles south east of the city.

[59] Nash, Worcs., i, 209. The suggestion that Walter was the founder is followed in VCH Worcs., ii, 154.

[60] For chronicle evidence of Bishop Walter in action see Ann. Mon., i (Ann. Tewkesbury), 146. His statutes are printed in Councils and Synods with Other Documents Relating to the English Church, II, 1205–1313, ed. F. M. Powicke and C. R. Cheney (Oxford, 1964), i, 1205–65, 294–321. For a discussion of these and their significance see C. R. Cheney, English Synodalia of the Thirteenth Century (Oxford, 1941, repr. 1968), chap. iv.

cause.[61] There is no direct evidence that the bishop was the founder of the community at Whistones. The nunnery was situated in the manor of Northwick and the bishop was recorded as holding land there in 1086.[62] The cartulary of the cathedral shows that the church at Whistones belonged to the prior and chapter in 1149.[63] There is no evidence that it was ever granted to the nunnery, but in 1255 the site of the priory was confirmed to the nuns by the prior and monks of Worcester.[64] Bishop Walter seems to have granted some land to the house, as the *Red Book of Worcester* records that the nuns of Whistones were given two acres by him.[65] It is not clear whether this refers to a gift or a confirmation, and it hardly provides evidence that the bishop was the founder of the house. At an earlier date, however, nuns had been associated with the cathedral church of Worcester. A grant of Ethelbald, King of Mercia, made in 743 refers to the presence of nuns there, as well as monks, and suggests the existence of some form of double establishment.[66] William of Malmesbury records the tradition that Wulfgifu, mother of St Wulfstan, took the veil at a nunnery in the city at the same time as his father entered religion.[67]

It is not possible, in the absence of evidence, to decide whether there was any link between an earlier group of women associated with the church of Worcester and the nuns of Whistones. It has been suggested in a previous chapter that links between nuns and monasteries of monks and canons were by no means uncommon.[68] A community of nuns was certainly in existence by 1241, when a reference on the close rolls records a grant by the king to the 'white sisters of Worcester'.[69] This probably refers to the nuns of Whistones who were sometimes described in this way.[70] The confirmation of

---

[61] *Councils and Synods II*, i, 312, no. 66; cf. ibid. 269–70, no. 11 for a similar decree in the Lincoln statutes of ?1239.

[62] VCH *Worcs.*, i, 294, 325.

[63] *Cartl. Worc.*, 42, no. 73. See also ibid. 47, no. 77.

[64] Nash, *Worcs.*, i, 209.

[65] *The Red Book of Worcester containing Surveys of the Bishops' Manors and Other Records*, ed. M. Hollings, 2 vols. (Worcs. Hist. Soc.; London, 1934–9), i, 87.

[66] KH, 81.

[67] *Vita Wulfstani of William of Malmesbury*, ed. R. R. Darlington (Camden, 3rd ser. 40; London, 1928), 7 and 4. For a further note on the early nunnery at Worcester see J. W. Lamb, *Saint Wulfstan, Prelate and Patriot* (London, 1933), 12, n. 1.

[68] See Chapter 4.

[69] *Cal. Close Rolls 1237–42*, 310 (1241). The same entry records that a grant of wine was also to be made to the nuns of Cook Hill. Another entry on the close rolls for the same year records a grant by the king of six oaks to the 'sorores penitentes' of Worcester (ibid. 274). This could also refer to the community which became established at Whistones.

[70] In the 15th cent. they were apparently sometimes described as white nuns of the order of St Benedict: see Nash, *Worcs.*, i, 222, no. 8. Cf. description as white nuns of order of St Bernard, ibid., no. 7.

the site at Whistones to the nuns by the prior and church of Worcester, and the dedication of the church to Saint Mary Magdalene in 1254,[71] may refer to the resettlement of an earlier group on a new site, or to the provision of new buildings and a new church for an already existing community. Later bishops seem to have acted as patrons of the nunnery. A grant of twelve acres of land was apparently made by Bishop Godfrey Giffard (1268–1301),[72] and in the early fourteenth century it was stated in the *Registrum Sede Vacante* that the bishop was patron of the house and a licence was granted by the bishop-elect for the election of a new prioress.[73]

If the claim of Bishop Walter of Worcester to have founded a nunnery rests only on indirect evidence, and may reflect episcopal support rather than an initial act of foundation, the possibility that Bishop Nigel of Ely (1133–69) founded the priory of St Radegund, Cambridge,[74] is even less clearly substantiated. The statement that the house was an episcopal foundation was made by Bishop Alcock in 1496 when he was trying to convert the convent to a college.[75] There seems to be little to suggest that Bishop Nigel was generally concerned to support monastic vocation. According to the *Liber Eliensis* he blatantly and diligently despoiled his own cathedral priory.[76] The bishop undoubtedly issued confirmation charters to the nuns of St Radegund, one in general terms to 'the cell of women recently founded outside Cambridge', and another confirming an early grant made by a certain William *Monachus*, a goldsmith. Bishop Nigel also acted as a witness to a charter of Countess Constance, wife of King Stephen's son Eustace, confirming grants to the nuns; moreover, the charter was in the form of a notification to him.[77] It is possible that William played an important part in providing the early endowment of the nuns of St Radegund. He featured in the *Liber Eliensis* as a friend of the bishop who eventually came to realize the error of his ways and repent of his evil-doing towards the monks.[78] He may have enlisted the support of the bishop on behalf of the community of women. It would seem, however, that the bishop was being called merely to add the weight

---

[71] *Ann. Mon.*, iv (*Ann. Worc.*), 443. This charter is preserved in the *Liber Albus* of Worcester, fo. 62.

[72] *Red Book of Worc.*, i, 27.

[73] *Register of the Diocese of Worcester during the Vacancy of the See usually called 'Registrum Sede Vacante' 1301–1435*, ed. J. W. Willis Bund (Worcs. Hist. Soc.; Oxford, 1897), 112 (1308). For the rights of patrons in elections see Chap.9, esp. p. 184–5.

[74] The main sources for this house are the charters preserved at Jesus College, Cambridge: see Gray, *St Radegund*. For a background history see VCH *Cambs.*, ii, 218–19.

[75] VCH Cambs., ii, 218.

[76] *Liber Eliensis*, ed. E. O. Blake (Camden, 3rd ser. 92; 1962), 294–9.

[77] Gray, *St Radegund*, 74, no. 1 and 75, nos. 2b and 3a.

[78] *Liber Eliensis*, 325 and 340. For a note on William see Gray, *St Radegund*, 4–6.

of his authority to grants made by others. The vagueness of the description in the episcopal charter of the land given to the nuns[79] hardly suggests a specific grant made by the bishop, and there is no real indication that he founded this community.

In the case of Minster in Sheppey, the claim that the house was founded by a member of the episcopate probably reflects a re-foundation associated with scandal. The original community had been established by a royal widow in *c*.670 and was probably destroyed by the Danes.[80] According to Hasted, nuns who had previously been living at Newington in Kent moved into the ruined abbey at Minster after the murder of the prioress.[81] Thorne's chronicle has a similar story, stating that the prioress was strangled by her cook when in bed at night and her body hidden in a well. The king then took the manor into his own hands and removed the nuns to Sheppey.[82] The version of the incident given in the chronicle attributed to Sprott strains credibility even further. In this the culprit who caused the prioress's death was not her cook but her cat.[83]

But the tradition of a move from Newington to Minster may have some validity, even if the details of the disturbance at Newington invite a measure of scepticism.[84] Hasted follows Leland in stating that Archbishop William Corbeil was the founder of the new settlement at Minster.[85] Evidence for his playing a decisive part in the re-foundation is indirect. A charter of King John refers to grants made to Minster by Archbishop William.[86] This must refer to William of Corbeil, an Augustinian monk, who was prior of the house of St Osyth, Essex.[87] The archbishop seems to have taken active measures to improve the quality of monastic life,[88] and may have been responsible for establishing regular canons at St Gregory's,

[79] 'Carta mea confirmasse quandam terram sanctimonialibus cellule extra villam Cantebruge noviter institute prope terram eiusdem cellule iacentem', Gray, *St Radegund*, 74, no. 1.

[80] KH, 261; VCH *Kent*, ii, 149.

[81] E. Hasted, *The History and Topographical Survey of the County of Kent*, 12 vols. (Canterbury, 1797–1801), vi, 218. [82] *Chron. Will. Thorne*, 273–4.

[83] *Thomae Sprotti Chronica*, ed. T. Hearne (Oxford, 1719), 162–3; see also *MA*, vi (iii), 1620. For a note on the doubts surrounding Sprott and Thorne see *Councils and Synods I* (ii), 1066–1204, 807.

[84] Thorne records another tradition of murder and scandal among canons at Newington (*Chron. Will. Thorne*, 274). The church of Newington near Sittingbourne (not to be confused with Newington in Folkestone Hundred) seems to have occupied an exceptional position: see *The Domesday Monachorum of Christ Church Canterbury*, ed. D. C. Douglas (London, 1944), 13–14 and n. 7.

[85] Leland, *Coll.*, i (i), 89; Hasted, *Kent*, vi, 218.

[86] *Rot. Chart.*, 148b (1205). A later *inspeximus* of Archbishop William Courtenay (1395 × 1396) refers to charters granted to the nuns by Archbishops William and Theobald (*Cal. Pat. Rolls 1399–1401*, 340).

[87] HRH, 183.

[88] For a legatine council held by him which promulgated decrees including one about the clothing of nuns see *Councils and Synods I* (ii) 1066–1204, 743–9, esp. 749, no. 11.

Canterbury, as well as St Martin's, Dover.[89] He was also said to be a close friend of Archbishop Anselm.[90] There was some confusion as to the order of the nuns at Minster, but in 1400 the archbishop claimed to have found documents proving the community had been founded for Augustinian canonesses. He was sufficiently convinced by the evidence to restore the nuns of Minster, then following the Benedictine rule, to the Augustinian fold.[91] It is possible that this may reflect the original foundation of William of Corbeil and his links with the Augustinians. The date given by Hasted for the restoration of religious life in Minster is 1130, while he suggests that the scandal at Newington may have occurred in the reign of the Conqueror.[92] But Thorne's chronicle leaves the chronology of the disturbance vague,[93] and it would seem a reasonable assumption that Archbishop William played an important part in the re-foundation of a community of nuns after some scandal, and as part of the introduction of a stricter monastic observance. The charter of King John, which provides the earliest evidence of the archbishop's involvement, is interesting in the detail it records about grants to Minster and the number which are associated with the entrance of a nun into the community. It is possible that the mother of justiciar Richard de Lucy was one of them,[94] and that, through her, land in Newington was transferred to Minster. The clear association of grants with the reception of nuns suggests that they may refer to early donations made at a time when anxieties about simony were less clearly formulated.

The nunnery of 'Ramstede' in Sussex provides an interesting example both of the obscurity of foundations said to have been established by a bishop, and of episcopal intervention in the face of scandal. Archbishop Richard of Dover (1174–84) confirmed to the nuns land on which their buildings were erected and lands granted by three named donors.[95] Very little is known of this nunnery—even the exact site and its dedication are uncertain.[96] It is not clear how

---

[89] KH, 152, 156.

[90] *Symeonis Monachi Opera Omnia*, ed. T. Arnold, 2 vols. (Rolls ser. 75; 1882–5), ii, 269.

[91] *Cal. Pat. Rolls 1399–1401*, 340–1.

[92] Hasted, *Kent*, vi, 218.

[93] *Chron. Will. Thorne*, 273–4.

[94] *Rot. Chart.*, 148b. Richard de Lucy was justiciar under Henry II until 1178 × 1179. He eventually entered his foundation of the Augustinian abbey of Lesnes in Kent (KH, 164).

[95] *Acta II Canterbury 1162–1190*, 157–8, nos. 183 and 184. See also 255, no. 300. For a background history of the priory see VCH *Sussex*, ii, 63.

[96] The site of the house is probably Ramscombe in Sussex: see *Acta II Canterbury 1162–1190*, 158. A note of grants made to 'Ramstede' is in the list preserved in PRO Misc. Books E36/137: see I. J. Churchill, 'Table of Canterbury Archbishopric Charters', *Camden Miscellany XV* (3rd ser. 41; 1929), 8. This suggests the nunnery was dedicated to St James; the dedication given in KH is St Mary Magdalene (KH, 263).

far the archbishop was making his own donation rather than simply confirming the grants of others. The house was eventually suppressed by Archbishop Hubert Walter, and in so doing he claimed it had been founded by his ancestors.[97] The lands and buildings of the nuns were granted by him to the prior and canons of St Gregory, Canterbury,[98] and it is stated that the women were deprived because of their scandalous behaviour. The suppression seems to have attracted little attention, gaining no mention in the chronicles.[99] It is not clear whether Archbishop Richard was the main founder, and the history of Ramstede seems to illustrate the problems of the nuns rather than the benefits of archiepiscopal patronage.

It is not surprising that several nunneries developed a tradition of episcopal foundation. In some cases this probably reflected their lack of a decisive lay founder and the involvement of a bishop at some time in the foundation process. Such involvement may have been considerable. At the dedication of the church of the abbey of Godstow, a lengthy charter of Bishop Alexander of Lincoln reveals the attendance of Archbishop Theobald, five other bishops, and the papal legate, as well as King Stephen and his queen.[100] In addition to gracing the occasion with their presence, the bishops made grants to the new foundation, with Bishop Alexander himself giving 100 shillings from the toll of his market at Banbury.[101] The involvement of so many bishops was probably unusual, perhaps reflecting the energy of Edith and the prestige of the foundation. At the dedication of the church at Markyate only the Bishop of Lincoln and the Bishop of Limerick appear to have been present.[102] But a sizeable number of nunneries, many of them relatively small and obscure foundations, obtained general confirmations from archbishop or bishop.[103]

In addition to such episcopal charters, the early endowment of

---

[97] *Cartulary of the Priory of St Gregory Canterbury*, ed. A. M. Woodcock (Camden, 3rd ser. 88; 1956), 6–7, no. 9. The word used is *antecessores*. This could indicate that he was referring to his ancestors rather than his predecessors in office, but it is not clear.

[98] Ibid.

[99] It is suggested in *MA*, iv, 658 that Archbishop Edmund re-established nuns there, but this is probably based on the mistaken identification of Archbishop 'B' as Boniface, rather than Baldwin.

[100] *Acta I Lincoln 1067–1185*, 20–2, no. 33.

[101] Ibid. 21, 23–4, no. 35.

[102] Ibid. 31, no. 49.

[103] e.g. general confirmations of endowments were obtained from Archbishop Theobald by: Clerkenwell (London), Greenfield (Lincs.), Littlemore (Oxon.), Malling (Kent), Nun Appleton (Yorks.), Nuneaton (Warwicks.), St Radegund (Cambs.), and Wintney (Hants.). See Saltman, *Archbishop Theobald*, 296–7, no. 72; 344, no. 122; 383–4, no. 160; 395–7, no. 173; 412, no. 189; 409–10, no. 187; 522, no. 296; 509–10, no. 280. The bishops of Lincoln granted general confirmations to: Godstow (Oxon.), Greenfield (Lincs.), Harrold (Beds.), Langley (Leics.), Nun Cotham and Stixwould (Lincs.): see *Acta I Lincoln 1067–1185*, 20–2, no. 33; 80–1, no. 129; 82, no. 132; 88–9, no. 142; 127, no. 203; 37–8, no. 57 and 160, no. 257.

several nunneries was notified to the bishop or archbishop by the lay founder or patron.[104] Sometimes these charters attempted to safeguard the new foundation by invoking ecclesiastical sanctions. At Legbourne, the charter of one of the founders, Robert fitz Gilbert, addressed to the Bishop of Lincoln, stated that all who harmed the endowments of the house were to be excommunicated.[105] There is a reference to episcopal sanctions in a charter of William de Liseurs for the nunnery of Crabhouse. William referred to the wrath of the bishop of Norwich which would be turned against any who threatened the community.[106] In addition to general confirmations, bishops also frequently ratified particular grants. Many of these were of churches or tithes, spiritual sources of revenue which clearly came within episcopal jurisdiction.[107] But it also seems that the bishop and chapter played an important part in ratifying individual grants, not all of which referred clearly to spiritual sources of revenue.[108] Some of these may have been linked with the entrance of a new recruit into the community. A charter of Jordan de Bricett and his wife, the founders of Clerkenwell, which was addressed to the Bishop of London, clearly refers to a grant made to facilitate the entry of their daughter into the nunnery.[109] The donation of a half mark, notified to the Archbishop of York at Marrick, was given when the grantor's sister became a nun.[110] Nevertheless, the general impression is that episcopal concern was not limited to new foundations, or to grants of churches with tithes, or to donations linked with the entrance of women into the nunnery.

The granting of an episcopal charter could reflect need on the part of the nuns as well as concern on the part of the bishop. There may

[104] These are extant for at least eight nunneries: Castle Hedingham (*MA*, iv, 437–8, no. 1); Gokewell (*EYC*, vi, 202, no. 103); Greenfield (BL Harl. chart. 50 I 30, printed in *MA*, v, 579–80; see also *Danelaw Docs.*, 99–100, nos. 150–1); Henwood (*MA*, iv, 212, no. 1); Heynings (*Cal. Chart. Rolls* 1257–1300, 106); Legbourne (Oxford, Bodleian MS Dodsworth lxxv, fo. 23ᵛ); Marrick (*EYC*, v, 76–7, no. 173); and Redlingfield (*Reg. Regum*, iii, 262, no. 712). At Oldbury (later Polesworth) an early grant was made in the presence of the bishop who then confirmed it (*MA*, ii, 367, nos. 8 and 9).

[105] Oxford, Bodleian MS Dodsworth, lxxv, fo. 23ᵛ.

[106] *MA*, v, 69, no. 4.

[107] Some examples of original charters recording episcopal grants or confirmations of churches are: *Acta IV Lincoln 1186–1206*, 32, no. 40 (Catesby nunnery), PRO E210/2060 (Wroxall nunnery). In one example the choice of which religious house was to receive the church seems to have been made by the bishop not the lay donor: see BL Addit. chart. 47,573 (Nuneaton).

[108] e.g. at Nun Cotham (*Acta I Lincoln 1067–1185*, 128–9, nos. 205, 206); Stixwould (BL Addit. MS 46,701, fos. 9ᵛ, 64, and 65ᵛ). For examples of episcopal charters ratifying more general grants, see BL Addit. charts. 33,442, and 33,595. For examples of episcopal charters confirming grants made by a predecessor, see PRO, E326/11,536; 11,537; 11,538 (Newcastle nunnery).

[109] *Cartl. Clerkenwell*, 51–2, no. 74 (1156 × 1162).

[110] 'Marrick Charts.', *Coll. Top. et Gen.*, v. 231, no. 1.

have been particular reasons why nuns needed to avail themselves of episcopal help. As suggested in the story of Christina of Markyate, the support and general patronage of a member of the spiritual hierarchy could make the difference between the success and failure of an individual woman's vocation. Once Christina had aroused the enmity of Bishop Robert of Lincoln, she was only openly able to follow the religious life after his death.[111] She eventually made her solemn profession at St Albans in front of his successor, Bishop Alexander.[112] It is not clear whether such a profession could, at that date, be made only to a bishop or to his representative. The doctrine that the care of virgins consecrated to God should be entrusted to the ordinary, or to someone designated by him, seems to have evolved early in the history of the Christian church.[113] The role of the bishop in assisting with the foundation of a religious community probably became more central. Instead of a mere notification of the foundation, the foundation charters of the nunnery of Flixton, established in the middle of the thirteenth century, make clear the part played by the prelate in veiling the women and ensuring that they followed the Augustinian rule. The bishop also decreed that they were to be enclosed and provided with sufficient sustinence.[114]

Such practicalities as the poverty of the women may frequently have resulted in their seeking episcopal help.[115] The idea that material difficulties provided a particular cause for concern is sometimes expressed in preambles to bishops' charters[116] and in synodal decrees. Such concern led to regulation and control. At the Council of Oxford, held in 1222, it was stated that the bishops should ensure that the nuns were adequately provided for, and not allow a greater number to enter the convent than could be provided for.[117] Although for the twelfth and first half of the thirteenth centuries, the lack of bishops' registers means that evidence about episcopal visitation and control is scanty,[118] injunctions have survived for two nunneries. The cartulary of Nun Cotham contains

[111] Talbot, *Life of Christina*, 118.

[112] Ibid. 146.

[113] J. Rambaud Buhot, 'Le Statut des moniales chez les Pères de l'Église dans les règles monastiques et les collections canoniques, jusqu'au XIIe siècle', in *Sainte Fare et Faremoutiers. Treize siècles de vie monastique* (Faremoutiers, 1956), 163. For the importance of the tradition of the consecrated virgin, see Hunt, 'Benedictine and Cistercian Nuns', 155–77, partic. 159.

[114] BL Stowe chart. 292; BL Stowe chart. 293.

[115] Grants of churches to nuns were frequently justified in episcopal charters on the grounds of poverty, e.g. *Foliot Letters and Charters*, 245, no. 172.

[116] See the charter of Archbishop Thomas to Ivinghoe Priory, *Acta II Canterbury 1162–1190*, 9–10, no. 16.

[117] *Councils and Synods II* (i), 123–4, no. 55.

[118] For later visitations of nunneries by bishops see Power, 635.

injunctions which were issued by Bishop Hugh of Lincoln.[119] Both these and a set of regulations extant for the priory of Marrick reveal the bishops' concern to control numbers within the community to ensure adequate resources.[120] The decree of the council of 1222 itself reveals the possibility of further episcopal intervention in an effort to obtain a balance between inmates and resources. It goes on to state that if the abbess, prioress, *magister*, or prior of a house contravened limitations of size set for the community, they were to be deposed.[121]

Another focal point for episcopal intervention in a nunnery was the provision of chaplains. The Oxford synod decreed that nuns were to confess to priests chosen by the bishop.[122] It is possible that a measure of episcopal control over the chaplains of nuns had existed in the twelfth century. A charter of Bishop Alexander of Lincoln allowed the abbess of Godstow control over her chaplains and granted that she should exercise care and correction over her nuns without being liable to episcopal or archidiaconal intervention.[123] Such a privilege may have been unusual. The evidence certainly suggests that Godstow was an unusually powerful foundation.[124] A theme of this book is that the provision of chaplains and masculine support for the nuns often caused difficulties. Double orders had failed to provide a solution, and episcopal intervention was probably increasingly necessary. Sometimes monks from nearby houses were appointed by the bishop to help with the administration of particular nunneries.[125] Unease about individual monks undertaking the *cura monialium*, however, is implicit in a decree of the synod of Salisbury which forbade monks to live alone in cells and went on to prohibit anyone in a nunnery from combining offices which had previously been held by several people.[126] This would seem to suggest episcopal unease at the possibility of individual monks being isolated in a convent of women.

In the second half of the thirteenth century it would seem that

[119] Oxford, Bodleian MS Top Lincs. d 1, fo. 38, printed in *MA*, v, 677–8, no. 7. Whether these derive from Hugh of Avalon or Hugh of Wells they are still the earliest known: see C. R. Cheney, *Episcopal Visitation of Monasteries in the Thirteenth Century* (Manchester, 1931; 2nd edn., 1983), 98.

[120] BL Egerton chart. 406. Reference is made to such returns in VCH *Yorks.*, iii, 117, where it is noted that search had failed to find the original document; see also Burton, *Yorks. Nunneries*, 29 and 52. The Egerton charter, written in a 13th-cent. hand, would seem to be the missing source.

[121] *Councils and Synods II* (i), 123–4, no. 55.

[122] Ibid. 124, no. 55.

[123] *Acta I Lincoln 1067–1185*, 22–3, no. 34.

[124] See above, pp. 167–8.

[125] For examples in Yorks. dating from *c.*1267–90, see Burton, *Yorks. Nunneries*, 35.

[126] *Councils and Synods II* (i), 93, no. 101 (1217 × 1219). A later alteration to the text makes it less clear that this refers to nuns: see ibid., 93, note a.

secular clergy were increasingly used by the bishop to help with the task of providing oversight and support for the nunneries. For example, in 1279 Archbishop Pecham entrusted the custody of the priory of Davington, Kent, to the vicar of Faversham.[127] It is also possible that clerics who were presented to churches where nuns held the advowson sometimes acted as chaplains to the women.[128] Such an arrangement would provide for their maintenance. It would also mean that such chaplains were under the authority of the bishop.

If financial problems and difficulties over the provision of chaplains may have been practical reasons leading to episcopal involvement in the affairs of nunneries, another factor was the lack of an alternative authority. In the case of men's houses, many monasteries obtained exemption from episcopal jurisdiction by virtue of their own power or by virtue of their order. This was generally not true of the nunneries. At Marham, founded as a Cistercian abbey, there is no evidence of contact with the Bishop of Norwich, apart from matters concerning the nuns' ownership of churches. The conventual church was dedicated by the Bishop of Chichester rather than the diocesan. This probably reflects the claims of the Cistercian order, and the house was visited by Cistercian abbots,[129] but efforts on the part of other English nunneries to obtain freedom from episcopal intervention by virtue of being Cistercian seem to have met with little success.[130] The houses of the order of Fontevrault were probably visited and controlled by members of the order rather than by the bishop. Yet the distance of the English nunneries from the mother house weakened such links, and the bishop seems to have come to replace the authority of the order. In 1320 he intruded his own candidate rather than the lady selected by the abbess of Fontevrault as head of Nuneaton, and in 1412 the Bishop of Salisbury was commissioned by the pope to visit the priory as often as was necessary, as long as the abbess of Fontevrault was unable to do so because of the war between France and England.[131]

---

[127] *Reg. epistolarum Peckham*, i, 72–3. For numerous other examples of the appointment of *custodes* in the latter part of the 13th and 14th centuries see Power, 228–36. She implies that their role was largely concerned with the supervision of temporal affairs, but as the Pecham entry makes clear, this was not always the case.

[128] In the absence of evidence this must remain a tentative suggestion. The description of the clerics presented as *capellani* can certainly not automatically be taken to mean that they were chaplains to the nuns.

[129] Nichols, 'Marham Abbey', 124.

[130] See above pp. 107–8. See also Nichols, 'Cistercian Nunneries and Bishops', 237–49. Although Cîteaux was not founded as exempt from diocesan authority, by the middle of the 12th cent. houses of the order were generally independent of episcopal intervention.

[131] VCH *Warwicks.*, ii, 68.

A study of the convents founded by monks and canons also illustrates the tendency of bishops to increase their control over nunneries at the expense of other ecclesiastical authorities. At Stamford, established as a cell of Peterborough, it would seem that the nuns were visited by both bishop and abbot. An enquiry carried out by Robert Grosseteste into the rights of the abbey over the women, apparently showed that Hugh of Lincoln had previously visited the dependent community.[132] The evidence suggests that the bishop increasingly came to replace the abbot as mentor of the nuns.[133] It would be misleading to suggest that bishop and abbot were necessarily in competition for the *cura monialium*. At Thetford, the Bishop of Norwich appears to have played a part in persuading Abbot Hugh of Bury to take responsibility for the care of the women who had previously been at Ling.[134] At Derby, the bishop granted the abbot the *cura virginum* and licence to consecrate virgins.[135] At Kilburn, founded by the abbot of Westminster, an early charter, probably of Bishop Gilbert the Universal of London (1128–34), stated that the abbey rather than the bishop was to have jurisdiction over the priory.[136] By the thirteenth century, however, there are hints of problems. A detailed agreement, drawn up in 1231, set out the rights of the bishop. If matters needed correction and the abbot failed to take action, the bishop could intervene. He might enter the convent to pray and hear confessions, but was to bless or consecrate nuns only by invitation of the abbot.[137] This settlement was probably worked out in response to the complaint of the abbey about interference by Bishop Eustace de Fauconberg.[138] It suggests that by this date the diocesan was seeking more actively to intervene.

As links with the founding order or the founding monastery were loosened, there would have been an opening for the bishop to play an increasingly important role. At Harrold in Bedfordshire, Hugh de Wells played an important part in settling the controversy between the nunnery and the abbey of Missenden and in obtaining the independence of the nuns from the Arrouaisian order.[139] At Derby, the bishop obtained the agreement whereby the nuns obtained a

---

[132] S. Gunton, *The History of the Church of Peterburgh set forth by Symon Patrick D D now Dean of the same* (London, 1686), 328–9. Unfortunately no precise reference is made to sources.

[133] Sturman, 'Stamford', 58 and 64. See also Power, 481.

[134] BL Harl. MS 743, fos. 271ᵛ–272ᵛ; *MA*, iv, 478, no. 1.

[135] *Cartl. Darley*, ii, 596, no. 02.

[136] *Foliot Letters and Charters*, 491, no. 463. For the dating of this charter see above, Chap. 2, n. 73.

[137] BL Cotton MS Faust. A. iii, fo. 329; see also *MA*, iii, 428, no. 9.

[138] BL Cotton MS Faust. A. iii, fo. 204–204ᵛ, printed *MA*, iii, 427–8, no. 8.

[139] *Records of Harrold Priory*, 57, no. 69.***

degree of independence from the canons.[140] The women were taken under episcopal protection, a gesture which would open up the possibilities of more intervention. Only at St Albans does the power of the abbot seem to have been retained undiminished over the dependent communities of women, and there it was clearly resented. In 1490 a letter of Archbishop Moreton, probably instigated by the prioress of Sopwell, accused the abbot of exercising tyrannical power over the nuns.[141]

The reasons underlying contact between bishops and nuns were probably many and varied. Gerald of Wales (whose reliability can be questioned), tells of a member of the episcopate who was always accompanied by a young and comely nun.[142] The motives behind this choice of companion can only be guessed at. Some bishops had personal reasons for involvement with particular nunneries. In the thirteenth century, the sister of Bishop Robert Grosseteste was apparently a nun at Northampton,[143] while Archbishop Edmund Rich placed his sisters at Catesby and sent bequests to them.[144] Bishop Richard Poore (1217–28) became the patron of the nunnery of Tarrant, and probably played an important part in obtaining its affiliation to the Cistercian order.[145] At Flixton, the foundress transferred the patronage of the house to the Bishop of Norwich who had himself played an important part in the establishment of the community.[146]

But also of interest is the earlier involvement of bishops such as Roger of Chester and Nigel of Ely in the foundation and support of several small nunneries. Apart from the abbey of Malling, founded at the end of the eleventh century by a monk-bishop who seems to have made the welfare of the women his particular concern, the other houses founded or assisted by members of the episcopate were small and poor. Bishops, unless wealthy in their own right or lord of a rich see, would not find it easy to make sizeable grants of land to found a religious house. The claim of several nunneries to have an episcopal founder probably has little basis, and reflects an involvement by the bishop which resulted in part from the particular problems of the nuns. Adam Marsh wrote to Bishop Robert Grosseteste on behalf of

[140] *Cartl. Darley*, i, 176–8, no. D15. The bishop was probably Richard Poore.

[141] *VCH Herts.*, iv, 425.

[142] *Giraldi Cambrensis*, ii, *Gemma Ecclesiastica*, 249.

[143] An *inspeximus* charter of Edward III for Northampton refers to a grant made by Geoffrey, father of Bishop Robert with his sister (*MA*, v, 212). This could refer to Grosseteste as his sister was a nun: see *Roberti Grosseteste episcopi quondam Lincolniensis epistolae*, ed. H. R. Luard (Rolls ser. 25; 1861), 43–5, no. 8.

[144] Lawrence, *St Edmund*, 107, 270.

[145] See pp. 97–8.

[146] BL Stowe chart. 308.

the nuns of Grace Dieu in Leicestershire. The community was poor and struggling, and the friar implored the bishop's help.[147] The example of the ephemeral convent of Spinney, where the only extant evidence for the existence of such a community of nuns is an episcopal confirmation charter, shows that help from the bishop did not always ensure survival,[148] but the prominent featuring of bishops in the obituary list of the nunnery of Wintney, a house which claimed to be Cistercian, illustrates their probable importance.[149] In the middle of the thirteenth century the nuns of Studley Priory in Oxfordshire resigned one of their churches to the bishop.[150] The reason they gave for this action was that they could not, because of the frailty of their sex, choose a suitable vicar. This is indicative of the difficulties of the nuns and of their attempted solution in turning to the bishop.

[147] *Monumenta Franciscana*, ed. J. Brewer, 2 vols. (Rolls ser. 4; London, 1858–82), i, 115, 119, 130–1.

[148] *Acta I Lincoln 1067–1185*, 160, no. 256 (1148 × 1166).

[149] BL Cotton MS Claud. D. iii, fos. 140ᵛ–162ᵛ, printed in Trokelowe, *Annales*, 384–93. Six bishops of Winchester, two bishops of Bath, and a bishop of Lincoln feature in the obits.

[150] *Reg. Ant. Linc.*, III, 272–3, nos. 932, 933.

Conclusion

WHEN Hugh of Flavigny, writing at the end of the eleventh century, considered what he thought would be the order of precedence at the Last Judgement, he regarded women as a special category. The order of celestial preference was described as follows: Peter, Paul, John the Baptist, the rest of the Apostles, holy hermits, perfect monks, good bishops, good priests, good laymen, and—last of all—women.[1] A study of the nunneries founded after the Norman Conquest endorses the implicit suggestion that in the search for sanctity, women as a group had particular problems and difficulties. At an exhibition of Benedictine Monasticism held at the British Museum in 1980, the vast bulk of the evidence related to monks, with only two documents of the 128 exhibits specifically being concerned with nuns.[2] The shortage of sources for a study of women leading the religious life during the twelfth and first half of the thirteenth century must cause problems for the historian. It is also an indication of the problems of the women themselves, reflecting poverty, lack of learning, and the vagaries of their intrinsic dependence on men.

The story of Christina of Markyate illustrates the strength of one woman's vocation to the religious life. Little is known of the motives of the other thousands of women entering religious communities in twelfth- and thirteenth-century England. The *Life* of Christina hints how the dedication of one could inspire or shame others. Christina's sister entered Markyate, and apparently other ladies came to embrace the religious life as penance for their attempts to dissuade the recluse from following her vocation.[3] A handful of charters suggest the motives behind an individual's desire to enter a community. Sometimes it appears to have been the shadow of illness. At Nuneaton, an ailing lady, wife of Robert the cook, seems to have taken out an insurance policy when she gave the nuns a mantle, a cap, a gold ring, eight pigs, eleven beasts, nineteen sheep, and two houses, on condition that if she recovered and wanted to return to

---

[1] 'Chronicon Hugonis monachi Virdunensis et Divionensis abbatis Flaviniacensis', *MGH Scriptores*, viii, 384.

[2] *The Benedictines in Britain* (British Library ser. 3; London, 1980), exhibits nos. 51 and 81. The nuns' documents were the Castle Hedingham mortuary roll (BL Egerton MS 2849); and a letter of appeal on behalf of the nunnery of Kingsmead, Derby (BL Wolley chart., xi, 25). For this see R. Graham, 'An appeal for the church and buildings of Kingsmead priory, circa 1218', *Antiquaries Journal* 11 (1931), 51–4. The only other exhibit linked with nuns was the letters patent of Henry VIII granting the site of the priory of Henwood to its new owner (no. 111).

[3] Talbot, *Life of Christina*, 141, 45.

the world she could do so. As a further safeguard the prioress agreed to receive her as a nun whenever she did decide to renounce the worldly life.[4] There are occasional hints of more sinister pressures. Isolated cases preserved in legal records suggest that some women were forced to enter a nunnery so their inheritance could be claimed by others. This apparently happened at Ankerwyke in Buckinghamshire, and similar accusations are made in a case in Hertfordshire.[5] Sometimes for men entering the community a motive appears to have been provision for their female dependants. At Clerkenwell in London, a certain William became a brother there and made a grant to provide for his wife to have free board at the nunnery if she outlived him.[6] In Anglo-Norman society, organized to a large extent on a military basis, the dependence of women may have been intensified. The position of women in families holding by military tenure was different from that of the sokemen and burgess families in post Conquest England. The limited rights of women over land may have been a factor in the establishment of nunneries as a provision for them and the reason for making a grant to ensure the reception of a dependant.[7]

The large number of religious communities for women established after the Norman Conquest, and the probability that there were other small, ephemeral groups which have left no trace on the records, should be taken as a corporate testimony to the strength of vocation among women religious as well as a possible reflection of their dependence.[8] Charters recording the formalization of an endowment to a monastery have traditionally been taken to mark the origin of the community. In some cases this may have been true. The role of patrons and the granting of endowments was vital to provide an economic base for a religious community and to ensure its survival. But many nunneries seem to have developed slowly. Some grew up round anchoresses or recluses, others evolved from earlier communities, monasteries, or hospitals, where the sexes were associated. The religious fervour of the new orders attracted women as well as men, and gave impetus to the development of new religious communities for women. But the stabilization of these groups and the provision of masculine support remained a problem. When

---

[4] *Danelaw Docs.*, 247, no. 329.

[5] *Curia Regis Rolls*, i, 118, v, 183–6 (Ankerwyke); ibid., ix, 65–8 (? Sopwell).

[6] *Cartl. Clerkenwell*, 125, no. 200.

[7] I am grateful to Dr Chibnall for pointing out the possible significance of the different land tenures. This subject would repay further study.

[8] It is interesting that in Wales, where the legal status of women was possibly higher than in England, there was less provision in terms of nunneries than in comparable areas elsewhere: see F. G. Cowley, *The Monastic Order in South Wales 1066–1349* (Cardiff, 1977), 37–8.

women sought to follow a vocation and form religious communities, they had to depend on men to act for them as priests and to help with their temporal affairs. This had long been recognized, and it was decreed at the Council of Seville in 619 that nunneries should be protected and governed by monks.[9]

During the period studied in this book, the ways in which masculine protection and help for women religious was articulated underwent significant modifications. It appears that at first there may have been a relatively free partnership between the sexes. Many communities of women seem to have been associated initially with monasteries. Such association between the sexes seems to have been a feature of the eremitical movement. Hermits seeking to lead a life dedicated to God attracted women wishing to follow the same road to holiness. When Bishop Roger de Clinton confirmed a grant of land to the hermits at Red Moor and approved their vocation, he went on to state that if women should be attracted to their community, the brothers would have jurisdiction over them.[10] In the first half of the twelfth century, therefore, men and women probably frequently lived the religious life in association, both in cenobitic communities and in groups with a more eremitical orientation. Orders such as that of Fontevrault and the Gilbertines gave organizational expression to this association of the sexes. Such partnership provided a solution to the *cura monialium*—the need of nuns for priestly and masculine help. It is possible that the women's vocation sometimes incorporated a practical element, dispensing charity to the sick or to travellers, or contributing to their side of the partnership by caring for the men's practical needs. But such an association of the sexes depended on an uneasy foundation, one undermined by distrust of sexuality and fears of scandal.

The history of the new orders reflects this tension. The Cistercians at first totally excluded the female sex from their search for sanctity, and were only unwillingly forced to incorporate communities of women within their order in the second half of the thirteenth century. The Premonstratensian and Arrouaisian canons, after welcoming women converts, subsequently came to distance them from their masculine communities and ultimately tried to exclude them. Towards the end of the twelfth century, increasing efforts seem to have been made by the ecclesiastical hierarchy to ensure that communities of women were organized on a separate basis which would allow of no breath of scandal. The establishment of nunneries such as Crabhouse, Buckland, St Mary de Pré, Kingsmead Derby,

---

[9] *Mansi*, x, 560–1. [10] *MA*, v, 446, no. 2.

and many others has to be set against this background. One of the reasons for the pope allowing Aconbury to transfer from the order of the Hospitallers to the Augustinian rule was concern about the proximity of the sexes.[11] By the later twelfth century there are fewer references in charters to men as well as women, and houses such as Blackborough, Swine, and Legbourne develop into convents of nuns. Even the Gilbertine order modified its initial vision, and the majority of the later foundations were for canons only.

The problem remained as to who was to exercise the *cura monialium* and provide the necessary masculine support. For some time this may still have been given by monks and canons living in separate communities. A probable explanation of the changes of order found at many nunneries is that they sometimes obtained help from Augustinian canons and sometimes from Benedictine monks.[12] Nor were their links with the newer orders secure. It is within the double orders of Fontevrault and Sempringham that affiliation to a particular Rule seems to have remained most clear and constant, for their provision of chaplains was safeguarded. It is notable that references to the order of the nunnery are most frequent in the charters for the Gilbertine and Fontevraldine houses. In many other cases the order of the house is not referred to at all or delineated in ambiguous terms such as *ordo sanctimonialium*.[13] The degree of confusion is further illustrated by Canon 26 of the Second Lateran Council in 1139, which declared that some women lived under no rule and yet still claimed to be nuns.[14]

The lack of firm association with a particular order would have increased the vulnerability of women's communities. As the emphasis moved away from the religious to the secular church, the role of bishops became more important in the effort to control and regulate women seeking a religious vocation. Whereas Bishop Roger de Clinton had delegated this duty to a community of hermits, bishops came later to be more directly involved. They intervened to regulate numbers, to secure endowment, and to provide chaplains and *magistri*, who were drawn increasingly from the secular clergy.[15]

---

[11] *Cal. Pap. Lett.*, i, 134.

[12] This conclusion is also reached by Sharon Elkins: see Elkins, *Holy Women*, 66–7.

[13] For example the phrase 'ordo sanctimonialium' is used in a charter of Bishop Alvred of Worcester (1158–60) for Pinley (*MA*, iv, 115, no. 1). When attempts were being made to found a cell of Nun Appleton at Coddenham it was described as being of the order of the nuns of Appleton 'de ordine sanctimonialium de Apeltuna'—(BL Cotton MS Nero C. iii, fo. 227, printed in *EYC*, i, 426, no. 546).

[14] *Conciliorum Decreta*, 203, canon 26.

[15] For synodal decrees regulating numbers in nunneries and decreeing that the nuns should confess to priests chosen by the bishop, see *Councils and Synods II* (i) *1205–65*, 123–4, no. 55 (Council of Oxford, 1222). See also pp. 205–6 above.

Regulations promulgated by the ecclesiastical hierarchy sometimes sought to impose organizational links on communities of women. A bull of Pope Honorius III (1216–27) addressed to the abbots of Fountains and Rievaulx, referred to the poverty and difficulty of the nuns in the northern diocese. A possible solution suggested by the archbishop and the pope was to unite small cells to form larger and more viable units.[16] It is possible that measures such as this can explain the links between Seton in Cumberland and Nunburnholme in Yorkshire. In the fourteenth century, Seton was described as a cell of Nunburnholme.[17] There is no evidence to suggest that the two communities were linked at their foundation, and it may be that the association was a later one, imposed by the ecclesiastical authorities in an attempt to achieve greater stability. Other attempts had been made to unite communities of nuns. Archbishop Geoffrey of York tried to link the nunnery of Clementhorpe with Godstow, although the Yorkshire nuns seem to have maintained their independence.[18] Also in the late twelfth century, the Earl of Chester apparently granted the community of nuns at Chester to Clerkenwell nunnery, London.[19] Both Godstow and Clerkenwell were relatively prosperous communities, and although there is no evidence to suggest the links became a reality, such measures probably represent attempts to increase the support for particular nunneries.

The organizational difficulties of the nuns are also reflected in their failure to maintain links between mother and daughter houses. As with the monasteries, it was clearly a possibility that a nunnery could found dependent communities. The papal bull issued by Pope Eugenius for the house of Godstow in 1145 decreed that only a member of their order should be made head of any dependent cell founded from Godstow.[20] But no dependent communities of Godstow are known. The attempt of Nun Appleton to found a cell at Coddenham proved abortive.[21] The community of Langley in

---

[16] *Mem. Fountains*, i, 175–6. See also *Cal. Pap. Lett.*, i, 114.

[17] *Reg. Greenfield*, iii, 211–12.

[18] The nuns appealed to the pope, stating that from their foundation they had been free of any such dependence, and there is no evidence to suggest the Archbishop was successful. The story of this attempt by Archbishop Geoffrey is recorded in several chronicles. The fullest account is given in *Gesta Henrici II*, ii, 240. See also *Chron. Howden*, iii, 188 and *Mem. Walter de Coventry*, ii, 22.

[19] *Cartl. Clerkenwell*, 6, no. 6; See also VCH *Cheshire*, iii, 146. The editor of the Clerkenwell cartulary was puzzled at this apparent granting of property in Chester to the London nuns; see W. O. Hassall, 'The Chester Property of the Nunnery of St Mary Clerkenwell in the Twelfth Century', *Journal of the Chester and North Wales Archit., Archaeol. and Hist. Soc.*, 36 (ii), 178–9. A probable explanation is that it represents an attempt to link the two houses rather than a simple granting of property.

[20] *PUE*, i, 261, no. 32.

[21] See p. 175.

Leicestershire was initially founded from Farewell in Staffordshire.[22] But the claims of Farewell to exercise control over the daughter house soon caused problems.[23] It is possible that other communities of women were initially offshoots of older nunneries, but the failure to maintain any organizational links means that no evidence survives.

In the first half of the twelfth century, Geoffrey de Clinton II made a grant of 150 acres to found a community of nuns. The donation was made to a certain Naomi, and the women were to follow the rule and customs which she would institute.[24] The subjectivity and vagueness of this description is striking—no reference is made to the Benedictine or Augustinian rule or to any other established order. A later charter of Geoffrey reveals that the permanence envisaged in the charter proved illusory. At his request and with his assent, Naomi and one companion transferred their endowment to the canons of Kenilworth and the community of women religious at Bretford apparently came to an end.[25] It was this grant of land to the men's house which resulted in the charters' preservation by being transcribed in the Kenilworth cartulary. The study of women religious and the foundation of English nunneries after the Conquest has to be set against this background of vulnerability.

[22] VCH *Leics.*, ii, 3; *MA*, iv, 221, no. 1.

[23] Disputes soon arose and eventually papal judges delegate decreed in 1209 that the prioress of Langley should be elected by the prioress of Farewell and the convent of Langley, and that the mother house would renounce all other rights over the Leicestershire community (Sayers, *Papal Judges Delegate*, 175).

[24] 'Ut ordo et institutio quam ipsa constituerit imperpetuum ibidem conservetur', BL Harl. MS 3650, fo. 69ᵛ printed in *MA*, iv, 158, no. 1. Naomi is described in Geoffrey's charter as 'charissima amica mea domina Noemi monialis'.

[25] BL Harl. MS 3650, fo. 5, printed *MA*, iv, 158, no. 3.

Appendix A
Dates of Foundations and Founders

This Appendix lists the nunneries alphabetically and gives the earliest surviving reference for the existence of each house (column 3). In some cases, as at Godstow, Lacock, and Clementhorpe at York, this date is that of the foundation of the house. For other convents such as Armathwaite, Barrow Gurney, Broomhall, and Pinley, this evidence merely shows that the priory was in existence by that date, leaving the possibility that the formation of the community had taken place much earlier. For these, a minus sign precedes the given date.

The names of the founders or principal benefactors of the house are also given where they are known, or where there is a clear tradition identifying them. As discussed in chapters 9 and 10 of this book, claims to have 'founded' a nunnery have to be treated with caution, and may obscure an earlier and more complex genesis. Column 3 also gives the main source for claims of such 'founders'. Where a foundation charter is in existence, or where the life-span of the founder provides the evidence of the date of the nunnery, one source is given for date and founder. In many cases, however, two or more sources are cited as together providing the evidence for what is known of the earliest history of the house. Where the source is printed using modern scholarship, reference is made to this; for charters printed in *MA* where possible the MSS are also cited.

Previous lists of nunneries have generally classified them by order (as in KH), by date (as in Burton, *Yorks. Nunneries*), or by chronology and geography (as in Elkins, *Holy Women*). Categories of order and date have not been used in this Appendix in view of the uncertainties and probable instability of the nunneries' order, and the lack of knowledge about exact dates of their foundation, with many convents probably developing slowly. A north–south classification also seems to present problems, with Chicksands having to be considered separately from the Gilbertine houses in the north, and the possibility of changes of site also complicating the picture. An alphabetical classification, therefore, seems to provide the easiest means of reference and avoids questionable lines of demarcation.

Place and Date	Probable Founders	Source
ACONBURY, Hereford 1216	Margaret de Lacy	*Rot. Lit. Pat.*, 199b

Place and Date	Probable Founders	Source
ALVINGHAM, Lincs. 1148 × 1154	Roger fitz Jocelin (brother of St Gilbert); Hamelin; Amfredus of Legbourne; Hugh de Scoteni; William of Friston	*Gilbertine Charts.*, 103, no. 2; *Acta I Lincoln 1067– 1185*, 43–4, no. 67
AMESBURY, Wilts. 1177 (refoundation) 1186 nuns installed	Henry II	*Cal. Docs. France*, 378, no. 1,069; *Gesta Henrici II*, i, 135–6, 354
ANKERWYKE, Bucks. ? Anchoretic origin – 1163	Gilbert de Muntfichet	See p. 36; *MA*, iv, 230–1
ARDEN, Yorks. c.1147 × 1169	Peter de Hoton	*Mowbray Charts.*, 20–1, no. 20
ARMATHWAITE (INGLEWOOD), Cumberland. ? Anchoretic origin – c.1201	Unknown	See p. 29; *Gervase of Canterbury*, ii, 441
ARTHINGTON, Yorks. c.1150 × 1158[1]	Peter de Arthington	*MA*, iv, 520, no. 1
BARROW GURNEY (MINCHIN BARROW), Somerset – c.1201	Unknown; ? Hawise de Gournay	*Gervase of Canterbury*, ii, 423
BAYSDALE, Yorks. Earlier sites at HUTTON and NUNTHORPE c.1139 × c.1159	Ralph de Neville	*MA*, v, 508, no. 3[2]
BAYSDALE c.1190 × 1211	Guy de Bovingcourt	*EYC*, i, 443–5
BLACKBOROUGH, Norfolk c.1150 monks 1200 nuns	Roger de Scales and Muriel his wife	*MA*, iv, 206–7; (BL Egerton MS 3137, fos. 30–1)
BLITHBURY, Staffs. ? Eremitical origin 1120 × 1147	Hugh de Ridware	*MA*, iv, 160; (BL Harl. MS 2044, fo. 123)

[1] Warin fitz Gerold, who made a grant to the nunnery, appears to have died in 1158; see *Reg. Regum*, iii, 391.

[2] For the dating of Ralph, an early archdeacon of York, who witnesses this charter, see *Acta V York 1070–1154*, 126.

Place and Date	Probable Founders	Source
BRETFORD, Warwicks. (ephemeral, see p. 216) – 1167	Geoffrey de Clinton and Agnes his wife	*MA*, iv, 158; (BL Harl. MS 3650, fos. 69^v and 5^{r-v})
BREWOOD BLACK LADIES, Staffs. – *c.*1150 ? – 1147	? Bishop Roger de Clinton	Mander, 'Brewood Black Ladies', 178, 182–3
BREWOOD WHITE LADIES (BOSCOBEL), Salop. – 1186	Unknown	*Cartl. Haughmond*, 48, nos. 149, 151
BRISTOL, Glos. – 1173[3]	Eva fitz Harding; ? hospital linked with St Augustine's	*Ricart's Kalendar*, 22; see pp. 45–7
BROADHOLME, Notts. 1148 × 1154 ? – 1167 (for sisters)	? Agnes de Goxhill; ? linked with Newhouse	*Acta I Lincoln 1067– 1185*, 105–6; see pp. 141–2; *MA*, vi, (ii), 919
BROOMHALL (BROMHALL), Berks. – 1157 × 1158	Unknown	*PR 2–4 Henry II*, 151
BUCKLAND (MINCHIN BUCKLAND), Somerset *c.*1186	Linked with the order of Knights Hospitallers	*Cartl. Buckland*, 5–6, 8; see pp. 156–7
BULLINGTON, Lincs. 1148 × 1154	Simon son of William de Kyme	*Gilbertine Charts.*, 91
BUNGAY, Suffolk 1175 × 1176 1183 nuns installed	Countess Gundreda and Roger de Glanville	*Cal. Chart. Rolls 1327–41*, 225–6; *Chron. Oxenedes*, 69
BURNHAM, Bucks. 1266	Richard, King of the Romans	*MA*, vi (i), 546, no. 1
CAMBRIDGE ST RADEGUND, Cambs. *c.*1147 × 1154	? William Monachus, ? Bishop Nigel of Ely	*Reg. Regum*, iii, 51, no. 138; see pp. 200–1.
CAMPSEY ASH, Suffolk – 1195	Theobald de Valoignes II	*Feet of Fines Henry II, Richard I*, 61; *Rot. Chart.*, 116b
CANNINGTON, Somerset ? *c.*1129 × *c.*1153	? Robert de Curci[4]	Leland, *Coll.*, i (i), 78

[3] Eva is said to have died on 13 March 1173 or 'neer thereabouts': see *HRH*, 209.

[4] A Robert de Curci occurs as steward in *c.*1129 × 1132, 1142 and 1153: see *Handbook of British Chronology*, ed. E. B. Fryde, D. E. Greenway, S. Porter and I. Roy (3rd edn., London, 1986), 74.

Place and Date	Probable Founders	Source
CANONSLEIGH, Devon 1284 refoundation from house of canons	Matilda, Countess of Gloucester	*Cal. Pap. Lett.*, i, 478; *Cartl. Canonsleigh*, xi–xii
CANTERBURY ST SEPULCHRE, Kent ? – 1087	? William Calvel; ? Archbishop Anselm	*Domesday Book*, i, 12; Urry, *Canterbury*, 62–3; see pp. 36–7
CARROW, see Norwich		
CASTLE HEDINGHAM (HEDINGHAM), Essex – 1191	? Member of the de Vere family; ? Lucy de Vere	*MA*, iv, 437–8; see pp. 180–1
CATESBY, Northants. c.1150 × 1176	Robert de Esseby	PRO, E326/694; *MA*, iv, 637, no. 1
CATLEY, Lincs. 1148 × 1154	Peter de Billinghay	*Gilbertine Charts.*, 72; *Acta I Lincoln 1067–1185*, 65
CHESHUNT, Herts. ? Anchoretic origin – 1165 × 1166	Unknown; ? Conan, Earl of Richmond	See p. 27; *PR 12 Henry II*, 77
CHESTER, Cheshire c.1141 × 1153	Hugh son of Oliver; ? Earl Rannulf de Chester	*MA*, iv, 313–14, no. 1; see p. 165
CHICKSANDS, Beds. 1147 × 1153	Countess Rose and her husband Pain de Beauchamp	BL Harl. chart. 45.I.7
COOK HILL, Worcs. (previously at SPERNALL) – 1155 × 1156	Unknown	*PR 2–4 Henry II*, 62; *Cal. Pap. Lett.*, v, 405
CORNWORTHY, Devon – 1238	Unknown; ?Eva de Braose	*Devon Fines*, 158, no. 318
CRABHOUSE, Norfolk Anchoretic origin c.1181	? Linked with canons of Normans Burrow	Bateson, 'Reg. Crabhouse', 12–13; *MA*, v, 69–70 (BL Harl. MS 2110, fos. 82^v, 125^v) and see pp. 24–5
DAVINGTON, Kent ? 1153 1150 × 1161	Fulk de Newenham	Tanner, Kent xviii; Lambeth Palace Library, Reg. Warham, fo. 154^v
DELAPRÉ, see Northampton		

Place and Date	Probable Founders	Source
DERBY KINGSMEAD (DE PRATIS) – 1154 × 1159	Linked with the canons of St Helens	*Cartl. Darley*, ii, 595–7, no. 02; see pp. 47–8.
EASEBOURNE, Sussex – 1248	? Member of the de Bohun family	PRO Just 1 909A., memb. 3
ELLERTON, Yorks. c.1189 × 1204	? Egglesclive or Barden family	*EYC*, v, 32–3, no. 132
ELSTOW, Beds. 1076 × 1086	Judith, widow of Earl Waltheof	Leland, *Coll.* i, (i), 41
ESHOLT, Yorks. – 1184	? Linked with SINNINGTHWAITE; ? Member of the Ward family	*EYC*, i, 168, no. 200; *EYC*, vi, 156–7, no. 67
FAREWELL, Staffs. ? Eremitical origin c.1139 × 1147	Bishop Roger de Clinton	See p. 27; *MA*, iv, 111, no. 1
FLAMSTEAD (ST GILES IN WOOD, WOODCHURCH). Herts. ? Anchoretic origin – 1157 × 1162, ? c.1150	Probably Roger de Tosny III	See p. 28; *MA*, iv, 300, no. 1 (Herts. Record Office, MS 17,465, fo. 3)
FLIXTON, Suffolk 1258 × 1259	Margery, widow of Bartholomew de Crek	BL Stowe Charts. 291, 292
FOSSE, Lincs. – 1184	? Inhabitants of Torksey; ? Linked with canons	BL Cotton MS Vesp. E. xviii, fo. 214^v; see pp. 30–1
FOUKEHOLME (ST STEPHEN'S THIMBLEBY), Yorks. – 1203 × 1204	? Member of the Coleville family	*Yorks. Assize Rolls John and Henry III*, 6; see p. 186
GODSTOW, Oxon. – 1133	Edith de Lancelene; John de St John	*Cartl. Godstow*, i, 26–7[5]; *Acta I Lincoln 1067–1185*, 20–2
GOKEWELL (ESKDALE, MANBY), Lincs. ? Anchoretic origin 1147 × 1175[6]	William de Alta Ripa and his wife Juetta	*EYC*, vi, 204–5, no. 106 (BL Egerton Chart., 624); *EYC*, vi, 201–2, no. 103

[5] According to this account Henry I helped with the foundation, suggesting a date of – 1133 when he went abroad.

[6] It is not clear that the William de Romara referred to in a later charter as making a grant to the nunnery is the one who died in 1161 (cf. KH, 273).

Place and Date	Probable Founders	Source
GORING, Oxon. ? – 1135	? Thomas de Druval	*Goring Charts.*, i, 103, no. 1[7]
GRACE DIEU (BELTON), Leics. – 1236 × 1242	Rose de Verdon	*Monumenta Franciscana*, i, 115, 119, 403; *MA*, vi, 567, no. 1
GREENFIELD, Lincs. 1148 × 1166 ? – 1153	Eudo de Grainsby	*MA*, v, 579–80; (BL Harl. Chart., 50, I. 30)
GRIMSBY, Lincs. – 1171 × 1180	Unknown; tradition of royal foundation; ? linked with canons of Wellow	*PUE*, iii, 402, no. 274; see p. 67
GUYZANCE (BRAINSHAUGH), Northumberland – 1152 × 1167	? Richard Tyson. Linked with the abbey of Alnwick	*Northumberland Pleas*, 217, no. 655; *Cal. Chart. Rolls 1300–26*, 87; see pp. 142–3
HAMPOLE, Yorks. – 1156	William de Clerfai and his wife Avicia de Tany	*PUE*, iii, 16; *MA*, v, 487
HANDALE (GRENDALE), Yorks. ? 1133 c.1150 × 1170	William, son of Richard de Percy of Dunsley	*EYC*, ii, 240–1, no. 897; ibid. 301
HARROLD, Beds. c.1136 × c.1138	? Hilbert Pélice; Sampson le Fort; linked with Abbot Gervase and abbey of Arrouaise	*Records of Harrold Priory*, 8, 16, no. 2 (i); see pp. 150–2
HAVERHOLME, Lincs. 1139	Bishop Alexander of Lincoln	*Acta I Lincoln 1067– 1185*, 24–5
HENWOOD (ESTWELL), Warwicks. 1149 × 1157	Ketelburne de Langdon	*MA*, iv, 212
HEYNINGS, Lincs. – c.1147 × 1152	Reyner de Evermue	*MA*, v, 723

[7] This confirmation charter of Henry II refers to a charter of his grandfather indicating—if the charter was to the nuns—that the community was in existence in the reign of Henry I. Thomas de Druval was clearly an important benefactor if not the founder. A Thomas de Druval—probably this one—died c.1150 suggesting the nunnery was founded pre-Henry II.

Place and Date	Probable Founders	Source
HIGHAM (LILLECHURCH), Kent *c.*1150 × 1152	King Stephen and Queen Matilda	Saltman, *Archbishop Theobald*, 379–80 (SJC MS D46. 98)
HINCHINGBROOKE (ST JAMES WITHOUT HUNTINGDON), Hunts. Tradition of foundation *temp.* William I Earlier site at ELTISLEY (PAPLEY) HINCHINGBROOKE 1186 × 1190	? Roger de Cundy	*Valor Eccl.*, iv, 256; *Mowbray Charts.*, 123–4
HOLYSTONE, Northumberland ? – 1124[8] 1124 × 1152	? Member of the Umfraville family	*Cal. Close Rolls 1337–9*, 223; *Reg. Pal. Dunelmense*, ii, 1153[9]
HORSELY, Surrey – *c.*1201	Unknown	*Gervase of Canterbury*, ii, 420
ICKLETON, Cambs. – 1158	? Member of the de Vere family ? Member of the de Valoignes family	*Spicilegium Liberianum*, ed. F. Liverani (Florence, 1864), 761;[10] see VCH *Cambs.*, ii, 223; vi, 233
IVINGHOE ST MARGARET, Herts. (formerly Bucks.) 1107 × 1129	? Bishop William Giffard of Winchester	*Acta II Canterbury 1162–90*, 9–10
KELDHOLME (DUVA), Yorks. 1154 × 1166	Robert de Stuteville III and his wife Helewise	*EYC*, ii, 64; ix, 92–4
KILBURN, Middlesex Anchoretic origin – 1128 × 1134	Hermit Godwyn; linked with the abbey of Westminster	*MA*, iii, 426, no. 1 (BL Cotton MS Faust. A. iii, fos. 325^v–326^v; see pp. 25–6

---

[8] See *A History of Northumberland*, xv, ed. M. Hope-Dodds (Newcastle, 1940), 459–60.

[9] *The Register of Richard de Kellawe, Lord Palatine and Bishop of Durham 1314–16*, ed. T. D. Hardy, 4 vols. (Rolls ser. 62; 1873–8).

[10] This evidence is wrongly cited in KH as applying to Swaffham Bulbeck. For the sources see Z. N. Brooke, 'The Register of Master David of London, and the part he played in the Becket Crisis', in *Essays in History presented to R. L. Poole*, ed. H. W. C. Davis (Oxford, 1927), 227–45.

Place and Date	Probable Founders	Source
KINGTON ST MICHAEL, Wilts. – 1142 × 1156 ? c.1142	Robert son of Wayfer de Brinton and Eva his wife; ? Empress Matilda	*PR 2–4 Henry II*, 59; *MA*, iv, 399–400, nos. 3 and 10; see p. 164
KIRKLEES, Yorks. c.1135 × 1140 or 1166 × c.1190	Reiner le Fleming I or II	Clay 'Seals';[11]*EYC*, viii, 203–4, no. 145
LACOCK, Wilts. 1229 1231 × 1232 first nuns	Ela, Countess of Salisbury	*Lacock Charts.*, 10, no. 1 (PRO, E40/ 9350); BL Cotton MS Vitellius A. viii, fo. 127
LAMBLEY, Northumberland – 1187 × 1188	Adam de Tindale I and his wife Helewise	*Rot. Chart.*, 87; *PR 34 Henry II*, 5
LANGLEY, Leics. 1148 × 1166 ? c.1150	William Pantulf and his wife Burgia	*Acta I Lincoln 1067– 1185*, 88–9
LEGBOURNE, Lincs. ? Early site at KEDDINGTON[12] LEGBOURNE – 1148 × 1166; ? 1150	Robert fitz Gilbert and Matilda his wife; his brother, Berengar Falconer	*MA*, v, 634–5, no. 3; Oxford, Bodleian Dodsworth MS lxxv, fos. 26ᵛ–27; *Acta I Lincoln 1067–1185*, 45–6
LILLECHURCH, see HIGHAM		
LIMEBROOK, Hereford ? Earlier anchoretic origin – 1221	? Ralph de Lingen; ? member of Mortimer family	See pp. 34–5; *Eyre Rolls Lincs. and Worcs.*, 647, no. 1524
LITTLE MARLOW (MARLOW), Bucks. – 1194 × 1195	Unknown	*Waltham Abbey Charts.*, 390–1
LITTLEMORE (SANDFORD), Oxon. – 1156	Robert de Sandford[13]	Oxford, Bodleian MS Oxon Chart. a8 no. 4; *Rot. Hund.*, ii, (ii), 723a

[11] See C. T. Clay, 'The Seals of the Religious Houses of Yorkshire', *Archaeologia* 78 (1928), 23; see also Burton, *Yorks. Nunneries*, 6.

[12] For the problems of the apparent changes of site at Legbourne and the link with Keddington which became a grange of the Gilbertine house of Alvingham see p. 179 and n. 138.

[13] The earliest extant pipe rolls for the reign of Henry II reveal that by this date Robert had been succeeded by his son Jordan.

Place and Date	Probable Founders	Source
LONDON CLERKENWELL c.1141 × 1144[14]	Jordan de Bricett and Muriel his wife	*Cartl. Clerkenwell*, 270, 30–3.
LONDON HALIWELL – 1158 × 1162[15]	Robert fitz Generannus, canon of St Paul's	BL Cotton MS Vitellius F. viii, fo. 84^v; *MA*, iv, 393, no. 1
LONDON ST HELENS 1212 × c.1214	William, son of William the Goldsmith	*HMC Ninth Report* App. i, 57a[16] (Guildhall MS 25, 121/2038); *Early Charts. of St Paul's*, 186, no. 235
LYMINSTER, Sussex Tradition of late 11th cent. foundation[17] – c.1201	? Earl Roger de Montgomery	PRO, C143/410(22) *Gervase of Canterbury*, ii, 419
MALLING, Kent c.1095[18]	Gundulf, Bishop of Rochester	*Life of Gundulf*, 58
MARHAM, Norfolk 1249	Isabel, Countess of Arundel	Nichols, 'Marham Abbey', 9–12, *MA*, v, 744, no. 1
MARKYATE (ST TRINITY DE BOSCO, CELLA), Herts. (formerly Beds.) Earlier anchoretic origin 1145	Christina of Markyate; Geoffrey, Abbot of St Albans; Canons of St Paul's	See pp. 17–18, 57–8 *Early Charts. of St Paul's*, 119–20
MARRICK, Yorks. 1154 × 1158	Roger de Aske	*EYC*, v, 76–7, no. 173

[14] For a rebuttal of an earlier date of *c.*1100 see Round, 'Clerkenwell', 223–8.

[15] The foundation date for Haliwell is sometimes given as – 1127. This is a possibility, but only if the Bishop Richard referred to in a charter of Richard I as making a grant to the nunnery was Richard Belmeis I rather than II. *LCC Survey of London*, viii, 153 dates a charter to the house as *c.*1158, but the witnesses suggest a date of *c.*1158 × 1162.

[16] *Ninth Report of the Royal Commission of Historical Manuscripts Report and Appendix* (London, 1883).

[17] It is clear that Lyminster was granted to Almenèches at an early date, but it is not possible to determine when it developed into a priory. It is sometimes suggested that the name 'Nonneminstre' recorded in Domesday Book suggests the presence of nuns there in the 11th cent., but another possibility is that the name derives from the personal name 'Nunna': see *English Place Name Society*, vi, *The Place Names of Sussex*, ed. A. Mawer and F. M. Stenton, with the assistance of J. E. Gover (Cambridge, 1929; repr. 1969), i, 170.

[18] The editor of the *Life* suggests a date of *c.*1090, but if Archbishop Anselm helped with the foundation as suggested, a later date is more likely.

Place and Date	Probable Founders	Source
MINSTER IN SHEPPEY (ST SEXBURGA), Kent Earlier foundation ? 1130 refounded	Archbishop William de Corbeil	Hasted, *Kent*, vi, 218; *Rot. Chart.*, 148b
MOXBY, Yorks. − 1158	Bertram de Bulmer; Linked with Marton (founded 1135 × 1154)	*EYC*, i, 328, no. 419; see pp. 65–6
NEASHAM, Durham − 1157	Emma de Teise	*PUE*, i, 317–18, no. 67
NEWCASTLE, Northumberland Tradition of earlier foundation 1143 × 1149; ? 1144	? Linked with hospital	KH, 262; see pp. 43–5; *Durham Episcopal Charts.*, 131–2, no. 33
NORTHAMPTON DELAPRÉ, Northants. Earlier site at FOTHERINGHAY c.1145 × 1153 c.1145	Simon de Senlis II, Earl of Northampton	Leland, *Itin.*, i, 4; *Reg. Regum*, iii, 226, no. 614; *Northants. Charts.*, 144–5, no. 55
NORTH ORMSBY (NUN ORMSBY, ORMSBY), Lincs. 1148 × 1154	Gilbert fitz Robert of Ormsby	*Gilbertine Charts.*, 39–40
NORWICH CARROW, Norfolk ? Moved from earlier site c.1136, site I c.1145 × 1147, site II	? Seyna and Lescelina; ? Developed from a hospital	*Reg. Regum*, iii, 226–7; Oxford, Bodleian MS Tanner 342, fo. 149ᵛ; see p. 49
NUN APPLETON, Yorks. c.1148 × 1154[19]	Alice de St Quentin	*EYC*, i, 419–20, no. 541
NUNBURNHOLME, Yorks. − 1199[20]	? Member of the de Merlay family	*EYC*, x, 129–30, no. 81; *MA*, iv, 279, no. 2
NUN COTHAM (COTHAM), Lincs. 1148 × 1153; probably −1149	Alan de Monceaux and Matilda his wife	*EYC*, iii, 51–2, no. 1,329; *Acta V York 1070–1154*, 96–7

[19] For this dating see Burton, *Yorks. Nunneries*, 40.

[20] If William (d.1170) or Roger (d.1188) were the founders, the nunnery must have been founded by 1188 or earlier: see Burton, *Yorks. Nunneries*, 43.

Place and Date	Probable Founders	Source
NUNEATON, Warwicks. Earlier site KINTBURY *c.*1147 × 1155 *c.*1155 × 1157	Robert, Earl of Leicester and Amicia his wife	BL Addit. Chart. 47,384 *Cal. Docs. France*, 376, no. 1,062; for dating see p. 123 n. 78
NUNKEELING, Yorks. 1143 × 1147; or 1153 × 1154	Agnes de Arches	*EYC*, iii, 53–4, nos. 1,331, 1,332; *Acta V York 1070–1154*, 76–7
NUN MONKTON, Yorks. 1151 × 1153	William de Arches and Juetta his wife	*EYC*, i, 414–15, no. 535; *Acta V York 1070–1154*, 97–9
ORFORD (IRFORD), Lincs. 1153 × *c.*1156 ? 1189 as a separate establishment	Linked with Newhouse; Ralph d'Aubigny and his wife Sybil de Valoignes	*Acta I Lincoln 1067–1185*, 108; Colvin, 'Irford Priory', and see pp. 140–1
PINLEY, Warwicks. − 1125 × 1150	Robert de Pillarton	*MA*, iv, 115, no. 1
POLESWORTH, Warwicks. Earlier foundation and change of site OLDBURY *c.*1129 × 1138 × 1144 POLESWORTH *c.*1138 × 1144[21]	Walter de Hastings and Hawise his wife; Robert de Marmion II and Millicent his wife	KH, 263; *MA*, ii, 365–7 *Reg. Regum*, iii, 245, no. 662; BL Lansdowne MS 447, fos. 28^v–29
POLSLOE, Devon − 1160	? William Brewer	Exeter Dean and Chapter MS 1374; see HMC, *Various Coll.*, iv, 49[22]
RAMSTEDE (RAMSCOMBE), Sussex 1174 × 1184	? Archbishop Richard of Canterbury	*Acta II Canterbury 1162–90*, 157–8, nos. 183–5

[21] Robert Marmion's charter is witnessed by Abbot Ralph I of Shrewsbury who occurs 1138 × 1148: see *The Cartulary of Shrewsbury Abbey*, ed. U. Rees, 2 vols. (Aberystwyth, 1975), i, p. xxiii. Robert died in 1144; see *Reg. Regum*, iii, 245.

[22] HMC, *Report on Manuscripts in Various Collections*, iv, *The Manuscripts of Bishop of Salisbury, Bishop of Exeter, Dean and Chapter of Exeter*, 55 (London, 1907).

Place and Date	Probable Founders	Source
REDLINGFIELD, Suffolk 1120	Manasses, Count of Guisnes and Emma his wife	*MA*, iv, 26, no. 1
ROSEDALE, Yorks. *c*.1130 × *c*.1160	? William son of Turgis de Rosedale	*EYC*, ix, 199, nos. 111 and 195–6
ROTHWELL, Northants. – 1249	Unknown; ? Member of the Clare family	*Cal. Lib. Rolls 1245– 51*, 224
ROWNEY, Herts. ? Earlier anchoretic origin *c*.1146 × *c*.1160	? Conan, Duke of Brittany and Earl of Richmond	See pp. 27–8; *Cal. Pat. Rolls 1452–61*, 503–4
RUSPER, Sussex ? – 1174	Unknown; ? member of the Braose family	Reference to grant by Ela de Warenne, see *Acta Chichester*, 181
ST MARY DE PRÉ, Herts.? Earlier linked with St Albans hospital 1194	Warin, Abbot of St Albans	See pp. 39–40; *Gesta Abbatum*, i, 202–4
SEMPRINGHAM, Lincs. 1131 St Andrew ? 1139 St Mary[23] 1147 × 1154	Gilbert of Sempringham; ? Gilbert de Gant; Roger fitz Jocelin	*MA*, vi, (ii), 947, no. 1; (*Rot. Hundred*, i, 254 b); Poynton, 'Sempingham Charts.', xv, 158–9, no. 1
SETON (LEKELAY), Cumberland – 1210	? Henry son of Arthur	*Reg. Holm Cultram*, 31, no. 83
SEWARDSLEY, Northants. 1148 × 1166	Richard de Lestre	PRO, E326/3229
SHOULDHAM, Norfolk *c*.1197 × 1198	Geoffrey fitz Peter, Earl of Essex	*MA*, vi, (ii), 974–5, no. 1
SINNINGTHWAITE, Yorks. – 1155	Bertram Haget	*MA*, v, 468, no. 13[24]

[23] The date traditionally given for the foundation of St Mary Sempringham is 1139, and the founder Gilbert de Gant (see *Book of St Gilbert*, pp. xx–xxi; Graham, *St Gilbert* 12). But earliest charter evidence can only be dated 1140 × 1154 (Poynton, 'Sempringham Charts.', xv, 223, no. 13). Nor does either this charter or one of his daughter (ibid. 161, no. 8) suggest that Gilbert de Gant was a major benefactor, whereas Roger fitz Jocelin made sizeable grants. I am grateful to Dr Brian Golding for help with this point.

[24] For the dating of this charter see *Mowbray Charts.*, 179.

Place and Date	Probable Founders	Source
SIXHILLS, Lincs. 1148 × 1154	William son of Hacon and Edith his wife; ? member of the Greslei family	*Gilbertine Charts.*, 1, no. 1; *MA*, vi (ii), 964, no. 1
SOPWELL, Herts. Earlier anchoretic origin c.1140	? Linked with abbey of St Albans; Geoffrey, Abbot of St Albans	See pp. 23–4, 56–7 *Gesta Abbatum*, i, 80–1
SPINNEY, Leics. 1148 × c.1154	? Gundreda, de Gournay	*Acta I Lincoln 1067–1185*, 160
STAINFIELD, Lincs. – 1168	? William de Percy II and Sybil de Valoignes his wife	*HRH*, 220; *MA*, iv, 309; *EYC*, xi, 60
STAMFORD, Northants. ? 1135 × 1154	? Earlier linked with the abbey of Peterborough; Abbot William of Waterville	*Book of Fees*, i, 196; see pp. 61–2; *MA*, iv, 260 (BL Cotton MS Vesp. E. xxii, fo. 39ᵛ)
STIXWOULD, Lincs. 1139 × 1142²⁵	Lucy, Countess of Chester	BL Addit. MS 46,701, fos. 1 and 11; *Acta I Lincoln 1067–1185*, 37–8
STRATFORD-AT-BOW, Middlesex – 1122	Unknown	*Rouleaux des Morts*, 341, no. 201
STUDLEY, Oxon. – 1175 × 1179²⁶ or 1187 × 1189	Bernard de St Valéry	*MA*, iv, 248 and 252, no. 1
SWAFFHAM BULBECK, Cambs. – 1199	Unknown; ? Isabel de Bolebec I or II	*Placitorum Abbreviatio*, 7b
SWINE, Yorks. c.1143 × 1153	? Brother Robert de Verli	*EYC*, iii, 75–6, no. 1,360²⁷
TARRANT (? CAMESTURNE), Dorset – 1169 × 1176	Ralph de Kahaines II²⁸	*MA*, v, 621, no. 6

²⁵ The nunnery must have been founded by 1142 as a charter in the cartulary bears this date (BL MS 46,701, fo. 11).
²⁶ This charter is witnessed by Robert the Sheriff but this could refer to Robert de Turvill or Robert de La Mara, see Eyton, *Itin.*, 339.
²⁷ For the dating of this charter see Burton, *Yorks. Nunneries*, 47, n. 25.
²⁸ For the probable date of Ralph's death see p. 97 n. 20.

Place and Date	Probable Founders	Source
THETFORD, Norfolk Earlier site at LING THETFORD – *c.*1163 × 1180	Abbot Hugh of Bury St Edmunds	*MA*, iv, 477–8, no. 1 (from Camb. UL MS Ff ii, 29; see also BL Harl. MS 743, fos. 271^v– 272^v)
THICKET, Yorks. – 1180	Roger fitz Roger	*EYC*, ii, 423–4, no. 1131
TUNSTALL (DUNSTALL), Lincs. *c.*1148 × 1160 – *c.*1170 joined to BULLINGTON	Reginald de Crèvecœur	BL Harl. Chart. 48 I. 49; *Danelaw Docs.*, 62–3, no. 96
WALLINGWELLS (DE PARCO), Notts. *c.*1144	Ralph de Chevercourt	*Danelaw Docs.*, 332– 3, no. 452[29]
WATTON, Yorks. ? Earlier foundation 1151 × 1153	Eustace fitz John and Agnes his wife	*MA*, vi, (ii), 955; *EYC*, ii, 404, nos. 1,107–8; *Acta V York 1070– 1154*, 100–2
WESTWOOD, Worcs. 1155 × 1158	Eustacia de Say	*Recueil Henri II*, i, 175–6; no. 73
WHISTONES (WHITE SISTERS), Worcs. – 1241 church dedicated 1254	? Bishop Walter de Cantilupe	*Cal. Close Rolls 1237–42*, 310; *Ann. Mon.*, iv (*Ann Worc.*) 443
WILBERFOSS, Yorks. 1147 × 1153	Alan son of Elias de Catton; Jordan fitz Gilbert	*MA*, iv, 356, no. 5
WINTNEY, Hants. – 1154 × 1161	Geoffrey fitz Peter; see p. 108	Saltman, *Archbishop Theobald*, 509–10; *Cal. Chart. Rolls 1327–41*, 392
WIX (SOPWICK), Essex 1123 × 1133 ? 1132	Walter Mascherell, Alexander and Edith his brother and sister	*Reg. Regum*, ii, 258, no. 1,739 (PRO E42/316)[30]
WOTHORPE, Northants. ? Earlier tradition *c.*1160	? Linked with the abbey of Bourne	See pp. 155–6; *Reg. Ant. Linc.*, ii, 39

[29] For the dating of this charter see *HRH*, 124, s.v. Herbert, prior of Pontefract.
[30] For the question of forgery see Brooke, 'Wix Charts.', 46.

Place and Date	Probable Founders	Source
WROXALL, Warwicks. ? 1141 1123 × 1153	Hugh fitz Richard and Margaret his wife	Leland, *Coll.*, iv, 73; PRO E210/7431; *MA*, iv, 90–2
WYKEHAM, Yorks. – 1153	Pain fitz Osbert	*MA*, v, 669–70
YEDINGHAM (LITTLE MAREIS), Yorks. – 1158	Helewise de Clere	*EYC*, i, 484, no. 613;[31] *Cal.* *Chart. Rolls 1226–* *57, 312*
YORK CLEMENTHORPE c.1125 × 1133	Archbishop Thurstan	*Acta V York 1070–* *1154, 60–1*

[31] For the correct dating of this charter see Burton, *Yorks. Nunneries*, 48, n. 28.

For the dating of the early charters of Cambridge St Radegund I am grateful for the help of Dr Elisabeth van Houts.

Appendix B
List of Abbesses, Prioresses, and Magistri

The majority of heads of nunneries for the period *c*.1100 to *c*.1216 are listed in *HRH*. In this Appendix reference is made to a name which dates pre-1216 only if it is not included in the *HRH* lists or gives additional information to that provided there: the bulk of the heads listed below therefore occur in the later period of *c*.1216 to *c*.1265. The Victoria County Histories list prioresses and abbesses at the end of their articles on the religious houses, but in general they have little information for the twelfth and thirteenth centuries, and their references for each head are not in modern form, for example citing manuscript material which is now published. The exceptions are the more recent VCH articles which incorporate modern scholarship: *Cheshire, Middlesex, Salop, Staffordshire,* and *Wiltshire*. In the case of these I have referred to their lists for individual heads rather than giving the original source.

This list, which includes male heads, makes it clear that the presence of priors and *magistri* (the titles often seem to have been interchangeable) was by no means uncommon. Such heads are listed for thirty-two houses, in addition to the Gilbertine double foundations.

ABBREVIATIONS

app.	appointed	n.d.	no date
d.	died	occ.	occurs
dep.	deposed	pal.	palaeography
el.	elected	res.	resigned
		temp.	in the time of

ACONBURY
Constancia (given the title of *magistra* see p. 51), occ. *c*.1232 (PRO, E315/55, fo. 42ᵛ).
H, occ. 1258 (PRO, E326/8696).
Margery, occ. 1262 (PRO, E326/9770).
Petronilla, occ. ? late 13th cent. (BL Harl. chart., 48 C. 33).

ALVINGHAM (list in VCH *Lincs.*, ii [1906], 194.

Priors
William, occ. 1240 (*Lincolnshire Records. Abstracts of Final Concords temp. Richard I, John and Henry III*, ed. W. O. Massingberd and W. Boyd, 2 vols. (privately printed, London 1896) ii 329, no. 104).
Richard, occ. 1247 (Oxford, Bodleian Laud Misc. 642, fo. 142ᵛ).
Alexander, occ. 1256 (*Final Concords of the County of Lincoln from the Feet of Fines preserved in the PRO 1244–72, with Additions from Various Sources 1176–1250*, ed. C. W. Foster [Lincs. Record Soc. 17; 1920], 120, no. 24); 1256 × 1257 (ibid. 148, no. 63).

Ralph, occ. 1267 and 1282 (Oxford, Bodleian Laud Misc. 642, fos. 161ᵛ and 162).

Amesbury (list in VCH *Wilts.*, iii, 258).

Prioresses
Felicia, occ. 1227, 1228 (*HRH*, 207); 1237 (*A Calendar of the Feet of Fines relating to the County of Wiltshire . . . from the Reign of Richard I (1195) to the End of Henry III (1272)*, compiled by W. A. Fry [Wilts. Archaeol. and Nat. Hist. Soc.; 1930], 29 no. 2).
Ida, occ. 1256, 1273 (VCH *Wilts.*, iii, 258).

Priors
Thomas, occ. 1255 (ibid.).
Peter, occ. 1293 (ibid.).

Ankerwyke (list in VCH *Bucks.*, i [1905, repr. 1969], 357).
Emma, d. ? 1236 (*MA*, iv, 230, but the ref. given [Cole's Collections, xxvi] suggests she died in 1326; see BL Addit. MS 5827, fo. 178ᵛ).
Celestria, app. 1238 × 1239 (*Reg. Grosseteste*, 345, 346); occ. 1239 × 1241 (*Reg. Ant. Linc.*, iii, 18–20, no. 656).
Juliana, el. 1243 × 1244 (*Reg. Grosseteste*, 369).
Joan of Rouen, el. 1250 × 1251 (ibid. 381).
Margery, occ. 1270 (PRO, E40/1590).

Arden (list in VCH *Yorks.*, iii [1913, repr. 1974], 115–16).
Muriel, occ. 1187, 1189 (*HRH*, 207); occ. 1212 (*Abstracts of the Charters and Other Documents Contained in the Chartulary of the Cistercian Abbey of Fountains*, ed. W. T. Lancaster, 2 vols. [privately printed, Leeds, 1915], ii, 626, no. 10).
Agatha, occ. 1262 (*MA*, iv, 286, no. 4).

Armathwaite (list in VCH *Cumberland*, ii [1905], 192).
No names known for this period.

Arthington (list in VCH *Yorks.*, iii [1913, repr. 1974], 190).
Sarah, occ. 1241 (*The Thirty-Sixth Report of the Deputy Keeper of Public Records* [London, 1874], app. 1, 182, no. 179).

Barrow Gurney (list in VCH *Somerset*, ii [1911, repr. 1969], 109).
No names known for this period.

Baysdale (list in VCH *Yorks.* [1913, repr. 1974], 160).

Prioresses
As listed in *HRH* 208.

Custos
William de Bardney, monk of Whitby, app. as *custos* 1267 × 1268 (*Reg. Walter Giffard*, 54; see also Handale).

BLACKBOROUGH (list in VCH *Norfolk*, ii [1906], 351).
Katherine de Scales, occ. 1238 (BL Egerton MS 3137, fo. 62).
Margaret, occ. 1221 × 1222, 1228 (ibid., fos. 65, 49ᵛ).
Alice, occ. n.d., probably 13th cent. (ibid., fos. 95ᵛ, 165, 171ᵛ).
Mary, occ. 1259, 1261 × 1262 (ibid., fos. 177, 170).
(The order of the last two is uncertain).

BLITHBURY (list in VCH *Staffs.*, iii [1970], 220).
The only known name is Alice, occ. *c.*1275 (VCH *Staffs.*, iii, 220).

BRETFORD
Naomi (not given title of prioress, but probably head of the community
there), occ. −1167 (*MA*, iv, 158, no. 1).

BREWOOD BLACK LADIES (list in VCH *Staffs.*, iii [1970], 222).
Isabel, occ. 1258 × 1295 (VCH *Staffs.*, iii, 222).

BREWOOD WHITE LADIES (list in VCH *Salop*, ii [1973], 84).
Aldith, occ. *c.*1225 (VCH *Salop*, ii, 84).
Cecilia, occ. *c.*1225 × 1233 (ibid.)
Agnes, occ. 1254, 1256 (ibid.)

BRISTOL (list in VCH *Glos.*, ii [1907], 93).

Prioresses
As in *HRH*.

Magister
John, occ. 1233 × 1240 as *Mag.* of the Hospital of St Mary Magdalene
(*Cartl. St Mark's Hospital*, 33, no. 32 and 205–6, no. 328). For the
probable identification of this house with the nunnery, see p. 46.

BROADHOLME (list in VCH *Notts.*, ii [1910], 140).
As listed in *HRH* 209.

BROOMHALL (list in VCH *Berks.*, ii [1907], 81).
Juliana, described as predecessor of Agnes (SJC MS D 14: 167).
Agnes de St Edmund, occ. 1268 (BL. Addit. MS 5829, fo. 66ᵛ); also occ. in
13th cent. charters, e.g. SJC MS D 13:7).

BUCKLAND
Preceptors / magistri
For the links of the masculine community at Buckland with the women see
pp. 156–7.
Hugh de Binford, occ. 1187 (*Cartl. Buckland*, 189, no. 350).
Greg(ory), occ. ? 1216 × *c.*1229 (ibid. 54, no. 86).
Richard de Morton, occ. 1253 (ibid. 143, no. 251).
Richard de Brampford, occ. 1267–81 (ibid. 110, no. 190; 37, no. 48; 134,
no. 234; 151, no. 268).

BULLINGTON (list in VCH *Lincs.*, ii [1906], 192).

Priors
William, occ. 1218 (*HRH*, 201); 1226 (BL Harl. Chart. 50 A. 46); 1242 (BL Harl. Chart. 44 E. 49); 1231 *Linc. Final Concords i* Boyd and Massingberd, ii, 231, no. 36); 1240 (ibid., ii, 306, no. 23A); 1245 (*Linc. Final Concords ii*, 7, no. 19).
Simon, occ. *temp.* Henry III (BL Harl. Charts. 44 A. 40 and 41).
Walter, occ. 1254 (*Linc. Final Concords ii*, 106, no. 22); 1258 × 1259 (ibid. 169, no. 30); 1261 × 1263 (BL Harl. Chart. 44 A. 44) (The order of the last two is unclear.)
William, occ. 1263 (BL Harl. Chart. 44 I. 17).
Patrick, occ. *c.*1270 (BL Harl. Chart. 44 A. 36).

BUNGAY (list in VCH *Suffolk*, ii [1907], 82).
Anastasia, occ. 1183 (*HRH*, 209).
Mary of Huntingfield, occ. early 13th cent. (*HRH*, 209).
A, occ. *c.*1212 × 1221 (Bungay charters preserved at Elveden Hall, no. 15),[1] probably the same as:
Alice, occ. 1228 (BL Addit. MS 19,111, fo. 161).
Mary, occ. 1270 (ibid., fos. 160, 161).

BURNHAM (list in VCH *Bucks.*, i [1905], repr. 1969), 384.

Abbesses
Margery of Aston, el. 1266 (*Reg. Gravesend*, 240–1, res. 1274 when:
Matilda of Dorchester, el. (ibid. 251).

CAMBRIDGE ST RADEGUND (list in VCH *Cambs.*, ii [1946], 219; based on Gray, *St Radegund*, 30–1).
E., occ. −1214 (*HRH*, 209). It is possible she is earlier than:
Lettice, occ. 1198 × *c.*1202 (SJC MS D. 98.49); 1228 × 1229 (*HRH*, 209).
Millicent, occ. 1246 × 1247, 1249 × 1250 (*Pedes Finium . . . relating to the County of Cambridge (Calendar 7 Richard I–1485)*, ed. W. Rye [Camb. Antiquarian Soc. 26; 1891], 27, no. 7 and 32, no. 11).
Dera, occ. 1258 (Gray, *St Radegund*, 30).
Agnes de Burgeylun, occ. 1274 (ibid.).

CAMPSEY ASH (list in VCH *Suffolk*, ii [1907], 115).
Joan de Valoignes, occ. 1211, 1220 × 1221 (*HRH*, 210). Also occ. ? 1230 × 1232 (*Cartl. Clerkenwell*, 227, no. 344).
Agnes de Valoignes, occ. 1232 (*HRH*, 210). Also occ. 1242 (*Feet of Fines for Essex (1182–1272)*, i, ed. R. E. G. Kirk [Essex Archaeol. Soc.; 1899–1910], 142, no. 750).
Basilia, occ. 1253 × 1254 (*Linc. Final Concords ii*, 106, no. 24); 1256 (ibid. 122, no. 32).

---

[1] I am grateful to Dr Philippa Brown for this information.

CANNINGTON (list in VCH *Somerset*, ii [1911, repr. 1969], 111).
No names known for this period.

CANONSLEIGH (for Canonsleigh abbey, refounded for nuns in 1284, see list in *Cartl. Canonsleigh*, 177).

CANTERBURY ST SEPULCHRE (list in VCH *Kent*, ii [1926], 143–4).
Juliana, occ. ? 1227 (*HRH*, 210); 1255 (BL Harl. Chart. 75 F. 60); d. 1258 (*Gervase of Canterbury*, ii, 208).
Lettice, el. 1258 (ibid.).
Benedicta, occ. 1272 × 1280 (BL Harl. Chart. 76 G. 34).

CASTLE HEDINGHAM (list in VCH *Essex*, ii [1907], 123).
Agnes, occ. as second prioress *c*.1230 (BL Egerton MS 2849).
Agnes, possibly same as above , occ. 1243, 1248 (*HRH*, 210).
Christiana, occ. 12th–13th cent. (ibid.).
Juliana de Chepford, occ. ? 13th cent. (BL Cotton MS Nero E. vi (ii), fo. 401^{r}–^{v}).

CATESBY (list in VCH *Northants.*, ii [1906], 125).
Prioresses
A, occ. 1209 × 1235 (PRO, E326/10,338); probably the same as:
Amice, occ. 1226 (W. Farrer, *Honors and Knights Fees*, 3 vols. [London, 1923–5], i, 169).
Margery Rich, el. 1244 × 1245 (*Reg. Grosseteste*, 222); occ. 1251 × 1252, 1252 × 1253 (PRO, E326/8499 and E326/10,389); d. after 1257 (*M. Paris Chron. Majora*, v, 621).
? **Alice**: according to Matthew Paris, Alice, sister of Margery Rich, also became prioress, but there is no other evidence to support this: see ibid., v, 642. The entry is suspiciously like that for **Margery**.
Felicia, occ. 1266 × 1267 (PRO, E326/10,421 and E326/12,465); d. 1276 (*Reg. Gravesend*, 129) when:
Amabilia el.
Magistri
Hugh, app. 1266 (*Reg. Gravesend*, 108); occ. 1276 (ibid. 129).

CATLEY (list in VCH *Lincs.*, ii [1906], 197).
Priors
Thomas, occ. 1245 (*Linc. Final Concords ii*, 16, no. 52; 1250 (ibid. 64, no. 42).
William, occ. 1271 (ibid. 259–60, no. 77).

CHESHUNT (list in VCH *Herts.*, iv [1914], 428).
Clemencia, occ. −1223 (BL Harl. MS 4809, fos. 171^{r}–^{v} [dated by Dr Ransford]).
Alice, occ. −1223 (probably after Clemencia [ibid., fo. 171]); *c*.1211 × 1230 (*HMC, Ninth Report*, app. i, 26a [Guildhall MS 25, 121/1068]).

Isabel, occ. 1236 × 1240 (*MA*, iv, 329, no. 2).
Cassandra, occ. 1250 (Norfolk Feet of Fines, PRO CP 25/1/157/75 [1037]).
Dionysia, occ. 1256 × 1257 (*A Calendar of the Feet of Fines for London and Middlesex, Richard I–12 Elizabeth*, ed. W. Hardy and W. Page, 2 vols., [London, 1892–3], i, 37, no. 362).

CHESTER (list in VCH *Cheshire* iii (1980), 150).
M., occ. 1190 × 1206 (BL Addit. chart. 49,969). Probably same as:
Mary, occ. *c*.1200 (VCH *Chester*, iii, 150).
Lucy, occ. 1199 × 1216 (ibid.).
Alice, occ. 1202 × 1229 (ibid.).
Alice (? II) of Stockport, d. 1253 (ibid.).
Alice de la Haye, el. 1253, d. 1283 (ibid.).

CHICKSANDS (list in VCH *Beds.*, i [1904], 393).
Prioress
As in *HRH*, 202.

Priors
Thomas, occ. 1232 (*A Calendar of the Fines for Bedfordshire Preserved in the PRO of the Reigns of Richard I, John and Henry III*, ed. G. H. Fowler [Beds. Hist. Rec. Soc. 6; 1919], 94, no. 349); 1240 (ibid. 118, no. 436).
Hugh de Ledenham, occ. 1244 (ibid. 130, no. 467); 1247 (ibid. 136–7, no. 490).
Richard le Blunt, occ. 1262 (*Reg. Gravesend*, 9).

COOK HILL (list in VCH *Worcs.*, ii [1907], 158).
Sarah, occ. 1220 (*Warwickshire Feet of Fines, 7 Richard I 1195–12 Edward I 1284*, abstracted by E. Stokes, and ed. F. C. Wellstood [Dugdale Soc. 11; 1932], 50, no. 248); 1227 (*Cal. Pat. Rolls 1225–32*, 167).

CORNWORTHY
Hawise, occ. 1238, 1242 (*Devon Feet of Fines, 1 Richard I–Henry III, 1196–1272*, ed. O. Reichel [Devon and Cornwall Rec. Soc. 1912], 158–9, no. 318 and 183, no. 368).

CRABHOUSE (list in VCH *Norfolk*, ii [1906], 410).
Leva (not called prioress but named as if head of the community), *c*.1180 (BL Harl. MS 2110, fos. 82ᵛ and 83).
For subsequent prioresses see *HRH* 210.
Katherine, occ. as predecessor of:
Cecilia, occ. 1249 (F. Blomefield, *An Essay towards a Topographical History of the County of Norfolk* [2nd edn.], 11 vols. [London, 1805–10], 174 [no ref. given]; also listed in VCH *Norfolk*, ii, 410, citing an Assize Roll ref. which appears to be incorrect).
Christiana de Tilney, occ. *c*.1271 (see G. H. Dashwood, 'Notes of Deeds and Survey of Crabhouse Nunnery', *Norfolk Archaeology* 5 [1859], 257).

DAVINGTON (list in VCH *Kent*, ii [1926], 145).

Names of prioresses are given in the obituary of the house (BL Cotton MS Faustina B. vi (i), see p. 30.). The following names may refer to 12th and 13th century prioresses of Davington, although it is not possible to ascertain their order or date:

Beatrice, Gunnora, Sarah (BL Cotton MS Faustina B. vi (i), fo. 102ᵛ).

Dionysia (ibid. 103ᵛ); **Matilda**, twice (ibid., fos. 103ᵛ and 106ᵛ); **Constancia** (ibid., fo. 104ᵛ); **Joanna** (ibid., fo. 106ᵛ).

Matilda (? same as above), occ. 1216 × 1227 (Lambeth Palace Library Reg. Warham i, fo. 157); 1232 (*HRH*, 210).

Joan (? same as Joanna), occ. 1259 (*Calendar of Kent Feet of Fines to the End of Henry III's Reign*, prepared in collaboration by I. J. Churchill, R. Griffin and F. W. Hardman [Kent Archaeol. Soc., 15; 1956], 305); 1263 (ibid. 332).

DERBY KINGSMEAD (list in VCH *Derby*, ii [1907], 44–5).

Prioresses

Rametta, occ. 1236 (*HRH* 211); (the name **Raimon** given in *Derby Charts.*, 303, no. 2,385, probably refers to the same lady).

Sybil, occ. *c.*1248 × 1261 (*Cartl. Darley*, i, 178–9, no. D.16).

Priors

R (prior), occ. 1213 × 1228, ? *c.*1218 (Wolley chart., xi, 25, calendared *Derby Charts.*, 119–20, no. 969).

William de Russell (*custos*), occ. *c.*1220 (*Cartl. Darley*, i, 120–1, no. B27).

EASEBOURNE (VCH *Sussex*, ii [1907], 85).
No heads known for this period.

ELLERTON (list in VCH *Yorks*, ii [1913, repr. 1974], 161).

Alice, occ. *c.*1227 (*Cal. Pat. Rolls 1225–32*, 207).

Aubreye, occ. 1228 (*Feet of Fines for the County of York from 1218 to 1231*, ed. J. Parker [Yorks. Archaeol. Soc., Rec. ser. 62; 1921], 116–17, no. 435).

Petronilla, occ. 1251 (*Feet of Fines for the County of York from 1246–72*, ed. J. Parker [Yorks. Archaeol. Soc., Rec. ser. 82; 1932], 18, no. 1,299).

Ellen, occ. 1268 (ibid. 157–8, no. 1,772).

ELSTOW (list in VCH *Beds.*, i [1904], 357; I am grateful to Sister Maura O'Carroll who is working on Elstow Abbey for information about abbesses).

Abbesses

Wymarca, el. 1233 (*Cal. Pat. Rolls 1232–47*, 8); d. 1241 (*Reg. Grosseteste*, 318).

Agnes of Westbury, el. 1241 (*Cal. Pat. Rolls 1232–47*, 254); res. 1250 (*Reg. Grosseteste*, 335).

Albreda de Fécamp / Saunford, el. 1251 (*Cal. Pat. Rolls 1247–58*, 90); res. or d. before 1258 (*Cal. Pat. Rolls 1247–58*, 623).

Anora de Baskerville, el. 1258 (ibid.); d. 1281 (*Cal. Pat. Rolls 1272–81*, 443).

ESHOLT (list in VCH *Yorks.*, iii [1913, repr. 1974], 162–3).
Agnes, occ. 1218 × 1219 (*Yorks. Fines 1218–31*, 30, no. 129); 1231 (PRO Just 1/1042, memb. 16ᵛ).

FAREWELL (list in VCH *Staffs.*, iii [1970], 224–5).
Serena, occ. 1248 (VCH *Staffs.*, 224).
Julia, occ. *temp*. Henry III (ibid.).
Matilda, occ. −1275 (ibid.).

FLAMSTEAD (list in VCH *Herts.*, iv [1914], 433).
Matilda, occ. 1163 (*PUE*, iii, 586, no. 494).
Alette, occ. 1162 × 1209 (*Cartl. Beauchamp*, 210, no. 370); ? d. 1201 (*Curia Regis Rolls*, i, 432).? Same as:
Alice, occ. early 13th cent. (pal.) (*HRH*, 211).
Joan, occ. 1228 (Flamstead Cartl., Herts. Record Off., MS 17,465, fo. 29).
Agnes, occ. 1242 × 1243 (ibid., fo. 1); d.1255 × 1256 (*Reg. Grosseteste*, 511–12).
Petronilla de Lucy, el. 1255 × 1256 (ibid.).
Sybil, d. 1267 × 1268 (*Reg. Gravesend*, 173).
Lauretta, el. 1267 × 1268 (ibid.); occ. 1270 (Bucks. Feet of Fines, PRO CP 25/1/16/41 [24]).
Other names which occur in the cartulary but cannot be dated are:
Lucy (fo. 23) and **Agatha** (fo. 28ᵛ).[2]

FLIXTON (list in VCH *Suffolk*, ii [1907], 117).
Beatrice de Ratlesden, occ. as first prioress 1262 × 1263 (BL Stowe Chart., 294); 1293 (BL Campbell Chart., iii, 16).
VCH *Suffolk*, ii, 117 lists **Eleanor** as occ. 1258, citing Tanner MS. There is, however, no reference to her in the early charters, and Beatrice is described as first prioress.

FOSSE (list in VCH *Lincs.*, ii [1906], 157).
Katherine, el. 1236 × 1237 (*Reg. Grosseteste*, 137).
Hawise, d. 1272 (*Reg. Gravesend*, 93).
Goda, el. 1272 (ibid.); d. 1278 (ibid. 97) when:
Ala of Canterbury, app.

Magistri
Godfrey, occ. *c*.1198 × *c*.1200 (*Cal. Chart. Rolls 1257–1300*, 107).

FOUKEHOLME (list in VCH *Yorks.*, iii [1913, repr. 1974], 116).
Acilla, occ. ? *c*.1190 × *c*.1240 (Yorks. Record Office, Mauleverer-Brown archive MS ZFL 8).

---

[2] I am grateful to Chris Butterill, who is working on the Flamstead Cartulary, for these references.

GODSTOW (list in VCH *Oxon.*, ii [1907], 74–5).

Abbesses (for the possibility that the foundation was not originally an abbey see pp. 168, 182.)
Amphelisa, el. 1225 (*Cal. Pat. Rolls 1216–25*, 533); occ. 1233 (*The Feet of Fines for Oxfordshire, 1195–1291*, transcr. and calendared by H. E. Salter [Oxfordshire Rec. Soc. 12; 1930], 91, no. 75); occ. 1235 × 1236 (*Reg. Grosseteste*, 448).
Flandrina, el. 1241 (*Cal. Pat. Rolls 1232–47*, 268); dep. 1248 (*Cal. Pat. Rolls 1247–58*, 12).
Emma Bloet, el. 1248 (ibid.); res. 1269 when:
Isolda of Durham, el., (*Reg. Gravesend*, 221).

Magistri / custos
Herbert, formerly vicar of St Giles, Oxford, occ. as *custos* ? *c.*1235 × 1236 (*Reg. Grosseteste*, 448).
Robert, vicar of Dunington, app. 1270 (*Reg. Gravesend*, 222).

GOKEWELL (list in VCH *Lincs.*, ii [1906], 156–7).
Avice, occ. 1234 (*Linc. Final Concords i*, Boyd and Massingberd, ii, 257, no. 121).
Olive,? 13th cent. (*Cal. Chart. Rolls 1300–1326*, 262).
Isabel, el. 1279 on resignation of last prioress (no name given) (*Reg. Gravesend*, 84, 87).

GORING (list in VCH *Oxon.*, ii [1907], 104).
Matilda, occ. 1227 (*HRH*, 212); 1229 (*Oxford Fines*, 85, no. 51).
Eularia, occ. 1261 (ibid. 190, no. 26); res. 1268 (*Reg. Gravesend*, 220).
Christiana de Marsh, el. 1268 (ibid.); res. 1271 when Eularia el. (ibid. 222).

GRACE DIEU (list in VCH *Leics.*, ii [1954], 28).
Mary of Stretton, el. 1242 × 1243 (*Reg. Grosseteste*, 420).
Agnes de Greslei, occ. 1268 × 1269 (*Derby Charts.*, 51, no. 399).

GREENFIELD (list in VCH *Lincs.*, ii [1906], 155–6).
Prioresses
Amabilia, occ. 1237 (BL Harl. Chart. 44 D. 57); probably the same as:
Mabel, occ. 1240 (*Linc. Final Concords i*, Boyd and Massingberd, ii, 320, no. 71).
Alice of Lincoln, el. 1250 × 1251 (*Reg. Grosseteste*, 122).
Matilda, occ. 1260 (BL Harl. Chart. 44 D. 60).
Joan Heyworth, el. 1275 (*Reg. Gravesend*, 66).
The **Sarah** listed in *HRH* as n.d. probably dates from 1286 (see BL Harl. Chart. 44 D. 62).

Magistri / Priors
Roger, occ. *c.*1225 × 1228 (BL Cotton Chart. xxix, 72).
Benedict, occ. 1237 (BL Harl. Chart. 44 D. 57).
Robert, occ. 1268 (BL Harl. Chart. 48 A. 12).

GRIMSBY (list in VCH *Lincs.*, ii [1906], 179).

Prioresses
Alice and Emma n.d. but possibly late 12th or 13th cent. (BL Lansdowne MS 207A, fos. 204 and 216ᵛ).
Philippa, occ. 1256 (*Linc. Final Concords ii*, 119, no. 19).

Magistri
John of Lincoln (once canon of St Augustine's, Grimsby), el. 1231 × 1232 (*Rot. Wells*, iii, 202).
Robert, n.d. and may be of later date (BL Lansdowne MS 207 A, fos. 203 and 205).
Philip, occ. 1265 (*Reg. Gravesend*, 19).

GUYZANCE
No names known for this period.

HAMPOLE (list in VCH *Yorks.*, iii [1913, repr. 1974], 165).

Prioresses
Alice, occ. 1230 (*EYC*, ii, 166).
Joan, n.d., possibly 13th cent. (*EYC*, iii, 366).

Magistri
Peter, occ. +1166–early *temp.* John (*The Cartulary of Blyth Priory*, ed. R. T. Timson, 2 vols. [Thoroton Soc., Rec. ser. 27 and 28; London, 1973], i, 194, no. 303).
Albinus, occ. 1188 × c.1205 (*EYC*, viii, 168, no. 119).
Ralph, occ. c.1241 × 1247 (*Cartl. Fountains*, i, 259, no. 4).

HANDALE (list in VCH *Yorks.*, iii [1913, repr. 1974], 166–7).

Prioresses
Bella, occ. 1240 (*HRH*, 212).
Avicia, occ. 1262, 1269 (*Cartularium Prioratus de Gyseburne*, ed. W. Brown, 2 vols. [Surtees Soc. 86, 89; 1889, 1894 for 1891], ii, 201, 223).

Magistri / custos
William de Bardney (monk of Whitby), app. 1267 × 1268 (*Reg. Walter Giffard*, 54; see also Baysdale).

HARROLD (list in VCH *Beds.*, i [1904], 389–90; *Records of Harrold Priory*, 13–14).

Prioresses
Gila, occ. 1188 (*HRH*, 213); also occ. (G.) 1199 × 1205 (*Letters of Pope Inn. III*, 101, no. 606).
Jelita, occ. c.1200 × 1210 (*HRH*, 213).
Agnes, occ. 1227 (*HRH*, 213); d. 1245 × 1246 (*Reg. Grosseteste*, 325).
Basilia de la Lee, el. 1245 × 1246 (ibid.); occ. 1254 (*Beds. Fines*, 159, no. 567).
Amice, occ. 1262, 1268 (*Records of Harrold Priory*, 24, no. 13, 27–8, no. 17).

Priors

? **Hilbert Pélice** (not given title of prior but named as head of the community: see *Cartl. Missenden*, iii, 182, no. 809).

Guy, occ. *c.*1147 × 1155 (BL Egerton MS 3033, fo. 1); 1161 × 1164 (*Reg. Regum Scot.*, i, 238).

HAVERHOLME (list in VCH *Lincs.*, ii [1906], 188).

Prioresses
As in *HRH*, 202.

Priors

Simon, occ. 1226 (*HRH*, 202); occ. 1234 (*Linc. Final Concords i*, Boyd and Massingberd, ii, 260, no. 133).

Odo, occ. 1241 (ibid. ii, 341, no. 140); 1252, 1254 × 1255, 1258 (*Linc. Final Concords ii*, 93, no. 10, 111, no. 43, and 165, no. 15).

Alan, occ. 1271 (ibid. 240, no. 56); 1271 × 1272 (ibid. 264, no. 95).

HENWOOD (list in VCH *Warwicks.*, ii [1908, repr. 1965], 66).
Elena, occ. 1252 (*Warwicks. Fines*, 150, no. 713).
Matilda, occ. ?late Henry III (pal.) (BL Cotton Chart. xxi, 18).
Juliana, ? 13th cent. (Madox, *Form. Ang.*, 377, no. dclxxxiii).

HEYNINGS (list in VCH *Lincs.*, ii [1906], 151).

Prioresses
? 1236 × 1237 (change of prioress, name blank, indicated in *Reg. Grosseteste*, 137).
Alice de Ballivo, el. 1241 (*Reg. Grosseteste*, 143–4).
Isolda, el. 1264 (*Reg. Gravesend*, 90).
Margery, occ. ?late Henry III (BL. Addit. Chart. 20,698); 1271 × 1272 (*Linc. Final Concords ii*, 257, no. 68).

Priors
Walter, occ. *c.*1234 (BL Harl. Chart. 45 D 12).

HIGHAM (LILLECHURCH) (list in VCH *Kent*, ii [1926], 146).
Amphelisa, occ. 1185 × 1214 (SJC MS D10. 22B, and D46.41; see also p. 11 n. 26).
Alice, occ. 1243 × 1244 (SJC MS D46.93).
Joan de Meriston, el. 1247 (*Cal. Pat. Rolls 1247–58*, 2); occ. 1255 (*Kent Fines*, 268).

HINCHINGBROOKE (list in VCH *Hunts.*, i [1926], 390).
(For Lettice, occ. *c.*1160 × 1169, see *HRH*, 238).
Lucy de Sibtoft, res. 1258 × 1259 (*Reg. Gravesend*, 167).
Emma de Bedford, el. 1258 × 1259 (ibid.); d. 1274 (ibid. 180) when:
Elena Walensis el.

HOLYSTONE

Prioresses

Beatrice, occ. *c.*1230 (*Newcastle Deeds,* 122–3, no. 196); 1240 (*The Chartulary of Brinkburn Priory,* ed. W. Page [Surtees Soc. 90; 1893 for 1892], 126, no. 151).

Agnes, occ. *c.*1261 × 1264, 1272 (*Newcastle Deeds,* 123).

Magister

William, occ. *c.*1230 (ibid. 122–3). It is probable he is *magister* of the nunnery, although this is not certain.

ICKLETON (list in VCH *Cambs.,* ii [1948], 226).

Ellen, occ. 1232 (PRO E326/11,550).

Lettice, occ. 1256 × 1257 (*Cambs. Fines,* 36, no. 9).

Margaret de St Andrew, occ. 1272 (BL Addit. MS 5823, fo. 82^v).

IVINGHOE ST MARGARET (list in VCH *Bucks.,* i [1905, repr. 1969], 354).

Alice, occ. 1237 (*Cal. Chart. Rolls* 1226–57, 226).

Isolda, occ. *c.*1250 (*MA,* iv, 269); d. 1261 × 1262 (*Reg. Gravesend,* 237).

Cecilia, el. 1261 × 1262 (ibid.); res. 1275 when:

Matilda, el. (ibid. 252).

KELDHOLME (list in VCH *Yorks.,* iii [1913, repr. 1974], 169–70).

Prioresses

Sybil, occ. 1224 × 1269 (*EYC,* ix, 93).

Ellen, occ. second half of 13th cent. (BL Cotton Claudius D xi, fo. 4).

Magister

Geoffrey, occ. 1166 × 1183 (*EYC,* ix, 207–8, no. 121); 1175 × 1185 (*EYC,* i, 387, no. 504).

KILBURN (list in VCH *Middlesex,* i [1969], 181–2).

Prioresses

Alice occ. ? 1190+ (*Cartl. Clerkenwell,* 237, no.355); 1207 × 1208 (*HRH,* 213).

Margaret (? same as **Margery,** occ. 1232 [*HRH,* 213]); occ. 1243 × 1248 (VCH *Middlesex,* i, 181).

Joan, occ. 1248 × 1249, *c.*1254 × 1257 (ibid.).

Matilda, occ. 1269 (ibid.).

Magister

Alexander of St Paul's, occ. 1207 (*Curia Regis Rolls,* v, 22).

KINGTON ST MICHAEL (list in VCH *Wilts.,* iii [1956], 261).

Names are given in the 15th-cent. obit list preserved in the Cambridge University Library MS Dd viii 2, fos. 11–20^v. The majority of these are probably of later date, but the following names may refer to 13th-cent.

prioresses: **Susanna, Edith** (*HRH*, 214). The absence of a second name may indicate that **Amicia** also belongs to an earlier period. For a list of the names see VCH *Wilts.*, iii, 261, n. 42.

Mary, occ. 1228 (PRO E164/19 [Torre Cartl.], fo. 60ᵛ); 1243 (VCH *Wilts.*, iii, 261).

KIRKLEES (list in VCH *Yorks.*, iii [1913, repr. 1974], 170).

Lecia, occ. *c*.1190 × 1210 (*EYC*, iii, 389, no. 1,765).

Sybil, occ. 1234 (*Yorkshire Deeds*, ed. W. Brown, C. T. Clay, and M. J. Hebditch, 10 vols. [Yorks. Archaeol. Soc. 39, 50, 63, 65, 69, 76, 83, 102, 111, 120; 1909–55], i, 82, no. 218); 1240 × 1241 (S. J. Chadwick, 'Kirklees Priory', *Yorks. Archaeol. Journal* 16 [1902], 321).

LACOCK (list in VCH *Wilts.*, iii [1956], 315).

Prioress
Wymarca, occ. 1233, 1239 (VCH *Wilts.*, iii, 315).

Abbesses
Ela (foundress), abbess elect 1239 × 1240; res. 1257 (ibid.).
Beatrice of Kent, app. 1257; d. in or after 1280 (ibid.).

LAMBLEY
No names known.

LANGLEY (list in VCH *Leics.*, ii [1954], 4).

Rose, occ. 1229 (*MA*, iv, 222–3, no. 5, and see VCH *Leics.*, ii, 3, n. 17 for date).

Burgia, el. 1229 × 1230 (*Rot. Wells*, ii, 312).

Isabella of Leicester, el. 1236 × 1237 (*Reg. Grosseteste*, 393); occ. (**Isabella**), 1265 (PRO E326/212).

Juliana of Winchester, app. 1269 (*Reg. Gravesend*, 149).

LEGBOURNE (list in VCH *Lincs.*, ii [1906], 155).

Prioresses
Beatrice, occ. 1226 (*HRH*, 214); res. 1246 × 1247 (*Reg. Grosseteste*, 88).
Alice of Holland, el. 1246 × 1247 (ibid.); occ. 1250 (*Linc. Final Concords ii*, 87, no. 123).
Joan, occ. 1256 (ibid. 158, no. 96); 1260 (*Reg. Ant. Linc.*, ii, 115–16, no. 400).
Alice de Coningsholme, el. 1275 (*Reg. Gravesend*, 65).

Magistri / Priors
Robert, occ. 1182 (*Gilbertine Charts.*, 102, no. 1); 1202, 1203, 1208, 1228, 1231 (*HRH*, 214).
Robert ?II, occ. 1260 (*Reg. Ant. Linc.*, ii, 115–16, no. 400).

LIMEBROOK
No names known.

LITTLE MARLOW (list in VCH *Bucks.*, i [1905, repr. 1969], 360).

Margaret, occ. *c.*1194 × 1195 (*Waltham Abbey Charts.*, 390–1); 1220 (*HRH*, 214), probably 1217: see 'A' below.

A, occ. 1217 (*Cartl. Missenden*, ii, 102, no. 427). Probably the same as:

Alice, occ. 1227 (*Calendar of the Roll of the Justices on Eyre 1227*, ed. J. G. Jenkins [Bucks. Rec. Soc. 6; 1942], 8, no. 125); d. 1229 × 1230 (**A**) (*Rot. Wells*, ii, 33).

Matilda d'Auvers, el. 1229 × 1230 (ibid.); occ. 1232 (*A Calendar of the Feet of Fines for the County of Buckingham, 7 Richard I–44 Henry III*, ed. M. W. Hughes [Bucks Rec. Soc. 4; 1942 for 1940], 63, no. 25).

Admiranda, el. 1236 × 1237 (*Reg. Grosseteste*, 344); occ. ?1247 (VCH *Bucks.*, i, 360, citing a reference I cannot trace).

Cecily de Turville, occ. 1257 (*Bucks. Fines*, 109, no. 13); res. 1258 × 1259 (*Reg. Gravesend*, 236).

Christiana de Whitemers, el. 1258 × 1259 (ibid.).

Felicia of Kimble, el. 1264; res. 1265 (*Reg. Gravesend*, 239).

Gunnora, el. 1265 (ibid.); res. 1273 when:

Margery of Waltham el. (ibid. 250).

LITTLEMORE (list in VCH *Oxon.*, ii [1907], 77).

Isabel de Henred, el. 1230 (*HRH*, 214); occ. (**Isabel**) 1241 (*Oxford Fines*, 116, no. 44).

Isabel de Stures, occ. 1265 (Oxford, Bodleian MS Oxon Chart. 36), d. 1266 (*Reg. Gravesend*, 219).

Amabilia de Sandford, el. 1266 (ibid.); d. 1274 (ibid. 226).

Amice de Sandford, el. 1274 (ibid.); d. 1276 × 1277 when:

Matilda, el. (ibid. 231).

LONDON CLERKENWELL (list in VCH *Middlesex*, i [1969], 174; see also *Cartl. Clerkenwell*, 270–1 and 281–3).

Prioresses

Isabel, occ. 1202 × 1204 (*Cartl. Beauchamp*, 178, no. 314); 1206 (*HRH*, 214);

1208, vacancy (ibid.).

Alice, occ. 1216 × 1220; 1221 × 1222 (*Cartl. Clerkenwell*, 187, 281).

Eleanor, occ. 1221 × 1223 (ibid. 181, 281).

Hawise, occ. 1231 × 1232, 1237, 1240, 1244 (ibid. 209, 281).

Cecily, occ. 1245, 1248 (ibid. 281).

Margery (or **Margaret**) **de Whatvyll**, occ. 1251 × 1252, 1254, 1264 × 1265 (ibid. 281–2).

Magistri

Alexander (probably *magister* of the nunnery), occ. 1176, 1185, *c.*1190 × 1196 (*Cartl. Clerkenwell*, 26, no. 33, 93, no. 145, 76, no. 114).

Matthew (*procurator*), occ. 1230 × 1231; *c.*1231 × 1245 (ibid. 218, no. 331 and 231, no. 347).

Martin (*procurator*), occ. 1244 × 1245 (ibid. 219, no. 333).

Richard (*magister*), *c.*1248 × *c.*1265 (ibid. 243, no. 362).

LONDON HALIWELL (list in VCH *Middlesex*, i [1969], 178).
Matilda, occ. 1224; 1225 (VCH *Middlesex*, i, 178).
Agnes, occ. 1239, 1245 × 1246 (ibid.).
Juliana, occ. 1248, 1262 (ibid.).
Benigna, occ. *temp* Henry III (ibid.).
Isabel, occ. 1261 (ibid.).
Christina, occ. 1269 × 1284 (ibid.).

LONDON ST HELENS (list in VCH *London*, i [1909], 460–1).
D, occ. *c*.1212 × *c*.1216 (*HRH*, 215).
Matilda, occ. *c*.1200 × 1225 (PRO, E40/2213; (could be before 'D').
Helen, occ. 1229 × 1230 (*HRH*, 215); d. (**H**.) *c*.1255 (*HMC Ninth Report*, app. i, 27b; Guildhall MS 25,121 / 1108).
Scholastica, occ. 1256 (*Beds. Fines*, 160, no. 571); 1265 (PRO E40/791); d. 1269 when:
Felicia de Basinges, el. (*HMC Ninth Report*, app. i, 57a; Guildhall MS 25,121/2039).

LYMINSTER (list in VCH *Sussex*, ii [1907], 121).
Mabel, occ. 1262 × 1263 as predecessor of then prioress (PRO Just 1/912A, memb. 4^v).

MALLING (list in VCH *Kent*, ii [1926], 148).

Abbesses
Avice, app. early 1108; occ. (A). 1108 × 1114 (*HRH*, 215); probably the same as:
Azeliz, occ. 1115 × 1122 (*Cal. Chart. Rolls 1341–1417*, 62, no. 34).
Ermelina, occ. 1159 × 1160 (not 1145 × 1150: see *HRH*, 215); 1153 × 1167 (Urry, *Canterbury*, 400–1, no. 20).

MARHAM (list in VCH *Norfolk*, ii [1906], 370).

Abbess
Mary, first abbess, occ. 1276 (Nichols, 'Marham Abbey', 27).

MARKYATE (list in VCH *Beds.*, i [1904], 360–1).
Christina I (foundress), occ. 1145 (*HRH*, 215), see p. 18. for uncertainties as to the date of her death.
Christina II, occ. 1188 × 1198 (BL Cotton Chart. xi, 36, printed *MA*, iii, 372, no. 8); 1202 × 1203 (*HRH*, 215).
Isabel I and II, occ. early 13th century, 1220, 1230 (*HRH*, 215).
Joan de Syret', el. 1238 × 1239 (*Reg. Grosseteste*, 312); occ. 1251 × 1252 (*Warwicks. Fines*, 152, no. 719).
Agnes Gobion, occ. 1260 (*Gesta Abbatum*, i, 387); d. 1274 when:
Isabella Gobion, el. (*Reg. Gravesend*, 200).

MARRICK (list in VCH *Yorks.*, iii [1913, repr. 1974], 118).
Isabel, occ. 1240 (*HRH*, 215), ? same as:

Isabella de Surrais, occ. 1250, 1257, 1263 ('Marrick Charts', *Coll. Top. et Gen.*, v, 239).

MINSTER IN SHEPPEY (list in VCH *Kent*, ii [1926], 150).

Prioresses

The names of prioresses, possibly dating from this period, are given in the Davington obituary list (BL Cotton MS Faustina B vi): **Eustacia** (ibid., fo. 104), **Agnes** and **Christina** (ibid., fo. 106ᵛ), occ. 1186, 1187 (*HRH*, 216). Gunnora, listed in VCH *Kent*, ii, 150, was prioress of Davington (see BL Cotton MS Faustina B. vi, fo. 102ᵛ).

Prior

As in *HRH*, 216.

MOXBY (list in VCH *Yorks*., iii [1913, repr. 1974], 240).

Prioresses

No names known for this period.

Magister

Peter, occ. *c.1225* (*Curia Regis Rolls*, xii, 168, no. 827).

NEASHAM

No names known.

NEWCASTLE

Christiana, occ. 1233 (Madox, *Form. Ang.*, 132, no. 224).

Emma, occ. *c.1250* (*Northumberland and Durham Deeds*, ed. A. Oliver [Newcastle on Tyne Records ser. 7; 1929], 135–6, no. 1); 1257 (*Feet of Fines Northumberland and Durham (abstracts 1196–1228)*, ed. A. M. Oliver and C. Johnson, from transcripts by P. Oliver [Newcastle on Tyne Record ser. 10; 1931 (1933)], 98).

Agnes, ? 13th cent. (PRO, E326/6624).

Sybil ? 13th cent. (PRO, E326/9848).

NORTHAMPTON DELAPRÉ (list in VCH *Northants*., ii [1906], 115–16).

Abbesses

Cecilia de Daventry, el. 1220 (*HRH*, 216); d. 1242 (*Cal. Pat. Rolls 1232–47*, 299).

Agatha de Navesby, el. 1242 (ibid.); d. 1275 when:

Emma Malore, el. (*Cal. Pat. Rolls 1272–81*, 75, 76).

NORTH ORMSBY (list in VCH *Lincs*., ii [1906], 196).

Priors

Thomas, occ. 1164, 1182 × 1200 (*HRH*, 204); 1188 (*Linc. Final Concords ii*, 331).

Robert, occ. 1209 × 1210, 1212 × 1213 (*HRH*, 204).

Vivian, occ. 1222 (ibid.).

William, occ. 1224 (*Linc. Final Concords i*, Boyd and Massingberd, i, 170, no. 46); 1225 × 1226 (ibid., ii, 177, no. 65).

Robert, occ. 1231 (ibid., ii, 226, no. 16); 1234 (ibid., ii, 261, no. 134).

Adam, occ. 1239 × 1240 (ibid., ii, 311, no. 39).

Thomas, occ. 1245 × 1246, 1250 (*Linc. Final Concords ii*, 34, no. 2 and 75, no. 82).

Robert, occ. 1255, 1263 (ibid. 111, no. 45 and 208, no. 85).

NORWICH CARROW (list in VCH *Norfolk*, ii [1906], 354).

Agnes de Monte Caenesi, occ. early 13th cent. (*HRH*, 216); *c.*1230 × 1247 (Rye, *Carrow Abbey*, 38).

Magdalen, occ. 1264 (Blomefield, *Norfolk*, iv, 525).

NUN APPLETON (list in VCH *Yorks.*, iii [1913, repr. 1974], 173–4).

Alice, occ. 1234 (*Yorks. Fines 1232–46*, 9, no. 622); 1256 (*Linc. Final Concords ii*, 293, no. 127).

Mabel, occ. 1262 (*Calendar of Charters and Rolls Preserved in the Bodleian Library*, ed. W. H. Turner, under direction of H. O. Coxe [Oxford, 1878], 697).

NUNBURNHOLME (list in VCH *Yorks.*, iii [1913, repr. 1974], 119. As in *HRH*, 216.

NUN COTHAM (list in VCH *Lincs.*, ii [1906], 153).

Prioresses

Emma, el. 1230 × 1231 (*Rot. Wells*, iii, 195); occ. 1234 (*Linc. Final Concords i*, Boyd and Massingberd, ii, 277–8, no. 187).

Joan de Thorne, el. 1265 (*Reg. Gravesend*, 19).

Lucy, occ. *c.*1268 (dated by Adam, see below; Oxford, Bodleian MS Top Lincs. d 1, fo. 51).

Magistri / Priors

Sampson, occ.(S), 1176 × 1203 (*HRH*, 216; for full name see Oxford, Bodleian MS Top Lincs. d 1, fo. 9).

Walter, occ. 1218 × 1219 (ibid., fo. 20); 1228 (BL Harl. Chart. 44 E. 20, *magister et rector*); *temp.* Henry III (BL Harl. Chart. 46 C. 24—in this charter he is called *prior*).

John, occ. 1246 (Oxford, Bodleian MS Top Lincs. d 1, fo. 47^v).

The next known *magister*, **Adam**, a canon of the house, was placed in this office in 1268 (*Reg. Gravesend*, 35).

NUNEATON (list in VCH *Warwicks.*, ii [1908, repr. 1965], 69–70).

Prioresses

For a note on the problems of the order of these heads see *HRH*, 217. It is possible that Alice was earlier than Agnes, and the references to 'A' listed in *HRH* refer to Agnes.

Agnes, occ. *c.*1160; ? late 12th cent. (*HRH*, 217).

Alice, occ. 1163 (BL Addit. Chart. 47,398 [4]); 1159 × 1181 (*PUE*, iii, 408–9, no. 283).

A, occ. 1186, 1188 × 1198 (*HRH*, 217).

Juliana, occ. late 12th cent. (ibid.).
Mabel, occ. 1202 (*HRH*, 217).
Emma, occ. 1206, 1206 × 1207 (ibid.).
M, occ.– 1213 (BL Addit. Chart. 20,872); probably same as:
Mabel, occ. 1213 × 1214 (*HRH*, 217).
Ida, occ. 1214, 1226 (ibid.).
Sybil, occ. 1227, 1227 × 1228 (ibid.), 1232 (BL Addit. Chart. 48,152).
Ida, occ. 1238 (*Bucks Fines*, 73–4, no. 6—wrongly described as prioress of
   Oxford); 1240 (BL Addit. Chart. 49,149); 1247 (BL Addit. Chart.
   48,497).
Cecilia de Lexington, occ. 1256 (Cecilia) (BL Addit. Charts. 47,961–2);
   1260 (BL Addit. Chart. 48,501).
Cecilia de Sutton, occ. *c.*1272 (BL Addit. Chart. 48,335).

Priors
Simon, occ. 1206 (*Curia Regis Rolls*, iv, 140).
A. occ. – 1213 (BL Addit. Chart. 20,872); see also *HRH*, 217.
N, occ. *c.*1206 × *c.*1207 (BL Addit. Chart. 47,646); *c.*1213 × 1214 (*HRH*,
   217). ? same as **Nicholas**, occ. 1221 (ibid.).
G, occ. early 13th cent. (ibid.).
Richard, occ. *c.*1227 (BL Addit. Chart. 48,490).
The order of these priors, particularly the last three is very uncertain.
Robert, occ. 1227 × 1228 (*HRH*, 217); 1240 (BL Addit. Chart. 49,149);
   1240 × 1247 (BL Addit. Chart. 48,088).
Gilbert, occ. 1247 (BL Addit. Chart. 48,497).
William de Verney, occ. 1256, 1257 (BL Addit. Chart. 47,594); 1260 (BL
   Addit. Chart. 48,501).
Peter de Palermo, occ. *temp.* Henry III (BL Addit. Chart. 48,151).
Henry, occ. *c.*1272 (BL Addit. Chart. 48,335).

NUNKEELING (list in VCH *Yorks.*, iii [1913, repr. 1974], 121–2).

Prioresses
Avice, occ. 1235 × 1236 (Oxford, Bodleian MS Dodsworth, vii, fo. 258);
   1252 (Assize Roll, PRO, Just 1/1046, memb. 62).
Sybil, occ. ? 1251 (*Yorks. Fines 1246–72*, 45, no. 1, 390).
Agnes de Mapleton, occ. 13th century (BL Harl. Chart. 44 E. 56).
Agnes de Beverley, el. 1267 (*Reg. Walter Giffard*, 50).
(The order of these three prioresses is not clear).

Magistri / custos
Ivo, occ. 13th century (BL Harl. Chart. 44 E. 56).
Gregory de Lesset, monk of Newburgh, app. 1267 as *custos* (*Reg. Walter
   Giffard*, 108–9).

NUN MONKTON (list in VCH *Yorks.*, iii [1913, repr. 1974], 123).
Matilda de Arches, occ. 1147 × 1153 (*HRH*, 218); see also p. 178 n.
   above.
(M), ? the same, occ. *c.*1198 × 1203 (*Cartl. Fountains*, ii, 723, no. 20).
Agnes, occ. 1224, 1226 (*HRH*, 218).

Amabel, occ. 1240 (*Yorks. Fines 1232–46*, 72, no. 892).
Avice, occ. 1251 (*Yorks. Fines 1246–72*, 17, no. 792); 1268 (*Reg. Walter Giffard*, 27).
Mary, occ. 1278 (BL Addit. Chart. 17,962 [i]).

ORFORD (list in VCH *Lincs.*, ii [1906], 209).

Prioresses
As in *HRH*, 218.

Priors / magistri
Ralph (not given the title prior or *magister*, but probably was the male head of the community), occ. c.1155 × 1167 (*Danelaw Docs.*, 185, no. 248).
Thomas, occ. 1228 × 1232 (*HRH*, 218).
Robert, occ. *temp.* Henry III (BL Cotton Chart. v, 71).

PINLEY (list in VCH *Warwicks*, ii [1908, repr. 1965], 83).

Prioresses
Margery, occ. 1226 (*Warwicks. Fines*, 76, no. 395).
Amicia, occ. 1235 × 1236 (ibid. 105–6, no. 528); 1239 (ibid. 112–13, no. 564).
The next known prioress, **Lucy de Sapy**, was el. 1269 (*Reg. Godfrey Giffard*, ii, 27).

Prior
Thomas, occ. c.1184 × 1196 (probably prior of Pinley, though full title is not given) (BL Cotton Chart. xi, 16).

POLESWORTH (list in VCH *Warwicks.*, ii [1908, repr. 1965], 64).
This community appears to have developed from a priory at Oldbury, although the original site was probably Polesworth: see KH, 263.

Abbesses
Osanna, occ. as prioress of Oldbury − 1147 (*MA*, ii, 367, no. 8); occ. as abbess of Polesworth. 1171 × c.1174 (*HRH*, 218).
Muriel, occ. 1220 × 1221 (ibid.).
Cecily, el. 1234 (*Cal. Pat. Rolls 1232–47*, 45).
Margaret de Appleby, el. 1237 (*Cal. Pat. Rolls 1232–47*, 188); occ. 1254 (*Warwicks. Fines*, 158, no. 749).
Sarah of Manchester, el. 1269 (*Cal. Pat. Rolls 1266–72*, 398); d. 1276 when:
Albreda de Camvill was el. 1277 (*Cal. Pat. Rolls 1272–81*, 186, 188).
(A **Sarah**, prioress of Oldbury, occ. n.d. [Oxford, Bodleian MS Dodsworth lxv, fo. 41ᵛ]).

POLSLOE (list of prioresses given in E. Lega-Weekes, 'History of St Katherine's Priory, Polsloe, Part I', *Transactions of the Devon Archaeol. Soc.* 66 [1934], 195–6).
Avelina, occ. 1218 (Lega-Weekes, 195).
Isabella of Brent, occ. 1256 (ibid.).
Margaret de Morchard, app. 1267 (ibid.).

RAMSTEDE (Ramscombe) (VCH *Sussex*, ii [1907], 63).
No heads known for this period.

REDLINGFIELD (list in VCH *Suffolk*, ii [1907], 85).
Emma, occ. early 13th cent. (pal.) (BL Addit. Chart. 10,640).
The names given in the extract BL Addit. MS 19,090, have to be treated
with caution: see *HRH*, 218. It is possible that **Agnes** and **Alice** (BL
Addit. MS 19,090, fos. 74^v and 70^v) date from the 13th cent.

ROSEDALE (list in VCH *Yorks.*, iii [1913, repr. 1974], 176).
Aubreye, occ. 1246 (*Yorks. Fines 1232–46*, 148–9, no. 1,175).
Juliana, occ. 1251 (*Yorks. Fines 1246–72*, 43, no. 1,380).

ROTHWELL (list in VCH *Northants.* [1906], 138).
No heads known for this period.

ROWNEY (list in VCH *Herts.*, iv [1914], 435).
Rose, occ. 13th cent. (pal.) (BL Campbell Chart. iv, 2); res. 1257 × 1258
(*Reg. Grosseteste*, 513).
Nichola, el. 1257 × 1258 (ibid.); res. 1277 (*Reg. Gravesend*, 183), when
the next prioress:
Ascelina of Brockhall was elected.

RUSPER (list in VCH *Sussex*, ii [1907], 64).
Katherine, occ. 1232 (VCH *Sussex*, ii, 64, citing a reference I have been
unable to trace).
Alice, occ. 1239 × 1247 (*The Chartulary of the High Church of Chichester*,
ed. W. D. Peckham [Sussex Rec. Soc. 6; 1946 for 1942–3], 155, no. 596);
1256 (*An Abstract of Feet of Fines relating to the County of Sussex from
34 Henry III to 35 Edward I*, ii, ed. L. F. Salzman [Sussex Rec. Soc. 7;
1907], 13, no. 555).

ST MARY DE PRÉ (list in VCH *Herts.*, iv [1914], 431).

Prioresses
No names known.

Magistri
John of Walden, occ. 1194 × 1195 (*Gesta Abbatum*, i, 201).
Richard, occ. 1235 (ibid. 305).
William (*custos*), occ. 1228 (*Curia Regis Rolls*, xiii, 188, no. 853); 1248
(*magister*) (Herts. Feet of Fines, PRO, CP 25/1/85/21, no. 344).
Richard, occ. 1278 (Herts. Feet of Fines, PRO, CP 25/1/86/37 [97]).

SEMPRINGHAM (list in VCH *Lincs.*, ii [1906], 186–7).

Priors of the House
For others in 12th cent. see *HRH*, 204.
Reginald, occ. 1222 (ibid. 205).

Alan, occ. 1223 (*Linc. Final Concords i*, Boyd and Massingberd, i, 167, no. 36).

Thomas, occ. 1226 (ibid., ii, 182, no. 82); 1231 (ibid., ii, 244, no. 83); 1234 (ibid., ii, 262, no. 142); 1240 (ibid., ii, 313, no. 48); 1242 (BL Cotton Chart. iv 57 [29]); 1245 (*Linc. Final Concords ii*, 24, no. 76).

Robert, occ. 1250 (ibid. 55, no. 12); 1258 × 1259 (ibid. 169, no. 32); 1263 (ibid. 223, no. 152).

Roger, occ. *c.*1270 (BL Harl. Chart. 44 A. 36); 1271 × 1272 (*Linc. Final Concords ii*, 275, no. 132).

SETON (VCH *Cumberland*, ii [1905], 194).
No names known.

SEWARDSLEY (list in VCH *Northants.*, ii [1906], 127).
Felicia, occ. early 13th cent. (BL Egerton MS 3033, fo. 6ᵛ).
Alice, d. 1247 × 1248 (*Reg. Grosseteste*, 234).
Juliana de Sewell, el. 1247 × 1248 (ibid.); res. 1260 × 1261 when:
Florence, el. (*Reg. Gravesend*, 100).
Juetta de Pavilly, occ. 13th cent. (PRO, E326/ 2919 and 1191).

SHOULDHAM (list in VCH *Norfolk*, ii [1906], 414).

Priors
William, occ. 1250 × 1251 (Blomefield, *Norfolk*, vii, 424).
Richard, occ. *c.*1270 (ibid.).

SINNINGTHWAITE (list in VCH *Yorks.*, iii [1913, repr. 1974], 178).
Matilda, occ. ? late 12th cent. (*Cartl. Fountains*, ii, 766, no. 7).
Sapiencia, occ. as predecessor of Euphemia (*Yorks. Assize Rolls John and Henry III*, 85).
Euphemia, occ. 1218 (*HRH*, 219); 1229 (*Yorks. Deeds*, vi [lxxvi], 165–6, no. 544).
Isabella, occ. 1267 (*MA*, v, 464, no. 5).

SIXHILLS (list in VCH *Lincs.*, ii [1906], 195).

Priors
T, occ. early 13th cent. (BL Harl. Chart. 45 C. 31).
Nicholas, occ. 1224 (*Linc. Final Concords i*, Boyd and Massingberd, i, 173, no. 56); 1231 (ibid., ii, 245, no. 90); 1234 (ibid., ii, 285, no. 214); 1235 (BL Harl. Chart. 44 H. 48); 1240 (*Linc. Final Concords, i*, Boyd and Massingberd, ii, 329–30, no. 106); 1245 (BL Harl. Chart. 44 G. 49).
Reginald, occ. 1252 (*Linc. Final Concords ii*, 100, no. 5); 1256 (ibid. 118, no. 17); 1271 (ibid. 270, no. 118); – 1279 (BL Harl. Chart. 56 A. 12).

SOPWELL (list in VCH Herts., iv [1914], 425–6).
Agnes, occ. 1156 (*PUE*, iii, 244, no. 107).
Amicia, occ. 1173 × 1174 (ibid. 384, no. 214). Probably the same as:
Avicia, occ. 12th cent. (*HRH*, 220).

Cecily, occ. *c.*1200 (PRO, E42/380 [i]).

Estr(avia), occ. n.d. ? early 13th cent. (pal.) (PRO, E210/3272), probably same as:

E, occ. 1233 (PRO, E210/285).

SPINNEY

Susanna (not given title of prioress but the charter suggests she was head of the community), occ. 1148 × 1154 (*Acta I Lincoln 1067–1185*, 160, no. 256).

STAINFIELD (list in VCH *Lincs.*, ii [1906], 132).

Prioresses

New prioress (no name given), el. 1236 × 1237 (*Reg. Grosseteste*, 11).

Agnes of Thornton, app. 1243 × 1244 (*Reg. Grosseteste*, 72); occ. 1245 (*Linc. Final Concords ii*, 6, no. 16; 1250 (ibid. 78, no. 92).

Matilda, d. 1258 × 1259 (*Reg. Gravesend*, 2).

Euphemia de Constable, el. 1258 × 1259 (ibid.); d. 1258 × 1259 when:

Katherine of Durham, el. (ibid.); ? same as:

Katherine, occ. 1272 (BL Harl. MS 6954, fo. 25^v).

Magistri / Priors

Alan (prior), occ. *temp.* prioress Margaret, i.e. 1168 × 1203 (see *HRH*, 220) (*Reg. Ant. Linc.*, x, 276, no. 2,940).

Richard, occ. 1200 (*Curia Regis Rolls*, i, 346).

William of Appleby, occ. 1225 (*HRH*, 220).

Robert de Sammar', monk of Whitby, installed 1223; occ. 1226 (*HRH*, 220).

Gilbert of Kingston, monk of Whitby, app. 1238 × 1239 (*Reg. Grosseteste*, 35); occ. *c.*1243 × *c.*1250 (*temp.* Prioress Agnes (*The Register or Rolls of Walter Gray, Lord Archbishop of York*, ed. J. Raine [Surtees Soc., 56; 1872], 11 n.).

Gilbert de Paunton, monk of Bardney, el. 1258 × 1259 (*Reg. Gravesend*, 2).

John of Barton, monk of Bardney, el. 1263 (ibid. 14).

Benedict of Billingborough, monk of Whitby, el. 1270 (ibid. 41).

STAMFORD (list in VCH *Northants.*, ii [1906], 100–1).

Prioresses

Amabilia, occ. *c.*1214 × 1222 (Madox, *Form. Ang.*, 371, no. 1,666); ? same as:

A, occ. 1174 × 1181 (*HRH*, 220).

Agnes de Boby, confirmed by bishop ? 1219 × 1220 (*HRH*, 220).

Dionysia, el. 1238 × 1239 (*Reg. Grosseteste*, 32–3).

Alice, occ. 1238 × 1240 (PRO E210/3614); d. 1240 (London Soc. of Antiquaries MS 60, fo. 205).

Petronilla, el. 1240 (ibid.).

Sybil, app. 1247 × 1248 (*Reg. Grosseteste*, 104).

Amicia, occ. 1251 × 1252 (PRO, E210/3672); res. 1272 when:
Elizabeth, el. (*Reg. Gravesend*, 52).

Priors

Richard de Scoter, monk of Peterborough, installed 1223 (*custos*) (*Rot. Wells*, iii, 126).
Henry of Fiskerton, res. 1228 × 1229 (*custos*) (ibid., iii, 173).
Serlo, monk of Peterborough, installed 1228 × 1229 (ibid.); occ. *c.*1238 × 1240 (PRO E210/3614).
Roger de Keten, precentor of Peterborough, installed 1243; d. 1247 × 1248 (*Reg. Grosseteste*, 69, 97).
Henry of Caversham, monk of Peterborough, installed 1247 × 1248 (ibid. 97); res. 1250 (ibid. 121–2).
Thomas of Grimsby, monk of Peterborough, installed (*magister*) 1250 × 1251 (ibid. 122).
J. de Keten, res. 1259 × 1260 (*Reg. Gravesend*, 4).
Hugh of Leicester, monk of Peterborough, installed 1259 × 1260 (ibid.); d. 1266 when:
William of Weston, monk of Peterborough, installed (ibid. 22).

STIXWOULD (list in VCH *Lincs.*, ii [1906], 149).

Prioresses

Lucy, occ. 1160, 1168 (BL Addit. MS 46,701, fos. 11^v, 104).
L, ? Different from above, occ. 1184 (*HRH*, 220).
Matilda, occ. late 12th century; 1209 × 1235 (ibid. 220).
Beatrice, occ. 1206 (*Curia Regis Rolls*, iv, 87), 1191 × 1223 (*temp.* Hugh) (BL Addit. MS 46,701, fo. 100). An alternative possibility is that Beatrice preceded Matilda.
New prioress (name not given), el. 1236 × 1237 (*Reg. Grosseteste*, 11).
Ivetta de Chauret, app. 1244 × 1245 (ibid. 74).
Lucy de Pincebeck, el. 1248 × 1249 (ibid. 111).
Isabella de Brus, occ. 1262 × 1263 (*Reg. Gravesend*, 89); d. 1265 (ibid. 19).
Isabella of Lavington, el. 1265 (ibid.).

Magistri

Simon, occ. *c.*1150 × 1160 (*HRH*, 220); 1172 (BL Addit. MS 46,701, fo. 70^v).
Hugh, occ. 1191; 1205; 1195 × 1223 (*HRH*, 221).
Matthew, occ. 1209 × 1235 (ibid.).
Geoffrey, app. *c.*1218 × 1219 (*Rot. Wells*, i, 117); occ. 1227 (*HRH*, 221); 1232 × 1233 (*Linc. Final Concords i*, Boyd and Massingberd, ii, 252, no. 107); 1235 BL (Harl. Chart. 44 H 48); 1247 (*Linc. Final Concords ii*, 45, no. 33); 1251 (ibid. 90, no. 2).
Roger, occ. 1262 × 1263 (*Reg. Gravesend*, 89).

STRATFORD (list in VCH *Middlesex*, i [1969], 159).
Alice, occ. 1226 × 1227 (*Rot. Lit. Claus.*, ii, 206b).
Lucy, occ. *c.*1264 × *c.*1284 (VCH *Middlesex*, i, 159).

STUDLEY (list in VCH *Oxon.*, ii [1907], 79).
Alice of Crowcombe, el. 1250 × 1251 (*Reg. Grosseteste*, 499).
Elizabeth, occ. 1258 (*Oxford Fines*, 175, no. 4); d. 1276 when:
Margery Clement, el. (*Reg. Gravesend*, 228).

SWAFFHAM BULBECK (list in VCH *Cambs.*, ii [1948], 228);
see also W. M. Palmer, 'The Benedictine Nunnery of Swaffham Bulbeck',
[*Cambs. Antiq. Soc. . . . Proceedings and Communications* 31; 1928],
38–9).
Agnes, occ. *temp.* John (BL Addit. MS 5819, fo. 139); 1234 × 1235
(*Cambs. Fines*, 19, no. 42).
Sybil, ? succeeded Agnes (E. Hailstone, *History of Swaffham Bulbeck*,
unpubl. proofs held in Cambridge Univ. Library, MS Bb 892 1).
Matilda, occ. 1242 × 1243 (*Cambs. Fines*, 25, no. 2), 1252 × 1253 (ibid.
34, no. 28).
Alice, occ. 1249 × 1250 (Hailstone, 54); 1272 (Assize roll, PRO, Just 1/84,
memb. 2^v).

SWINE (list in VCH *Yorks.*, iii [1913, repr. 1974], 182).
Prioresses
Sybil, occ. 1236 (*Yorks. Fines 1232–46*, 43, no. 776).
Matilda, occ. 1240 (ibid. 86, no. 963).
Sybil, occ. 1246 (ibid. 151, no. 1,190), 1251 (*Yorks. Fines 1246–72*, 48,
no. 1,403).

Priors / Magistri
Robert, occ. 1170 × 1175 (*HRH*, 221); as prior (*Cartl. Bridlington*, 364).
Philip, occ. *c.*1184 × 1189 (Oxford, Bodleian MS Linc. Chart. 1167), late
Henry II (*Danelaw Docs.*, 286, no. 382).
Hamo, canon of Healaugh Park, occ. 1235 × 1249 (*Chron. Meaux*, ii, 13).

TARRANT (list in VCH *Dorset*, ii [1908], 90).
Abbesses
Claricia, el. − 1228 (declaration to the bishop preserved in Salisbury
Chapter records, press 2, box 1).
Emelina, ? early 13th cent. (declaration, undated, preserved in Salisbury
Chapter records).
Matilda, occ. 1240, 1245 (*Cal. Chart. Rolls 1226–57*, 250, 285); 1246
(PRO, E132/3/30).
Isolda, occ. −1280 (*Cal. Chart. Rolls 1257–1300*, 229).
Proctor
William, occ. 1237 (*Cal. Lib. Rolls 1226–40*, 280).

THETFORD (list in VCH *Norfolk*, ii [1906], 355–6; VCH *Suffolk*, ii [1907],
86).
Agnes, occ. 1253 × 1254 (*A Calendar of the Feet of Fines for Suffolk
Richard I–Edward IV*), ed. W. Rye [Suffolk Inst. of Archaeol. and Nat.
Hist., 1900]; 56, no. 209).

THICKET (list in VCH *Yorks.*, iii [1913, repr. 1974], 125).
Alice, occ. *c.*1252 × 1269 (W. P. Baildon, *Notes on the Religious and Secular Houses of Yorkshire*, 2 vols. [Yorks. Archaeol. Soc., Record ser., 17; 1895, and 81; 1931], ii, 44).

TUNSTALL (later joined to Bullington).
Priors
Alan, sometimes described as prior of this house, was probably prior of Haverholme: see *HRH*, 202, n. 5.

WALLINGWELLS (list in VCH *Notts.*, ii [1910], 90).
Isolda, occ. 1240 (*Yorks. Fines 1232–46*, 61, no. 832).
Agnes, occ. 1262 (*Reg. Walter Giffard*, 327).
Alice de Montenay, ? late 13th cent. (BL Harl. Chart. 112 F. 30).

WATTON (list in VCH *Yorks.*, iii [1913, repr. 1974], 255).
Priors
William, occ. 1226 (*HRH*, 205); 1229 (*Yorks. Fines 1218–31*, 121–2, no. 442).
Roger, occ. 1240 (*Yorks. Fines 1232–46*, 85, no. 958).
Patrick, occ. 1251 × 1252 (*Yorks. Fines 1246–72*, 64, no. 1,455); –1261 when el. *magister* of the order of Sempringham (*Reg. Gravesend*, 7–8).

WESTWOOD (list in VCH *Worcs.*, ii [1907], 151).
No prioresses known for this period.
Priors
Nicholas, occ. –1260 (*Cal. Close Rolls 1259–61*, 212).

WHISTONES (list in VCH *Worcs.*, ii [1907], 156).
The first known, **Juliana,** occ. 1262 (VCH *Worcs.*, ii, 156).

WILBERFOSS (list in VCH *Yorks.*, iii [1913, repr. 1974], 126).
Christiana, occ. 1231 (*Yorks. Fines 1218–31*, 144, no. 522); 1234 × 1235 (*Yorks. Fines 1232–46*, 37, no. 752).
Lettice, occ. 1240 (ibid. 58, no. 818).
The next known prioress, **Isabella,** occ. 1276 (Baildon, i, 226).

WINTNEY (list in VCH *Hants.*, ii (1903), 151).
The following names are given in the obituary list of the house (BL Cotton Claud. D. iii), but it is not possible to ascertain their date or chronological order:
Emma, Sabina, Isilia, Claricia, Lucy I, Juliana, Alice, Lucy II, Hawise, Cecilia (ibid., fos. 140ᵛ, 147, 148, 148ᵛ, 151ᵛ, 155, 155ᵛ, 156ᵛ, 157). It has been suggested that **Rose,** whose name is written in red (ibid., fo. 158), may have been the first prioress (*HRH*, 223), but the name of Cecilia is also written in red.

Lucy ? I (the name of the other Lucy is written in a later hand), occ. 1223 ✕ 1224 (*HRH*, 223).
It is possible that Alice and Cecilia date from later than 1250 (VCH *Hants.*, ii, 151).

WIX (list in VCH *Essex*, ii [1907], 124).
Idonia, occ. 1198 (*HRH*, 224); 1199 (PRO, E40/13,772); 1202 (*HRH*, 224).
Christina, occ. early 13th cent. (ibid.).
Constance, occ. 1235 (ibid.); 1247 (*Essex Fines*, 156, no. 837).
Basilia, occ. 1257 (PRO, E40/3563).
Isabel, occ. 1262 (PRO, E40/3350); 1295 (PRO, E40/3353).

WOTHORPE (list in VCH *Northants.*, ii [1906], 101–2).
Dionysia, el. 1224 (*Rot. Wells*, ii, 120).
Claricia, el. 1244 ✕ 1245 (*Reg. Grosseteste*, 221).
Isabella, occ. 1257 (PRO, E210/195).

WROXALL (list in VCH *Warwicks.*, ii [1908, repr. 1965], 72–3).
For an early antiquarian list of prioresses see *MA*, iv, 89. The names given
   are: **Erneburga, Helena, Sabina, Helena, Matilda, Emma, Matilda,
   Cecilia, Ida, Amicia, Sibilia** (see also *HRH*, 224).
Sabina, occ. 1163 (ibid.).
Matilda, occ. 1221, and before **Helena** (*Rolls of the Justices in Eyre, Being
   the Rolls of Pleas and Assizes for Gloucestershire, Warwickshire and
   Staffordshire (recte Shropshire) 1221, 1222*, ed. D. M. Stenton [Selden
   Soc. 59; 1940], 182).
Helen, occ. 1221 (ibid.); 1236 (*Warwicks. Fines*, 104, no. 518).
Ida, occ. 1240 (ibid. 118, no. 593).
Avicia, occ. ? *c.*1270 (PRO, E210/216, dated Ryland, *Wroxall*, 219–20, no. 395).

WYKEHAM (list in VCH *Yorks.*, iii [1913, repr. 1974], 184).

Prioresses
Alice, occ. ? 13th cent. (Oxford, Bodleian MS Dodsworth, vii, fo. 293).
Eva, occ. 1234 (*HRH*, 224).

Magistri
Alan, occ. *c.*1160 ✕ 1176 (*EYC*, i, 300, no. 383).
Simon, occ. 1203 ✕ 1214 (*HRH*, 224).
Walter de Harpham, occ. 1233 ✕ 1234 (Oxford, Bodleian MS Dodsworth
   vii, fo. 293).

YEDINGHAM (list in VCH *Yorks.*, iii [1913, repr. 1974], 128).

Prioresses
Emma de Humbleton, occ. 1231 (Oxford, Bodleian MS Dodsworth, vii,
   fo. 183); 1241 (*MA*, iv, 275, no. 3).

Magister

Andrew, Prior of Kirkham, occ. *c.*1198 × *c.*1214 (*EYC*, i, 306, no. 390; for
   date, see *HRH*, 168).

YORK, CLEMENTHORPE (list in VCH *Yorks.*, iii [1913, repr. 1974], 130–1).
Agnes, occ. 1234 (*Yorks. Fines 1232–46*, 16–17, nos. 663 and 666); 1246
   (Assize Roll, PRO, Just 1/1045, memb. 44^v).
Margaret, occ. 1268 (*Yorks. Fines 1246–72*, 146, no. 1,730).

BIBLIOGRAPHY

1. Manuscript Sources

LONDON, BRITISH LIBRARY (BL)

Additional Charters
1050; 6518; 7524; 10,640; 17,962(i); 19,279; 19,962; 20,544; 20,622; 20,698; 20,872; 33,442; 35,595; 47,072; 47,381; 47,382; 47,384; 47,389; 47,398; 47,418; 47,423; 47,573; 47,594; 47,604; 47,615; 47,627; 47,646; 47,854; 47,871; 47,961; 47,962; 48,000; 48,027; 48,088; 48,093; 48,151; 48,152; 48,335; 48,488; 48,490; 48,497; 48,498; 48,501; 49,149; 49,969, 53,102; 53,108; 53,109

Additional MSS
4733: Register of Crabhouse
5516: Fragment of Canterbury, St Sepulchre's Cartulary
5819: vol. xviii of Cole's Collections
5823: vol. xxii of Cole's Collections
5827: vol. xxvi of Cole's Collections
5829: vol. xxviii of Cole's Collections
19,090: David Davy Collections
19,111: David Davy Collections
46,701: Stixwould cartulary

Arundel MS
29: Transcripts of Book of Walden

Campbell Charters
iii 1; iii 16; iv 2; xii 20

Cotton Charters
iv 57; v 71; xi 16; xi 36; xxi 18; xxix 72

Cotton MSS
Claudius (Claud.) D. iii, fos. 140ᵛ–160ᵛ: Witney obit calendar (printed Trokelowe, *Annales*, 384–93)
Claud. D. xi: Malton cartulary
Faustina (Faust.) A. iii: Westminster cartulary
Faust. B. vi: Davington obit calendar
Faust. B. vii: List of Cistercian foundations
Nero C. iii: Charters
Nero D. iii: St Leonard's Hospital (York) cartulary
Nero E. vi: Cartulary of the Hospitallers of St John of Jerusalem
Otto C. viii: Nunkeeling cartulary
Tiberius (Tib.) C ix: Waltham cartulary
Tib. E. i (ii): Life of Christina of Markyate
Tib. E. vi (ii): St Albans cartulary

Vespian (Vesp.) B. xxiv: Evesham cartulary
Vesp. E. vi: Transcripts of book of foundation of Walden
Vesp. E. ix: Westwood cartulary
Vesp. E. xvii: St Andrew, Northampton cartulary
Vesp. E. xviii: Kirkstead cartulary
Vesp. E. xxii: Peterborough register
Vitellius A. viii: Annals of Lacock Abbey
Vitellius E. viii: Miscellaneous collections

Egerton Charters
406; 622; 623; 624

Egerton MSS
2849:   Mortuary roll of Castle Hedingham
3033:   Canons Ashby cartulary
3137:   Blackborough cartulary

Harleian (Harl.) Charters
43 A. 34; 44 A. 36; 44 A. 40; 44 A. 41; 44 A. 44; 44 D. 57; 44 D. 60; 44 D.
    62; 44 E. 20; 44 E. 49; 44 E. 56; 44 G. 49; 44 H. 48; 44 I. 17; 45 C. 31;
    45 D. 12; 45 I. 7; 46 C. 24; 48 A. 12; 48 B. 3; 48 C. 33; 48 I. 49; 50 A.
    46; 50 I. 30; 52 H. 28; 54 C. 47; 55 A. 11; 55 E. 20; 56 A. 12; 58 G. 40;
    75 F. 60; 76 G. 34; 112 F. 30

Harleian MSS
391:    Waltham cartulary
743:    Bury St Edmunds register
1087:   Wigmore genealogy
1240:   *Liber Niger de Wigmore*
2044:   Randulph Holme's transcripts
2110:   Castle Acre cartulary
3650:   Kenilworth cartulary
3977:   Bury St Edmunds, register of custumaries
4809:   Waltham cartulary
6954   Extracts from registers of Lincoln diocese

Lansdowne MSS
207A: Collections of Gervase Holles
391:    Harrold cartulary
447:    Collections of Sir Richard St George Clarenceaux

Sloane Charter
xxx ii 64

Stow Charters
291; 292; 293; 294; 308

Wolley Charters
viii 51; xi 25

LAMBETH PALACE LIBRARY

Register of Archbishop Warham (1503–32)

LONDON, COLLEGE OF ARMS

MS L 17: Hospitaller MS

LONDON, GUILDHALL MSS

9531/9: Register of Bishop Richard fitz James (1506–22)
25,121/1068; 1108; 2038; 2039 (charters formerly in archives of St Paul's
  Cathedral)

LONDON, PUBLIC RECORD OFFICE (PRO)

C53/124: Charter roll calendared in *Cal. Chart. Roll 1327–41*, 391–7
C62/12 (memb. 9): Liberate roll calendared in *Cal. Lib. Rolls 1226–40*, 322
C143/410: Inquis. ad quod damnum 14 Richard II
CP 25/1/16/41: Bucks. Feet of Fines
CP 25/1/85/21: Herts. Feet of Fines
CP 25/1/86/37: Herts. Feet of Fines
CP 25/1/157/75: Norfolk Feet of Fines
E 36/137: Table of Canterbury Archbishopric Charters: see Churchill,
  'Canterbury Charts.'
E 40 (Ancient Deeds series A, Exchequer T R): 791; 996; 1590; 2213;
  3350; 3353; 3563; 9350; 11,069; 11,538; 13,772; 15,365
E 42 (Ancient Deeds series AS) 316; 380 (i); 419 (1)
E 132/2/11: Transcripts of Aconbury charters
E 132/2/19: Rowney charters
E 132/3/21: Stamford deeds
E 132/3/30: Tarrant deeds
E 132/3/51: Stamford deeds
E 164/19: Torre cartulary
E 164/20: Godstow cartulary
E 210 (Ancient Deeds series D, Exchequer T R): 125; 139; 195; 216; 285;
  331; 2060; 3272; 3614; 3672; 7431
E 211/301, 303, 307, 312: Rowney deeds
E 315/55: Aconbury cartulary
E 326 (Ancient Deeds series B, Exchequer Augmentations): 212; 421; 694;
  891; 1191; 2919; 3229; 4020; 5774; 6158; 6624; 8499; 8696; 8712;
  8713; 8779; 9770; 9848; 10,338; 10,389; 10,421; 11,356; 11,537;
  11,538; 11,550; 12,465
Just 1/84: Cambridge Eyre Roll of 1272
Just 1 909A: Sussex Eyre Roll of 1248
Just 1/912A: Sussex Eyre Roll of 1262
Just 1/1045: Yorks. Eyre Roll of 1246
Just 1/1046: Yorks. Eyre Roll of 1251–2
Scll/46: inventory of charts (Stamford)

LONDON SOCIETY OF ANTIQUARIES

MS 60: Register of Peterborough

LONDON WESTMINSTER ABBEY

Westminster Abbey Muniments Book 1: *Liber Niger Quaternus*

CAMBRIDGE UNIVERSITY LIBRARY

MS Dd viii 2: Obit calendar of Kington St Michael
MS Ff ii 29: Register of Bury St Edmunds

CAMBRIDGE, ST JOHN'S COLL. (SJC)

MS 271: (Lillechurch Mortuary Roll)
Charters (SJC archives) D.10: (Drawer 10): 29; 22B
D 13 (Drawer 13): 7
D 14 (Drawer 14): 167
D 46 (Drawer 46): 6; 21; 22; 41; 93; 98; 138
D 98 (Drawer 98): 29; 49

ALNWICK, DUKE OF NORTHUMBERLAND MSS

Alnwick Castle X div. 6

ELVEDEN HALL, SUFFOLK

Iveagh Collection, Bungay Charter no. 15

GLOUCESTER, GLOS. RECORD OFFICE

MS 1071: Microfilm of cartulary of St Augustine's Abbey, Bristol

WORCESTER, HEREFORD AND WORC. RECORD OFFICE

MS b716.093–BA 2648/1(i): Register of Bishop Godfrey Giffard (1268–1302)

HERTFORD, HERTS. RECORD OFFICE

MS 17,465: Flamstead cartulary

LINCOLN, LINCS. ARCHIVES OFFICE

Episcopal Register III John Dalderby

OXFORD, BODLEIAN LIBRARY MSS

Bodl. 451: Winchester manuscript
Dodsworth Collections, vols. vii, viii, lxiii, lxv, lxxv
Hatton 101: Ailred *De Institutis Inclusarum*
Laud Misc. 642: Alvingham cartulary
Tanner 342
Top Lincs d 1: Nun Cotham cartulary

Charters
Linc. Charters: 1165; 1167
Oxon. Charters: a8, no. 4; 36; 2740

SALISBURY, DIOCESAN RECORD OFFICE

Chapter records, press 2, box 1

NORTHALLERTON, NORTH YORKS. RECORD OFFICE

Charter from Mauleverer Brown Archives Z FL 8

Printed Books and Articles cited with abbreviated references

'Abbot Newland's Roll of the Abbots of St Augustine's Abbey by Bristol', ed. I. H. Jeayes, *Bristol and Glos. Archaeol. Soc. Trans.* 14 (1889–90), 117–30.

An Abstract of Feet of Fines relating to the County of Sussex from 34 Henry III to 35 Edward I, ed. L. F. Salzman (Sussex Rec. Soc. 7; 1907).

Acta Chichester = *The Acta of the Bishops of Chichester 1075–1207*, ed. H. Mayr-Harting (Canterbury and York Soc.; 1964).

Acta I Lincoln 1067–1185 = *English Episcopal Acta I, Lincoln 1067–1185*, ed. D. Smith (London, 1980).

Acta II Canterbury 1162–1190 = *English Episcopal Acta II, Canterbury 1162–1190*, ed. C. R. Cheney and B. A. Jones (London, 1986).

Acta III Canterbury 1193–1205 = *English Episcopal Acta III, Canterbury 1193–1205*, ed. C. R. Cheney and E. John (London, 1986).

Acta IV Lincoln 1186–1206 = *English Episcopal Acta IV, Lincoln 1186–1206*, ed. D. M. Smith (London, 1986).

Acta V York 1070–1154 = *English Episcopal Acta V, York 1070–1154*, ed. J. E. Burton (Oxford, 1988).

'Anchorites in Faversham Churchyard' (no author given), *Archaeologia Cantiana* 11 (1877), 24–39.

Ancren Riwle, ed. Moreton = *The Ancren Riwle: A Treatise on the Rules and Duties of Monastic Life*, ed. T. Moreton (Camden Soc.; London, 1853).

Ann. Dunstable = *Ann. Mon.*, iii.

Ann. Mon. = *Annales Monastici*, ed. H. R. Luard, 5 vols. (Rolls. ser. 36; London, 1864–9).

Ann. Tewkesbury = *Ann. Mon.*, i.

Ann. Waverley = *Ann. Mon.*, ii.

Ann. Winchester = *Ann. Mon.*, ii.

Ann Worc. = *Ann. Mon.*, iv.

The Archives of the Abbey of Bury St Edmunds, ed. R. M. Thomson (Suffolk Rec. Soc. 21; 1980).

BACKMUND = N. Backmund, *Monasticon Praemonstratense*, 3 vols. (Straubing, 1949–56; 2nd edn. Berlin and New York, 1983), i (2 parts).

BAILDON = W. P. Baildon, *Notes on the Religious and Secular Houses of Yorkshire*, 2 vols. (Yorks. Archaeol. Soc., Record ser. 17; 1895, and 81; 1931).

BAILEY, S. J., 'The Countess Gundred's Lands', *Cambridge Law Journal*, 10 (1948–50), 84–103.

BAKER, D., ' "A Nursery of Saints". St Margaret of Scotland Re-considered', in id. (ed.), *Medieval Women, Studies in Church History*, Subsidia I (Oxford, 1978), 119–42.

—— 'Patronage in the Early Twelfth-Century Church: Walter Espec, Kirkham and Rievaulx', in *Traditio-Krisis-Renovatio aus Theologischer sicht. Festschrift Winifried Zeller* (Marburg, 1976), 92–100.

BARBIER, *L'Abbaye de Floreffe* = V. and J., *Histoire de L'Abbaye de Floreffe de l'Ordre de Prémontré* (Namur, 1880).

BARRATT, A., 'Anchoritic Aspects of *Ancrene Wisse*', *Medium Aevum* 49 (1980), 32–56.

BATESON, M., 'Origin and Early History of Double Monasteries', *TRHS*, N.S. 13 (1899), 137–98.

BATESON, 'Reg. Crabhouse' = M. Bateson, 'The Register of Crabhouse Nunnery', *Norfolk Archaeology*, 11 (1892), 1–71.

BECQUET, J., 'La Première Crise de l'Ordre de Grandmont', *Bulletin de la Société Archéologique et Historique du Limousin* 87 (Limoges, 1960), 283–324.

Beds. Fines = *A Calendar of the Fines for Bedfordshire Preserved in the PRO of the Reigns of Richard I, John, and Henry III*, ed. G. H. Fowler (Beds. Hist. Rec. Soc. 6; 1919).

The Benedictines in Britain (British Library ser. 3; London, 1980).

BERLIÈRE, U., 'L'Ancien Monastère des Norbertines de Rivreulle', *Messager des sciences historiques ou archives des arts et de la bibliographie de Belgique* (Gand, 1893), 381–91.

BERLIÈRE, 'Les Monastères doubles' = U. Berlière, 'Les Monastères doubles au 12ᵉ et 13ᵉ siècles', *Mémoires de l'Académie Royale des Sciences etc. de Belgique*, 2nd ser., 18 (Brussels, 1923), 1–32.

Bibl. Cluniacensis = *Bibliotheca Cluniacensis*, ed. A. Quercetanus and M. Marrier (Paris, 1614).

BIENVENU, J., 'Aliénor d'Aquitaine et Fontevraud', *Cahiers de civilisation médiévale* 29 (1986), 15–27.

—— 'Aux origines d'un ordre religieux' = J. Bienvenu, 'Aux origines d'un ordre religieux. Robert d'Arbrissel et la fondation de Fontevraud (1101)', *Cahiers d'histoire* 20 (Grenoble, 1975), 226–51.

—— *Robert d'Arbrissel* = J. Bienvenu, *L'Étonnant Fondateur de Fontevraud, Robert d'Arbrissel* (Paris, 1981).

BINNS, *Dedications* = A. Binns, *Dedications of Monastic Houses in England and Wales 1066–1216* (Studies in the History of Medieval Religion, 2, Woodbridge, 1989).

BIRCH, W. 'Account of Nunnery of Little Marlow', *Records of Buckinghamshire* 4 (Aylesbury, 1870), 64–73.

—— 'On the Date of Foundation Ascribed to Cistertian Abbeys of Great Britain', *Journal of the British Archaeol. Association*, 26 (London, 1870), 281–99, 352–69.

BLOMEFIELD, *Norfolk* = F. Blomefield, *An Essay towards a Topographical History of the County of Norfolk* (2nd edn.), 11 vols. (London, 1805–10).

BOLTON, B. M., 'Mulieres Sanctae', in D. Baker (ed.), *Sanctity and Secularity. The Church and the World. Studies in Church History* 10 (Oxford, 1973), 77–95.

Book of Fees = *Liber Feodorum. The Book of Fees Commonly Called Testa de Neville*, PRO Texts and Calendars, 2 vols. in 3 (1920–31).

Book of St Gilbert = *The Book of St Gilbert*, ed. R. Foreville and G. Keir (Oxford, 1987).

BOWLES, W. L. and NICHOLS, J. G., *Annals and Antiquities of Lacock Abbey in the County of Wilts with Memorials of the Foundress Ela Countess of Salisbury* (London, 1835).

BRETT, *English Church* = M. Brett, *The English Church under Henry I* (Oxford, 1975).

BRIDGES, *Northants.* = J. Bridges, *The History and Antiquities of Northamptonshire Compiled from the Manuscript Collections of John Bridges*, ed. P. Whalley, 2 vols. (Oxford, 1791).

BROOKE, C. N. L., 'Approaches to Medieval Forgery', *Journal of the Society of Archivists*, 3 (1965–9), 377–86.

—— 'Princes and Kings as Patrons of Monasteries, Normandy and England in *Il Monachesimo e la Riforma Ecclesiastica (1049–1122) Miscellanea del Centro di Studi Medievali*, 6, (Milan, 1971), 125–44.

—— 'St Albans: the Great Abbey', in R. Runcie (ed.), *Cathedral and City, St Albans Ancient and Modern* (Thetford, 1977), 43–70.

—— *The Monastic World, 1000–1300* (London, 1974).

—— and KEIR, G. *London 800–1216: The Shaping of a City* (London, 1975).

—— 'Wix Charts' = C. N. L. Brooke, 'Episcopal Charters for Wix Priory', in *A Medieval Miscellany for D. M. Stenton*, ed. P. Barnes and C. Slade (Pipe Roll Soc.; London, 1962), 45–62.

BROOKE, Z. N., 'The Register of Master David of London and the Part he Played in the Becket Crisis' in *Essays in History Presented to R. L. Poole*, ed. H. W. C. Davis (Oxford, 1927), 227–45.

BROWN, 'Thimbleby', = W. Brown, 'The Nunnery of St Stephen's of Thimbleby', *Yorks. Archaeol. Journal* 9 (London / Leeds, 1886), 334–7.

Bucks. Fines = A Calendar of the Feet of Fines for the County of Buckingham, 7 Richard I–44 Henry III, ed. M. W. Hughes (Bucks. Rec. Soc. 4; 1942 for 1940).

BUGGE, J., *Virginitas. An Essay in the History of a Medieval Ideal* (The Hague, 1975).

BUHOT, J. RAMBAUD, 'Le Statut des moniales chez les Pères de l'Église dans les règles monastiques et les collections canoniques, jusqu'au xiie siècle', in *Sainte Fare et Faremoutiers. Treize siècles de vie monastique* (Faremoutiers, 1956), 149–74.

BURTON, *Yorks. Nunneries* = The Yorkshire Nunneries in the Twelfth and Thirteenth Centuries, Borthwick Papers, no. 56 (York, 1979).

Cal. Chart. Rolls = Calendar of the Charter Rolls preserved in the Public Record Office, 6 vols. (PRO texts and calendars; London, 1903–27).

Cal. Close Rolls = Calendar of the Close Rolls preserved in the Public Record Office (PRO texts and calendars; London, 1896–   ).

Cal. Docs. France = Calendar of Documents preserved in France illustrative of the History of Great Britain and Ireland, i, AD 918–1206, ed. J. H. Round (PRO texts and calendars; London, 1899).

Cal. Lib. Rolls = Calendar of the Liberate Rolls preserved in the Public Record Office (PRO texts and calendars; London, 1916–64).

Cal. Pap. Lett. = Calendar of Entries in the Papal Registers relating to

Great Britain and Ireland, i, *Papal Letters 1198–1304*, ed. W. H. Bliss (London, 1893).

Cal. Pat. Rolls = *Calendar of the Patent Rolls preserved in the Public Record Office* (PRO texts and calendars; London, 1891–   ).

Calendar of Charters and Rolls Preserved in the Bodleian Library, ed. W. H. Turner, under direction of H. O. Coxe (Oxford, 1878).

A Calendar of the Feet of Fines for London and Middlesex, Richard I–12 Elizabeth, ed. W. Hardy and W. Page, 2 vols. (London, 1892–3).

A Calendar of the Feet of Fines relating to the County of Wiltshire . . . from the Reign of Richard I (1195) to the end of Henry III (1272), compiled by W. A. Fry, (Wilts. Archaeol. and Nat. Hist. Soc.; 1930).

Calendar of the Register of Adam de Orleton, Bishop of Worcester 1327–1333, ed. R. M. Haines (Worcs. Hist. Soc., N.S. 10; London, 1979).

Calendar of the Roll of the Justices on Eyre 1227, ed. J. G. Jenkins (Bucks. Rec. Soc. 6; 1942).

Cambs. Fines = *Pedes Finium . . . relating to the County of Cambridge (Calendar 7 Richard I–1485)*, ed. W. Rye (Camb. Antiq. Soc. 26; 1891).

CANIVEZ = J. M. Canivez, *Statuta Capitulorum Generalium Ordinis Cisterciensis ab anno 1116 ad annum 1786*, 8 vols. (Louvain, 1933–41).

Cartl. Beauchamp = *The Beauchamp Cartulary Charters, 1110–1268*, ed. E. Mason (Pipe Roll Soc.; London, 1980).

Cartl. Bridlington = *Abstracts of the Charters . . . of Bridlington Priory*, ed. W. Lancaster (privately printed, Leeds, 1912).

Cartl. Buckland = *A Cartulary of Buckland Priory in the County of Somerset*, ed. F. W. Weaver (Somerset Rec. Soc. 25; 1909).

Cartl. Canonsleigh = *The Cartulary of Canonsleigh Abbey (Harleian MS 3660). A Calendar*, ed. V. London (Devon and Cornwall Rec. Soc., N.S. 1965 for 1962).

Cartl. Clerkenwell = *Cartulary of St Mary, Clerkenwell*, ed. W. O. Hassall (Camden., 3rd ser., 71; 1949).

Cartl. Cysoing = *Cartulaire de l'Abbaye de Cysoing et de ses dépendances*, ed. I. de Coussemaker (Lille, 1883).

Cartl. Darley = *The Cartulary of Darley Abbey*, ed. R. Darlington, 2 vols. (Derby Archaeol. Soc.; 1945).

Cartl. de l'Ordre des Hospitaliers = *Cartulaire général de l'Ordre des Hospitaliers de S. Jean de Jérusalem 1100–1310*, ed. J. Delaville le Roulx, 4 vols. (Paris, 1894–1906).

Cartl. Fountains = *Abstracts of the Charters and other Documents contained in the Chartulary of the Cistercian Abbey of Fountains*, ed. W. T. Lancaster, 2 vols. (privately printed, Leeds, 1915).

Cartl. Godstow = *The English Register of Godstow Nunnery*, ed. A. Clark, 2 vols. (EETS; London, 1911).

Cartl. Haughmond = *The Cartulary of Haughmond Abbey*, ed. U. Rees (Shropshire Archaeol. Soc.; Cardiff, 1985).

Cartl. Leiston = *Leiston Abbey Cartulary and Butley Priory Charters*, ed. R. Mortimer (Suffolk Rec. Soc.; 1979).

Cartl. Marcigny = J. Richard, *Le Cartulaire de Marcigny-sur-Loire (1045–1144). Essai de reconstitution d'un manuscrit disparu* (Dijon, 1957).

Cartl. Missenden = *The Cartulary of Missenden Abbey*, ed. J. G. Jenkins, 3 vols. (Bucks. Rec. Soc. 2, 10, 12; 1938–62).

Cartl. St Mark's Hospital = *Cartulary of St Mark's Hospital Bristol*, ed. C. D. Ross (Bristol Rec. Soc. 21; Bristol, 1959).

Cartl. Worc. = *The Cartulary of Worcester Cathedral Priory (Register 1)*, ed. R. R. Darlington (Pipe Roll Soc., N.S. 38; 1968 for 1962–3).

Cartulaire de l'Abbaye de Saint-Sulpice-La-Forêt, ed. P. Anger (Extrait du Bulletin archéologique d'Ille-et-Vilaine, 1911).

Cartularium Prioratus de Gyseburne, ed. W. Brown, 2 vols. (Surtees Soc. 86, 89; 1889, 1894 for 1891).

The Cartulary of Blyth Priory, ed. R. T. Timson, 2 vols. (Thoroton Soc. Record ser. 27, 28; London, 1973).

The Cartulary of the Knights of St John of Jerusalem in England, Secunda Camera: Essex, ed. M. Gervers (Records of Social and Economic Hist., N.S. 6; London, 1982).

Cartulary of the Priory of St Gregory Canterbury, ed. A. M. Woodcock (Camden 3rd ser. 88; 1956).

The Cartulary of Shrewsbury Abbey, ed. U. Rees, 2 vols. (Aberystwyth, 1975).

CASSASSOLES = F. Cassassoles, *Monographie du couvent de Boulauc dans le Canton de Saramon* (Auch, 1859).

CHADWICK, S. J., 'Kirklees Priory', *Yorks Archæol. Journal* 16 (1902), 319–68.

CHAMBERS, R. W., 'Recent Research upon the *Ancren Riwle*', *The Review of English Studies*, 1 (1925), 4–23.

Charters and Custumals of the Abbey of Holy Trinity Caen, ed. M. Chibnall (Oxford, 1982).

Chartrou, J., *L'Anjou de 1109 à 1151. Foulque de Jerusalem et Geffroi Plantegenet* (Paris, 1928).

The Chartulary of Brinkburn Priory, ed. W. Page (Surtees Soc., 90; 1893 for 1892).

The Chartulary of . . . Healaugh Park, ed. J. S. Purvis (Yorks. Archæol. Soc., Record ser. 92; 1936 for 1935).

The Chartulary of the High Church of Chichester, ed. W. D. Peckham (Sussex Rec. Soc. 46; 1946 for 1942–3).

CHARVIN, G., *Statuts, chapîtres généraux et visites de l'ordre de Cluny*, 9 vols. (Paris, 1965–   ).

CHENEY, C. R., *English Bishops' Chanceries 1100–1250* (Manchester, 1950).

—— *English Synodalia of the Thirteenth Century* (Oxford, 1941, repr. 1968).

—— *Episcopal Visitation of Monasteries in the Thirteenth Century* (Manchester, 1931; 2nd edn., 1983).

—— 'Gervase, Abbot of Prémontré: A Medieval Letter Writer', *Medieval Texts and Studies* (Oxford, 1973), 242–76.

—— 'Two Mortuary Rolls from Canterbury: Devotional Links of Canterbury with Normandy and the Welsh Marsh', in D. Greenway, C. Holdsworth, and J. Sayers (eds.), *Tradition and Change, Essays in Honour of Marjorie Chibnall Presented by her Friends on the Occasion of her 70th Birthday* (Cambridge, 1985).

—— 'Harrold Priory' = C. R. Cheney, 'Harrold Priory: A Twelfth-Century Dispute', *Medieval Texts and Studies* (Oxford, 1973), 285–313.

CHETTLE, H. F., 'The English Houses of the Order of Fontevraud', *Downside Review*, N.S. 61 (1942), 33–55.

CHIBNALL, 'L'Ordre de Fontevraud' = M. Chibnall, 'L'Ordre de Fontevraud en Angleterre au XIIe siècle', *Cahiers de civilisation médiévale*, 29 (1986), 41–7.

Chron. Howden = *Chronica Rogeri de Hovedene*, ed. W. Stubbs, 4 vols. (Rolls ser. 51; 1868–71).

Chron. Meaux = *Chronica Monasterii de Melsa a fundatione usque ad annum 1396*, ed. E. A. Bond, 3 vols. (Rolls ser. 43; 1866–8).

Chron. Newburgh = *Chronicles of the Reigns of Stephen, Henry II and Richard I*, i, *Historia Rerum Anglicarum of William of Newburgh*, ed. R. Howlett (Rolls ser., 82; London, 1884, repr. 1964).

Chron. Oxenedes = *Chronica Johannis de Oxenedes*, ed. H. Ellis (Rolls ser. 13; London, 1859, repr. 1969).

Chron. Will. Thorne = *William Thorne's Chronicle of St Augustine's Abbey, Canterbury*, ed. A. H. Davis (Oxford, 1934).

The Chronicle of Hugh Candidus, a Monk of Peterborough, ed. T. Mellows (London, 1949).

'The Chronicle of John Brompton', in R. Twysden, *Historiae Anglicanae Scriptores X* (London, 1652), 725–1,283.

The Chronicles of Elstow Abbey: see Wigram.

'Chronicon Hugonis monachi Virdunensis et Divionensis, abbatis Flaviniacensis' *MGH Scriptores* 8 (1848), 280–503.

CHURCHILL, 'Canterbury Charts' = 'Table of Canterbury Archbishopric Charters', ed. I. J. Churchill, *Camden Miscellany XV* (3rd ser. 41; 1929).

CLANCHY, *Written Record* = M. Clanchy, *From Memory to Written Record. England 1066–1307* (London, 1979).

CLARK, E. K., 'The Foundation of Kirkstall Abbey', *The Publications of the Thoresby Soc.* 4, *Miscellanea* (Leeds, 1895), 169–209.

CLARK-MAXWELL, 'Earliest Charts' = W. G. Clark-Maxwell, 'The Earliest Charters of the Abbey of Lacock', *Wilts. Archæol. Magazine* 35 (1907–8), 191–209.

CLAY, C. T., *Notes on the Family of Clere with a Bibliography of the Writings of Sir Charles Clay* (privately printed, 1975).

—— 'Two Charters Issued to Kirklees Priory', *Yorks. Archaeol. Journal* 38 (1952–5), 355–8.

CLAY, 'Seals' = C. T. Clay, 'The Seals of the Religious Houses of Yorkshire', *Archæologia* 78 (1928), 1–36.

CLAY, *Hermits and Anchorites* = R. M. Clay, *The Hermits and Anchorites of England* (London, 1914).

—— *Hospitals* = R. M. Clay, *The Medieval Hospitals of England* (London, 1909).

—— 'Recluses' = R. M. Clay, 'Further Studies on Medieval Recluses', *Journal of the British Archaeol. Assoc.*, 16, 3rd ser. (1953), 74–86.

Cluniac Monasticism in the Central Middle Ages, ed. N. Hunt (London, 1971).

COLE, R. E., 'The Priory, or House of Nuns, of St Mary of Brodholme of the Order of Prémontré', *Associated Archaeol. Soc. Reports and Papers* 28 (1) (1905), 48–86.

—— 'Priory of St Katherine' = R. E. Cole, 'The Priory of St Katherine without Lincoln, of the Order of St Gilbert of Sempringham', *Associated Archaeol. Soc. Reports and Papers*, 27 (2) (1904), 264–336.

Collectanea Anglo-Praemonstratensia, ed. F. A. Gasquet, 3 vols. (Camden 3rd ser. 6, 10, and 12; 1904–6).

COLVIN, 'Irford Priory' = H. M. Colvin, A Twelfth-Century Grant to Irford Priory', *Lincs. Archit. and Archaeol. Soc. Reports and Papers* 5 (2) (1953), 83–6.

—— *Kings Works* = *The History of the Kings' Works*, ed. H. M. Colvin, 6 vols. (London, 1963–82).

—— *The White Canons* = H. M. Colvin, *The White Canons in England* (Oxford, 1951).

Complete Peerage = *The Complete Peerage*, by G.E.C.; revd. edn. V. Gibbs, H. A. Doubleday, Lord Howard de Walden, G. H. White, and R. S. Lea, 12 vols. (London, 1910–59).

Conciliorum Decreta = *Conciliorum Oecumenicorum Decreta*, ed. G. Alberigo *et al.*, 3rd edn. (Bologna, 1973).

The Concise Oxford Dictionary of English Place Names, ed. E. Ekwall, 4th edn. (Oxford, 1960).

CONSTABLE, G., *Medieval Monasticism. A Select Bibliography* (Toronto, 1976).

—— 'Nun of Watton' = G. Constable, 'Aelred of Rievaulx and the Nun of Watton: An Episode in the Early History of the Gilbertine Order', in *Medieval Women*, 205–26.

Constitutiones Concilii Quarti Lateranensis una cum commentariis glossatorum. Monumenta Iuris Canonici, series A, *Corpus Glossatorum*, ii, ed. A. Garcia y Garcia (Vatican, 1981).

Corpus Iuris Canonici editio Lipsiensis secunda post Aemilii Ludovici Richteri curas . . . recognovit . . . Aemilius Friedberg, 2 vols., i, *Decretum Magistri Gratiani* (Lipsiae, 1879).

COTTINEAU, L. H., *Répertoire topo-bibliographique des Abbayes et Prieurés*, 3 vols.: i–ii (Mâcon, 1935–7), iii, ed. G. Poras (Mâcon, 1970).

Councils and Synods I = *Councils and Synods with Other Documents Relating to the English Church*, I, AD 871–1204, ed. D. Whitelock, M. Brett, and C. N. L. Brooke, 2 vols. (Oxford, 1981).

Councils and Synods II = *Councils and Synods with Other Documents*

Relating to the English Church, II, *1205–1313*, ed. F. M. Powicke and C. R. Cheney, 2 vols. (Oxford, 1964).

COWLEY, F. G., *The Monastic Order in South Wales 1066–1349* (Cardiff, 1977).

COX, J., 'The Priory of Bromhall', in VCH *Berks.*, ii (1907), 80–1.

CUCHERAT = F. Cucherat, *Cluny au onzième siècle* (2nd edn.; Autun, 1850).

Curia Regis Rolls = *Curia Regis Rolls* (PRO texts and calendars; London, 1922–79).

Danelaw Docs. = *Documents Illustrative of the Social and Economic History of the Danelaw from Various Collections*, ed. F. M. Stenton (British Academy; London, 1920).

DANIEL, W., *The Life of Ailred of Rievaulx*, ed. and trans. F. M. Powicke (London, 1950, repr. 1963).

DARWIN, F., *The English Mediaeval Recluse* (London, 1944).

DASHWOOD, G. H., 'Notes of Deeds and Survey of Crabhouse Nunnery', *Norfolk Archaeology* 5 (1859), 257–62.

DAUPHIN, 'L'Érémitisme en Angleterre' = H. Dauphin, 'L'Érémitisme en Angleterre aux XIᵉ et XIIᵉ siècles', in *Eremitismo in Occidente nei secoli xiᵉ et xiiᵉ Miscellanea del Centro di Studi Medievali* 4 (Milan, 1965), 271–310.

DAVIS, *Med. Cartls.* = G. R. C. Davis, *Medieval Cartularies of Great Britain. A Short Catalogue* (London, 1958).

'*De Institutis Inclusarum*' = C. H. Talbot, 'The *De Institutis Inclusarum* of Ailred of Rievaulx' *Analecta Sacri Ordinis Cisterciensis* 7 (Rome, 1951), 167–217.

DELAVILLE LE ROULX, J., 'Les Hospitalières de Saint Jean de Jérusalem', *Comptes rendus des séances de l'anneé 1894* Académie des inscriptions et belles lettres, (4th ser. 22; Paris, 1894), 137–46.

Derby Charts. = *Descriptive Catalogue of Derbyshire Charters in Public and Private Libraries*, ed. I. H. Jeayes (London, 1906).

Descriptive Catalogue of the Charters and Muniments . . . at Berkeley Castle, ed. I. H. Jeayes (Bristol, 1892).

DESHOULIÈRES = F. Deshoulières, 'Le Prieuré d'Orsan en Berri', *Mémoires de la Société des Antiquaires du Centre* 25 (1901), 51–137.

DEVOISINS = A. J. Devoisins, *Histoire de Notre Dame du Désert. L'Ermitage (460–1125), Le Prieuré (1125–1675), La Chapelle (1675–1900)* (Paris, 1901).

Devon Fines = *Devon Feet of Fines*, 1 Richard I–Henry III, *1196–1272*, ed. O. Reichel (Devon and Cornwall Rec. Soc; 1912).

'Dialogus inter Cluniacensem monachum et Cisterciensem', in E. Martène, and U. Durand, *Thesaurus Novus Anecdotorum . . .*, v (Paris, 1717), 1570–1654.

DICKINSON, J. C., 'English Regular Canons and the Continent in the Twelfth Century', *TRHS*, 5th ser. 1 (1951), 71–89.

—— *Austin Canons* = J. C. Dickinson, *The Origins of the Austin Canons and their Introduction into England* (London, 1950).

—— 'St Augustine's Bristol' = J. C. Dickinson, 'The Origins of St Augustine's Bristol', in P. McGrath and J. Cannon (eds.), *Essays in Bristol and Gloucestershire History* (Bristol and Glos. Archaeol. Soc.; 1976).

Dict. de droit canonique = *Dictionnaire de droit canonique*, ed. R. Naz (Paris, 1935–).

Dict. de théol. catholique = *Dictionnaire de théologie catholique*, ed. A. Vacant, xiii (Paris, 1936).

Dict. of Saints = *The Oxford Dictionary of Saints*, ed. D. H. Farmer (Oxford, 1978).

Dictionary of Medieval Latin from British Sources, i, fasc. iii, *D–E*, ed. R. E. Latham and D. R. Howlett, with assist. A. H. Powell and M. A. Sharpe (London, 1986).

Distant Echoes = *Distant Echoes. Medieval Religious Women*, i, ed. J. A. Nichols and L. T. Shank (Cistercian Publications; Kalamazoo, 1984).

DOBSON, E. J., 'The Affiliations of the Manuscripts of Ancrene Wisse', in N. Davis and C. L. Wrenn (eds.), *English and Medieval Studies presented to J. R. R. Tolkien* (London, 1962), 128–63.

—— *Ancrene Riwle* = *The English Text of the Ancrene Riwle edited from BM MS Cotton Cleopatra C. vi*, ed. E. J. Dobson (EETS 267; Oxford, 1972).

—— 'Date of AW' = E. J. Dobson, 'The Date and Composition of *Ancrene Wisse*', *Proceedings of the British Academy* 52 (1966), 181–208.

—— *Origins of AW* = E. J. Dobson, *The Origins of Ancrene Wisse* (Oxford, 1976).

DODWELL, B., 'A Papal Bull for Torksey Priory', *BIHR* 52 (1979), 87–90.

Domesday Book = *Domesday Book. Liber Censualis called Domesday Book*, 4 vols. (Record Commission; London, 1783–1816).

The Domesday Monachorum of Christ Church Canterbury, ed. D. C. Douglas (London, 1944).

DRAKARD, J., *The History of Stamford* (Stamford, 1822).

DUBOIS, J., 'L'Institution des convers au XIIᵉ siècle, forme de vie monastique propre aux laïcs', in *I Laici nella 'Societas Christiana' dei secoli xi e xii. Miscellanea del Centro di Studi Medievali*, 5 (Milan, 1965), 183–261.

DU CHESNE, A., *Histoire généalogique des maisons de Guines, d'Ardres, de Gand, et de Courcy*, 2 parts (Paris, 1631).

DUCKETT, G. F. 'Charters of the Priory of Swine in Holderness (among the Rawlinson MSS in the Bodleian Library)', *Yorks. Archaeol. Journal*, 6 (1879–80), 113–24.

—— *Monasticon Cluniacense Anglicanum, or Charters and Records Illustrative of the English Foundations of the Ancient Abbey of Cluny from 1077 to 1534*, 2 vols. (privately printed, Lewes, 1888).

—— *Visitations of English Cluniac Foundations* (London, 1890).

DUNNING, P. J., 'The Arroaisian Order in Medieval Ireland', *Irish Historical Studies* 4 (1945), 297–315.

Durham Episcopal Charts. = *Durham Episcopal Charters 1071–1152*, ed. H.S. Offler (Surtees Soc. 179; 1968).

DYSON, A. G., 'The Monastic Patronage of Bishop Alexander of Lincoln', *Journal of Ecclesiastical History* 26 (1975), 1–24.

Early Charts. of St Paul's = *Early Charters of the Cathedral Church of St Paul, London*, ed. M. Gibbs (Camden 3rd ser., 58; London, 1939).

Early Yorkshire Families, ed. C. Clay and D. Greenway (Yorks. Archaeol. Soc., Record ser., 135; 1973).

Ecclesiastical Documents viz I. A Brief History of the Bishoprick of Somerset from its Foundation to the Year 1174. II. Charters from the Library of Dr Cox Macro, ed. J. Hunter (Camden Soc., o.s. 8; 1840).

ECKENSTEIN, L., *Women under Monasticism* . . . (Cambridge, 1896).

ÉDOUARD = J. Édouard, *Fontevrault et ses monuments ou histoire de cette royale abbaye* . . . , 2 vols. in one (Paris / Marseilles, 1873–4).

ELKINS, *Holy Women* = S. Elkins, *Holy Women of Twelfth Century England* (University of North Carolina, 1988).

—— 'The Gilbertines' = S. Elkins, 'All Ages, Every Condition, and Both Sexes: The Emergence of a Gilbertine Identity', in *Distant Echoes*, 169–82.

English Place Name Society, vi, *The Place Names of Sussex*, ed. A. Mawer and F. M. Stenton, with the assistance of J. E. Gover (Cambridge, 1929; repr. 1969).

The English Text of the Ancrene Riwle. Ancrene Wisse, edited from MS Corpus Christi College Cambridge 402, ed. J. R. R. Tolkien (EETS, 249; 1962).

ERENS, 'Sœurs de Prémontré' = A. Erens, 'Les Sœurs dans l'ordre de Prémontré,' *Analecta Praemonstratensia* 5 (1929), 5–26.

Essex Fines = *Feet of Fines for Essex (1182–1272)*, ed. R. E. G. Kirk (Essex Archaeol. Soc.; 1899–1910).

Ex libro iii Hermanni Monachi: *see* Hermanni Monachi.

Eyre Rolls Linc. and Worcs. = *Rolls of the Justices in Eyre . . . for Lincolnshire 1218–19 and Worcestershire 1221*, ed. D. M. Stenton (Selden Soc. 53; 1934).

EYTON, *Itin.* = R. Eyton, *Court, Household and Itinerary of King Henry II* (London, 1878).

—— *Salop.* = R. Eyton, *Antiquities of Shropshire*, 12 vols. (London, 1854–60).

FAIRWEATHER, F. H., 'The Abbey of St Mary Malling, Kent', *Archaeological Journal* 88 (1931), 175–92.

Fälschungen im Mittelalter (Schriften der Monumenta Germaniae Historica, Band 33, 5 vols. (Hanover, 1988, vol. 6 to come).

FARRER, W., *Honors and Knights Fees*, 3 vols. (London, 1923–5).

Feet of Fines Henry II, Richard I = *Feet of Fines in the PRO in the Reign of Henry II and of the first seven years of the Reign of Richard I, AD 1182–AD 1196* (Pipe Roll Soc., 17; London, 1894).

Feodarium Prioratus Dunelmensis, ed. W. Greenwell (Surtees Soc. 58; 1871).

Flete = *The History of Westminster Abbey by John Flete*, ed. J. A. Robinson (Cambridge, 1909).

Foliot Letters and Charters = *The Letters and Charters of Gilbert Foliot*, ed. A. Morey and C. N. L. Brooke (Cambridge, 1967).

FONTETTE = M. Fontette, *Les Religieuses à l'âge classique du droit canon*.

Recherches sur les structures juridiques des branches féminines des ordres (Bibliothêque de la Société d'Histoire Ecclésiastique de la France 28; Paris, 1967).

FOWLER, G. H., 'De St Walery', *The Genealogist*, N.S. 30 (London, 1914), 1–17.

—— 'Turvey Records' = G. H. Fowler, 'Early Records of Turvey and its Neighbourhood' *Beds. Hist. Rec. Soc.* 11 (1927), 47–83.

GALBRAITH, 'Foundation Charters' = V. H. Galbraith, 'Monastic Foundation Charters of the Eleventh and Twelfth Centuries', *Cambridge Historical Journal* 4 (1934), 205–22, 296–8.

GANZ, D., 'The Buildings of Godstow Nunnery', *Oxoniensia* 37 (1972), 150–7.

GENICOT, L., 'L'Érémitisme du xie siècle dans son contexte économique et social', in *L'Eremitismo in Occidente nei Secoli xie xii. Miscellanea del Centro di Studi Medievali*, 4 (Milan, 1965), 45–70.

Gervase of Canterbury = *The Historical Works of Gervase of Canterbury*, ed. W. Stubbs, 2 vols. (Rolls ser. 73; 1879–80).

GERVERS, M., 'A History of the Cartulary of the Order of the Hospital of St John of Jerusalem in England (BM Cott. MS Nero E VI)', *Scriptorium* 28 (1974), 262–73.

Gesta Abbatum = *Gesta Abbatum Monasterii Sancti Albani*, ed. T. H. Riley, 3 vols. (Rolls ser. 28; 1867–9).

Gesta Henrici II = *Gesta Regis Henrici Secundi Benedicti Abbatis. The Chronicle of the Reigns of Henry II and Richard I (AD 1169–1192) known commonly under the name of Benedict of Peterborough*, ed. W. Stubbs, 2 vols. (Rolls ser. 49; 1867).

GIBSON, M., *Lanfranc of Bec* (Oxford, 1978).

GIEYSZTOR, A., 'La Légende de Saint Alexis en Occident: Un idéal de pauvreté', in *Études sur l'histoire de la pauvreté*, ed. M. Mollat (publications de la Sorbonne Série Études, 8, Paris, 1974).

Gilbert of Hoyland, Sermons = *The Works of Gilbert of Hoyland. Sermons on the Song of Songs*, ed. and transl. L. C. Braceland, 3 vols. (Cistercian Fathers, ser. 14, 20, 26; Kalamazoo, 1978–9).

Gilbertine Charts. = *Transcripts of Charters relating to the Gilbertine Houses of Sixle, Ormsby, Catley, Bullington, and Alvingham*, ed. F. M. Stenton (Linc. Rec. Soc. 18; Horncastle, 1922).

Giraldi Cambrensis = *Giraldi Cambrensis Opera*, ed. J. S. Brewer, J. F. Dimock and G. F. Warner, 8 vols. (Rolls ser. 21; 1861–91).

Glos. Charts. = *Earldom of Gloucester Charters. The Charters and Scribes of the Earls and Countesses of Gloucester to AD 1217*, ed. R. B. Patterson (Oxford, 1973).

GODFREY, J., 'The Double Monastery in Early English History', *Ampleforth Journal* 79 (1974), 19–32.

GOLD, 'Fontevrault' = P. S. Gold, 'Male/Female Co-operation: The Example of Fontevrault', in *Distant Echoes*, 151–68.

GOLDING, B., 'The Coming of the Cluniacs', in R. A. Brown (ed.), *Proceedings of the Battle Conference on Anglo-Norman Studies III 1980* (Woodbridge, 1981), 65–77.

—— 'Alvingham and Bullington' = B. Golding, 'The Gilbertine Priories of Alvingham and Bullington: their Endowments and Benefactors', Ph.D. thesis (Oxford, 1979).

—— 'St Bernard and St Gilbert' = B. Golding, 'St Bernard and St Gilbert', in B. Ward (ed.), *The Influence of St Bernard: Anglican Essays with an Introduction by Jean Leclercq* (Fairacres, Oxford, 1976), 42–54.

Goring Charts. = *A Collection of Charters relating to Goring, Streatley and the Neighbourhood 1181–1546 preserved in the Bodleian Library, with a supplement*, ed. T. R. Gambier-Parry, 2 vols. (Oxford Rec. Soc. 13, 14; 1931–2).

GOSSE = A. Gosse, *Histoire de l'abbaye et de l'ancienne congrégation des chanoines réguliers d'Arrouaise* (Lille, 1786).

GRAHAM, R., 'An Appeal for the Church and Buildings of Kingsmead Priory circa 1218', *Antiquaries Journal* 11 (1931), 51–4.

—— *English Ecclesiastical Studies* (London, 1929).

—— 'The Taxation of Pope Nicholas IV', *EHR* 23 (1908), 434–54.

—— *St Gilbert* = R. Graham, *St. Gilbert of Sempringham and the Gilbertines* (London, 1901).

GRAVES, C., 'English Cistercian Nuns in Lincolnshire', *Speculum* 54 (1979), 492–9.

GRAY, *St Radegund* = A. Gray, *The Priory of St Radegund Cambridge* (Cambridge Antiq. Soc., octavo ser. 31; Cambridge, 1898).

GRAZEAU, R., 'La Clôture des moniales au XIIe siècle en France', *Revue Mabillon* 58 (1974), 289–308.

GRELIER, 'Le Temporel de Fontevrault' = F. Grelier, 'Le Temporel de l'Abbaye de Fontevrault dans le Haut-Poitou des origines à la réforme du XVe siècle', *Ecole des Chartes. Positions des Thèses* (Paris, 1960), 35–40.

GUILLOREAU, L., 'Les Prieurés anglais de l'Ordre de Cluny', *Revue Mabillon* 8 (Paris, 1912–13), 1–42, 159–88.

GUNTON, S., *The History of the Church of Peterburgh . . . set forth by Symon Patrick DD now Dean of the same* (London, 1686).

HABINGTON, T., *A Survey of Worcestershire*, ed. J. Amphlett, 2 vols. (Worcs. Hist. Soc.; Oxford, 1895–9).

HAILSTONE = E. Hailstone, 'History of Swaffham Bulbeck' (unpubl. proofs held in Cambridge Univ. Library MS Bb 892. 1).

HALLAM, 'Henry II' = E. M. Hallam-Smith, 'Henry II as a Founder of Monasteries', *Journal of Ecclesiastical History* 28 (1977), 113–32.

—— 'Monastic Patronage' = E. M. Hallam-Smith, 'Aspects of the Monastic Patronage of the English and French Royal Houses c.1130–1270', Ph.D. thesis (London, 1976).

Handbook of British Chronology (3rd edn.) ed. E. B. Fryde, D. E. Greenway, S. Porter, and I. Roy, (London, 1986).

HANNING, R. W., *The Individual in Twelfth Century Romance* (New Haven and London, 1977).

HARRISON, Marshal General Plantagenet, *The History of Yorkshire* (London, 1835).

HARVEY, B., *Westminster Abbey and its Estates in the Middle Ages* (Oxford, 1977).

HASSALL, W. O., 'The Chester Property of the Nunnery of St Mary Clerkenwell in the Twelfth Century', *Journal of the Chester and North Wales Archit., Archaeol., and Hist. Soc.*, 36 (ii), 178–9.

HASTED, *Kent* = E. Hasted, *The History and Topographical Survey of the County of Kent*, 12 vols. (Canterbury, 1797–1801).

HÉLYOT = P. Hélyot and M. Bullot, *Histoires des ordres monastiques religieux et militaires et des congregations séculières de l'un et de l'autre sexe*, 8 vols. (2nd edn., Paris, 1721).

HERBERT, J., 'The Transformation of Hermitages into Augustinian Priories in 12th Century England', in W. J. Sheils (ed.), *Monks, Hermits and the Ascetic Tradition, Studies in Church History* 22 (Oxford, 1985), 131–45.

'Hermanni monachi. De miraculis S. Marie Laudunensis', *PL*, clvi (1880), 962–1,018.

'Ex libro iii Hermanni Monachi de Miraculis S Marie Laudunen.', *AASS*, Jun., i, 862–8.

HINNEBUSCH, *Jacques de Vitry* = *The Historia Occidentalis of Jacques de Vitry*, ed. J. F. Hinnebusch (Spicilegium Friburgense 17; Fribourg, 1972).

The History and Antiquities of Northamptonshire, Compiled from the Manuscript Collections of John Bridges, ed. P. Whalley, 2 vols. (Oxford, 1791).

A History of Northumberland, xv, ed. M. Hope Dodds (Newcastle, 1940).

HMC Ancaster = *Report on the Manuscripts of the Earl of Ancaster Preserved at Grimsthorpe* (Historical Manuscripts Commission 66; 1907).

HMC Fourteenth Report of the Royal Commission of Historical Manuscripts (London, 1895).

HMC Ninth Report = *HMC Ninth Report of the Royal Commission of Historical Manuscripts. Report and Appendix* (London, 1883).

HMC Various Coll. = *HMC Report on Manuscripts in Various Collections, iv The Manuscripts of Bishop of Salisbury, Bishop of Exeter, Dean and Chapter of Exeter*, 55 (London, 1907).

HODSON, J. H., 'Medieval Charters, the Last Witness', *Journal of the Society of Archivists* 5 (1974–5), 71–89.

HOLDSWORTH, C. J., 'The Blessings of Work: the Cistercian View', in D. Baker (ed.), *Sanctity and Secularity. The Church and the World, Studies in Church History* 10 (Oxford, 1973), 59–76.

—— 'Christina' = C. J. Holdsworth, 'Christina of Markyate', in *Medieval Women* (Oxford, 1978), 185–204.

HUGO, C. L., *Sacrae antiquitatis monumenta in historica dogmatica diplomatica* (Stivagii, 1725).

—— *Annales* = C. L. Hugo, *Sacri et canonici ordinis Praemonstratensis Annales*, 2 vols. (Nancy, 1734–6).

HUGO, T., *The Medieval Nunneries of the County of Somerset* (London, 1867).

HUNT, 'Benedictine and Cistercian Nuns' = N. Hunt, 'Notes on the History of Benedictine and Cistercian Nuns in Britain', *Cistercian Studies* 8 (1973), 157–77.

—— *St Hugh* = N. Hunt, *Cluny under St Hugh 1049–1109* (London, 1967).

HUTCHINS, J., *The History and Antiquities of . . . Dorset*, 3rd edn. by W. Shipp and J. W. Hodson, 4 vols. (London, 1861–70).

Index to the Charters and Rolls in the Department of Manuscripts, British Museum, ed. H. J. Ellis, ii. *Religious Houses and Other Corporations and Index Locorum for Acquisitions from 1882–1900* (London, 1912).

IOGNA-PRAT, D., 'La Femme dans la perspective pénitentielle des ermites du Bas-Maine (fin XIᵉ debut XIIᵉ siècle)', *Revue d'histoire de la spiritualité*, 53 (1977), 47–64.

IRVINE, W. F., 'Notes on the History of St Mary's Nunnery Chester', *Journal of the Chester and North Wales Archit., Archaeol. and Hist. Soc.*, N.S. 13 (1906), 67–109.

JACKSON, J. E., 'Kington St Michael', *Wilts. Archaeological Magazine* 4 (1858), 36–124.

JAFFÉ = P. Jaffé, *Regesta Pontificum Romanorum ab condita ecclesia ad. annum 1198* (2nd edn.), G. Wattenbach *et al.* 2 vols. (Leipzig, 1885–88, repr. Graz, 1958).

JAMES, M. R., *A Descriptive Catalogue of the Manuscripts in the Library of St John's College, Cambridge* (Cambridge, 1913).

JESSOPP, A., 'Ups and Downs of an Old Nunnery', *Frivola* (London, 1896), 28–67.

JUBIEN, Marie de Bretagne = A. Jubien, *L'Abbesse Marie de Bretagne et la réforme de l'Ordre de Fontevrault d'après des documents inédits* (Angers / Paris, 1872).

Kent Fines = *Calendar of Kent Feet of Fines to the end of Henry III's Reign*, prepared in collaboration by I. J. Churchill, R. Griffin, and F. W. Hardman, introd. F. W. Jessup (Kent Archaeol. Soc. 15; 1956).

KERLING, N. J., 'The Foundation of St Bartholomew's Hospital in West Smithfield, London', *The Guildhall Miscellany*, 4, no. 3 (1972), 137–48.

KING, E. J., *The Knights of St John in the British Realm*, rev. and cont. by Sir Harry Luke (London, 1967).

—— *The Rule, Statutes and Customs of the Hospitallers 1099–1310* (London, 1934).

The Knights Hospitallers in England being the Report of Prior Philip de Thame to the Grand Master Elyan de Villanova for AD 1338, ed. L. Larking (Camden Soc., 65; 1857).

KNOWLES, D., 'Gervase of Canterbury and the *Mappa Mundi*', *Downside Review* 48 (Exeter, 1930), 237–47.

—— *Monastic Order* = D. Knowles, *The Monastic Order in England* (Cambridge, 1940; 2nd edn., 1963).

—— *Relig. Orders* = D. Knowles, *The Religious Orders in England*, 3 vols. (Cambridge, 1948–59).

—— 'Revolt' = D. Knowles, 'The Revolt of the Lay Brothers of Sempringham', *EHR* 50 (1935), 465–87.

KNOWLES, W. H., 'The Hospital of St Mary the Virgin, Newcastle upon Tyne', *Archaeologia Aeliana*, N.S. 5 (1892), 194–207.

LACKNER, B. K., *The Eleventh Century Background of Cîteaux* (Cistercian Studies ser. 8; Washington, 1972).

Lacock Charts. = *Lacock Abbey Charters*, ed. K. H. Rogers (Wilts. Rec. Soc. 34; Devizes, 1979).

LAMB, J. W., *Saint Wulfstan, Prelate and Patriot* (London, 1933).

LAMY, *L'Abbaye de Tongerloo* = H. Lamy, *L'Abbaye de Tongerloo depuis sa fondation jusqu'en 1263* (Louvain / Paris, 1914).

LANCASTER, W. T., 'Four Early Charters of Arthington Nunnery', *Miscellanea VI* (Thoresby Soc., 22 Leeds, 1915), 118–28.

LATHAM, R., *Revised Medieval Latin Word List* (London, 1965).

The Latin Text of the Ancrene Riwle edited from Merton College MS 44 and BM MS Cotton Vitellius E. vii, ed. C. D'Evelyn (EETS 216; 1944).

LAWRENCE, *St Edmund* = C. H. Lawrence, *St Edmund of Abingdon. A Study in Hagiography and History* (Oxford, 1960).

LCC Survey of London = *London County Council Survey of London*, vol. viii, *St Leonard's Shoreditch* ed. Sir J. Bird and P. Norman, (London, 1922).

LECLERCQ, J., '*Eremus* et *eremita* pour l'histoire du vocabulaire de la vie solitaire', *Collectanea Ordinis Cisterciensium Reformatorum*, 25 (Rome / Westmalle, 1963), 8–30.

LEFÈVRE, *Les Statuts de Prémontré XIIe siècle* = P. Lefèvre, *Les Statuts de Prémontré au milieu du XIIe siècle* (Bibliotheca Analectorum Praemonstratensium, fasc. xii; Averbode, 1978).

—— *Les Statuts réformés XIIIe siècle* = P. Lefèvre, *Les Statuts de Prémontre réformés sur les ordres de Gregoire IX et d'Innocent IV au XIIIe siècle* (Louvain, 1946).

LEGA-WEEKES = E. Lega-Weekes, 'History of St Katherine's Priory Polsloe, Part I', *Transactions Devon Archaeol. Soc.* 66 (1934), 181–99.

LE GRAND, 'Statuts d'hôtels-Dieu' = L. F. Le Grand, 'Statuts d'hôtels-Dieu et de léproseries. Recueil de textes du xiie au xive siècle,' *Collections de textes pour servir à l'étude et à l'enseignement de l'histoire* (Paris, 1901).

LEKAI, L. J. 'Ideals and Reality in Early Cistercian Life and Legislation', in J. R. Sommerfeldt (ed.), *Cistercian Ideals and Reality* (Kalamazoo, 1978), 4–29.

LELAND, *Coll.* = *Joannis Lelandi antiquarii de rebus Britannicis Collectanea*, ed. T. Hearne, 6 vols. (2nd edn., London, 1770).

—— *Itin.* = *The Itinerary of John Leland*, ed. L. T. Smith, 5 vols. (London, 1907–10).

Le Neve, *Fasti* = *John Le Neve Fasti Ecclesiae Anglicanae 1066–1300*, rev. edn., 3 vols., i *St Paul's London*, ii, *Monastic Cathedrals (Northern and Southern provinces)*, iii *Lincoln*, compiled D. Greenway (London, 1968–77).

LE PAIGE, *Bibliotheca Praemonstratensis* = J. Le Paige, *Bibliotheca Praemonstratensis Ordinis*, 2 parts (Paris, 1633).

Letters and Papers Foreign and Domestic of the Reign of Henry VIII, ed. J. Gairdner, x (London, 1887).

Letters of Abelard and Heloise = *The Letters of Abelard and Heloise*, trans. B. Radice (Harmondsworth, 1974).

The Letters of Lanfranc, Archbishop of Canterbury, ed. H. Clover and M. Gibson (Oxford, 1979).

The Letters of Peter the Venerable, ed. G. Constable, 2 vols. (Cambridge, Mass., 1967).

Letters of Pope Inn. III = The Letters of Pope Innocent III (1198–1216) concerning England and Wales. A Calendar with an Appendix of Texts, ed. C. R. and M. G. Cheney (Oxford, 1967).

LEVETT, A. E. 'The Accounts of St Mary des Prés (Pray)', in H. M. Cam, M. Coate, and L. Sutherland (eds.), *Studies in Manorial History by Ada Elizabeth Levett* (Oxford, 1938), 287–99.

Libellus de diversis ordinibus = Libellus de diversis ordinibus et professionibus qui sunt in aecclesia, ed. G. Constable and B. Smith (Oxford, 1972).

Liber Albus of the Priory of Worcester, Parts I and II. Priors John de Wyke 1301–17 and Wulstan de Bransford 1317–39, ed. J. M. Wilson (Worcs Hist. Soc.; 1919).

Liber antiquus de ordinationibus vicariarum tempore Hugonis Wells, Lincolniensis episcopi 1209–35, ed. A. Gibbons (Lincoln, 1888).

'Liber de miraculis S. Marie Laudensis', *PL*, clvi (1880), 1,001–2.

Liber Eliensis = Liber Eliensis, ed. E. O. Blake (Camden 3rd ser. 92; 1962).

Liber Feodorum: see *Book of Fees*.

Life of Gundulf = The Life of Gundulf, Bishop of Rochester, ed. R. Thomson (Toronto, 1977).

Linc. Final Concords i, Boyd and Massingberd = *Lincolnshire Records. Abstracts of Final Concords temp. Richard I, John, and Henry III (1193–1244)*, ed. W. O. Massingberd and W. Boyd, 2 vols. (privately printed, London, 1896).

Linc. Final Concords ii = Final Concords of the County of Lincoln from the Feet of Fines preserved in the PRO 1244–72 with additions from Various Sources AD 1176–1250, ed. C. W. Foster (Linc. Rec. Soc. 17; 1920).

Lincoln Visitations = Visitations of Religious Houses in the Diocese of Lincoln. Records of Visitations held by William Alnwick, Bishop of Lincoln AD MCCCCXXXVI–MCCCCXLIX, ed. A. H. Thompson, 2 vols. (Cant. and York Soc. 24; London, 1919).

Literae Cant. = Literae Cantuarienses. The Letter Books of the Monastery of Christ Church Canterbury, ed. J. Sheppard Brigstocke, 3 vols. (Rolls. ser. 85, London, 1887–9).

LOBEL, M. D., *The Borough of Bury St Edmunds. A Study in the Government and Development of a Monastic Town* (Oxford, 1935).

LONGRAIS, J. DES, 'Le Statut de la femme en Angleterre dans le droit commun médiéval', in *La Femme* (ii), *Recueils de la Société Jean Bodin pour l'histoire comparative des institutions* 12 (Brussels, 1962), 135–241.

LOYD, L. C., 'The Origin of the Family of Aubigny of Cainhoe', *Beds. Hist. Rec. Soc.* 19 (1937), 101–10.

LYNCH, J. H., *Simoniacal Entry into Religious Life from 1000–1260: A Social, Economic and Legal Study* (Ohio, 1976).

MCHARDY, A. K., 'The Alien Priories and the Expulsion of Aliens from England in 1378', in D. Baker (ed.), *Church, Society and Politics, Studies in Church History* 12; (Oxford, 1975), 133–41.

Madox, *Form. Ang.* = T. Madox, *Formulare Anglicanum* (London, 1702).

Magnum Registrum Album. The Great Register of Lichfield Cathedral, ed. H. E. Savage (Staffs. Hist. Coll.; 1926 for 1924).

MANDER, 'Brewood Black Ladies' = G. P. Mander, 'The Priory of Black Ladies of Brewood co. Stafford. Some Charters and Records and Notes on the Same,' *Staffs. Hist. Collections,* (Staffs. Record Soc.; 1939), 175–220.

MANRIQUE, A., *Cisterciensium seu verius ecclesiasticorum annalium a condito Cistercio,* 4 vols. (Lyons, 1642–59).

MANSI = J. D. Mansi, *Sacrorum conciliorum nova et amplissima collectio,* ed. L. Petit and J. B. Martin, 54 vols. in 59 (Paris, 1901–27, repr. Graz, 1960–1).

Manuscripts from St Albans Abbey 1066–1235, ed. R. M. Thomson, 2 vols. (Woodbridge, 1982).

'Marrick Charts.', *Coll. Top et Gen.* = 'Charters of Marrick Priory', ed. T.S. (? Thomas Stapleton), *Collectanea Topographica et Genealogica,* 8 vols. (London, 1834–43), v, 100–24, 221–59.

MARTÈNE, *De ritibus* = E. Martène, *De antiquis Ecclesiae ritibus,* 3 vols. (Antwerp, 1736–7).

MARTIN, J. D., *The Cartularies and Registers of Peterborough Abbey* (Northants. Rec. Soc.; 1978).

MASSINGBERD, W. O., 'Lincoln Cathedral Charters', *Associated Societies Reports and Papers* 26 (2) (1902), 321–69.

MATTHEW, *Norm. Monasteries* = D. Matthew, *The Norman Monasteries and their English Possessions* (Oxford, 1962).

MAYR-HARTING, '12th Century Recluse' = H. Mayr-Harting, 'Functions of a Twelfth-Century Recluse', *History* 60 (1975), 337–52.

Medieval Women = D. Barker (ed.), *Medieval Women, Studies in Church History,* Subsidia 1 (Oxford, 1978).

Mem. Fountains = *Memorials of the Abbey of St Mary of Fountains,* ed. J. Walbran, 3 vols. (Surtees Soc. 42, 67, 130; 1863–1918).

Mem. Walter de Coventry = *Memoriale Fratris Walteri de Coventria. The Historical Collections of Walter of Coventry,* ed. W. Stubbs, 2 vols. (Rolls ser. 58; London, 1872–3).

MICHEL, H., 'Inventaire sommaire du cartulaire d'Arrouaise', *Bulletin de la Société des Antiquaires de Picardie* 28 (Amiens, 1917–18), 251–73.

MICHELET, J., *Histoire de France,* 17 vols. (2nd edn., Paris, 1835–67).

MILIS = L. M. Milis, *'L'Ordre des chanoines réguliers d'Arrouaise. Son histoire et son organisation de la fondation de l'Abbaye-Mère (vers 1090) à la fin des chapîtres annuels (1471),* 2 vols. (Bruges, 1969).

Monasticon = *Monasticon Anglicanum* (1st edn.), ed. R. Dodsworth and W. Dugdale, 3 vols. (London, 1655–73).

Monumenta Franciscana = *Monumenta Franciscana,* ed. J. Brewer, 2 vols. (Rolls ser. 4; London, 1858–82).

MOORE, 'Cartl. Fontevrault' = R. I. Moore, 'The Reconstruction of the Cartulary of Fontevrault', *BIHR* 41 (1968), 86–95.

MOREAU = E. de Moreau, 'Les "Monastères doubles". Leur histoire surtout en Belgique', *Nouvelle Revue théologique* 66 (Louvain, 1939), 787–92.

MOREY, A. and C. N. L. BROOKE, *Gilbert Foliot and his Letters* (Cambridge Studies in Medieval Life and Thought, N.S. II; Cambridge, 1965).

MORTIMER, R., 'Religious and Secular Motives for Some English Monastic Foundations', in D. Baker (ed.), *Religious Motivation: Biographical and Sociological Problems for the Church Historian, Studies in Church History*, 15 (Oxford, 1978), 77–85.

—— 'Glanville' = R. Mortimer, 'The Family of Rannulf de Glanville', *BIHR* 54 (1981), 1–16.

Mowbray Charts. = *Charters of the Honour of Mowbray 1107–1191*, ed. D. E. Greenway (London, 1972).

M. Paris Chron. Majora = *Matthaei Parisiensis, monachi St Albani, Chronica Majora*, ed. H. R. Luard, 7 vols. (Rolls ser. 57; London, 1872–84).

NASH, *Worcs.* = T. R. Nash, *Collections for the History of Worcestershire*, 2 vols. (Oxford, 1781–2).

Newcastle Deeds = *Early Deeds Relating to Newcastle upon Tyne*, ed. A. M. Oliver (Surtees Soc. 137; 1924).

New Palaeographical Society. Facsimiles of Ancient Manuscripts etc., ed. E. Thompson, G. Warner, F. Kenyon, and J. Gilson, 1st ser., 2 (London, 1903–12).

NICHOLL, *Thurstan* = D. Nicholl, *Thurstan, Archbishop of York, 1114–40* (York, 1964).

NICHOLS, 'Cistercian Nunneries and Bishops' = J. A. Nichols, 'Medieval Cistercian Nunneries and English Bishops', in *Distant Echoes*, 237–49.

—— 'Marham Abbey' = J. A. Nichols, 'The History and Cartulary of the Cistercian Nuns of Marham Abbey, 1249–1536', Ph.D. thesis (Ohio, 1974).

NIDERST = R. Niderst, *Robert d'Arbrissel et les origines de l'Ordre de Fontevrault* (Rodez, 1952).

NIQUET = H. Niquet, *Histoire de l'Ordre de Font Evraud* (Paris, 1642).

Northants. Charts. = *Facsimiles of Early Charters from Northamptonshire Collections*, ed. F. M. Stenton (Northants. Rec. Soc. 4; 1930).

Northumberland and Durham Deeds, ed. A. Oliver (Newcastle upon Tyne Record ser. 7; 1929).

Northumberland and Durham Fines = *Feet of Fines, Northumberland and Durham (abstracts 1196–1228)*, ed. A. M. Oliver and C. Johnson from transcripts by P. Oliver (Newcastle upon Tyne Record ser. 10; 1931 [1922]).

Northumberland Pleas = *Northumberland Pleas from the Curia Regis and Assize Rolls 1198–1272*, ed. A. H. Thompson (Newcastle upon Tyne Record ser. 2; 1922).

Orderic Vitalis = *The Ecclesiastical History of Orderic Vitalis*, ed. M. Chibnall, 6 vols. (Oxford, 1969–80).

OWEN, D. M., *Church and Society in Medieval Lincolnshire*, History of Lincolnshire, 5 (Lincoln, 1971).

Oxford Fines = *The Feet of Fines for Oxfordshire 1196–1291*, transc. and calendared by H. E. Salter (Oxfordshire Rec. Soc. 12; 1930).

PAGE, W., 'The History of the Monastery of St Mary de Pré', *St Albans and Herts. Arch. and Archaeol. Soc.*, Transactions, I, N.S. (1895–1902), 8–18.

PALMER, W. M., 'The Benedictine Nunnery of Swaffham Bulbeck', *Cambridge Antiq. Soc., Proceedings and Communications*, 31 (1928), 30–65.

Papal Decretals Relating to the Diocese of Lincoln in the Twelfth Century, ed. W. Holtzmann and E. Kemp (Linc. Rec. Soc. 47; 1954).

PARISSE, M., *Les Nonnes au Moyen Âge*, ed. Christine Bonneton (Paris, 1983).

—— *Les Religieuses en France au XIIIe siècle* (Nancy, 1985).

Paston Letters and Papers of the Fifteenth Century, ed. N. Davis, 2 vols. (Oxford, 1971).

PEERS, C. R., 'The Benedictine Nunnery of Little Marlow', *Archaeological Journal* 59 (1902), 307–25.

PETIGNY, J., 'Robert d'Arbrissel et Geoffroi de Vendôme,' *Bibl. École des Chartes*, 3rd ser. 15 (1853–4), 1–30.

PETIT, F., 'Les Vêtements des Prémontrés au 12e siècle', *Analecta Praemonstratensia* (Tongerloo / Averbode, 1925–   ), xv (1939), 17–24.

'Petri Blesensis continuatio ad Historiam Ingulphi', in *Rerum Anglicarum Scriptorum Veterum*, ed. W. Fulman (Oxford, 1684), i, 108–30.

PICARD = L. Picard, *L'Ordre de Fontevrault de 1115 à 1207* (Saumur, 1933).

The Place Names of Sussex: see *English Place Name Soc.*

Placita de quo warranto temporibus Edw. I, II, and III in curia receptae scaccarii Westm. asservata, ed. W. Illingworth (Record Commission; London, 1818).

Placitorum Abbreviatio = Placitorum in domo Capitulari Westmonasteriensi Asservatorum Abbreviatio temporibus Regum Ric.I, Johann., Henr. III, Edw. I, Edw. II, ed. W. Illingworth (London, 1811).

The Pontifical of Magdalen College, with Appendix of Extracts from other English MSS of the Twelfth Century, ed. H. A. Wilson (Henry Bradshaw Soc. 39; London, 1910).

PORÉE, A. A., *Histoire de l'Abbaye du Bec*, 2 vols. (Évreux, 1901).

POTTHAST = *Regesta Pontificum Romanorum inde ab a. post Christum natum 1198 ad a. 1304*, ed. A. Potthast, 2 vols. (1874–5, repr. Graz, 1957).

POWER = E. Power, *Medieval English Nunneries c.1275–1535* (Cambridge, 1922).

POYNTON, 'Sempringham Charts.' = E. M. Poynton, 'Charters Relating to the Priory of Sempringham', *The Genealogist*, N.S. 15 (1899), 158–61, 221–27; 16 (1900), 30–5, 76–83, 153–8, 223–8; 17 (1901), 29–35, 164–8, 232–9.

PR 2–4 Henry II = *The Great Rolls of the Pipe for the 2nd, 3rd and 4th Years of the Reign of King Henry II, 1155, 1156, 1157, 1158*, ed. J. Hunter (London, 1844).

PROCTER, 'Religious Life for Women' = Z. M. Procter, 'Religious Life for Women in Twelfth Century Canon Law, with Special Reference to English Houses', M.Phil. thesis (London, 1967).

Records of Harrold Priory = *Records of Harrold Priory*, ed. G. H. Fowler, *Beds. Hist. Rec. Soc.* 17 (1935).

Recueil des chartes de Cluny = *Recueil des chartes de l'Abbaye de Cluny. Collections de documents inédits*, ed. A. Bernard and A. Bruel, 6 vols. (Paris, 1876–1903).

Recueil Henri II = *Recueil des actes de Henri II, Roi d'Angleterre et Duc de Normandie concernant les provinces françaises et les affaires de France*, ed. L. Delisle and E. Berger, 4 vols. (Paris, 1909–27).

Red Book of Worc. = *The Red Book of Worcester Containing Surveys of the Bishops' Manors and Other Records*, ed. M. Hollings, 2 vols. Worcs. Hist. Soc.; London, 1934–9).

REES, W., *A History of the Order of St John of Jerusalem in Wales and on the Welsh Border* (Cardiff, 1947).

Reg. Ant. Linc. = *The Registrum Antiquissimum of the Cathedral Church of Lincoln*, ed. C. W. Foster and K. Major, 10 vols. (Linc. Rec. Soc. 27–9, 32, 34, 41, 42, 46, 51, 62, 67; 1931–73).

Reg. Concordia = *Regularis Concordia. The Monastic Agreement*, ed. T. Symons (Nelson Medieval Texts, 1953).

Reg. epistolarum Peckham = *Registrum epistolarum Fratris Johannis Peckham Archiepiscopi Cantuariensis*, ed. C. T. Martin, 3 vols. (Rolls ser. 77; 1882–5).

Reg. Godfrey Giffard = *Episcopal Registers. Diocese of Worcester. Register of Bishop Godfrey Giffard Sept. 23rd 1268–August 15th 1301*, ed. J. Willis Bund, 2 vols. (Worcs. Hist. Soc.; 1902 [1898–1902]).

Reg. Gravesend = *Rotuli Ricardi Gravesend diocesis Lincolniensis*, ed. F. N. Davis, additions by C. W. Foster and A. H. Thompson (Cant. and York Soc. 31; 1925).

Reg. Greenfield = *The Register of William Greenfield, Lord Archbishop of York, 1306–15*, transcr. by W. Brown, ed. A. H. Thompson, 5 vols. (Surtees Soc. 145, 149, 151, 152, 153; 1931–40).

Reg. Grosseteste = *Rotuli Roberti Grosseteste episcopi Lincolniensis AD MCCXXXV–MCCLIII*, ed. F. N. Davis (Cant. and York Soc. 10; 1913).

Reg. Holm Cultram = *The Register and Records of Holm Cultram*, ed. F. Grainger and W. G. Collingwood (Cumberland and Westmorland Antiq. and Archaeol. Soc., Record ser. 7; 1929).

Reg. Inn. III = *Die Register Innocenz' III*, ed. O. Hageneder and A. Haidacher, 2 vols. in 4 (Graz-Köln, 1964–79).

Reg. Pal. Dunelmense = *The Register of Richard de Kellawe, Lord Palatine and Bishop of Durham, 1314–16*, ed. T. D. Hardy, 4 vols. (Rolls ser.; 1873–8).

Reg. Pontissara = *Registrum Johannis de Pontissara, Episcopi Wyntoniensis AD MCCLXXXII–MCCCIV*, ed. and trans. C. Deedes, 2 vols. (Cant. and York Soc. 19, 30; 1915–24).

Reg. Regum = *Regesta Regum Anglo-Normannorum, 1066–1154*: i, 1066–1100, *Regesta Willelmi Conquestoris et Willelmi Rufi*, ed. H. W. C. Davis (Oxford, 1913); ii, *Regesta Henrici Primi 1100–1135*, ed. C. Johnson and H. A. Cronne (Oxford, 1956); iii, iv, *Regesta Stephani 1135–54* and *Facsimiles*, ed. H. A. Cronne and R. H. C. Davis (Oxford, 1968–9).

Reg. Regum Scot. = *Regesta Regum Scottorum*, ed. G. W. S. Barrow, 2 vols., i, *The Acts of Malcolm IV, King of Scots 1153–65*, ii, *The Acts of William I, King of Scots 1165–1214* (Edinburgh, 1960–71).

Reg. Sutton = *The Rolls and Register of Bishop Oliver Sutton 1280–99*, ed. R. M. T. Hill, 8 vols. (Linc. Rec. Soc.; 1948–86).

Reg. Walter Giffard = *The Register of Walter Giffard. Lord Archbishop of York 1266–79*, ed. W. Brown (Surtees Soc., 109; 1904).

Regesta Honorii Papae III, ed. P. Pressutti, 2 vols. (Rome, 1895).

Reginald of Durham. Libellus de vita et miraculis S. Godrici heremitae de Finchale, ed. J. Stevenson (Surtees Soc. 20; 1847).

Register of the Diocese of Worcester during the Vacancy of the See usually called 'Registrum Sede Vacante', 1301–1435, ed. J. W. Willis Bund (Worcs. Hist. Soc.; Oxford, 1897).

The Register of John le Romeyn, Lord Archbishop of York 1286–96, i, ed. W. Brown (Surtees Soc. 123; 1913).

The Register of the Priory of St Bees, ed. J. Wilson (Surtees Soc. 126; 1915).

The Register or Rolls of Walter Gray, Lord Archbishop of York, ed. J. Raine (Surtees Soc. 56; 1872).

Registrum Hamonis Hethe, Diocesis Roffensis AD 1319–52, ed. C. Johnson, 2 vols. (Cant. and York Soc. 48–9; Oxford, 1948).

Registrum Ricardi de Swinfield episcopi Herefordensis AD MCCLXXXIII–MCCCXVII, ed. W. Capes (Cantilupe Soc., and Cant. and York Soc.; 1909).

Registrum Roffense, ed. J. Thorpe (London, 1769).

Ricart's Kalendar = *The Maire of Bristowe is Kalendar by Robert Ricart Town Clerk of Bristol 18 Edward IV*, ed. L. T. Smith (Camden Soc. N.S. 5; 1872).

RICHOU, G., 'Essai sur la vie claustrale et l'administration intérieure dans l'Ordre et l'Abbaye de Prémontré au XIIe et au XIIIe siècles', *École Nationale des Chartes. Positions des thèses des élèves* (Paris, 1875), 23–9.

Roberti Grosseteste episcopi quondam Lincolniensis epistolae, ed. H. R. Luard (Rolls ser. 25; 1861).

Rolls of the Justices in Eyre, being the Rolls of Pleas and Assizes for Gloucestershire, Warwickshire and Staffordshire (recte Shropshire) 1221, 1222, ed. D. M. Stenton (Selden Soc. 59; 1940).

Rolls of Justices in Eyre . . . for Lincolnshire . . . and Worcestershire: see *Eyre Rolls Lincs. and Worcs.*

Rot. Chart. = *Rotuli Chartarum in Turri Londinensi asservati (1199–1216)*, ed. T. Hardy (Record Commission; London, 1837).

Rot. Hund. = *Rotuli Hundredorum temp. Hen. III and Ed. I. in Turr' Lond'*, 2 vols. (2 parts, vol. ii) (London, 1912–18).

Rot. Lit. Claus. = *Rotuli Litterarum Clausarum in Turri Londinensi asservati*, ed. T. Hardy, 2 vols. (Record Commission; London, 1833–4).

Rot. Lit. Pat. = *Rotuli Litterarum Patentium in Turri Londinensi asservati 1201–1216*, ed. T. Hardy (Record Commission; London, 1835).

Rot. Wells = *Rotuli Hugonis de Welles, episcopi Lincolniensis AD MCCXXIX–MCCXXXV*, ed. W. P. W. Phillimore and F. N. Davis, 3 vols. (Cant. and York Soc.; London, 1907 [1905]–1909).

Rotuli Curiae Regis. Rolls and Records of the Court held before the King's Justiciars or Justices. 6 Richard I–1 John, ed. F. Palgrave, i (Record Commission; London, 1835).

Rouleaux des Morts = *Rouleaux des Morts du IXᵉ au XVᵉ siècles recueillis et publiés pour la Société de l'histoire de France*, ed. L. Delisle (Paris, 1866).

ROUND, J. H., *Feudal England* (London, 1895, repr. 1964).

—— 'Clerkenwell' = J. H. Round, 'The Foundation of the Priories of St Mary and of St John Clerkenwell', *Archaeologia* 56 (2) (1899), 223–8.

—— *Geoff. de Mandeville* = J. H. Round, *Geoffrey de Mandeville* (London, 1892).

RUBIN, M., *Charity and Community in Medieval Cambridge* (Cambridge, 1987).

Rufford Charters, ed. C. Holdsworth, 4 vols. (Thoroton Soc., Rec. Ser. 29, 30, 32, 34; Nottingham, 1972–81).

RYE, *Carrow Abbey* = W. Rye, *Carrow Abbey . . . in the County of Norfolk* (privately printed, Norwich, 1889).

RYLAND, *Wroxall* = J. W. Ryland, *Records of Wroxall Abbey and Manor* (London, 1903).

St Albans Psalter = *The St Albans Psalter*, ed. O. Pächt, C. R. Dodwell, and F. Wormald (London, 1960).

SALTMAN, *Archbishop Theobald* = A. Saltman, *Theobald, Archbishop of Canterbury* (London, 1956).

SANDERS, *Baronies* = I. J. Sanders, *English Baronies. A Study of their Origin and Descent 1086–1327* (Oxford, 1960).

Sarum Charts. = *Charters and Documents Illustrating the History of the Cathedral, City and Diocese of Salisbury in the Twelfth and Thirteenth Centuries*, ed. W. R. Jones and W. D. Macray (Rolls ser. 97; 1891).

SAYERS, *Papal Judges Delegate* = J. Sayers, *Papal Judges Delegate in the Province of Canterbury 1198–1254* (Oxford, 1971).

—— 'Papal Privileges' = J. Sayers, 'Papal Privileges for St Albans Abbey and its Dependencies', in D. A. Bullough and R. L. Storey (eds.), *The Study of Medieval Records. Essays in Honour of Kathleen Major*, (Oxford, 1971), 57–84.

SAYLE, C. E., 'The Mortuary Roll of the Abbess of Lillechurch, Kent', *Proceedings of the Cambridge Antiquarian Soc.* 10 (1898–1903), 383–409.

SCHMITZ, *Ordre de St Benoît* = P. Schmitz, *Histoire de L'Ordre de Saint Benoît*, 7 vols. (Gembloux, 1942–6; 2nd edn., i–ii, Maredsous, 1948–56).

SCHULENBURG, J. T., 'Strict Active Enclosure and its Effects on the Female Monastic Experience (ca. 500–1100)', in *Distant Echoes*, 51–86.

SERJEANTSON, *Delapré* = R. A. Serjeantson, *A History of Delapré Abbey Northampton* (Northampton, 1909).

SIMPSON, A. W. B., *A History of the Land Law* (2nd edn., Oxford, 1986).

SMITH, D., *Guide to the Bishops' Registers of England and Wales. A Survey from the Middle Ages to the Abolition of Episcopacy, 1646* (Royal Hist. Soc.; London, 1981).

SMITH, J., 'Robert of Arbrissel: *Procurator Mulierum*', in *Medieval Women*, 175–84.

SMITH, R. A. L., 'The Place of Gundulf in the Anglo-Norman Church', *EHR* 58 (1943), 257–72.

SMYTH, J., *Lives of the Berkeleys*, ed. J. Maclean, 3 vols. (Gloucester, 1883).

SOUTHERN, R. W., *Western Society and the Church in the Middle Ages* (Harmondsworth, 1970).

Spicilegium Liberianum, ed. F. Liverani (Florence, 1864).

STAPLETON, T., 'Observations upon the Succession to the Barony of William of Arques in the County of Kent during the Period between the Conquest of England and the Reign of King John', *Archaeologia* 31 (1846), 216–37.

STENTON, D. M., *The English Woman in History* (London, 1957).

STURMAN, W. M., 'Barking Abbey; A Study in its Internal and External Administration from the Conquest to the Dissolution', Ph.D. thesis (London, 1961).

—— 'Stamford' = W. M. Sturman, 'History of the Nunnery of St Mary and St Michael outside Stamford', MA thesis (London, 1946).

Suffolk Fines = *A Calendar of the Feet of Fines for Suffolk Richard I–Edward IV*, ed. W. Rye (Suffolk Inst. of Archaeol. and Nat. Hist.; 1900).

Symeonis Monachi opera omnia, ed. T. Arnold, 2 vols. (Rolls ser. 75; 1882–5).

TALBOT, *Life of Christina* = *The Life of Christina of Markyate, a Twelfth-Century Recluse*, ed. and trans. C. H. Talbot, 1959, corr. repr. (Oxford, 1987).

TANNER = T. Tanner, *Notitia Monastica*, revised edn., J. Nasmith (London, 1787).

Textus Roffensis, ed. P. Sawyer, *Early English MSS in Facsimile* 11 [2] (Copenhagen, 1962).

The Thirty-Sixth Report of the Deputy Keeper of Public Records (London, 1874).

Thomae Sprotti Chronica, ed. T. Hearne (Oxford, 1719).

THOMPSON, A. H., 'Double Monasteries and the Male Element in Nunneries', in *The Ministry of Women. A Report by a Committee appointed by his Grace the Lord Archbishop of Canterbury* (London, 1919), app. viii, 145–64.

THOMPSON, S. P., 'Why English Nunneries had no History. A Study of the Problems of English Nunneries founded after the Conquest' in *Distant Echoes*, 131–49.

—— 'Cistercian Nuns' = S. P. Thompson, 'The Problem of the Cistercian Nuns in the Twelfth and Early Thirteenth Centuries', in *Medieval Women*, 227–52.

TROKELOWE, *Annales* = *Johannis de Trokelowe, Annales Edwardi II, Henrici de Blaneford Chronica et Edwardi II Vita*, ed. T. Hearne (Oxford, 1729).

TWYSDEN, R., *Historiae Anglicanae Scriptores X* (London, 1652). See also 'The Chronicle of John Brompton'.

URRY, *Canterbury* = W. Urry, *Canterbury under the Angevin Kings* (London, 1967).

Valor Eccl. = *Valor Ecclesiasticus temp. Henry VIII auctoritate regia institutus*, 6 vols. in 4 (London, 1810–34).

VALOUS = G. de Valous, *Le Monachisme clunisien des origines au XVᵉ siècle*, 2 vols. (Archives de la France monastique 39; Paris, 1935).

VAN WAEFELGHEM, 'Les Premiers Statuts' = R. Van Waefelghem, 'Les Premiers Statuts de l'Ordre de Prémontré', *Analectes de l'Ordre de Prémontré* 9 (1913), 1–74.

VAUGEOIS, J. F., *Histoire des antiquités de la Ville de L'Aigle et de ses environs* (L'Aigle, 1841).

VAUZELLES = L. Vauzelles, *Histoire du Prieuré de la Magdeleine-Lez-Orléans de l'Ordre de Fontevraud* (Paris, 1873).

VERDON, J., 'Les Sources de l'histoire de la femme en Occident aux Xᵉ–XIIIᵉ siècles', *Cahiers de civilisation médiévale* 20 (1977), 219–51.

—— 'Les Moniales' = J. Verdon, 'Les Moniales dans la France de l'Ouest au XIᵉ et XIIᵉ siècles. Étude d'histoire sociale', *Cahiers de civilisation médiévale* 19 (Univ. de Poitiers, 1976), 247–64.

VERHEIJEN, L., *La Règle de Saint Augustin*, 2 vols. (Paris, 1967).

Vie de S. Hugues Abbé de Cluny 1024–1109, by A. L'Huillier (Solesmes, 1888).

'Vita auctore Andrea' = 'Alia Vita B. Roberti sive extrema conversatio et transitus eius, auctore monachi Fontis Ebraldi Andrea', *AASS*, Feb., iii, 609–16.

'Vita auctore Baldrico' = 'Vita B. Roberti auctore Baldrico episc. Dolensi', *AASS*, Feb., iii, 603–8.

'Vita B. Giraldi de Salis', in E. Martène and U. Durand, *Veterum scriptorum et monumentorum historicorum, dogmaticorum, moralium, amplissima collectio*, vi (Paris, 1729), 990–1,014.

Vita Wulfstani of William of Malmesbury, ed. R. R. Darlington (Camden 3rd ser., 40; London, 1928).

WAKE, J. and PANTIN, W. A., 'Delapré Abbey, its History and Architecture', *Northants. Past and Present* (Northants. Rec. Soc. 2; 1954–9), 225–41.

WALTER, 'Wanderprediger' = J. von Walter, 'Die ersten wanderprediger Frankreichs', in N. Bonwetsch and R. Seeberg, (eds.), *Studien zur geschichte der Theologie und der Kirche*, ix (Leipzig, 1903).

Waltham Abbey Charts. = *Early Charters of the Augustinian Canons of Waltham Abbey, Essex, 1062–1230*, ed. R. Ransford (Studies in the History of Medieval Religion, ii, Woodbridge, 1989).

WARREN, *Anchorites and Patrons* = A. K. Warren, *Anchorites and their Patrons in Medieval England* (Univ. of California Press, 1985).

—— 'The Nun as Anchoress' = A. K. Warren, 'The Nun as Anchoress. England 1100–1500', in *Distant Echoes*, 197–212.

Warwicks. Fines = *Warwickshire Feet of Fines, 7 Richard I, 1195–12 Edward I, 1284*, abstracted by E. Stokes and ed. F. C. Wellstood, with an introduction and indexes by F. T. Houghton (Dugdale Soc. 11; 1932).

WATKIN, R. H. and WINDEATT, E., *The Priory for Nuns of St Mary, Cornworthy, Devon*, issued as an appendix to *Devon and Cornwall Notes and Queries* (1921).

WATT, J. A., *The Church in Medieval Ireland* (The Gill History of Ireland, 5; Dublin, 1972).

WIGRAM, S. R., *Chronicles of the Abbey of Elstow . . . with some notes of the Architecture of the Church by M. J. C. Buckley* (Oxford, 1885).

Willelmi Malmesbiriensis monachi. De Gestis Pontificum Anglorum, ed. N. E. S. A. Hamilton (Rolls ser. 52; 1870).

Willelmi Malmesbiriensis monachi. De Gestis Regum Anglorum, ed. W. Stubbs, 2 vols. (Rolls ser. 90; 1887–9).

WILLIAMS, D. H., 'Cistercian Nunneries in Medieval Wales,' *Cîteaux. Commentarii Cistercienses* 26 (Westmalle, 1975), 155–74.

WILLIAMS, RUSHBROOK L. F., *History of the Abbey of St Alban* (London, 1917).

WILLIAMS, W., 'A Dialogue between a Cluniac and a Cistercian', *Journal of Theological Studies* (1930), 164–75.

WOLLASCH, J., 'A Cluniac Necrology from the Time of Abbot Hugh', in N. Hunt (ed.), *Cluniac Monasticism in the Central Middle Ages* (London, 1971), 143–90.

WOOD, *Patrons* = S. Wood, *English Monasteries and their Patrons in the Thirteenth Century* (Oxford, 1955).

Yorks. Assize Rolls John and Henry III = *Three Yorkshire Assize Rolls for the Reigns of King John and Henry III*, ed. C. T. Clay (Yorks. Archaeol. Soc., Record ser. 44; 1911).

Yorks. Deeds = *Yorkshire Deeds*, ed. W. Brown, C. T. Clay, and M. J. Hebditch, 10 vols. (Yorks. Archaeol. Soc. 39, 50, 63, 65, 69, 76, 83, 102, 111, 120; 1909–55).

Yorks. Fines 1218–31 = *Feet of Fines for the County of York from 1218 to 1231*, ed. J. Parker (Yorks. Archaeol. Soc., Record ser. 62; 1921).

Yorks. Fines 1232–46 = *Feet of Fines for the County of York from 1232–46*, ed. J. Parker (Yorks. Archaeol. Soc., Record ser. 67; 1925).

Yorks. Fines 1246–72 = *Feet of Fines for the County of York 1246–72*, ed. J. Parker (Yorks. Archaeol. Soc., Record ser. 82; 1932).

YOUNGS, S. and CLARK, J., 'Medieval Britain in 1981', *Medieval Archaeology* 26 (1982), 164–227.

Index